For Gen Nav, IAS, RAS, CAS Same.

[illegible] < 300 kts.

Rhumb lines - On Chart always

Mercator - RL = Straight line

Plot = Straight line.

latitude

B x Scale denominator at A.

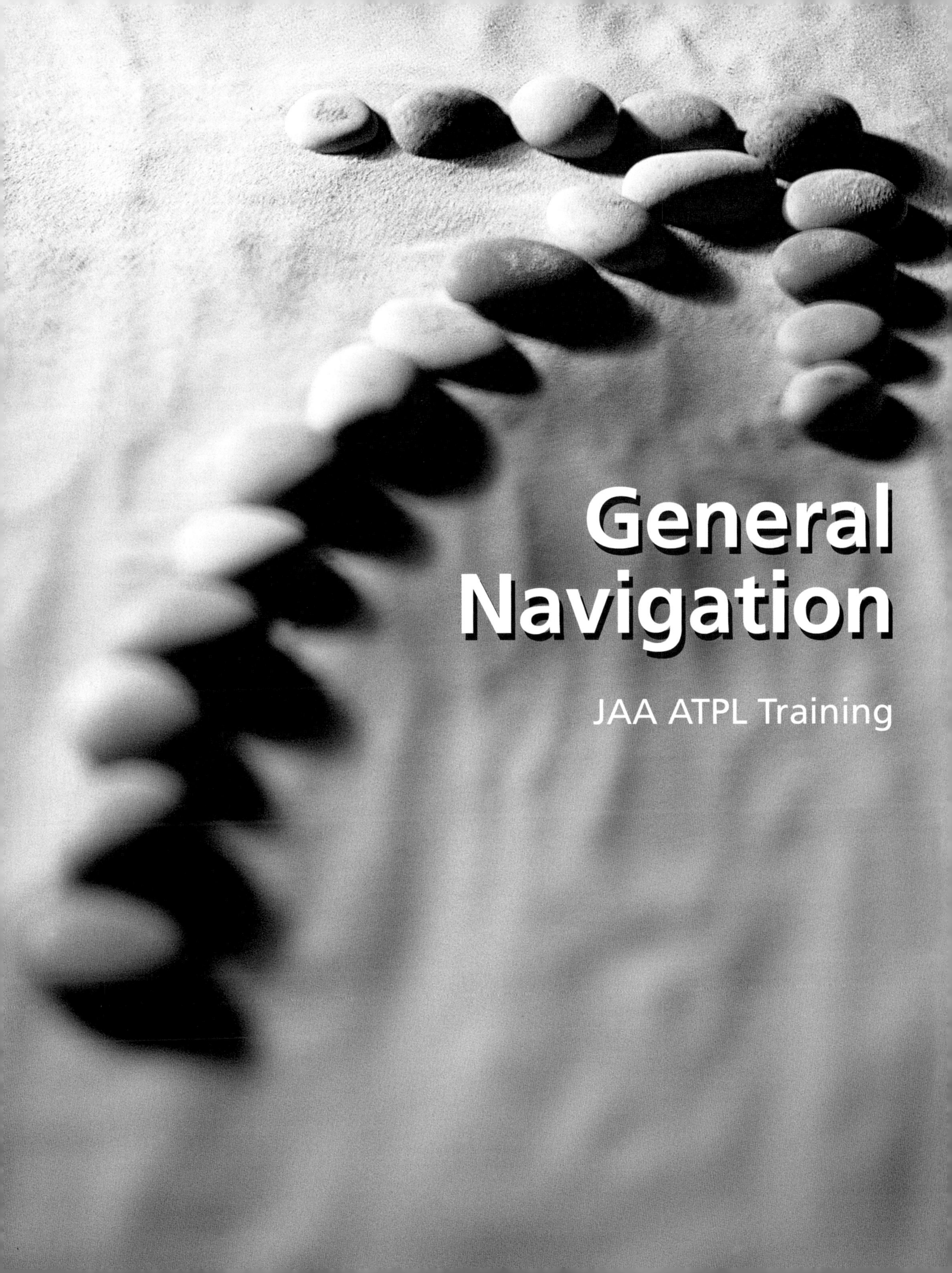

General Navigation

JAA ATPL Training

This book has been written and published to assist students enrolled in an approved JAA Air Transport Pilot Licence (ATPL) course in preparation for the JAA ATPL theoretical knowledge examinations. Nothing in the content of this book is to be interpreted as constituting instruction or advice relating to practical flying.

Whilst every effort has been made to ensure the accuracy of the information contained within this book, neither Jeppesen nor Atlantic Flight Training gives any warranty as to its accuracy or otherwise. Students preparing for the JAA ATPL theoretical knowledge examinations should not regard this book as a substitute for the JAA ATPL theoretical knowledge training syllabus published in the current edition of "JAR-FCL 1 Flight Crew Licensing (Aeroplanes)" (the Syllabus). The Syllabus constitutes the sole authoritative definition of the subject matter to be studied in a JAA ATPL theoretical knowledge training programme. No student should prepare for, or is entitled to enter himself/herself for, the JAA ATPL theoretical knowledge examinations without first being enrolled in a training school which has been granted approval by a JAA-authorised national aviation authority to deliver JAA ATPL training.

Contact Details:

Sales and Service Department
Jeppesen GmbH
Frankfurter Strasse 233
63263 Neu-Isenburg
Germany

Tel: ++49 (0)6102 5070
E-mail: fra-services@jeppesen.com

For further information on products and services from Jeppesen, visit our web site at:
www.jeppesen.com

JA310102-000
ISBN 0-88487-352-8
Printed in Germany

PREFACE

As the world moves toward a single standard for international pilot licensing, many nations have adopted the syllabi and regulations of the "Joint Aviation Requirements-Flight Crew Licensing" (JAR-FCL), the licensing agency of the Joint Aviation Authorities (JAA).

Though training and licensing requirements of individual national aviation authorities are similar in content and scope to the JAA curriculum, individuals who wish to train for JAA licences need access to study materials which have been specifically designed to meet the requirements of the JAA licensing system. The volumes in this series aim to cover the subject matter tested in the JAA ATPL ground examinations as set forth in the ATPL training syllabus, contained in the JAA publication, "JAR-FCL 1 (Aeroplanes)".

The JAA regulations specify that all those who wish to obtain a JAA ATPL must study with a flying training organisation (FTO) which has been granted approval by a JAA-authorised national aviation authority to deliver JAA ATPL training. While the formal responsibility to prepare you for both the skill tests and the ground examinations lies with the FTO, these Jeppesen manuals will provide a comprehensive and necessary background for your formal training.

Jeppesen is acknowledged as the world's leading supplier of flight information services, and provides a full range of print and electronic flight information services, including navigation data, computerised flight planning, aviation software products, aviation weather services, maintenance information, and pilot training systems and supplies. Jeppesen counts among its customer base all US airlines and the majority of international airlines worldwide. It also serves the large general and business aviation markets. These manuals enable you to draw on Jeppesen's vast experience as an acknowledged expert in the development and publication of pilot training materials.

We at Jeppesen wish you success in your flying and training, and we are confident that your study of these manuals will be of great value in preparing for the JAA ATPL ground examinations.

The next three pages contain a list and content description of all the volumes in the ATPL series.

ATPL Series

Meteorology (JAR Ref 050)

- The Atmosphere
- Wind
- Thermodynamics
- Clouds and Fog
- Precipitation
- Air Masses and Fronts
- Pressure System
- Climatology
- Flight Hazards
- Meteorological Information

General Navigation (JAR Ref 061)

- Basics of Navigation
- Magnetism
- Compasses
- Charts
- Dead Reckoning Navigation
- In-Flight Navigation
- Inertial Navigation Systems

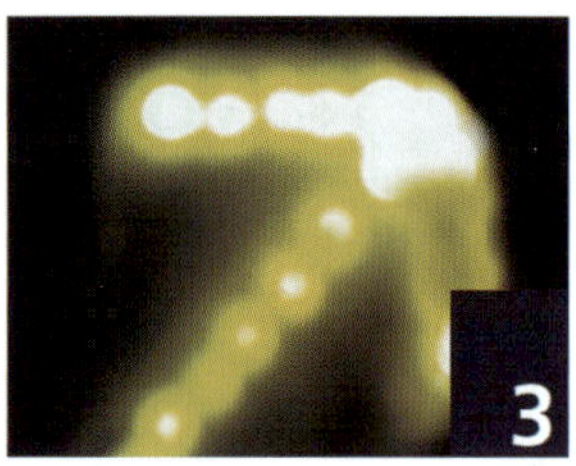

Radio Navigation (JAR Ref 062)

- Radio Aids
- Self-contained and External-Referenced Navigation Systems
- Basic Radar Principles
- Area Navigation Systems
- Basic Radio Propagation Theory

Airframes and Systems (JAR Ref 021 01)

- Fuselage
- Windows
- Wings
- Stabilising Surfaces
- Landing Gear
- Flight Controls
- Hydraulics
- Pneumatic Systems
- Air Conditioning System
- Pressurisation
- De-Ice / Anti-Ice Systems
- Fuel Systems

Powerplant (JAR Ref 021 03)

- Piston Engine
- Turbine Engine
- Engine Construction
- Engine Systems
- Auxiliary Power Unit (APU)

Electrics (JAR Ref 021 02)

- Direct Current
- Alternating Current
- Batteries
- Magnetism
- Generator / Alternator
- Semiconductors
- Circuits

Instrumentation (JAR Ref 022)

- Flight Instruments
- Automatic Flight Control Systems
- Warning and Recording Equipment
- Powerplant and System Monitoring Instruments

Principles of Flight (JAR Ref 080)

- Laws and Definitions
- Aerofoil Airflow
- Aeroplane Airflow
- Lift Coefficient
- Total Drag
- Ground Effect
- Stall
- C_{LMAX} Augmentation
- Lift Coefficient and Speed
- Boundary Layer
- High Speed Flight
- Stability
- Flying Controls
- Adverse Weather Conditions
- Propellers
- Operating Limitations
- Flight Mechanics

Performance (JAR Ref 032)

- Single-Engine Aeroplanes – Not certified under JAR/FAR 25 (Performance Class B)
- Multi-Engine Aeroplanes – Not certified under JAR/FAR 25 (Performance Class B)
- Aeroplanes certified under JAR/FAR 25 (Performance Class A)

Mass and Balance (JAR Ref 031)

- Definition and Terminology
- Limits
- Loading
- Centre of Gravity

Flight Planning (JAR Ref 033)

- Flight Plan for Cross-Country Flights
- ICAO ATC Flight Planning
- IFR (Airways) Flight Planning
- Jeppesen Airway Manual
- Meteorological Messages
- Point of Equal Time
- Point of Safe Return
- Medium Range Jet Transport Planning

Air Law (JAR Ref 010)

- International Agreements and Organisations
- Annex 8 – Airworthiness of Aircraft
- Annex 7 – Aircraft Nationality and Registration Marks
- Annex 1 – Licensing
- Rules of the Air
- Procedures for Air Navigation
- Air Traffic Services
- Aerodromes
- Facilitation
- Search and Rescue
- Security
- Aircraft Accident Investigation
- JAR-FCL
- National Law

Human Performance and Limitations (JAR Ref 040)

- Human Factors
- Aviation Physiology and Health Maintenance
- Aviation Psychology

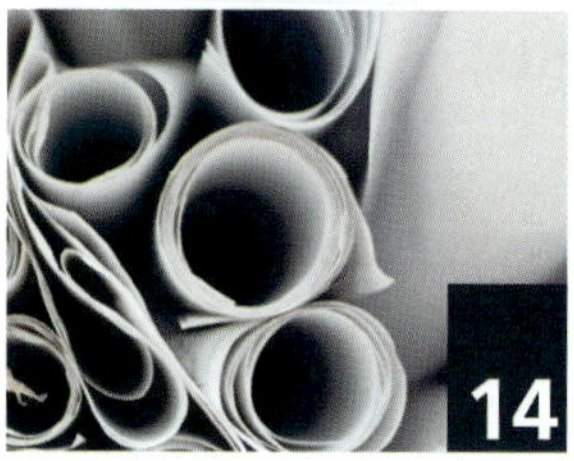

Operational Procedures (JAR Ref 070)

- Operator
- Air Operations Certificate
- Flight Operations
- Aerodrome Operating Minima
- Low Visibility Operations
- Special Operational Procedures and Hazards
- Transoceanic and Polar Flight

Communications (JAR Ref 090)

- Definitions
- General Operation Procedures
- Relevant Weather Information
- Communication Failure
- VHF Propagation
- Allocation of Frequencies
- Distress and Urgency Procedures
- Aerodrome Control
- Approach Control
- Area Control

CHAPTER 1

The Form of the Earth

CHAPTER 2

Position on the Earth

CHAPTER 3

Distance

CHAPTER 4

Direction

CHAPTER 5

Speed

CHAPTER 6

Triangle of Velocities

CHAPTER 7

Pooley's CRP 5 – Circular Slide Rule

CHAPTER 8

Pooley's – The Triangle of Velocities

CHAPTER 9

Maps and Charts – Introduction

CHAPTER 10

Maps and Charts – Mercator

CHAPTER 11

Maps and Charts – Lambert's Conformal

CHAPTER 12

Maps and Charts – Polar Stereographic

CHAPTER 13

Maps and Charts – Transverse and Oblique Mercator

CHAPTER 14

Maps and Charts – Summary

CHAPTER 15

Pilot Navigation Technique

CHAPTER 16

Relative Velocity

CHAPTER 17

Principles of Plotting

CHAPTER 18

Time

CHAPTER 19

Point of Equal Time and Point of Safe Return and Radius of Action

CHAPTER 20

Aircraft Magnetism

CHAPTER 21

Aircraft Magnetism - Compasses

CHAPTER 22

Inertial Navigation

Chapter 1
The Form of the Earth

SHAPE OF THE EARTH

For navigational purposes, the Earth is assumed to be a perfect sphere. In reality, it is slightly flattened at the poles and can be described as an ellipsoid or oblate spheroid. The Earth's polar diameter is approximately 23½ nm shorter than the equatorial diameter. When considering the full diameter of the Earth, this is negligible and can be disregarded for the purposes of practical navigation.

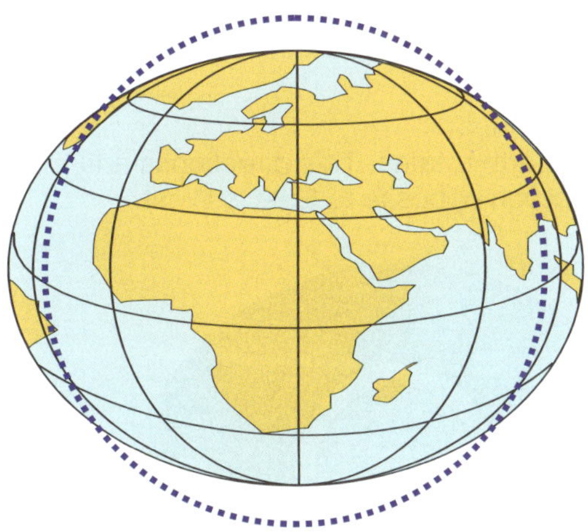

Polar Radius	6 356 752 metres	3432 nm
Equatorial Radius	6 378 137 metres	3443 nm

Note: In the diagram above, the compression is greatly exaggerated.

The **compression ratio** is the ratio between the polar diameter and the equatorial diameter and indicates the amount of flattening. The ratio is approximately $^{1}/_{297}$ but geodetic information obtained by satellite shows that the Earth is in fact pear-shaped with the larger mass being in the Southern Hemisphere.

For navigation and mapping purposes, World Geodetic System 1984 (WGS-84) is the current ICAO standard.

THE POLES

The Earth rotates about an invisible axis which passes through the Earth and cuts the Earth's surface at two points. These two points are called the poles, as shown on the diagram below.

NP North Pole
SP South Pole

EAST AND WEST

East is the direction in which the Earth rotates. This direction is anti-clockwise to a person looking down on the North Pole. The direction opposite to East is West.

NORTH POLE AND SOUTH POLE

The North Pole is the pole which lies to the left of an observer facing East.

If an observer stands:

- At the North Pole, all directions are South
- At the South Pole, all directions are North

CARDINAL DIRECTIONS

The directions North, East, South, and West are known as the Cardinal Directions.

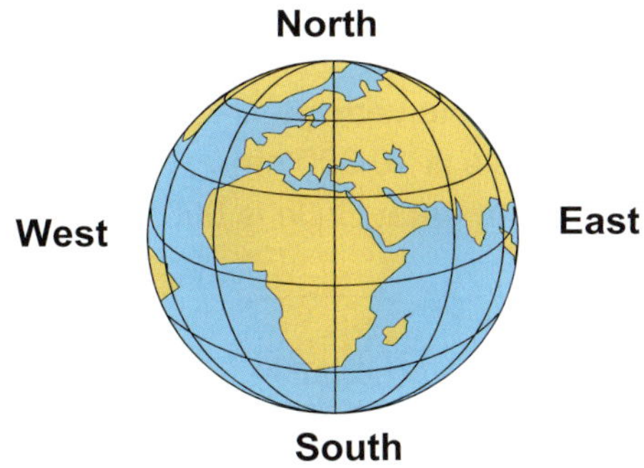

GREAT CIRCLE

A great circle is a circle drawn on the surface of a sphere which has the centre of the sphere as its origin. These circles are the largest that can be drawn on the sphere's surface.

A great circle can connect any two points on the Earth's surface. Normally, only one great circle can be drawn through any two points, as shown on the diagram below.

The exception to this rule is that if the two points are diametrically opposed - the North Pole and the South Pole, for example - an infinite number of great circles may be drawn.

The great circle joining two points has a long and a short path. The short path is always the shortest possible distance on the Earth's surface between the two points.

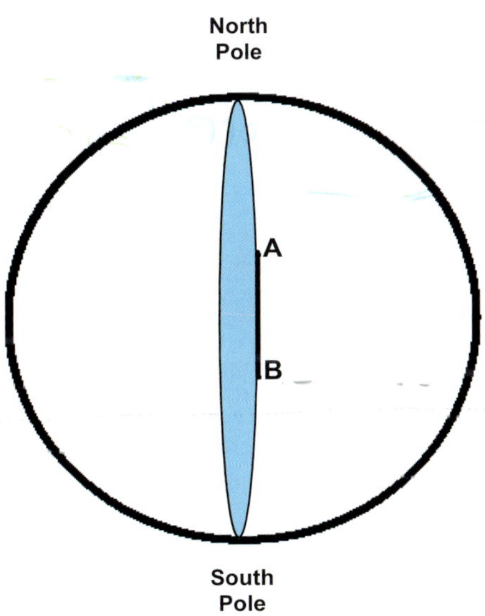

VERTEX OF A GREAT CIRCLE

The vertices of a great circle are the most northerly and southerly points on that great circle.

Vertex properties:

- The points are called antipodal; the vertices are diametrically opposed
- The distance between the points is 10 800 nm
- At the vertex the direction of the great circle is 090° - 270°

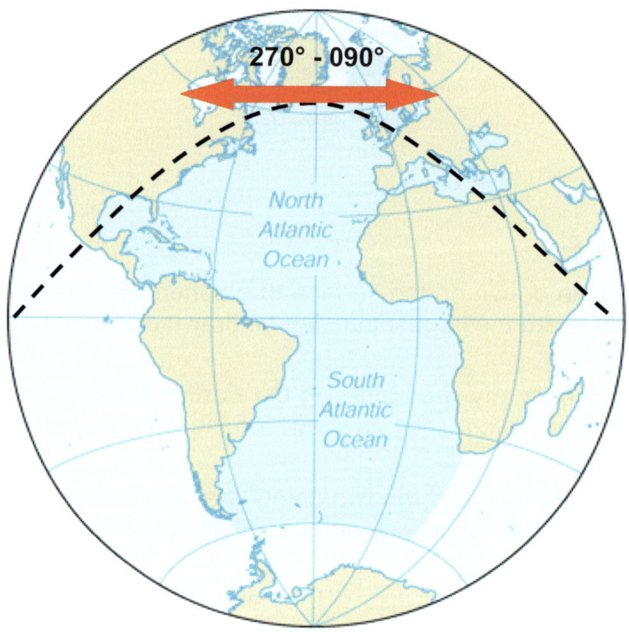

The great circle crosses the Equator at longitudes 90° from the vertex longitude.

Example 1: If the most northerly point is 73°N 020°W, what is its most southerly point?

Answer: 73°S 160°E

Example 2: Where the vertex is 73°N 020°W, the great circle cuts the Equator at which longitudes?

Answer: 110°W, 070°E

SMALL CIRCLE

A small circle is any circle drawn on the surface of a sphere which does not have the centre of the sphere as its origin.

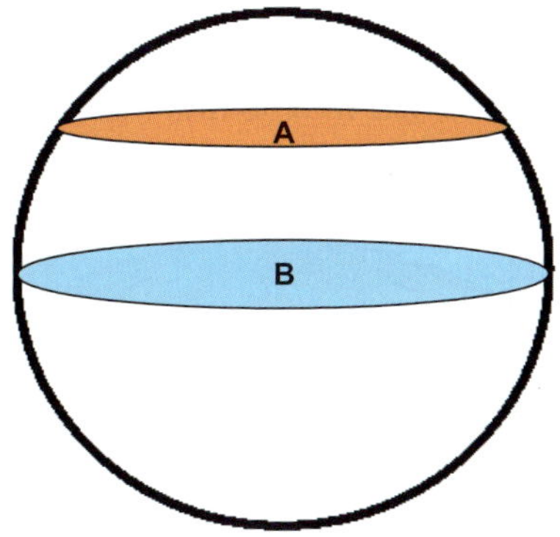

In the diagram above:

- Circle A is a Small Circle.
- Circle B is a Great Circle.

THE EQUATOR

The Equator is the great circle that cuts the Earth in half in an East – West direction. To the north of the Equator is the Northern Hemisphere; to the south, the Southern Hemisphere. The distance from the Equator to the North Pole is the same as the distance from the Equator to the South Pole.

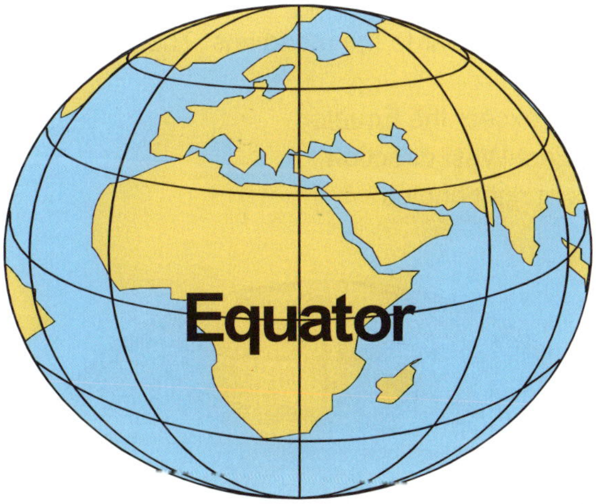

MERIDIANS

A meridian is half of a great circle that joins the poles. Each meridian:

- Runs in a North-South direction
- Cuts the Equator at right angles
- Has an anti-meridian
- forms the complete great circle with its anti-meridian

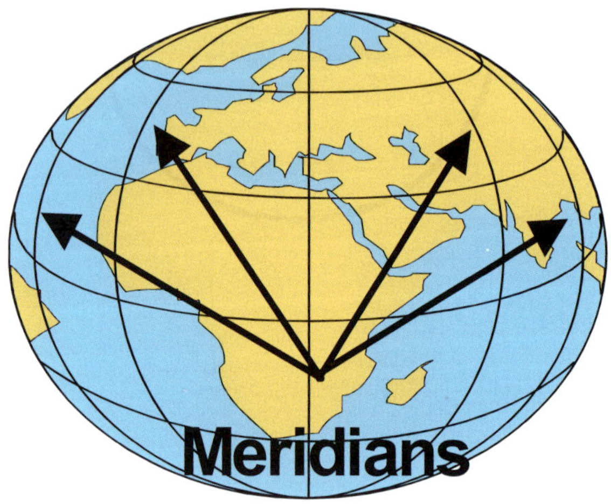

PARALLELS OF LATITUDE

The parallels of latitude run perpendicular to the meridians. The parallels of latitude:

- Are all small circles except the Equator
- Always run in an East-West direction
- Cut the meridians at right angles

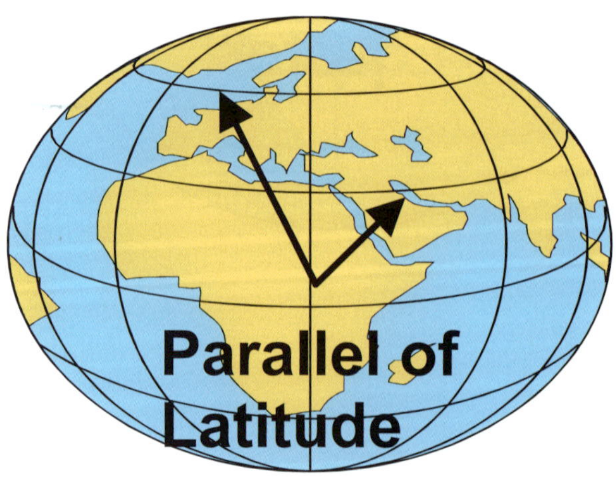

RHUMB LINE

A Rhumb line is a regularly curved line on the surface of the Earth that cuts all meridians at the same angle.

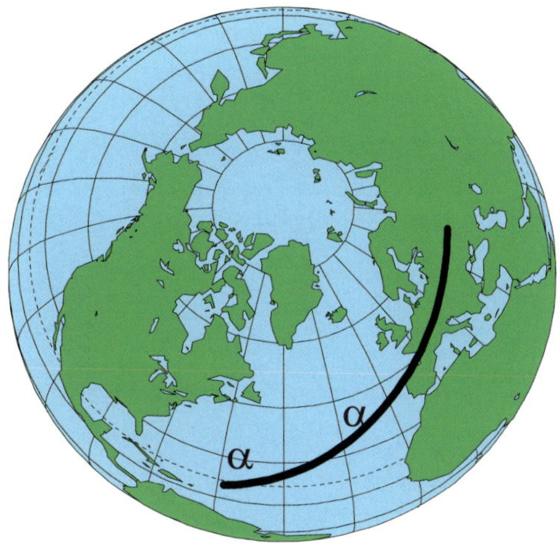

Only one Rhumb line can be drawn through two points on the Earth's surface. A Rhumb line is not a great circle with the exception of the meridians and the Equator. All parallels of latitude are Rhumb lines. Also, the distance along a Rhumb line is not the shortest distance between two points unless the Rhumb line is a meridian or a great circle.

The difference in distance between flying a Rhumb line track and a great circle:

- Is greatest over long distances
- Increases with latitude

The table below shows the difference in the Rhumb line and great circle distances along 60°N departing from 010°00'E.

Destination	Degrees	Rhumb Line Distance	Great Circle Distance	Difference	
				nm	%
010°00'W	20	600	597.7	2.3	0.4
030°00'W	40	1200	1181.6	18.4	1.5
050°00'W	60	1800	1737.3	62.6	3.5
110°00'W	120	3600	3079.1	520.9	14.5

Normally, flights of less than 1000 nm are flown along a Rhumb Line.

Chapter 2
Position on the Earth

ANGULAR MEASUREMENT

The Sexagesimal system of measuring angles is used in navigation.

Angles are expressed in terms of degrees, minutes, and seconds.

A degree (symbolised by °) is the angle subtended by an arc equal to $^{1}/_{360}$ part of the circumference of a circle.

- Each degree is split into 60 minutes (symbolised by ')
- Each minute is split into 60 seconds (symbolised by ")

Example 010°32'24"

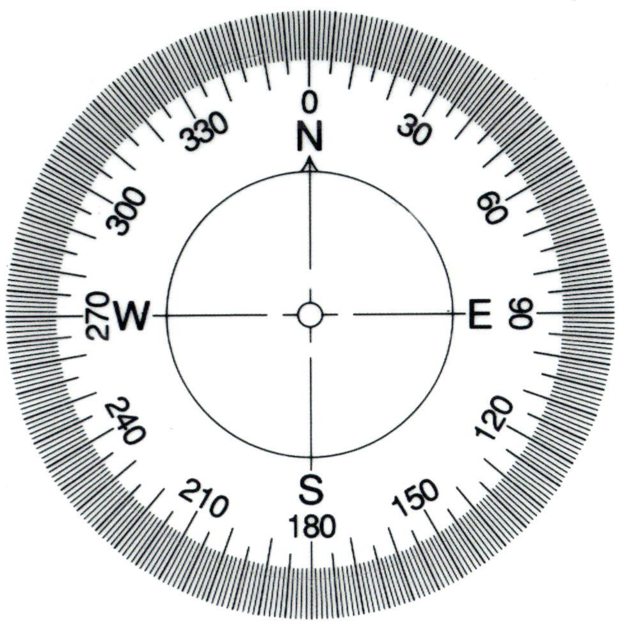

In navigation:

- North is 000°
- East is 090°
- South is 180°
- West is 270°

Where a direction is given, use three figures, e.g. 90° is reported as 090°. Angles are always measured in a clockwise direction from north.

POSITION REFERENCE SYSTEM

In navigation, it is necessary to pinpoint an aircraft:

1. Accurately
2. Unambiguously

The Cartesian System is the simplest and most effective position reference system.

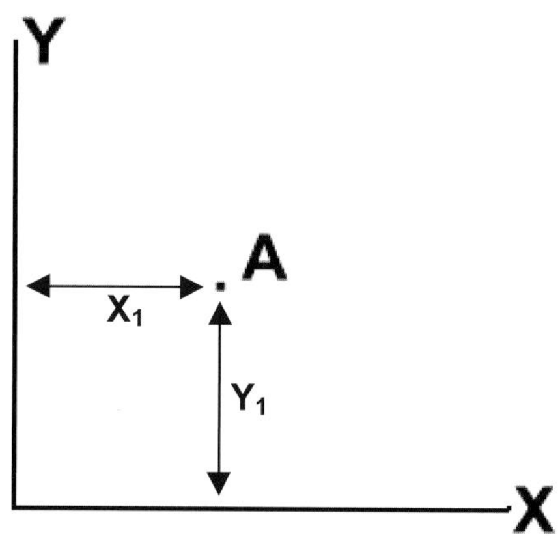

Point A can be defined as the position X_1Y_1.

The Cartesian System is good for work on a flat plane. For position on the Earth, a similar system can be employed.

LATITUDE AND LONGITUDE

On the Earth, position is described using latitude and longitude:

- The X-axis is the Equator and is defined as 0° Latitude.
- The Y-axis is aligned to the Greenwich Meridian (the Prime Meridian) and is 0° longitude.

LATITUDE

The latitude is expressed as the arc along the meridian between the Equator and that point.

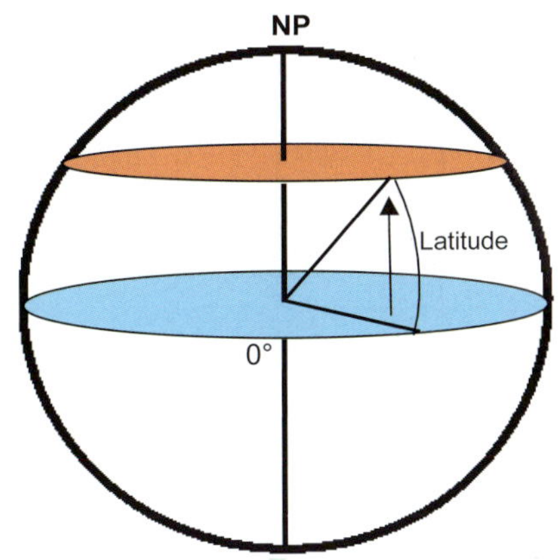

Latitude has values up to 90° and is annotated with the hemisphere where the point is situated.

Example 40°25'N or 40°25'S

LONGITUDE

The longitude of a point is the shorter angular distance between the Prime Meridian and the meridian passing through the point. Like latitude, longitude is expressed in degrees and minutes.

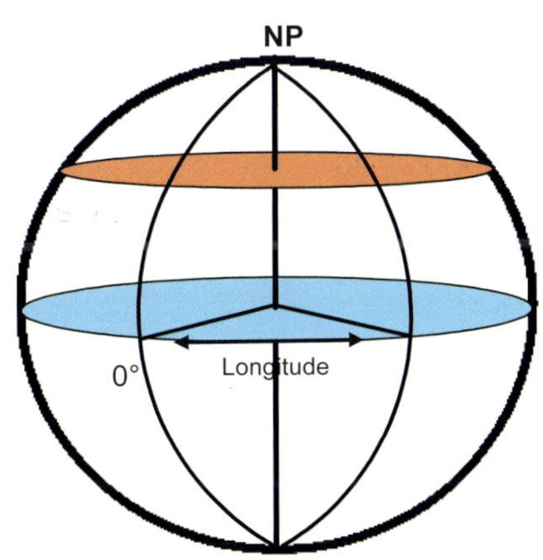

It is annotated east and west depending whether the point lies east or west of the Prime Meridian. Longitude cannot be greater than 180°W or 180°E. These two longitudes are coincident, and the meridian is referred to as the Greenwich Anti-Meridian.

Example 165°35'W or 165°35'E

POSITION USING LATITUDE AND LONGITUDE

Position on the Earth is always expressed as latitude first, then longitude. The lines that form the parallels of latitude and the meridians are called the **graticule**. By using the graticule, any position on the Earth can be determined.

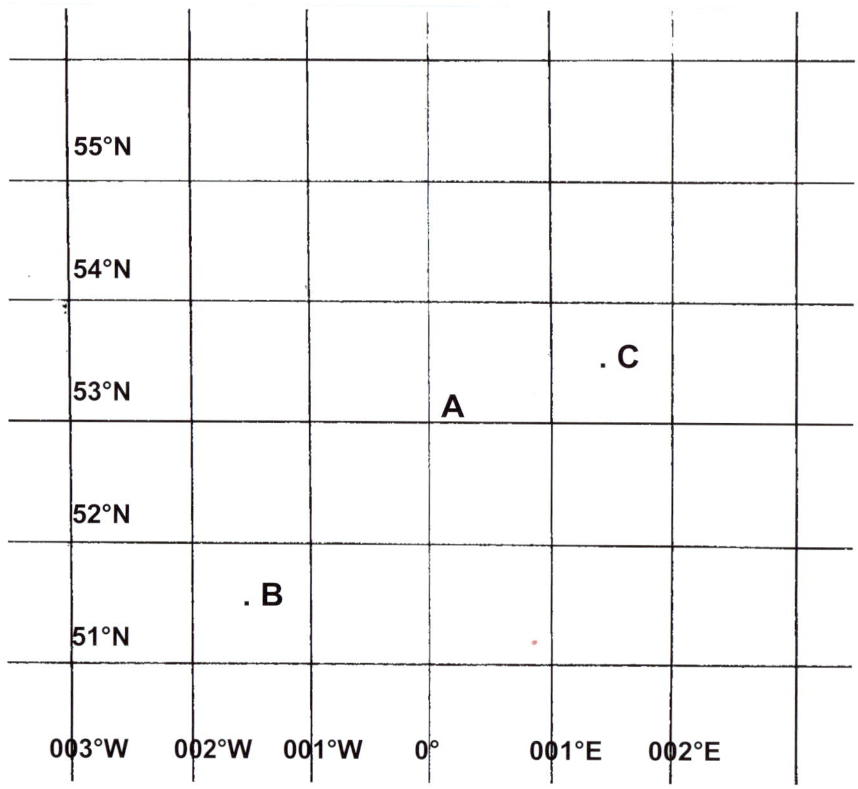

In the above diagram:

- Position A 53°N 0°E/W
- Position B 51°30'N 001°30'W
- Position C 53°30'N 001°30'E

CHANGE OF LATITUDE (CH LAT)

Ch Lat is the shortest arc along a meridian between two parallels of latitude. It is expressed in degrees and minutes.

CALCULATION OF CHANGE OF LATITUDE

Where two points are in the same hemisphere, the Ch Lat is the difference between the two points.

Example 1 Point A is 20°30'N and point B is 41°30'N. If an aircraft is travelling from A to B, what is the Ch Lat?

STEP 1 First calculate the difference between the two points in degrees and minutes. Simply subtract the smallest from the largest:

41°30' – 20°30' = 21°

STEP 2 Note the direction of the change.

In this case, the aircraft is travelling north so the Ch Lat is:

21°N

The term D Lat can also be used. Where Ch Lat is given in degrees and minutes, D Lat is given in minutes alone. For Example 1, the answer would change to:

STEP 3 The D Lat is the Ch Lat expressed in minutes alone.

Remember that there are 60' in 1°.

D Lat is:

21 x 60 = 1260'N

Where the two points are in different hemispheres, the solution is the sum of the two latitudes.

Example 2 Point A is 20°30'N and point B is 41°30'S. If an aircraft is travelling from A to B, what is the Ch Lat?

STEP 1 Calculate the difference between the two points. Simply add the two together:

41°30' + 20°30' = 62°

STEP 2 Note the direction of the change.
In this case, the aircraft is travelling south so the Ch Lat is:
62°S

Position Example 1 Calculate the Ch Lat and D Lat for the following (assume the aircraft is travelling from the first position to the second):

Answers can be found at the end of the chapter.

Position A	Position B	Ch Lat	D Lat
54°35'N	67°34'N		
23°33'S	47°56'S		
33°47'N	23°55'S		
27°25'N	07°44'N		
30°45'S	78°33'N		

MEAN LATITUDE: MEAN LAT (MLAT)

You may be required to calculate the mean latitude. Mean latitude is the mid-point between two latitudes. If the two latitudes are in the same hemisphere, find the Mlat by adding the two values, then dividing by 2.

Example 3 Calculate the Mlat for the positions 65°N and 25°N.

STEP 1 Add the two values of latitude:
65 + 25 = 90

STEP 2 Divide the figure found in STEP 1 by 2:
90 ÷ 2 = 45 = 45°N

If the positions are in different hemispheres, find the Mlat by first adding the two latitudes together, then dividing by two. This figure is then subtracted from the higher value. The higher latitude determines which hemisphere the Mlat is in.

Example 4 Calculate the Mlat for 65°N and 25°S.

STEP 1 Add the two values together:
65 + 25 = 90

STEP 2 Divide the figure found in STEP 1 by 2:
90 ÷ 2 = 45

STEP 3 Subtract the figure found in STEP 2 from the higher latitude:
65 - 45 = 20°N

Remember the higher value determines the hemisphere that Mlat is in.

CHANGE OF LONGITUDE (CH LONG)

To express the difference between two meridians, Ch Long, the smaller arc, is used. Values are expressed in exactly the same manner as Ch Lat. Remember that the value of Ch Long can never exceed 180°. The suffixes E and W are used in regard to the direction of travel.

Example 1 Calculate the Ch Long between position A 165°W and position B 103°W. Assume that the aircraft is flying from A to B.

Find the numerical difference between A and B. The two points are in the same hemisphere, so subtract the smaller from the larger:

165 – 103 = 62°E

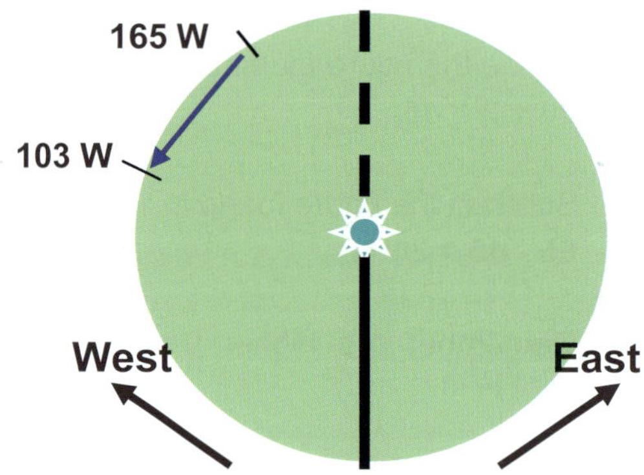

Remember that anti-clockwise measurement is east.

When the two positions are in different hemispheres, the situation is slightly more complicated.

Example 2 Calculate the Ch Long between position A 165°W and position B 170°E. Assume that the aircraft is flying from A to B.

It is obvious the shortest distance between the two points is by crossing the 180° meridian.

The difference between 165° and 180° is 15°.

The difference between 170° and 180° is 10°.

The Ch Long is therefore 25°W because the movement is clockwise.

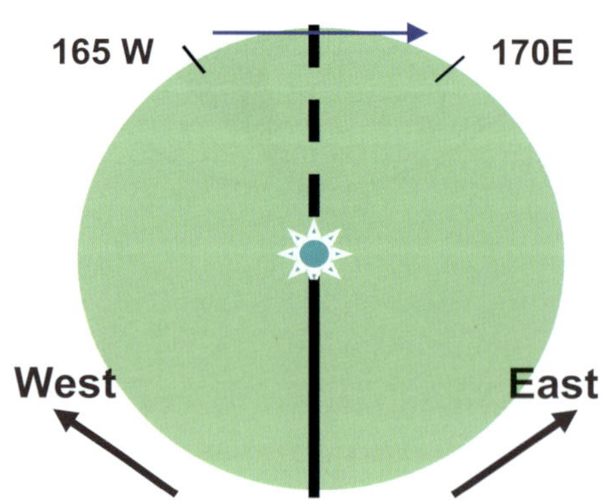

Position Example 2 Calculate the Ch Long and Dlong for the following (assume the aircraft is travelling from the first position to the second):

Position A	Position B	Ch Long	D Long
009°33W'	156°45'W		
153°33'E	078°44'E		
144°23'W	102°33'E		
077°55'W	178°44'E		
143°24'E	179°15'E		

MEAN LONGITUDE

Mean longitude is calculated in the same way as mean latitude. Rarely used in navigation, mean longitude is not discussed further.

ANSWERS TO POSITION EXAMPLES

Position Example 1

Position A	Position B	Ch Lat	D Lat
54°35'N	67°34'N	**12°59'N**	**779'N**
23°33'S	47°56'S	**24°23'S**	**1463'S**
33°47'N	23°55'S	**57°42'S**	**3462'S**
27°25'N	07°44'N	**19°41'S**	**1181'S**
30°45'S	78°33'N	**109°18'N**	**6558'N**

Position Example 2

Position A	Position B	Ch Long	D Long
009°33'W	156°45'W	**147°12'W**	**8832'**
153°33'E	078°44'E	**74°49'W**	**4489'**
144°23'W	102°33'E	**113°04'W**	**6784'**
077°55'W	178°44'E	**103°21'W**	**6201'**
143°24'E	179°15'E	**35°51'E**	**2151'**

Chapter 3
Distance

INTRODUCTION

This chapter describes the definitions and methods of calculating the distance between two points.

DEFINITIONS

Kilometre The length of $^1/_{10\,000}$ of the average distance between the Equator and a pole. The distance from the Equator to either pole is 10 000 km. The circumference of the Earth is 40 000 km.

Metre The length equal to $^1/_{1000th}$ of a kilometre.

Foot An Imperial measurement equal to 0.304 m.

Statute Mile A statute mile is defined as 5280 ft.

Nautical Mile Assuming that the Earth is a perfect sphere, the nautical mile is the length of arc which subtends an angle of one minute at the centre of the Earth.

However, the Earth is not a perfect sphere, and the length of the nautical mile varies:

- The Standard Nautical Mile is 6080 ft.
- At the pole, a Nautical Mile is 6108 ft.
- At the Equator, the Nautical Mile is 6046 ft.

The average value of the nautical mile is approximately 6076 ft. This is the International Nautical Mile, which is approximately 1852 m.

The ICAO Nautical Mile is 1852 m exactly.

CONVERSION FACTORS

The CRP-5 has the conversions required for the JAR-FCL examinations. Use of these scales is discussed in a later chapter.

54 nautical miles (nm) = 62 statute miles (sm) = 100 kilometres (km)

Or:

1 nm	1.85 km
1 nm	1.15 sm

Other useful conversion factors are:

1 metre	100 centimetres
1 centimetre	10 millimetres
1 metre	3.28 feet
1 foot	12 inches
1 foot	30.5 centimetres
1 inch	2.54 centimetres
1 yard	3 feet

GREAT CIRCLE DISTANCE

The definition of a nautical mile, which is the length of arc which subtends an angle of one minute at the centre of the Earth, helps in the calculation of the great circle distance between two points. For most great circle calculations, use spherical geometry. Where the two points are on a meridian or the Equator, the calculation is much easier.

Note: The use of spherical geometry is not required in the JAR examination.

Example 1 **Both positions in the same hemisphere** — What is the shortest distance between A (64°35'N 010°00'W) and B (53°15'N 010°00'W)?

STEP 1 If the points are on the same meridian, calculate the D Lat:
64°35' – 53°15' = 11°20' = 680'

STEP 2 Using the definition of the nautical mile, 1 minute of arc is equivalent to 1 nm:
680' is equal to 680 nm

Example 2 **Both positions in different hemispheres** — What is the shortest distance between A (64°35'N 010°00'W) and B (53°15'S 010°00'W)?

STEP 1 If the points are on the same meridian, calculate the D Lat:
64°35' + 53°15' = 117°50' = 7070'

STEP 2 Using the definition of the nautical mile, 1' is equivalent to 1 nm:
7070' is equal to 7070 nm

Example 3 **Both positions on the meridian and anti-meridian in the same hemisphere** — What is the shortest distance between A (64°35'N 010°00'W) and B (53°15'N 170°00'E)? If both positions are in the same hemisphere, the shortest distance of travel is over the North Pole.

STEP 1 Find the distance to travel from A to the North Pole and from B to the North Pole.

A: 90° – 64°35' = 25°25'= 1525' = 1525 nm

B: 90° – 53°15' = 36°45' = 2205' = 2205 nm

Example 4 **Both positions on the meridian and anti-meridian in different hemispheres** — What is the shortest distance between A (64°35'N 010°00'W) and B (53°15'S 170°00'E)?

It does not matter whether the calculation uses the South Pole or the North Pole.

STEP 1 If travel was by the North Pole, the approximate distance would be:

90° – 64°35' = 25°25' = 1525 nm

90° + 53°15' = 143°15' = 8595 nm

Total 10 120 nm

STEP 2 If the calculation had been done using the South Pole:

90° + 64°35' = 154°35'

90° - 53°15' = 36°45'

Total = 191°20'

The answer is more than 180°, which is the longer distance of the two, and therefore not of commercial use.

STEP 3 Subtract the answer found in STEP 2 from 360°.

360° - 191°20' = 168°40' = 10 120'

Total 10 120 nm

Example 5 **Two points on the Equator** — What is the great circle distance between A (00°00'N/S 012°00'W) and B (00°00'N/S 012°00'E)?

The calculation is the same as for two points on the same meridian.

STEP 1 Calculate D Long between A and B.

A to the Prime Meridian is 12°

B to the Prime Meridian is 12°

Total 24° = 1440' = 1440 nm

Distance Example 1 Calculate the shortest distances between the following points:

Position A	Position B	Distance
37°14'N 030°00'W	45°35'S 030°00'W	
58°34'N 120°34'E	19°45'N 120°34'E	
42°56'N 010°35'E	55°33'N 169°25'W	
00°00'N/S 123°35'E	00°00'N/S 003°26'W	
25°33'S 070°14'W	66°47'N 109°46'E	

DEPARTURE (EAST – WEST DISTANCE CALCULATION)

When calculating D Lat, a change in 1 minute of latitude was found to be equivalent to 1 nm. A change in 1 minute of longitude is only equivalent to 1 nm where the East – West direction follows a great circle – the Equator.

Because the meridians converge, the distance between them decreases with increasing distance from the Equator:

- At the Equator, the distance between two meridians is 60 nm
- At the poles, the distance between the meridians is 0 nm

An aviator requires a method of calculating the distance East-West between two points.

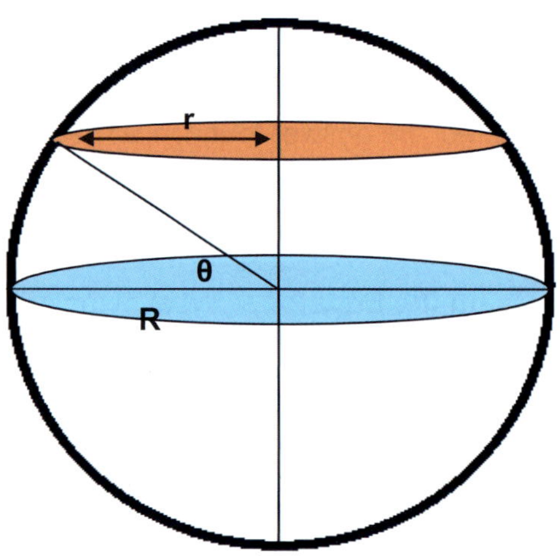

In the above diagram:

$$r = R \cos \theta$$

Where:

R	Radius of the Earth
r	Radius of the parallel of latitude to be found
θ	Latitude in degrees

The radius varies with the cosine of the latitude. The distance between two meridians varies at a constant rate. Therefore, the distance between two meridians 1 degree apart is:

60 cos Lat

Where 60 is the D Long between two meridians.

The formula can also be expressed as a function of D Long:

Departure = D Long cos Lat

Example Calculate the distance between two meridians that are 10° apart at latitude 60°N

STEP 1 D Long = 10 x 60 = 600'

STEP 2 Formula: Departure = D Long cos Lat
600 cos 60 = 600 x 0.5 = 300 nm

Distance Example 2 What is the distance between 00500W and 01000E at a latitude of 35°S?

Distance Example 3 The distance between 01000W and 00500W is 200 nm. What is the latitude?

Distance Example 4 Starting at position 5000N 00000E/W, an aircraft flies due west for 1000 nm. What is the final position?

DISTANCE EXAMPLE ANSWERS

Distance Example 1

Position A	Position B	Distance
37°14'N 030°00'W	45°35'S 030°00'W	**4969 nm**
58°34'N 120°34'E	19°45'N 120°34'E	**2329 nm**
42°56'N 010°35'E	55°33'N 169°25'W	**4891 nm**
00°00'N/S 123°35'E	00°00'N/S 003°26'W	**7621 nm**
25°33'S 070°14'W	66°47'N 109°46'E	**8326 nm**

Distance Example 2 D Long = 15 x 60 = 900'

900 cos 35 = 900 x .819

737 nm

Distance Example 3 Departure = D Long x cos Lat

cos Lat = Departure / D Long

cos Lat = $^{200}/_{300}$

Inverse cos 0.66 = 48.2

Latitude 48.2°

Distance Example 4 D Long = Departure / cos Lat

$^{1000}/_{\cos 50} = {}^{1000}/_{.642} = 1557.6'$

25°57.6' Ch Long

Final Position 50°00'N 025°57.6'W

Chapter 4 Direction

INTRODUCTION

Direction is used to:

- Provide a datum for following a line across the surface of the Earth
- Relate positions to each other

DEFINITIONS

Course	The intended track
Heading	The direction in which the fore-and-aft axis of the aircraft is pointing
Track	The flight path that the aircraft has followed (Also known as Track Made Good)

TRUE DIRECTION

True direction is a reference to the direction of the Geographic North Pole, whether the aircraft is in the Northern or Southern Hemisphere.

MAGNETIC DIRECTION

It is not possible to directly determine true direction in an aircraft. Instead, use what is called magnetic direction.

The Earth's magnetic field acts as if there are two magnetic poles. These magnetic poles are not co-located with the North and South Geographic poles, and unlike the geographic poles, they move annually. The magnetic North Pole and the geographic North Pole are separated by approximately 900 nm. The magnetic North Pole rotates around the True North Pole approximately every 960 years.

Unlike the geographic poles, the magnetic poles are not antipodal.

The Earth's magnetic field has a horizontal and a vertical component (this is described more fully in Chapter 20 – Aircraft Magnetism).

A magnet freely suspended indicates the position of the magnetic poles. Magnetic direction can be measured by reference to a freely suspended magnet. Aircraft compasses have a magnet which detects the horizontal component of the Earth's magnetic field, giving the magnetic direction.

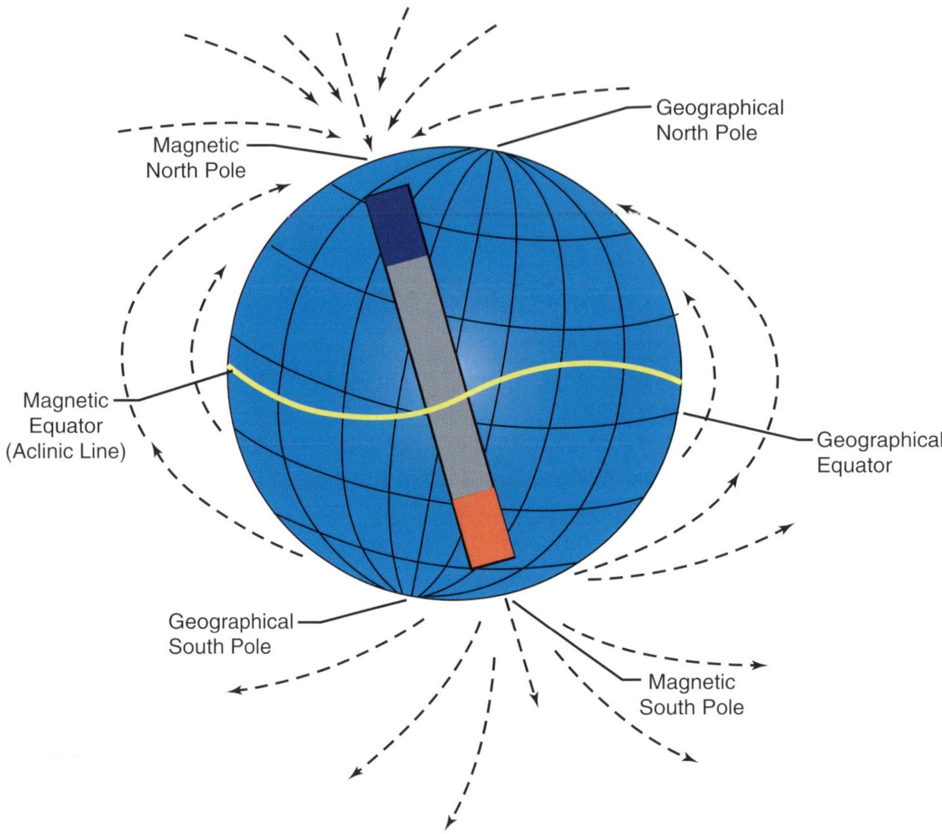

VARIATION

Variation is the angular difference between magnetic north and true north at any given point.

Variation is measured in degrees with the suffix W (west) or E (east).

VARIATION – WEST

When magnetic north lies to the west of true north, the variation is west.

For the following diagrams:

Arrow	Designation
———▶	Magnetic North
———◆	True North
———●	Compass North

The diagram below indicates that the magnetic heading is larger and:

Variation + True Heading = Magnetic Heading

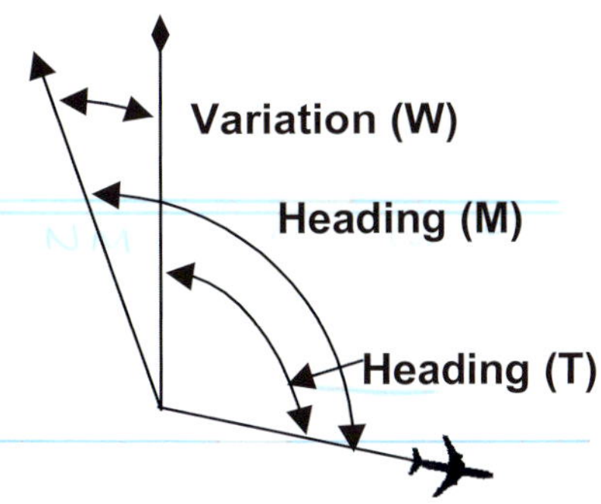

A useful aide memoire for this goes as follows:

VARIATION WEST	MAGNETIC BEST

Example 1 If the aircraft is heading 130°T and the variation is 15°W, what is the magnetic heading?

STEP 1 Variation (W) + True Heading = Magnetic Heading
15° + 130° = 145°M

VARIATION – EAST

When magnetic north lies to the east of true north, the variation is said to be east.

From the diagram below, notice that the magnetic heading is smaller and:

True Heading – Variation (E) = Magnetic Heading

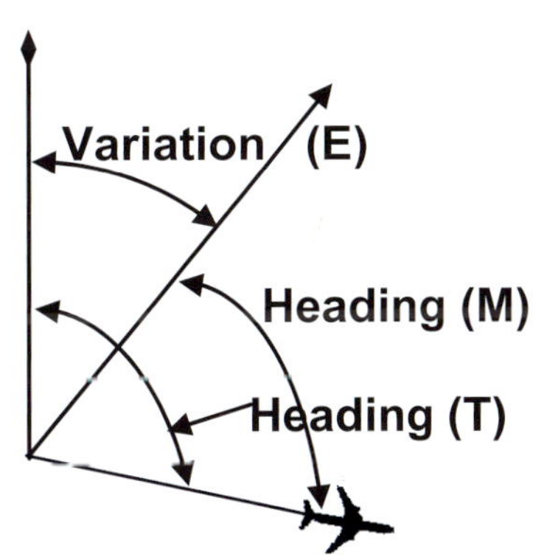

The equivalent aide memoire for this is:

VARIATION EAST	MAGNETIC LEAST

Example 2 If the aircraft is heading 130°T and the variation is 15°E, what is the magnetic heading?

STEP 1 True Heading - Variation (E) = Magnetic Heading
130° - 15° = 115°M

ISOGONAL

On all aeronautical charts, places of equal magnetic variation, **isogonals**, are marked. Variation is applied to the magnetic direction to give true direction and vice versa.

— 3° E —

A pecked or dashed blue line is used to indicate the isogonal on an aeronautical chart.

THE AGONIC LINE

The **Agonic Line** is an isogonal where the value of variation is zero. This is described more fully in Chapter 20 – Aircraft Magnetism.

DEVIATION

Because of the aircraft's inherent magnetic fields, a compass settles on what it interprets as magnetic north. The causes of aircraft magnetism are discussed the Chapter 20. The angle between what the compass indicates as magnetic north (compass north) and the real magnetic north is known as deviation.

Like variation, deviation is measured in degrees east (E) or west (W).

DEVIATION – WEST

Where compass north lies to the west of magnetic north, the deviation is west.

Magnetic Heading + Deviation (W) = Compass Heading

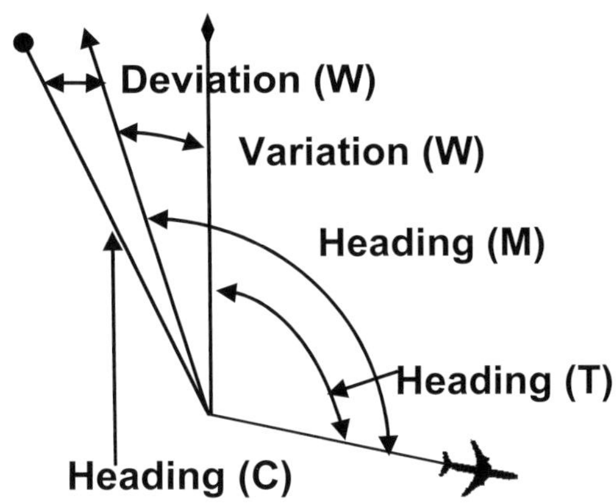

A useful aide memoire for this is:

DEVIATION WEST	COMPASS BEST

Example 3 An aircraft is flying a heading of 130°M; deviation is 10°W. What is the compass heading?

STEP 1 Magnetic Heading + Deviation (W) = Compass Heading
130° + 10° = 140°C

DEVIATION – EAST

Where compass north is to the east of magnetic north, the deviation is east.

Magnetic North – Deviation (E) = Compass Heading

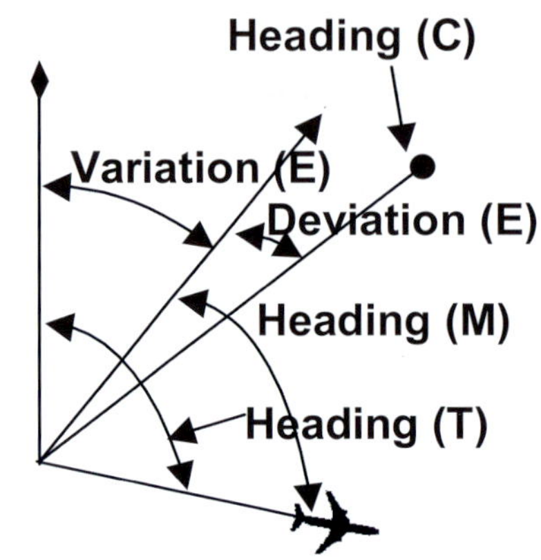

The equivalent aide memoire for this is:

DEVIATION EAST	COMPASS LEAST

Example 3 An aircraft is flying a heading of 130°M; deviation is 10°E. What is the compass heading?

STEP 1 Magnetic Heading - Deviation (E) = Compass Heading
130° - 10° = 120°C

In the JAR examinations, deviation can sometimes be given as a positive or negative numeric value (+3 or –3). Add or subtract the value from compass heading to get the magnetic heading:

+3 would be deviation 3E
-3 would be deviation 3W

Example 4 Compass heading is 250°; deviation +3°. What is the magnetic heading?

STEP 1 Compass Heading + Deviation = Magnetic Heading
250° + 3° = MH
MH = 253°

Example 5 Magnetic heading is 017°; deviation +4°. What is the compass heading?

STEP 1 Compass Heading + Deviation = Magnetic Heading
CH + 4° = 017°

STEP 2 Transpose the equation
CH = 017° – 4° = 013°

Direction Example 1 Complete the following table:

True Heading	Variation	Magnetic Heading	Deviation	Compass Heading
150°		170°	2°W	
	7°E	125°	4°W	
325°		333°		330°
247°	12°W			260°
001°	5°E		5°W	
	15°W	247°	2°E	
075°		095°	3°W	
213°	9°W		1E	
337°		330°		332°
	17°E	258°	3°W	

RELATIVE BEARING

The relative bearing is always measured clockwise from the nose of the aircraft. To obtain a true bearing from an aircraft:

True Bearing (TB) = Relative Bearing + Heading (T)

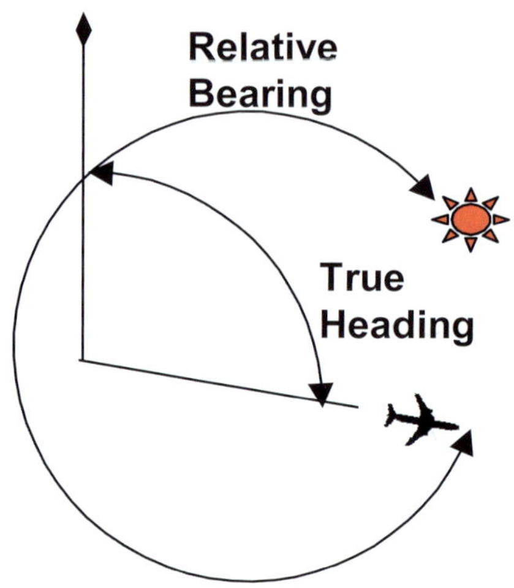

Example 6 Assume in the diagram above that the aircraft is heading 110°T. An island is seen on a relative bearing of 270° (remember that the relative bearing is measured from the nose clockwise). What is the true bearing of the island from the aircraft?

STEP 1 True Bearing = Relative Bearing + Heading
110° + 270° = 380°

STEP 2 Because the answer is greater than 360°, 360° has to be subtracted from the answer.
380° – 360° = 020°

The true bearing of the island from the aircraft is 020°T.

As an alternative, the island could be said to be 90° left of the aircraft. Using left as minus and right as plus the calculation goes as follows:

STEP 1 Aircraft Heading ± Bearing Left or Right = True Bearing
110° – 090° = 020°T

Use whichever method is the easiest.

DIRECTION EXAMPLE ANSWERS

Direction Example 1

True Heading	Variation	Magnetic Heading	Deviation	Compass Heading
150°	**20°W**	170°	2°W	**172°**
132°	7°E	125°	4°W	**129°**
325°	**8°W**	333°	**3°E**	330°
247°	12°W	**259°**	**1°W**	260°
001°	5°E	**356°**	5°W	**001°**
232°	15°W	247°	2°E	**245°**
075°	**20°W**	095°	3°W	**098°**
213°	9°W	**222°**	1°E	**221°**
337°	**7°E**	330°	**2°W**	332°
275°	17°E	258°	3°W	**261°**

Chapter 5
Speed

INTRODUCTION

Speed is the rate of change of position, or distance covered, per unit of time. It is expressed in linear units per hour. As there are three main linear units, there are three main expressions of speed:

Knotst (kt)	nautical miles per hour
Miles per hour (mph)	statute miles per hour
Kilometres per hour (kph)	

These speeds represent how far an aircraft travels in one hour (i.e. a speed of 300 kt means that in one hour an aircraft travels 300 nm).

Speed can be calculated from the formula:

SPEED = DISTANCE/TIME

Three groups of speed are used in air navigation:

Airspeed	The speed of the aircraft through the air
Groundspeed	The speed of the aircraft relative to the ground
Relative Speed	The speed of an aircraft relative to another aircraft

AIRSPEED

AIRSPEED INDICATOR READING (ASIR)

The speed measured by the pitot-static system connected to the airspeed indicator without any corrections.

INDICATED AIRSPEED (IAS)

Indicated airspeed is the ASIR, corrected for instrument error due to imperfections in manufacture. The aircraft is flown on IAS.

INSTRUMENT ERROR

Caused by inaccuracies during the manufacturing process. Normally, these errors are so small they are ignored.

RECTIFIED AIRSPEED (RAS)

Rectified Airspeed, sometimes known as Calibrated Airspeed (CAS), is IAS corrected for Position Error. RAS equals TAS (True Airspeed) in calibration conditions, sea level temperature +15°C, with pressure 1013.25 mb.

POSITION ERROR

When the air flow around the pitot-static system is disrupted, inaccuracies can occur. Position errors for different configurations are listed in the operating manual by using graphs or tables.

EQUIVALENT AIRSPEED (EAS)

Most ASIs are calibrated for an ideal incompressible air flow ($\frac{1}{2}\rho v^2$). As compression affects all speeds, EAS is RAS corrected for compressibility. In real terms, EAS is the speed equivalent to a given dynamic pressure in ISA conditions at mean sea level.

By using a compressibility factor, RAS/CAS can be corrected to give EAS. The CRP-5 can be used for the calculation. Normally, compressibility is only corrected for a TAS of greater than 300 kt.

TRUE AIRSPEED (TAS)

TAS is the speed of the aircraft relative to the air mass through which the aircraft is flying.True airspeed is EAS corrected for density error – pressure altitude and temperature.

TAS can be mentally calculated by adding 2 percent of the RAS/CAS for each 1000 ft of pressure altitude.

Example An aircraft is flying at 10 000 ft at an RAS/CAS of 150 kt. What is the TAS?

STEP 1 Apply the formula

TAS = CAS + ((2 x $^{CAS}/_{100}$) x Altitude in 1000s of ft)

TAS = 150 + ((2 x 1.5) x 10)

TAS = 150 + 30 = 180 kt

Note: The above is a rule of thumb only. A more accurate method for this conversion exists using the Pooley's flight computer and is described in a later chapter.

DENSITY ERROR

Air density decreases with:

- Higher temperatures
- Higher pressure altitude

Flying at the same groundspeed in still air, the ASI will indicate a lower speed if:

- The temperature increases
- The pressure altitude increases

The correction for air density can be calculated mathematically or by use of the CRP-5.

GROUNDSPEED

Groundspeed is the speed of the aircraft relative to the ground. It takes into account the aircraft's movement relative to the air mass (TAS and heading) and movement of the airmass (wind velocity).

MACH NUMBER

An alternative method of measuring speed is to express it as a fraction of the local speed of sound (LSS). This fraction is known as the **Mach Number** (MN). The relationship of TAS to Mach Number is much simpler than that of RAS to TAS, as the only variable factor is temperature. Therefore, at higher speeds it is usually easier to calculate TAS from Mach Number.

The LSS depends upon the air mass temperature and is calculated using the following formula:

$$LSS = 39\sqrt{T°K}$$

Where T is the temperature in degrees Kelvin.

An approximate calculation is:

$$LSS = (644 + 1.2t)$$

Where t is in degrees centigrade.

The formula for calculating the MN is based on TAS and the local speed of sound (LSS).

$$MN = TAS/LSS$$

SUMMARY OF SPEED

The following flow chart shows the relationship between the various speeds.

ASIR
| **Instrument Error**
IAS
| **Position Error**
RAS/CAS
| **Compressibility**
EAS
| **Density**
TAS
| **Wind**
Groundspeed

INTRODUCTION TO RELATIVE SPEED

Relative speed is the speed of one object in relation to another. In the diagram below, the two aircraft are at different speeds, and the relative speed is the difference between the two:
360 – 300 = 60 kt

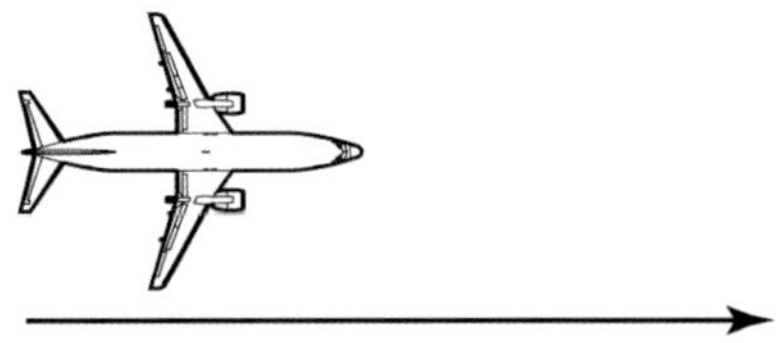

Aircraft A - 300 knots

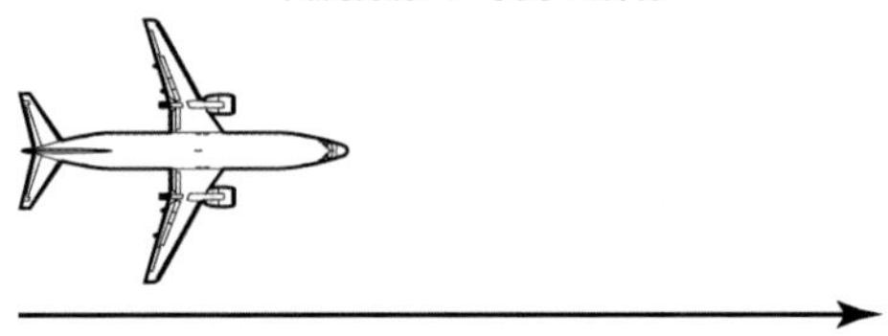

Aircraft B - 360 knots

Where the aircraft are on reciprocal tracks, the relative speed is the sum of the two speeds.

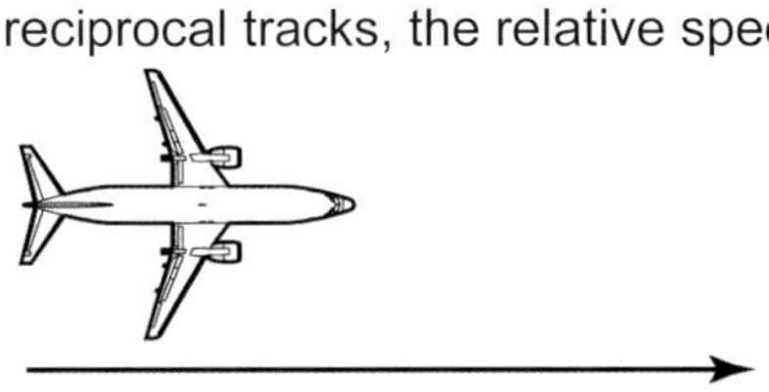

Aircraft A - 300 knots

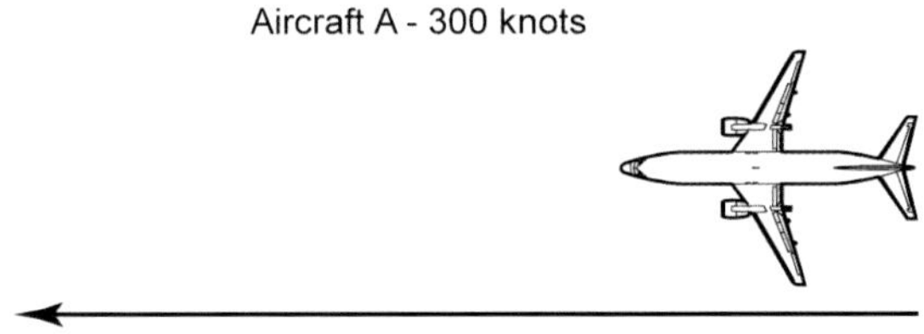

Aircraft B - 360 knots

In this case, the relative speed (closing speed) is 360 + 300 = 660 kt.

The relative speed can be used to calculate times of:

- Aircraft crossing
- When two aircraft will meet

Relative speeds and relative velocity are discussed more fully in Chapter 16 – Relative Velocity.

Chapter 6
Triangle of Velocities

INTRODUCTION

A velocity is a combination of speed and direction. Speed is a scalar quantity, whereas velocity is a vector quantity.

Velocity can be represented graphically by a straight line where:

- The length of the line represents the speed.
- The direction of the line is measured from a datum.

Any convenient scale can be used.

THE COMPONENTS OF THE TRIANGLE OF VELOCITIES

The components of the triangle of velocities are the **air vector**, the **wind vector**, and the **ground vector**. The ground vector is the vector sum, or resultant, of the other two components.

THE AIR VECTOR

This describes the path of the aircraft through the air. The heading is the direction the aircraft flies in relation to the air mass. The aircraft's speed through the air is the true airspeed. The two sub-components of the air vector are heading (HDG) and true airspeed (TAS).

The air vector is shown below:

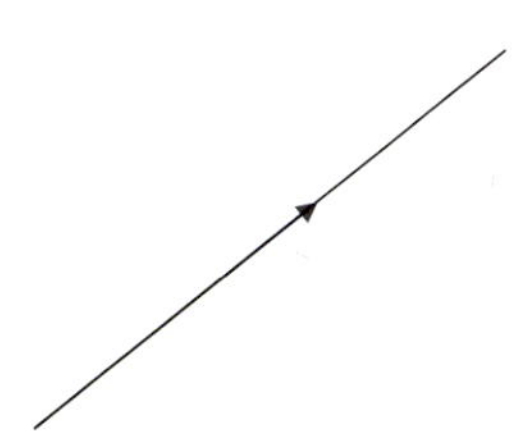

THE WIND VECTOR

The wind vector describes the movement of the air mass through which the aircraft is travelling, over the surface of the Earth. Wind velocity, when written, includes the direction from which the wind is blowing and the speed (usually in knots). It is written as a 5 or 6 figure group, as shown below:

330/25

330/125

The diagram shows the air vector and the wind vector:

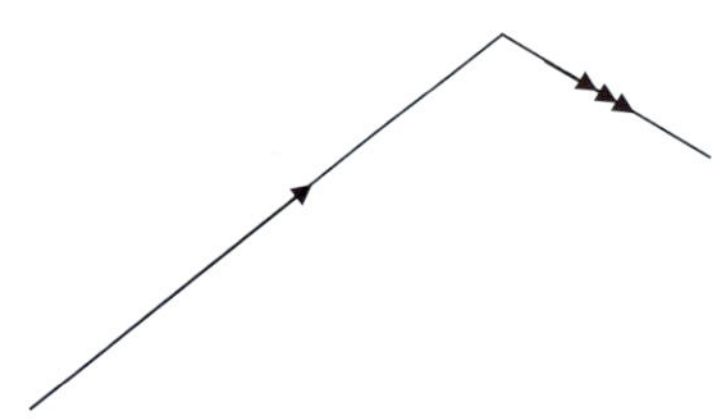

The vector summation of the air vector (heading and TAS) and wind velocity give the third component, the ground vector.

THE GROUND VECTOR

This describes the direction and speed of the aircraft over the ground. It comprises track (TRK) and groundspeed (GS).

The diagram below shows the completed triangle of velocities:

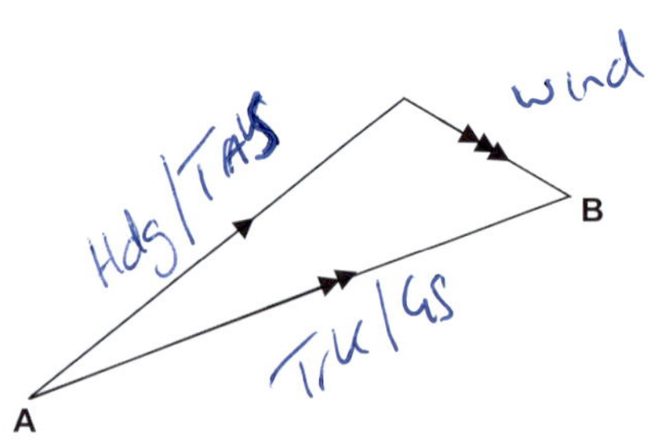

The angle between the heading and the track is the drift angle.

- If blown to the right, as in the case above, it is **Right Drift**
- If blown to the left, it is **Left Drift**

As the diagrams show, each vector is represented by its unique arrow convention:

One Arrow	Heading and TAS
Two Arrows	Track (Course) and Groundspeed
Three Arrows	Wind Velocity

Each of the three components is made up of two sub-components, a total of six sub-components. Given any four of these, it is possible to determine the other two. Chapter 8 describes how the CRP-5 can be used to solve the triangle of velocities.

To reinforce understanding of the chapter, solve the following problems graphically, using a sheet of plain paper:

Triangle of Velocities Example 1

Given:

Heading	100°T
TAS	210 kt
Wind Velocity	020/25

Find the track and groundspeed.

Triangle of Velocities Example 2

Given:

Heading	270°T
TAS	230 kt
Track	280°T
Groundspeed	215 kt

Find the wind velocity.

Triangle of Velocities Example 3

Given:

TAS	220 kt
Track	230°T
Wind Velocity	270/50

Find the heading and groundspeed.

ANSWERS TO THE TRIANGLE OF VELOCITIES EXAMPLES

Triangle of Velocities Example 1

STEP 1 From any origin, draw a vector of 100°T. Represent the TAS by drawing the line to a sensible scale (1 cm equal to 20 nm). The vector is then 10½ cm long.

STEP 2 From the end of the heading vector, draw the wind direction of 020°. Remember that the wind direction is always the direction from which the wind is blowing. Draw the line to 25 nm scale, using the same scale for the heading and TAS – 1.25 cm.

STEP 3 Measure the track and the length of the vector.

Track **107°**

Groundspeed **208 kt**

Triangle of Velocities Example 2

STEP 1 From any origin, draw a vector of 270°T. Represent the TAS (230 kt) by drawing the line to a sensible scale.

STEP 2 From the start of the heading vector, draw the track (280°), and mark off the groundspeed using the same scale as the heading/TAS vector.

STEP 3 Measure the wind velocity.

Wind Velocity **207/42**

Triangle of Velocities Example 3

STEP 1 From any origin, draw the wind velocity.

STEP 2 From the origin, draw the track (230°). Make the line of any length, as the groundspeed is unknown.

STEP 3 From the head of the wind velocity, draw an arc using dividers, which represents the TAS.

STEP 4 Where the arc intercepts the track, measure the heading and groundspeed.

Heading **239°**

Groundspeed **179 kt**

Chapter 7
Pooley's CRP-5 — Circular Slide Rule

INTRODUCTION

The circular slide rule found on the CRP-5 is depicted below. If used effectively, it can give reasonably accurate answers to calculations needed for both flight planning and general navigation. The JAR-FCL General Navigation examination requires numerous calculations which involve the CRP-5. It is important to learn to perform these calculations both quickly and accurately.

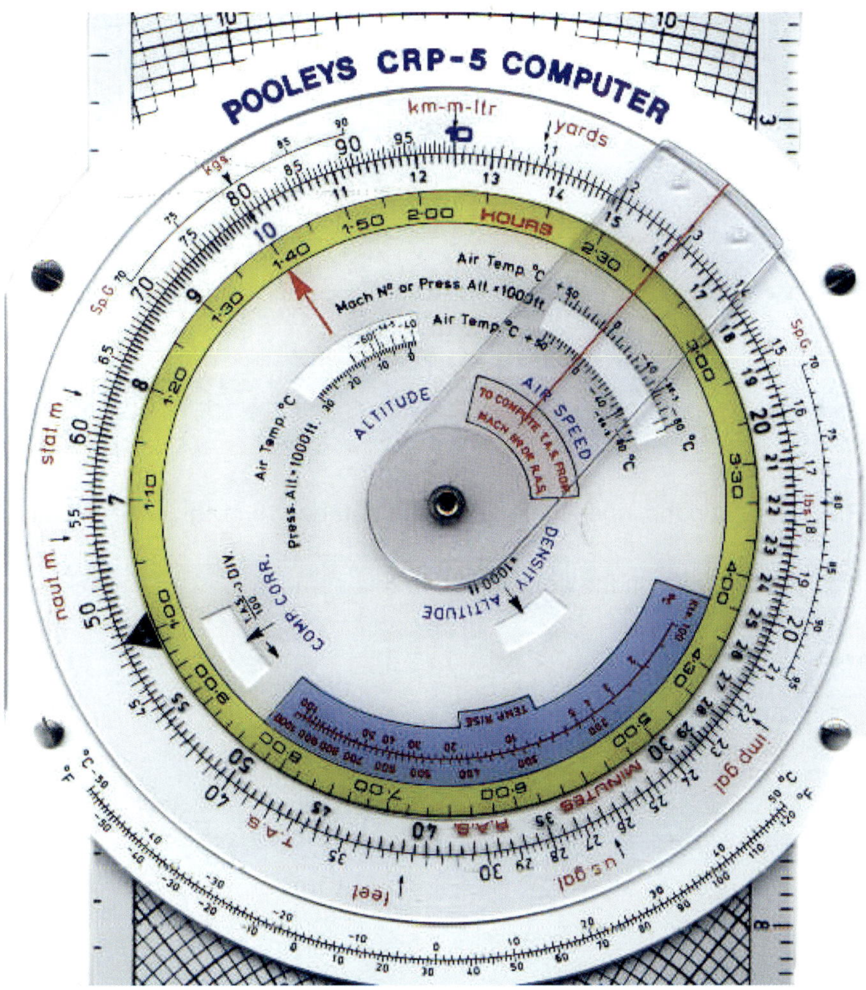

The slide rule consists of two circular scales, an outer fixed scale and an inner moveable scale. Numbers are printed on both scales from 10 to 99.9. When doing any calculation, the user mentally places the decimal point before reading the answer off the slide rule. So 25 can represent .0025, .025, .25, 2.5, 25, etc. Note that the scale around the slide rule is not constant but logarithmic.

MULTIPLICATION, DIVISION, AND RATIOS

MULTIPLICATION

Here are some simple examples to illustrate how the CRP-5 is used.

Example Consider the simple multiplication 8 X 1.5. Mental arithmetic says the answer is 12.

STEP 1 Rotate the inner scale so that the number 10 is under the number 80 (80 represents 8, and 10 represents 1).

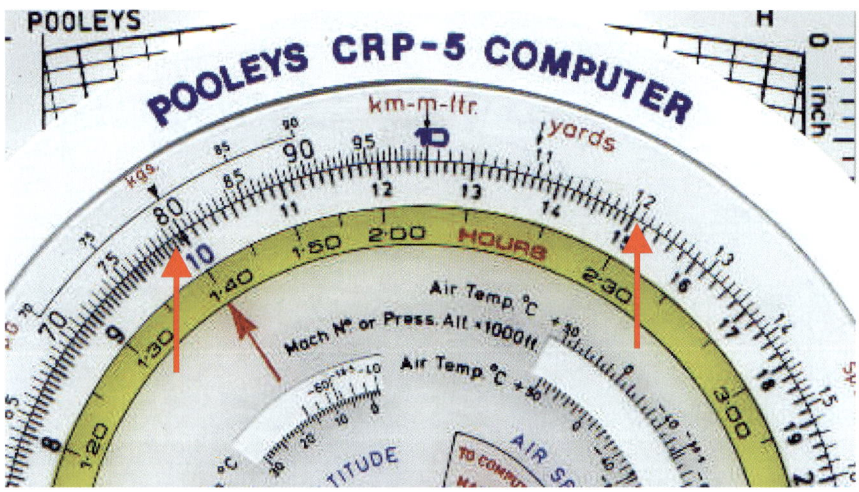

STEP 2 On the inner scale, go to the number 15 (1.5).

STEP 3 Read off the answer above this number.

Answer **12**

Example Multiply 1.72 by 2.

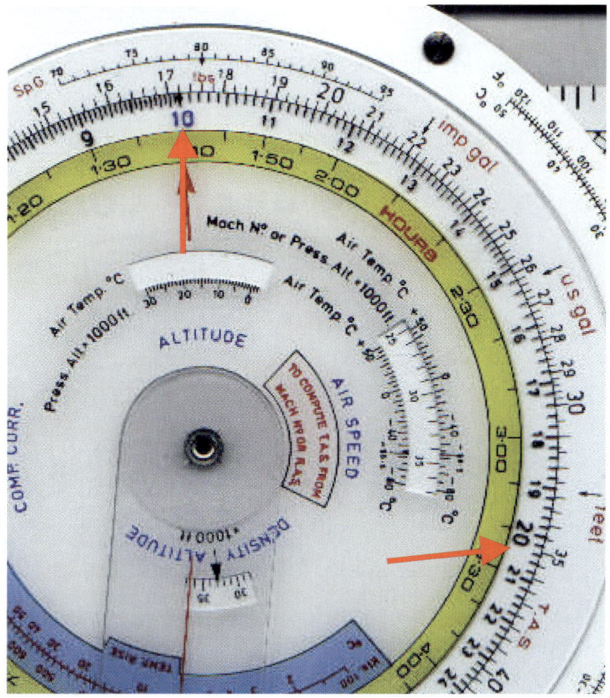

Answer **3.44**

CRP Example 1 Answer the following questions:

a. 70 x 213
b. .02 x .3
c. 31 x .75
d. 1.5 x 1.7
e. 46 x 57

DIVISION

Division is the exact opposite of multiplication.

Example Using the same numbers for the multiplication, divide 12 by 1.5.

STEP 1 Place 15 on the inner scale under 12 on the outer scale.

STEP 2 On the inner scale, follow the numbers to 10.

STEP 3 On the outer scale, read off the answer.
Answer: 8

Example Divide 34.4 by 20.

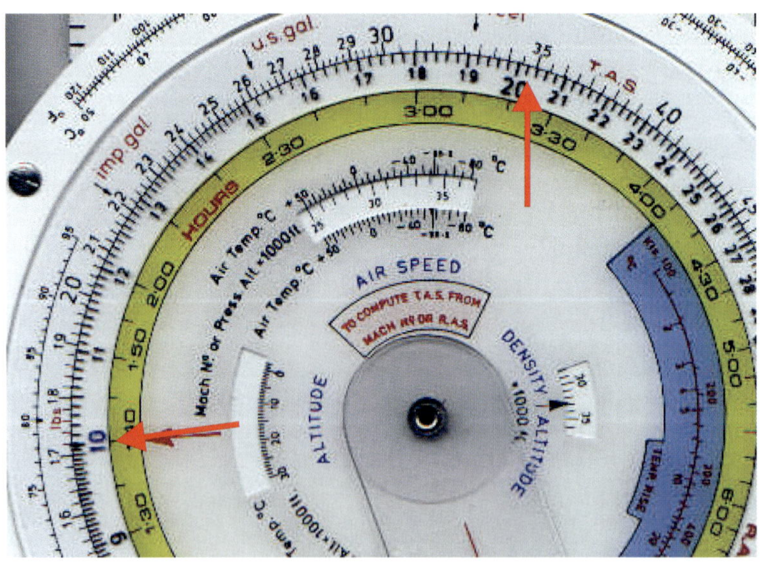

Answer **1.72**

CRP Example 2 Complete the following questions:

a. 70 ÷ 213

b. .02 ÷ .3

c. 31 ÷ .75

d. 1.5 ÷1.7

e. 46 ÷ 57

RATIOS

Any ratio can be read off the slide rule direct.

Example For $^{A}/_{B} = {}^{C}/_{D}$, assume that A = 30, B = 15, and D = 25. What is C?

STEP 1 Place 15(B) on the inner scale under 30(A) on the outer scale.

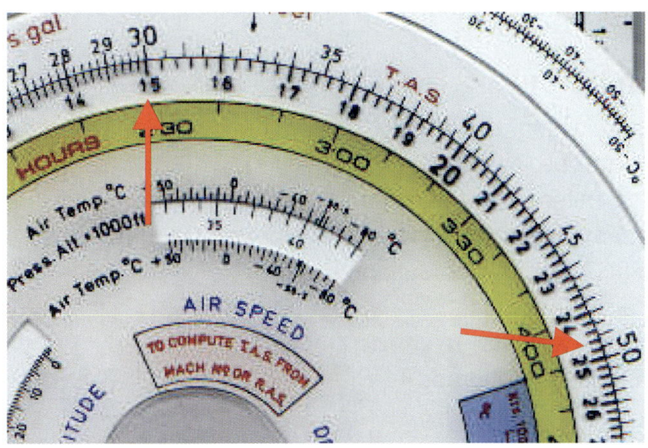

STEP 2 Follow the inner scale to 25(D).

STEP 3 Read off the answer on the outer scale.

Answer **50**

Example If A = 35, B = 20.4, and D = 14, what is C?

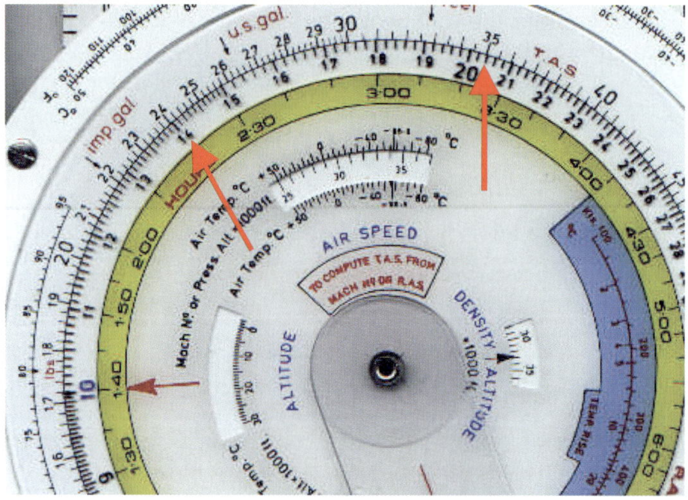

Answer **24**

Conversions use the same principle as the multiplication, division, and ratio calculations.

CONVERSIONS

The conversions required for the JAR-FCL examination include:

- Feet – metres – yards
- Nautical miles – statute miles – kilometres
- Knots – miles per hour (mph) – kilometres per hour (kph)
- Imperial Gallons – US Gallons – litres
- Kilograms – pounds
- Volumes – weights
- Fahrenheit to centigrade

In order to correctly place the decimal point in an answer, use the following rough conversion to get a ballpark estimate before doing the conversion on the CRP-5.

- 1 yard = 3 feet
- 1 metre = 3.3 feet
- 1 nm = 1.2 statute miles = 2 km
- 1 imp gal = 1.2 US gal = 4.5 litres
- 1 kilogram = 2.2 pounds

The above units are indicated in red on the outer scale of the slide rule with black arrows showing the datum point.

FEET – METRES – YARDS

Example Convert 3 feet into yards and metres.

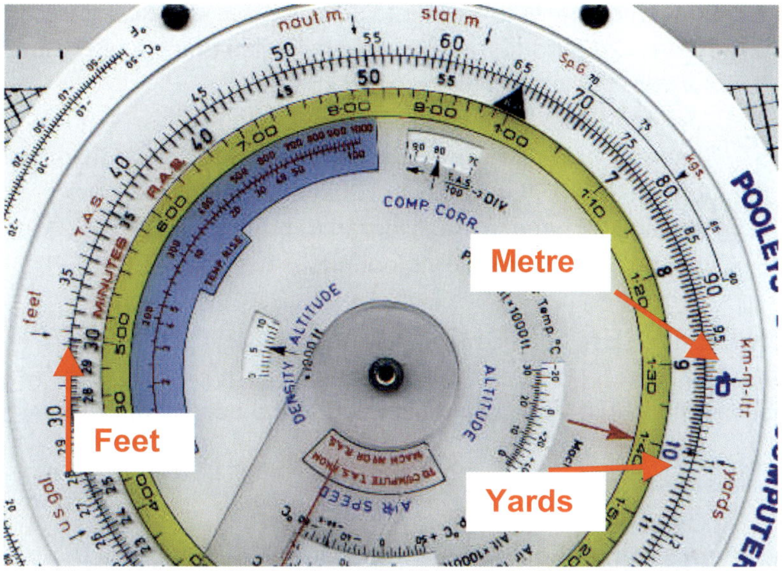

STEP 1 Under the feet arrow on the outer scale, place 3 on the inner scale.

STEP 2 On the inner scale, opposite the yards and metres datum arrows, read off the answers.

1 yard; 0.915 metres

CRP Example 3

	Feet	Yards	Metres
1.	19500	6500	5943
2.	230	76·6	70·1
3.	5577	1859.	1700
4.	51	153	16
5.	28500	9500	8686

The following conversions use exactly the same system as feet – yards – metres. Look for the red datum written on the outer scale, and read off the answer on the inner scale.

- Nautical miles – statute miles – kilometres
- Knots – miles per hour (mph) – kilometres per hour (kph)
- Imperial Gallons – US Gallons – litres
- Kilograms – pounds

CRP Example 4

Answer the following questions:

1. Convert 60 nautical miles into statute miles and kilometres.
2. Convert 200 kilometres into nautical miles and statute miles.
3. Convert 350 knots into mph and kph.
4. Convert 450 kph into knots and mph.
5. Convert 21 000 litres into US Gallons and Imperial Gallons.
6. Convert 300 US Gallons into litres and Imperial Gallons.
7. Convert 650 pounds into kilograms.
8. Convert 345 kilograms into pounds.

CONVERSION BETWEEN WEIGHT AND VOLUME

To convert between weight and volume, start with the specific gravity (SG) of the fuel. The SG expresses the density of the fuel as a decimal fraction of the density of water.

1 litre of water weighs 1 kilogram.

Fuel is less dense than water. For example, Avgas usually has an SG of 0.72. One litre of Avgas with an SG of 0.72 weighs 0.72 kilograms.

Both the volume datum point and the specific gravity datum points are used in these conversions. There are two SG datum points on the slide rule:

- One centred around the pounds datum
- One centred around the kilograms datum

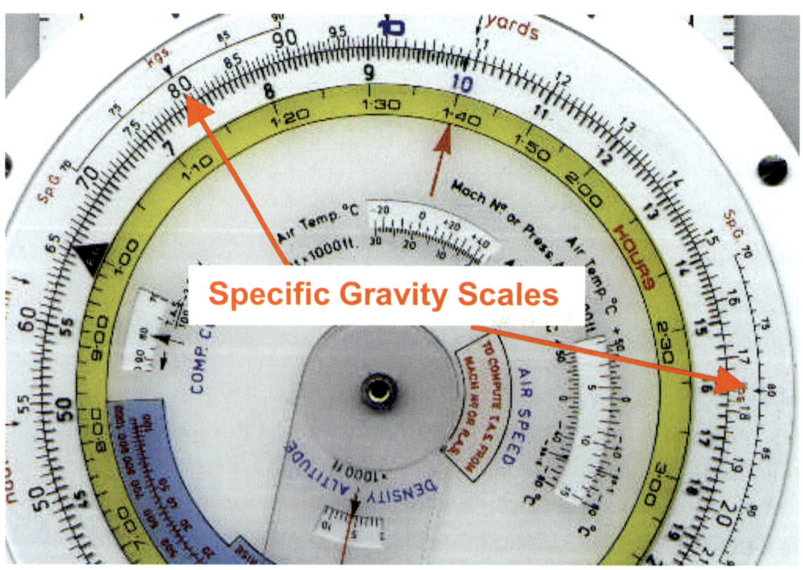

Example To convert 800 Imperial Gallons (SG 0.75) into kilograms and pounds.

STEP 1 Do a rough calculation first; 800 Imperial Gallons equates to about 3600 litres. Multiply by the SG, to obtain 2700 kilograms.

STEP 2 Against the Imperial Gallon datum, align 8 on the inner scale.

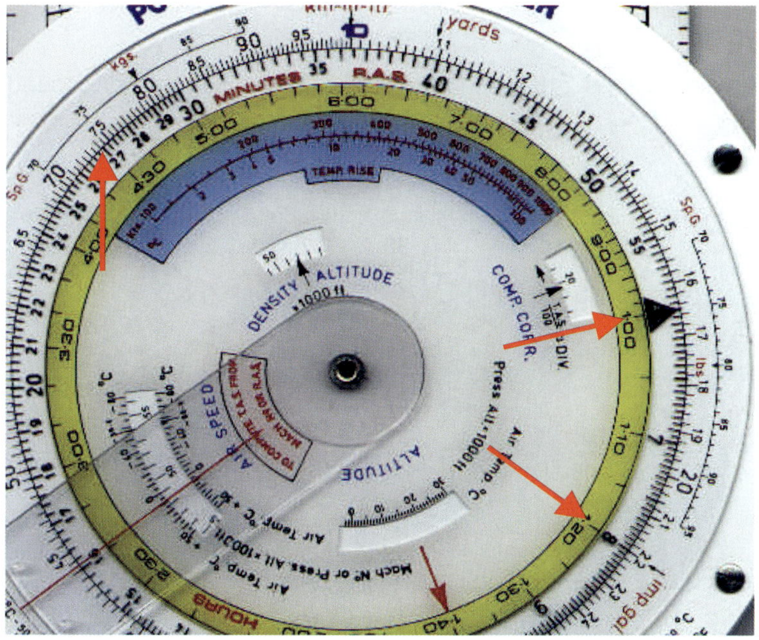

STEP 3 Against the SG scale for kilograms, read off the number of kilograms abeam 0.75 **2720**

STEP 4 From the SG datum for pounds, read off the number of pounds from the inner scale abeam 0.75 **6000**

FAHRENHEIT TO CENTIGRADE

The conversion scale found at the bottom of the slide rule makes this a simple operation.

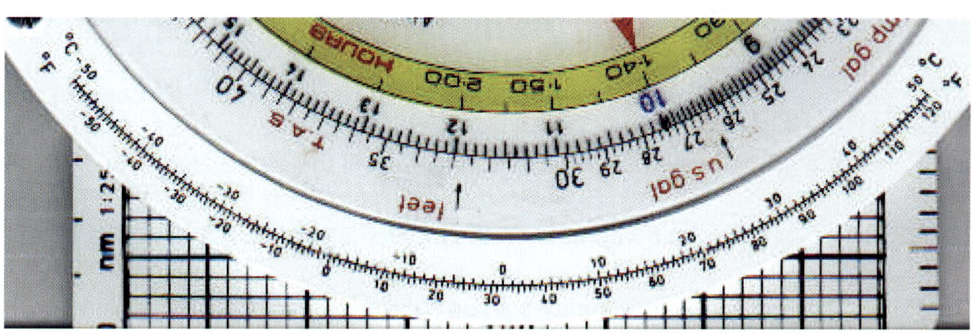

Example The temperature is 14 degrees centigrade. What is the temperature in Fahrenheit?

Answer Find 14 on the inner arc. Read off the temperature on the outer arc.
57°F

SPEED, DISTANCE, AND TIME

To calculate any of the variables, remember that minutes are always on the inner scale. To remind the user, the inner scale has "minutes" written in red between 30 and 35. The calculations work on the factor 60. All speeds are a distance travelled in 60 minutes (i.e. one hour), so all calculations revolve around this number. The number 60 is in white, surrounded by a black triangle, to make it more prominent and as a reminder of which scale to use.

GROUNDSPEED

Example An aircraft flies 210 nm in 25 minutes. What is the groundspeed?

STEP 1 Align the 25 on the inner scale against 210 on the outer scale.

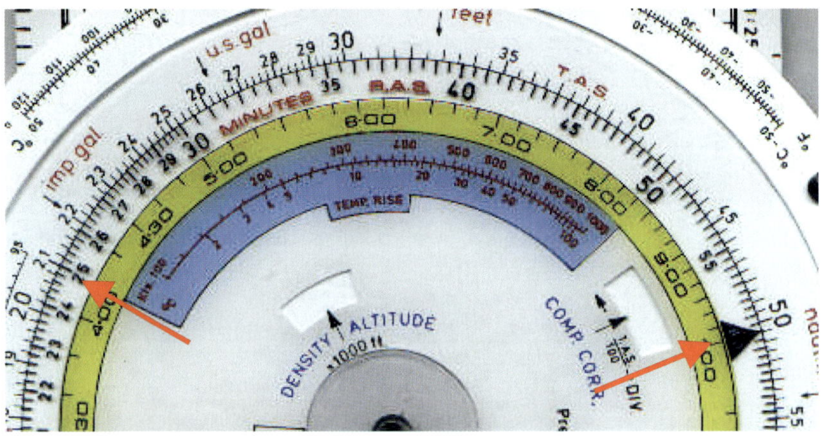

STEP 2 Read off the groundspeed against the 60 triangle. **503 knots**

TIME

Example Using the same settings; at the groundspeed of 503 knots, how long will it take the aircraft to travel 210 nautical miles?

STEP 1 Align the 60 triangle on the inner scale against 503 on the outer scale.

STEP 2 On the outer distance scale, go to 210. Read off the time on the inner scale. **25 minutes**

DISTANCE TRAVELLED

Example For a groundspeed of 503 knots, how far will the aircraft travel in 35 minutes?

STEP 1 Align the 60 triangle on the inner scale against 503 on the outer scale.

STEP 2 On the inner minutes scale, go to 35. Read off the distance travelled on the outer scale. **294 nautical miles**

Fuel consumption, fuel flow, and time calculations are performed in the same manner.

CRP Example 5 Complete the following table:

	Distance	Time	Groundspeed	Fuel Consumption	Fuel flow
1.	250 nm	25 minutes		200 lb	
2.		37 minutes	350 knots		200 imp gal/hr
3.	120 nm	17 minutes		500 kg	
4.	300 nm		270 knots		2000 lb/hr
5.	240 nm		210 knots	30 US Gallons	

CALCULATION OF TAS UP TO 300 KNOTS

There are three windows on the slide rule: the COMP CORR, ALTITUDE, and AIRSPEED. When calculating TAS from RAS, use the AIRSPEED window.

For all these calculations, remember that RAS is on the inner scale and TAS on the outer scale. They are written in red as a reminder.

Example The pressure altitude is 35 000 ft, and the corrected outside air temperature (COAT) is – 65°C. The RAS is 160 knots. What is the TAS?

STEP 1 In the AIRSPEED window, against the COAT of –65°C, place the altitude of 35 000 ft, as shown in the diagram.

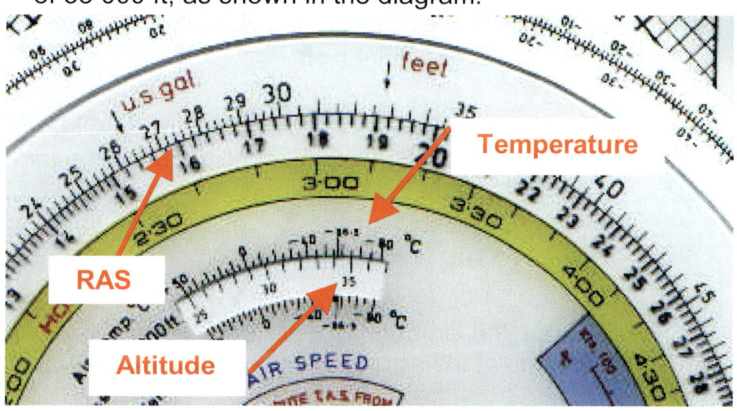

STEP 2 Find the RAS of 160 knots on the inner scale. Read off the TAS on the outer scale. **275 knots**

CALCULATION OF TAS OVER 300 KNOTS

At high TAS, the air becomes compressed and causes extra pressure, which is sensed by the ASI. This compressibility results in a higher-than-actual TAS being calculated. To correct for this, a compressibility correction must be made using the COMP CORR window.

Example The pressure altitude is 35 000 ft, and the corrected outside air temperature (COAT) is – 65°C. The RAS is 210 knots. What is the TAS?

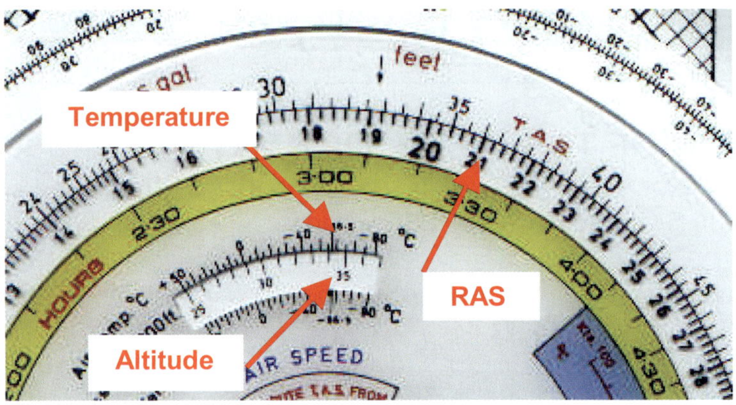

STEP 1 Against the COAT of –65°C, place the altitude of 35 000 ft as shown in the diagram.

STEP 2 Find the RAS of 210 knots on the inner scale. Read off the TAS on the outer scale. **360 knots**

STEP 3 Because the TAS is over 300 knots, the COMP CORR window has to be used to account for compressibility. Using the formula by the window, the TAS first calculated is used:

$$\mathbf{{}^{TAS}/_{100} - 3\ DIV = {}^{360}/_{100} - 3 = 0.6}$$

This is the number of divisions the computer must be moved in the direction of the arrow (to the left, or anti-clockwise).

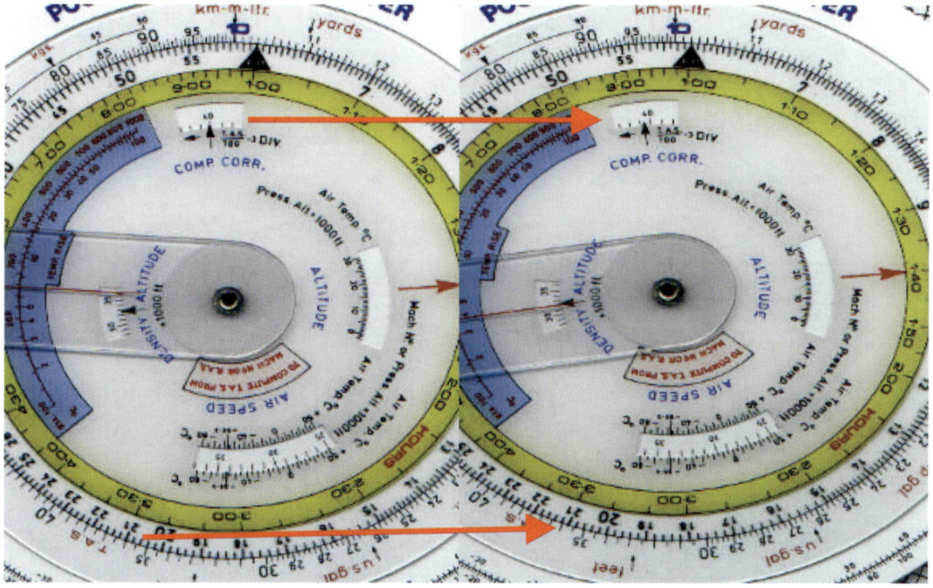

STEP 4 Read off the new TAS against the RAS of 210 knots **357 knots**

CALCULATION OF TAS FROM MACH NUMBER

Mach Number is the TAS expressed as a decimal fraction of the local speed of sound.

MACH NUMBER = TAS ÷ LOCAL SPEED OF SOUND

Turn the scale until the Mach Number index becomes visible in the AIRSPEED window.

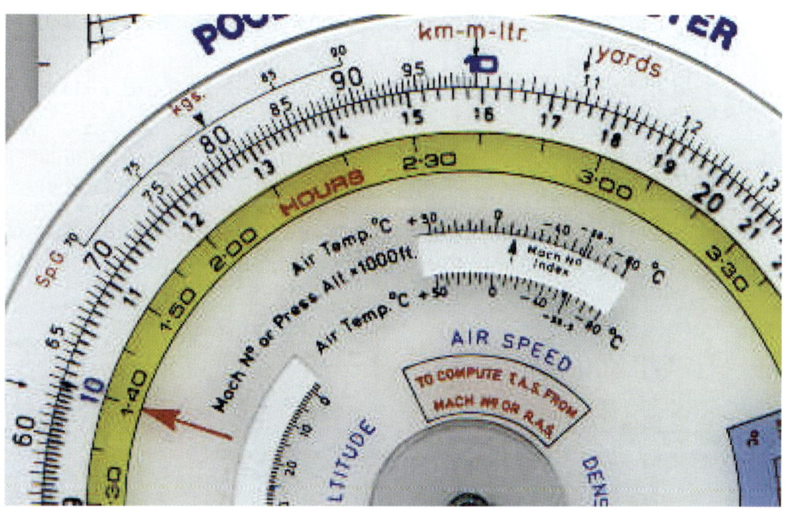

Example For a COAT –50°C and a Mach Number 0.83, what are the TAS and local speed of sound?

STEP 1 To calculate the TAS, align the Mach No Arrow with the COAT.

-50

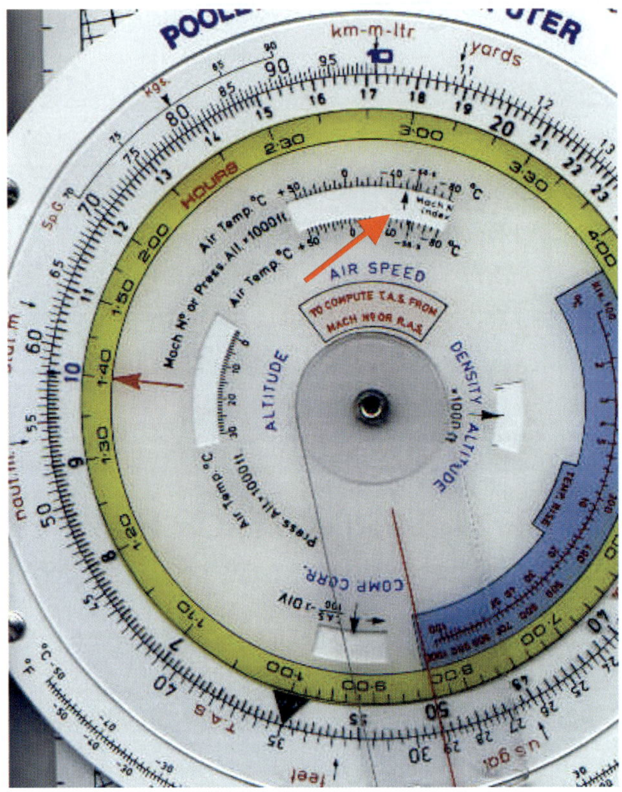

STEP 2 On the inner scale, go to 0.83, and read off the TAS on the outer scale.

483 kt

STEP 3 The local speed of sound equates to a Mach Number of 1.0. To find the LSS, go to 1 on the inner scale, and read off the speed on the outer scale.

582 knots

TEMPERATURE RISE SCALE

If an indicated outside air temperature is given, this must be adjusted to get a corrected outside air temperature. The indicated outside air temperature is higher due to the effects of compressibility and friction. For this, use the blue temperature rise scale.

Example Given an indicated temperature of –35°C, altitude of 25 000 ft, and RAS of 180 knots, what is the TAS?

STEP 1 Place the indicated temperature, –35, against the altitude in the AIRSPEED window and calculate the TAS for the RAS of 180 knots.
266 knots

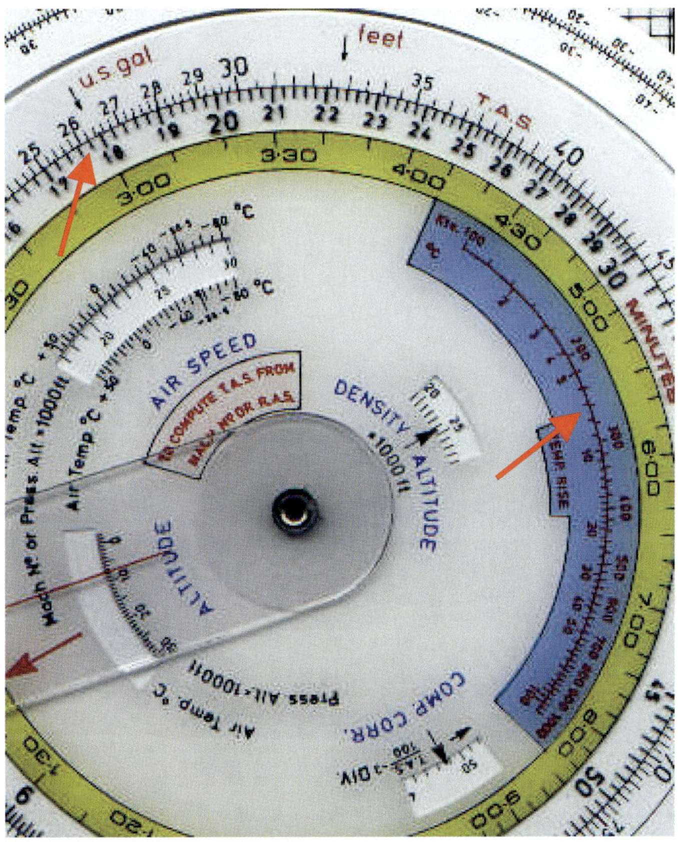

STEP 2 Go to the blue temperature rise scale, and read off the temperature rise for 266 knots.
7°

STEP 3 Subtract this figure from the indicated temperature to give the COAT.
-35 – 7 = -42°C

STEP 4 Recalculate the TAS using the COAT, using the normal method.
262 knots

CALCULATION OF TRUE ALTITUDE

Example For a temperature of –40°C and a pressure altitude of 25 000 ft, what is the true altitude?

STEP 1 In the ALTITUDE window, align the temperature and the altitude.

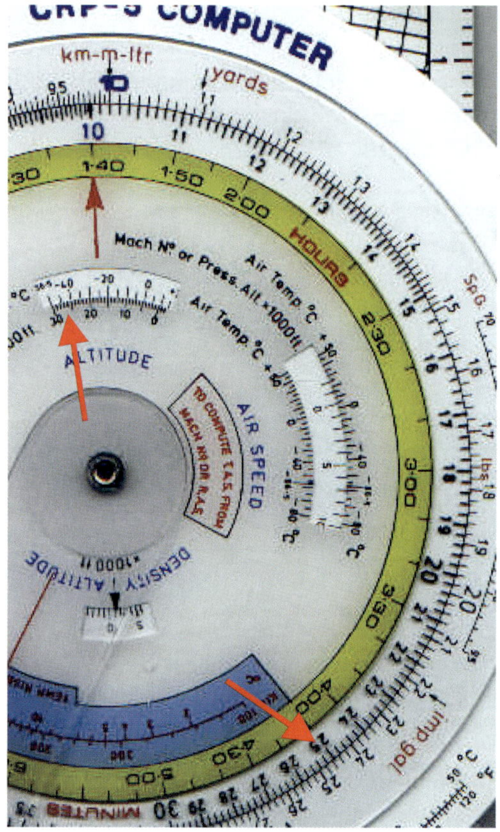

STEP 2 Go to the indicated altitude of 25 000 ft on the inner scale and read off the true altitude on the outer scale.

24 400 ft

CALCULATION OF DENSITY ALTITUDE

Density altitude can be calculated two ways, by using either the CRP-5 or a mathematical formula. Unlike the other calculations described in this chapter, the formula should be used in this case. The CRP-5 method is given for information only.

The formula is:

DENSITY ALTITUDE = PRESSURE ALTITUDE + (ISA DEVIATION X 120)

Alternatively, using the CRP-5:

Example An airfield 6000 ft amsl has a surface temperature of 10°C. What is the density altitude?

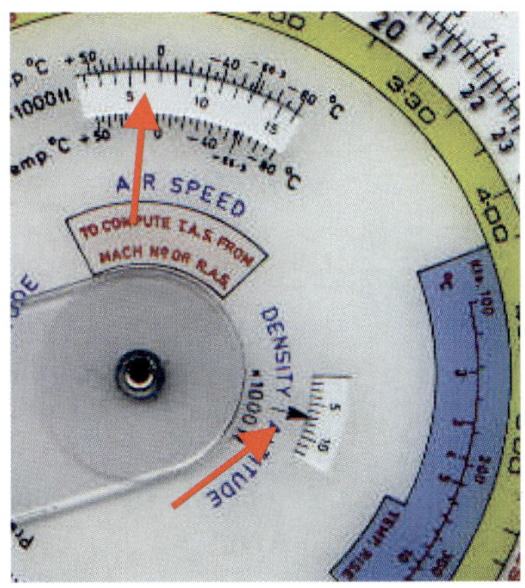

STEP 1 In the airspeed window set 6000 ft against 10°.

STEP 2 In the Density Altitude window, read off the density altitude.
7000 ft

ANSWERS TO CRP-5 EXAMPLES

CRP Example 1

a. 14 910
b. .006
c. 23.2
d. 2.55
e. 2622

CRP Example 2

a. .329
b. .0665
c. 41.3
d. .88
e. .807

CRP Example 3

	Feet	Yards	Metres
1.	**19 500**	6500	**5950**
2.	230	**76.6**	**70**
3.	**5580**	**1860**	1700
4.	51	**17**	**15.6**
5.	**28 500**	9500	**8700**

CRP Example 4

1. 69 statute miles 110 kilometres
2. 108 nautical miles 124 statute miles
3. 403 mph 648 kph
4. 244 knots 280 mph
5. 4620 Imperial Gallons 5580 US Gallons
6. 250 Imperial Gallons 1135 litres
7. 295 kilograms
8. 760 pounds

CRP Example 5

	Distance	Time	Groundspeed	Fuel Consumption	Fuel flow
1.	250 nm	25 minutes	**600 knots**	200 lb	**480 lb/hr**
2.	**216 nm**	37 minutes	350 knots	**123 gal**	200 Imp gal/hr
3.	120 nm	17 minutes	**423 knots**	500 kg	**1760 kg/hr**
4.	300 nm	**66.6 minutes**	270 knots	**2200 lb**	2000 lb/hr
5.	240 nm	**68.6 minutes**	210 knots	30 US Gallons	**26.6 US gal/hr**

Chapter 8
Pooley's — The Triangle of Velocities

INTRODUCTION

Chapter 6 demonstrated how to solve the triangle of velocities using construction, that is, by drawing a scale diagram on a piece of paper. However, this is time consuming. The wind side of the Pooley's CRP-5 Flight Computer solves the triangle of velocities more quickly.

COMPUTER TERMINOLOGY

a.	**Grid Ring**	The scale around the rotatable protractor
b.	**Computer Face**	The transparent plastic of the rotatable protractor
c.	**True or True Heading Pointer**	The reference mark at the top of the stock, reading against the grid ring
d.	**Drift Scale**	Scale on the top of the stock to the left and right of the true index. Note that the graduations are equal to those on the grid ring
e.	**The Grommet**	The point or circle at the exact centre of the rotatable protractor
f.	**Drift Line**	All the drift lines originate from one origin. The numbers on the drift lines indicate the degree of inclination to the centre line
g.	**Heading Line**	The central line or zero drift line
h.	**Speed Circles**	The arcs of concentric circles around the drift lines are equally spaced and graduated from zero knots up to any required speed. The scale is quite arbitrary. Each side of the sliding scale has a different speed scale, for the CRP-5 this is: **1.** 40 to 300 knots **2.** 150 to 1050 knots

TIPS FOR USAGE

There are various tips to help avoid any confusion:

1. The grommet is **always** used to represent true airspeed/TAS.
2. Heading is **always** aligned with the true heading pointer in the finished triangle of velocities.
3. Unless otherwise instructed, all working should be done in **true**. Exceptions are dealt with later in the chapter.
4. Always use the wind mark down method, as described in this chapter. PPL students are usually taught the wind mark up method. This works for the common calculation of finding heading and groundspeed, but does not work for several of the calculations required on the ATPL exam. It is best to learn the method described in the following pages, as it works for all calculations.
5. Buy a fine line pen to draw on the face of the computer. It allows very accurate work and rubs out easily. Pencils do not allow sufficiently accurate work for the JAR exams.

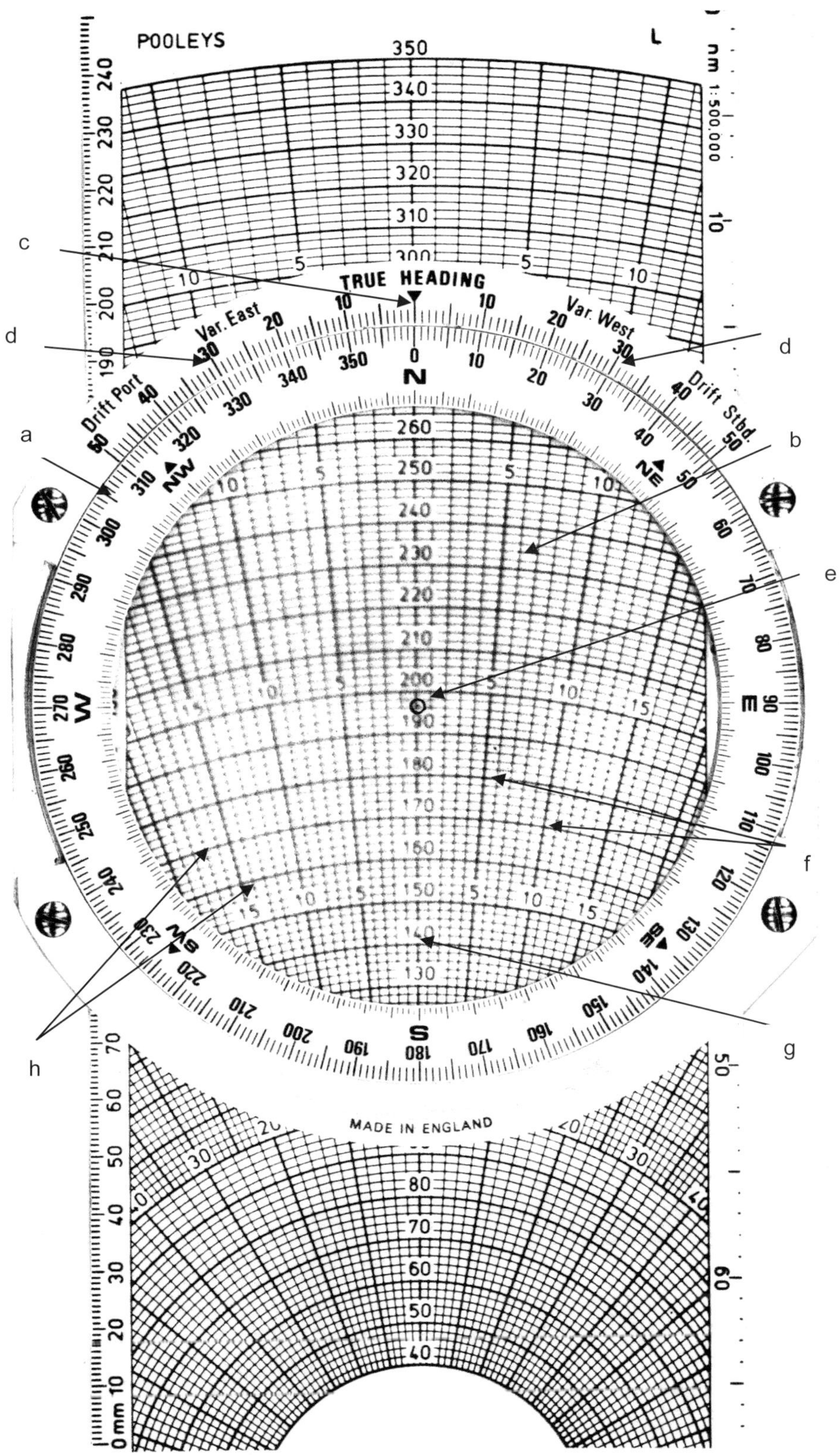
POOLEYS
TRUE HEADING
Var. East
Var. West
Drift Port
Drift Stbd.
MADE IN ENGLAND
a
b
c
d
d
e
f
g
h

DRIFT SCALE

The drift scale is only used in conjunction with the grid-ring scale. It has no direct relationship with the drift lines on the slide.

When a true heading is set against the true course index, the corresponding track can be read off the grid ring against the known drift value or vice versa.

Example
Heading 050°, Drift 20° right (Stbd)
Track 070°

Example
Track 090°, Drift 20° left (Port)
Heading 110°

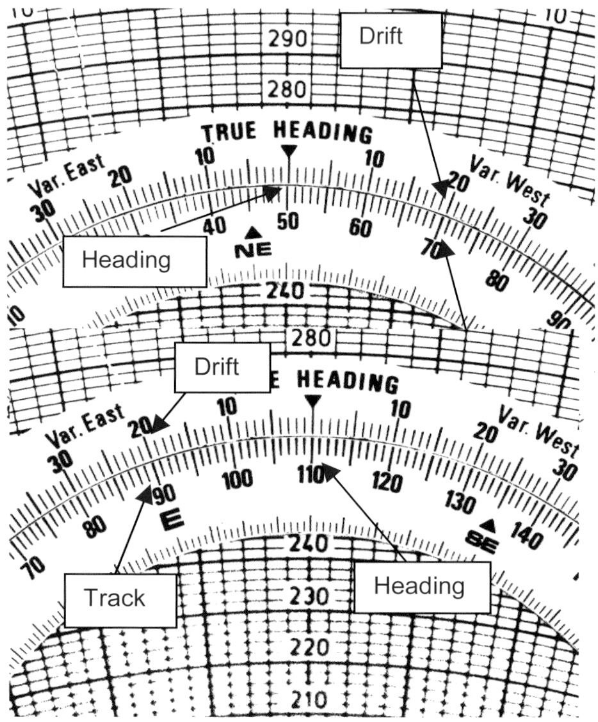

OBTAINING HEADING

The drift scales are also marked Var.East and Var.West. When the true or grid heading is set against the index, magnetic heading can be read against the grid ring. This applies when using either a grid heading or true heading.

Example
Heading (T) 110°, Variation 7°W
Magnetic Heading (M) 117°

Example
Heading (G) 236°, Grivation 21°W
Magnetic Heading (M) 257°

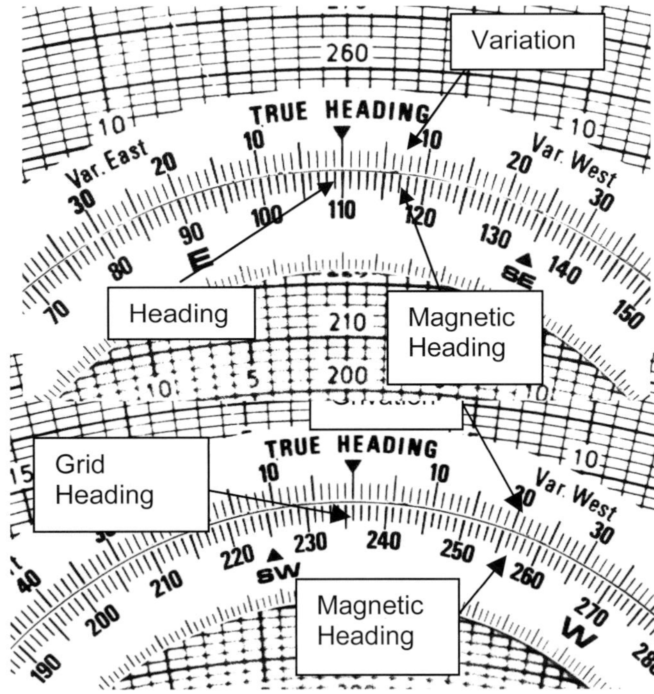

TO CALCULATE TRACK AND GROUNDSPEED

As discussed in Chapter 6, when four components of the triangle of velocities are known, the other two can be determined. In this section, the heading, TAS, and W/V are known.

Example Given that the heading is 000°T, the TAS is 350 knots, the wind velocity is 310/100, what is the track and groundspeed?

STEP 1 Be sure to use the correct side of the slide. The TAS and windspeed require the higher speed side.

STEP 2 Align the wind direction with the true heading pointer, as shown. Then draw a line down from the central grommet. This line should be 100 knots long, using the scale on the slide. Always mark the wind velocity down from the central grommet.

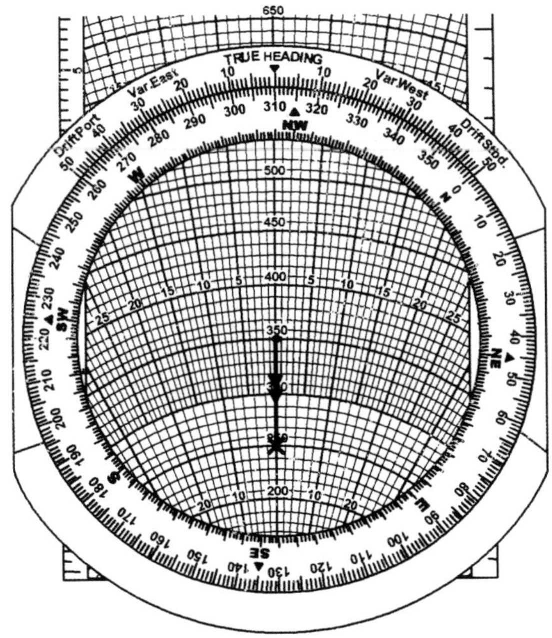

STEP 3 Set the heading under the true heading pointer. Place the central grommet on the true airspeed.

STEP 4 The end of the wind velocity line will represent the groundspeed. In this case, it is **296 knots.**

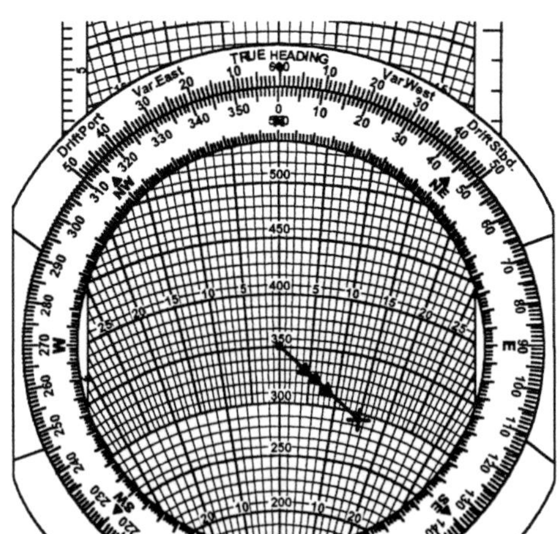

STEP 5 The end of the line also shows the drift, 15° right. Find 15° right on the drift scale, and read off the track **015ºT.**

TO FIND THE WIND VELOCITY

In this case, the heading, TAS, track (or drift), and groundspeed are given.

Example Given: Heading 060°T, TAS 332 kt, Drift 10° left, groundspeed 390 kt.

STEP 1 Set the heading and TAS on the slide. Remember, heading goes under the true heading pointer, and TAS goes under the grommet.

STEP 2 Mark off the intersection of 10° left drift and 390 knots groundspeed on the face of the computer. Draw a line from the grommet to this point. This represents the wind vector.

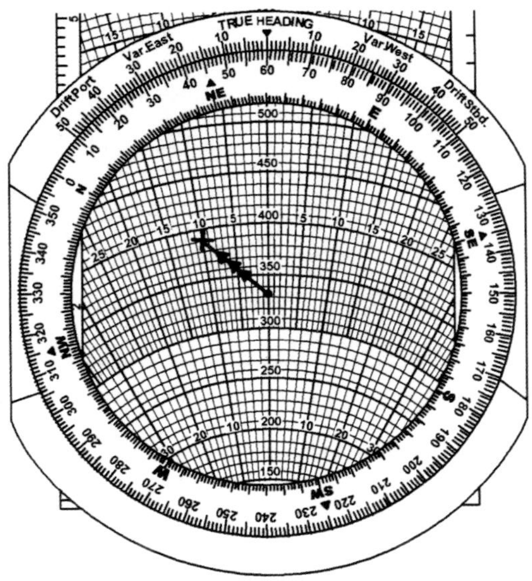

STEP 3 Rotate the ring until the wind line lies vertically down from the grommet. Set the grommet over a convenient speed and read off the wind velocity. **188°/84 knots.**

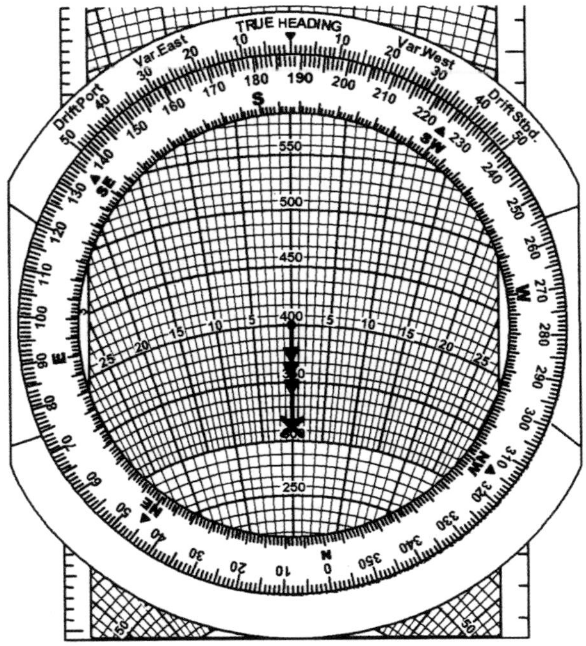

TO FIND HEADING AND GROUNDSPEED

This is one of the most common calculations performed on the CRP-5 during flight planning. It is also the most difficult. Remember that heading must always go under the true heading pointer. However, for this calculation, the heading is not known. A technique known as **shuffling** is used to compute the heading.

Example Given: Track 070°T, TAS 370 kt, and wind velocity 360/90.

STEP 1 Set the wind velocity down from the central grommet as normal.

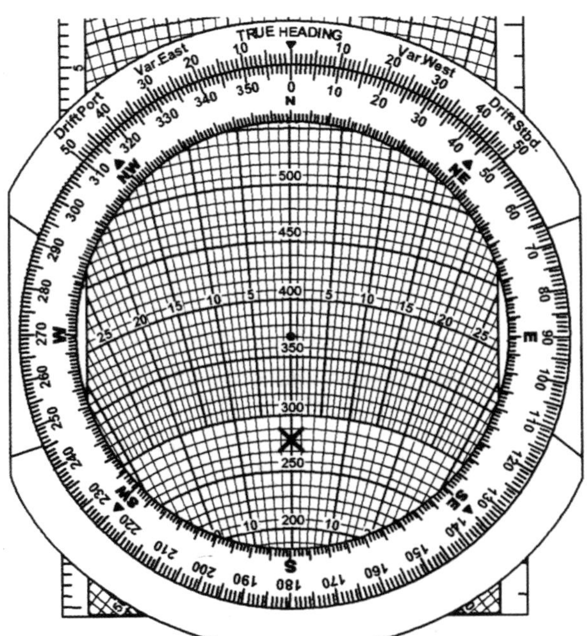

STEP 2 Since the heading is not known, start by calculating an approximation for drift using the track. Place the grommet on the TAS of 370 kt. Then, place the track under the true heading pointer. At this stage, the indicated drift is 14° right.

Remember, the wind always blows the aircraft from its heading to its track, so its heading must be 056°.

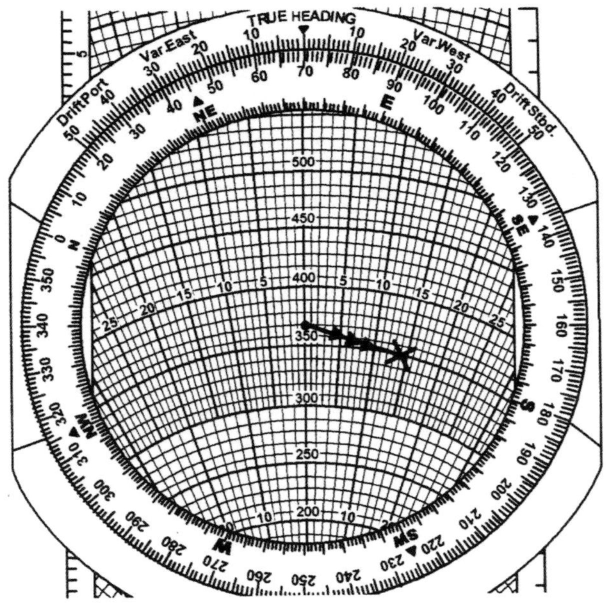

STEP 3 Set the heading of 056° under the true heading pointer. This now gives a drift of only 13° right. This would make the track 069°, which is not correct.

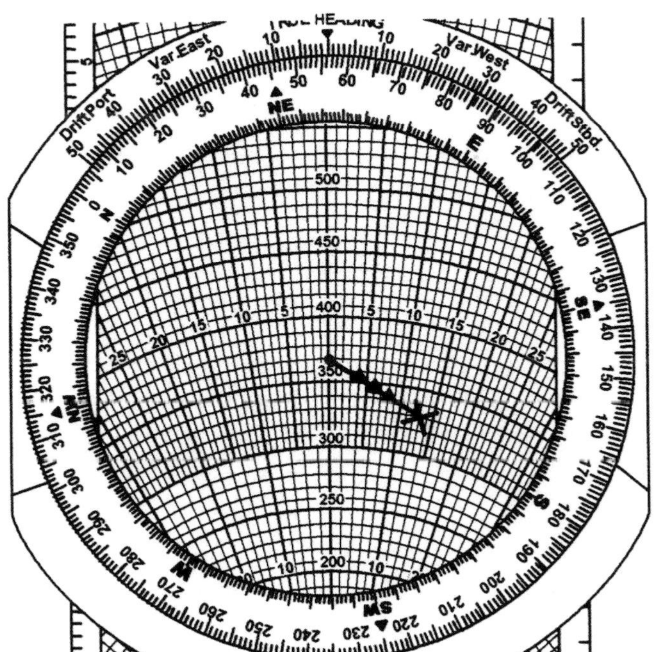

STEP 4 So move the ring round to a heading of 057°. This is called **shuffling**.

The drift now stays at 13°, so the heading, drift, and track all agree. The correct heading is 057°T.

It may take 2 or 3 shuffles to solve a problem.

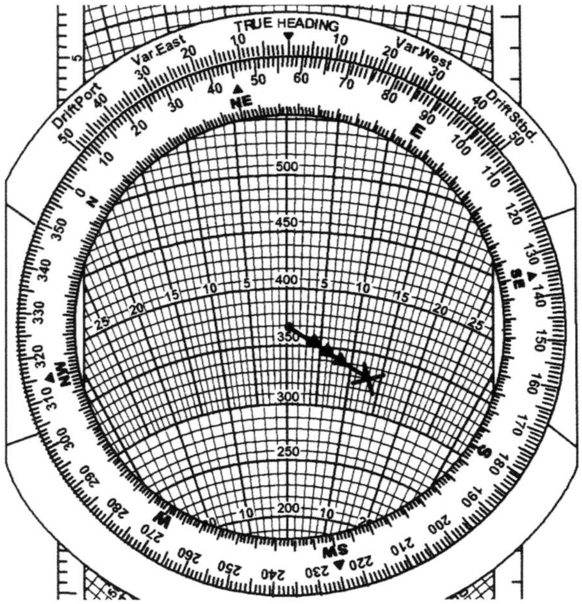

STEP 5 Read off the groundspeed, which is **328 knots.**

Note: The shuffling technique is only used when performing calculations where the heading is not known. There is no need to shuffle when calculating track.

TAKE-OFF AND LANDING WIND COMPONENT

Aircraft are subject to crosswind and tailwind maxima. Both can be calculated using the square scale at the bottom of the slide on the CRP-5.

For the next few examples, use the low-speed speed side of the slide. Also note that this is one of the rare occasions that magnetic headings are used.

Example Runway 31 is in use and the wind velocity reported by ATC is 270/40. Remember that the runway direction is in magnetic, and the wind velocity reported by ATC is in magnetic. What is the crosswind and headwind component?

STEP 1 Set the grommet on the zero point of the squared section as shown.

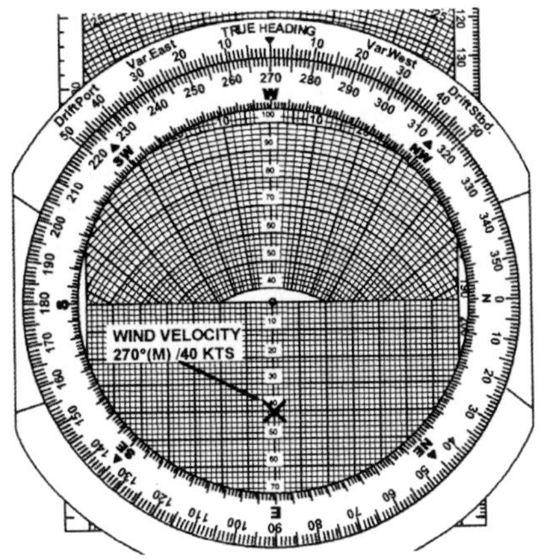

STEP 2 Mark in the wind velocity as normal.

STEP 3 Set the runway direction of 310 M against the heading index.

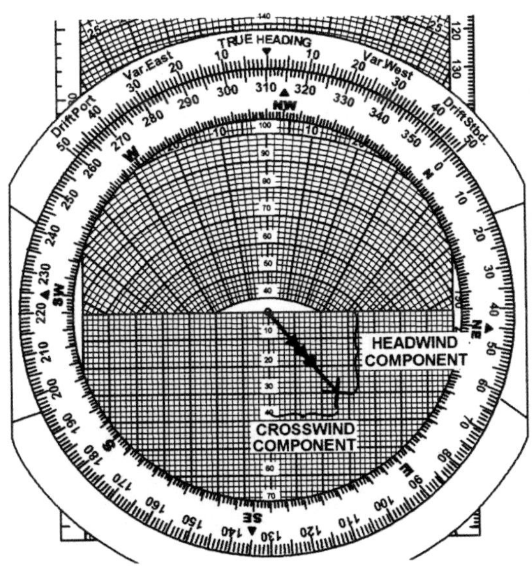

STEP 4 The headwind is read down from the horizontal zero line **30 knots**

The crosswind across from the vertical centre line **26 knots**

TAILWIND COMPONENT

Suppose that the wind velocity is 210/40 with runway 31 in use. Using the procedure above (steps 1 – 3), the answer shows that the wind point is above the zero line. This indicates a tailwind.

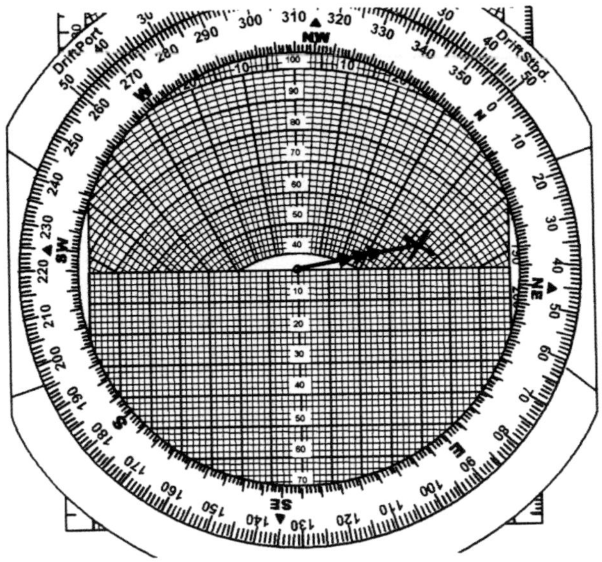

STEP 4 Bring the wind point to the zero horizontal line. The grommet gives the tailwind, in this case, 7 knots.

CROSSWIND AND HEADWIND LIMITS

Example Runway 21 in use. The wind direction is 180°M. A minimum headwind of 10 knots and maximum crosswind is 16 knots for this runway. What is the minimum and maximum windspeed?

STEP 1 Set the runway direction against the true heading index and place the grommet on the zero point.

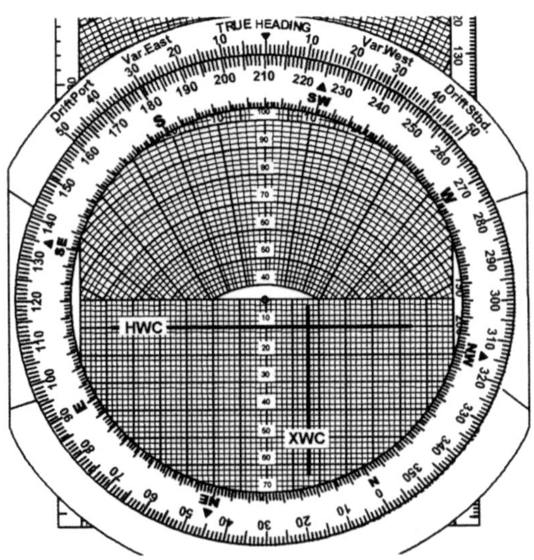

STEP 2 Mark in the maximum crosswind and minimum headwind for the runway using straight lines, as shown. The crosswind is blowing from the left. Wind always blows away from the grommet, so the crosswind is drawn on the right.

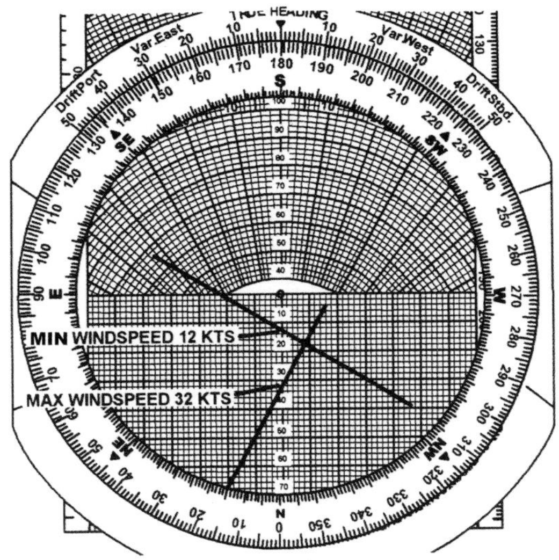

STEP 3 Set the wind direction against the true heading index.

STEP 4 Read off the maximum and minimum windspeed where the lines cut the heading line as shown.

Chapter 9
Maps and Charts — Introduction

INTRODUCTION

A map or chart is a representation of a part of the Earth's surface. Certain factors have to be taken into account when constructing a map or chart. A map is normally a representation of an area of land, giving details that are not required by the aviator, such as a street map or road atlas. A chart usually represents an area in less detail and has features which are identifiable from the air. In the following chapters, the text refers only to charts. Aviators are interested in:

1. What the chart is to be used for
2. What scale is required

To represent the spherical Earth on a flat sheet is difficult. It is important to understand how different areas are displayed. A map projection is the method the cartographer uses to display a certain portion of the Earth's surface.

PROPERTIES OF THE IDEAL CHART

The ideal chart would have the following properties:

1. Constant scale over the whole chart
2. Areas of the Earth correctly represented (Conformal – see definition later)
3. Great circles should be straight lines
4. Rhumb lines should be straight lines
5. Position should be easy to plot
6. Charts of adjacent areas should fit exactly
7. Each cardinal direction should point in the same direction on all parts of the chart
8. Areas should be represented by their true shape

The ideal chart is an impossibility. For navigation it is important that:

1. Bearing and distance are correctly represented
2. Both bearing and distance are easily measured
3. The course that is flown is a straight line
4. Plotting of bearings is simple

To obtain these properties, other properties must be sacrificed.

On any chart, certain properties cannot be achieved over the whole chart:

1. Scale is never constant and correct over large areas
2. The shape of a large area can never be fully correct

SHAPE OF THE EARTH

The Earth's surface is too irregular to be represented simply. Approximations have to be made by using less complicated shapes.

VERTICAL DATUM

The vertical datum, or zero surface, to which elevation is measured, is normally taken as mean sea level. When measuring elevation, three terms are used:

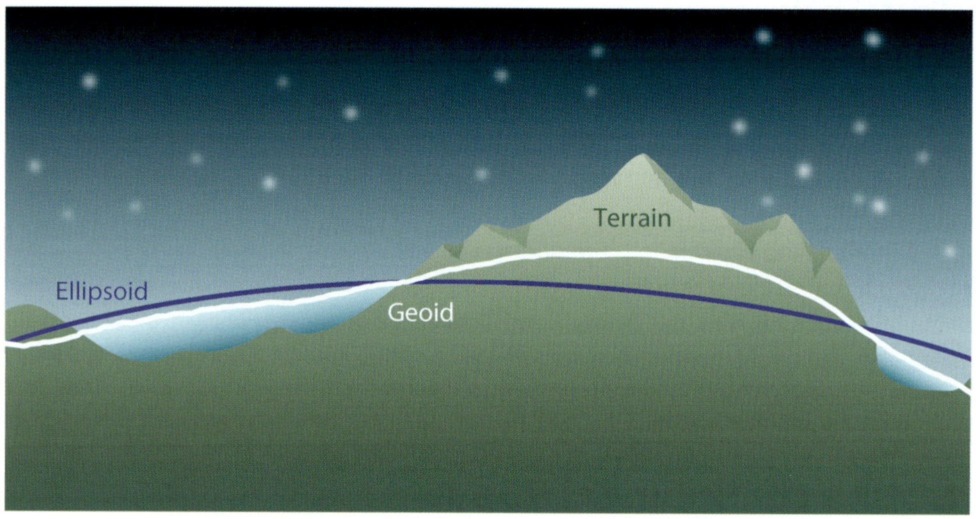

TOPOGRAPHIC SURFACE / TERRAIN

This describes the actual surface of the Earth, following the ocean floor, mountains, and other features of the terrain.

ELLIPSOID

This is a regular geometric representation of the shape of the Earth. This is also referred to as the spheroid, an abbreviation of the term oblate spheroid.

GEOID

An equipotential surface of the Earth's gravity field. It closely approximates mean sea level and is irregular.

Any zero surface can be used as the datum to measure height.

CHART CONSTRUCTION

Before the chart can be constructed, three processes must be completed:

1. The Earth needs to be reduced in size to the required scale. This is known as the reduced Earth.
2. A graticule needs to be constructed to represent latitude and longitude.
3. The land area is then drawn on the chart.

ORTHOMORPHISM

Orthomorphism is a Greek word meaning **correct shape**. Only on small areas of charts is this possible. The term is rarely used in context with maps and charts today.

CONFORMALITY

The word **conformal** is a more modern term used to describe the property of orthomorphism. It is associated with many of the charts described in the next few chapters.

Where charts are concerned, the terms **orthomorphism** and **conformality** mean that bearings are correctly represented.

For a chart to be conformal and to have bearings correctly represented:

1. Meridians of longitude and parallels of latitude must cut at right angles.
2. The scale must be correct in all directions.

EARTH CONVERGENCE

Looking at the representation of the Earth below, it is easy to see that as the meridians of longitude cross the Equator, they are parallel to each other. When looking at the poles, all the meridians come together and meet at the pole. This phenomenon is called **convergence**.

Convergence is the angle between two meridians.

When examining the Earth's surface, it is apparent that:

1. Convergence is zero at the Equator because the meridians cross the Equator at 90°.
2. Convergence is a maximum at the poles where all the meridians converge.

The following diagrams are courtesy of Black Hawk College, Illinois.

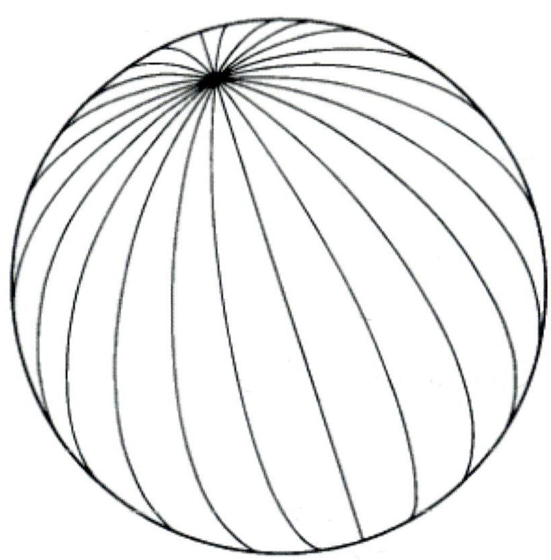

The convergence of the meridians determines the direction of a great circle.

The great circle direction is constantly changing because the meridians converge. In the diagram below, the initial great circle track at A is approximately 040°. The final track at B is approximately 090°.

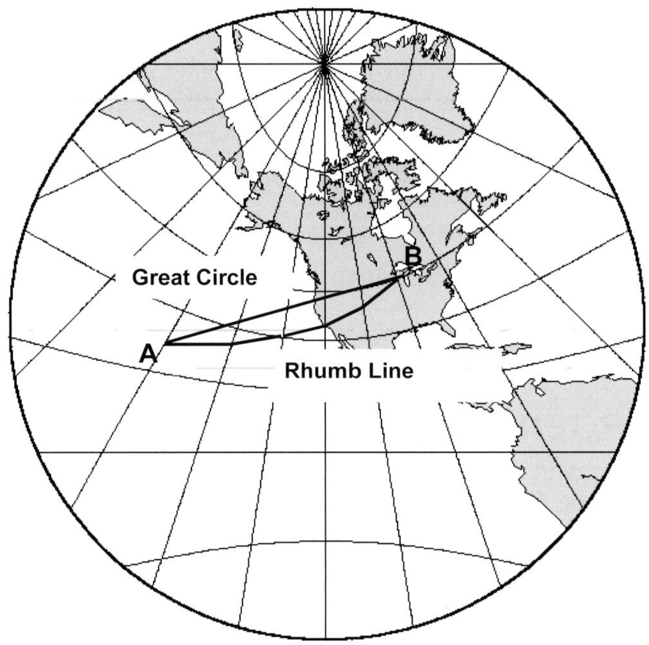

The rhumb line direction remains constant throughout.

The rhumb line between two points is always closer to the Equator than the great circle track between the same points. This applies to both hemispheres and is important when great circle and rhumb line tracks are calculated.

CALCULATION OF CONVERGENCE

As discussed, convergence is zero at the Equator and a maximum at the poles. However, the relationship is not linear. In fact, it follows a sine curve.

This is described by the formula:

CONVERGENCE = CH LONG X SIN LAT

Note: This formula is very important and must be remembered.

In this calculation, the Ch Long must be entered in degrees and decimal degrees.

Note that the formula is only valid for a specific latitude. To find the convergence between two points at different latitudes, Mean Lat may be substituted into the equation. In that case, the answer is an approximation because the relationship is not linear.

Consider the following diagram. On the diagram below at point A, the initial track is approximately 050°. At B, the track is approximately 100°. Although the route appears as a straight line on the diagram, in fact the track is constantly changing. This is because, although the aircraft appears to be travelling in a straight line, the meridians are converging, so its direction in relation to each local meridian changes as it travels along the line.

Consider a section of the above route.

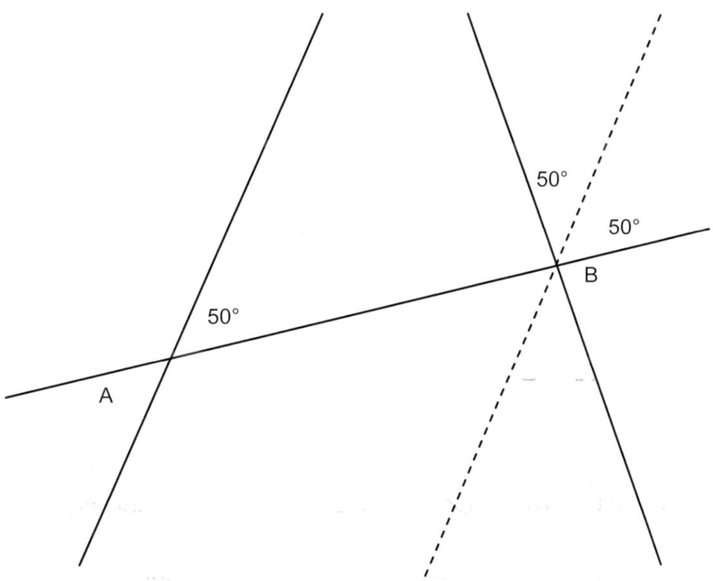

The diagram shows two meridians converging, and a great circle track drawn between them. The initial track is 50° (measured in relation to the local meridian). The final track is 100° (again, measured in relation to the local meridian). The difference between the two is 50°.

The dotted line represents the meridian from position A transferred over to position B. The diagram shows that the difference between the initial and final track is also the angle between the two meridians, that is, their convergence.

Convergence is the difference between the initial and final great circle tracks.

In the diagram below:

- The great circle initial track is 020°
- The great circle final track is 140°
- Convergence is 120°

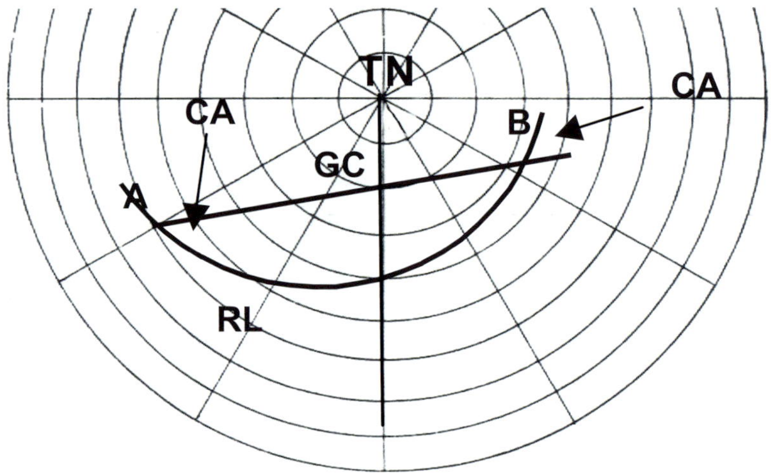

The rhumb line, although it looks curved, is crossing all meridians at the same angle. The rhumb line track is 080° and remains constant throughout.

In summary:

Great Circle Initial Track	020°	Rhumb Line Track	080°	Difference	60°
Great Circle Final Track	140°	Rhumb Line Track	080°	Difference	60°

The difference between the initial rhumb line track and the initial great circle track is 60°. The difference between the final rhumb line track and the final great circle track is 60°. In both cases this is ½ convergence.

This angular difference between the rhumb line track and the initial/final great circle track is called the Conversion Angle (CA). Half way between two points, the great circle and rhumb line tracks is briefly parallel. In the above example, the great circle track is 080° exactly halfway along the track.

MAP CLASSIFICATION

No map projection can fill all the criteria needed to make the ideal chart. Different charts have different classifications. Two styles of projection are used:

Perspective Projections — Otherwise known as a **geometric projection**.

This style of projection is constructed by casting the Earth's graticule onto a surface by using a transparent model Earth. The point of projection is usually tangential with the Earth.

Three types of projection can be said to be perspective:

Azimuthal	A projection onto a plane surface
Cylindrical	A projection onto a cylinder
Conical	A projection onto a cone

Conformal Projection — These are essentially perspective charts, but they have been produced using mathematical modelling rather than directly from a projection.

Where a Conformal Projection is used:

- All small features retain their original form or shape, but the size of an area may be slightly distorted in relation to another.
- All angles between intersecting lines or curves are the same, and all meridians and parallels cross at 90°.
- Conformality is achieved by increasing or reducing the spacing between the meridians and parallels at a constant rate.

The Lambert's Conformal, Mercator, and Polar Stereographic charts are examples of Conformal charts.

SCALE

Scale is defined as the ratio of the length on a chart to the length it represents on the Earth's surface. The most common way of representing the scale is by the use of the representative fraction (RF):

$$\textbf{Representative Fraction} = {}^{\text{Chart Length}}/_{\text{Earth Distance}}$$

Chart Length is abbreviated to CL and Earth Distance to ED.

Example 1:1 000 000 — 1 inch represents 1 000 000 inches on the Earth.

Example A chart has a scale of 1:1 000 000. How many nautical miles does 10 inches on the chart represent?

STEP 1 $ED = {}^{CL}/_{RF}$

ED = 10 ÷ ($^{1}/_{1\,000\,000}$) = 10 000 000 inches

STEP 2 Calculate the number of inches in a nautical mile.

1 nm = 6080 ft = 72 960 inches

STEP 3 Divide the answer from STEP 1 by the number of inches in a nautical mile.

10 000 000 ÷ 72 960 = 137.06 nm

DISTANCES

There are several relationships that must be remembered to ensure that any scale calculations are done quickly and accurately.

1 Nautical mile	72 960 in 1.852 km 1852 m
1 Kilometre	1000 m 100 000 cm 3280 ft
1 Metre	3.28 ft 100 cm
1 Centimetre	10 mm
1 Inch	2.54 cm
1 Foot	12 in
1 Statute Mile	5280 ft

Maps and Charts Example 1

The chart scale is given as 1 cm = 1 km. What is the scale of the chart?

Maps and Charts Example 2

Where the chart scale is 1:250 000, what is the distance in kilometres represented by 10 cm?

Maps and Charts Example 3

Where the chart scale is 1:400 000, how many inches represent 100 nm?

Maps and Charts Example 4

The chart length of 4 inches represents 150 nm. What is the scale?

Maps and Charts Example 5

The chart scale is 1:1 750 000. How many kilometres does a chart length of 6 inches represent?

Maps and Charts Example 6

The scale is 4.75 cm to the kilometre. What is the distance in centimetres that would represent the distance flown by an aircraft in 30 seconds at a groundspeed of 300 knots?

Maps and Charts Example 7

The chart scale is 1:3 600 000. How many kilometres does a chart length of 5 inches represent?

Maps and Charts Example 8

An Earth distance of 220 km is represented by a line measuring 2.9 inches. What is the scale of the chart?

Maps and Charts Example 9

An aircraft flying at a constant groundspeed obtains two fixes 40 minutes apart. The distance between the fixes is 28 cm on a chart with a scale of 1:2 000 000. What is the groundspeed in knots?

Maps and Charts Example 10

The chart scale is 1:4 000 000. How many statute miles does a line of 41.7 cm represent?

GEODETIC AND GEOCENTRIC LATITUDE

The difference between geodetic and geocentric latitude results from the fact that the Earth is not a perfect sphere, but an ellipsoid.

GEODETIC (GEOGRAPHIC) LATITUDE

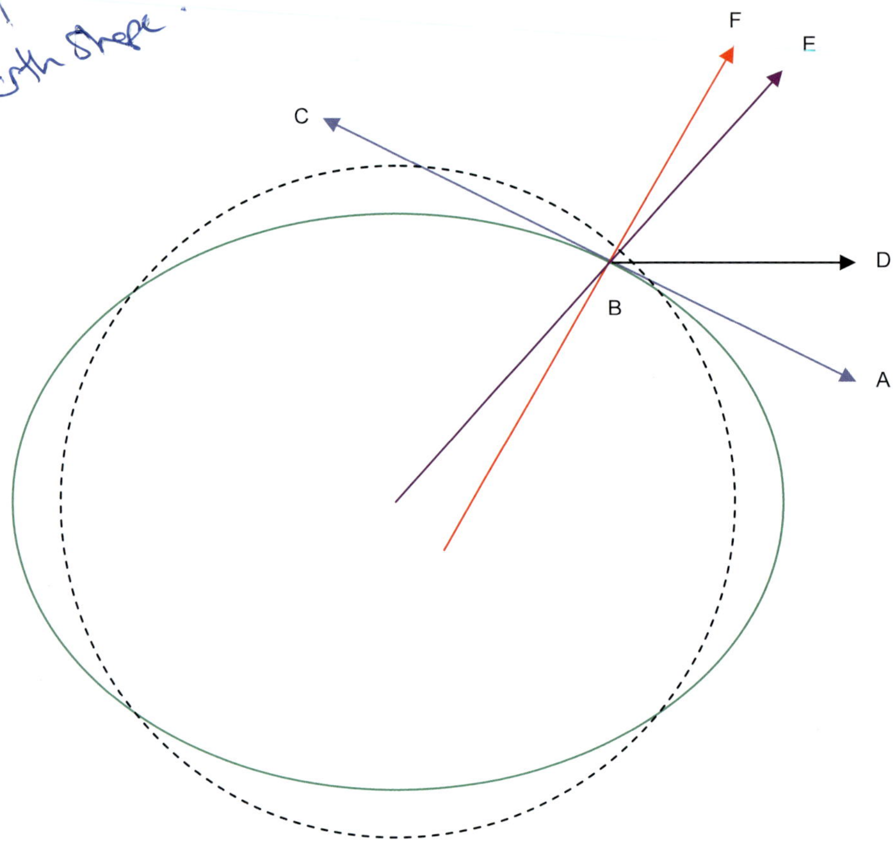

The line AC represents a tangent to the ellipsoid. The line BF is a normal (at 90 degrees) to this tangent. The line BD represents the local horizontal.

Continuing along the line from F through B into the Earth, notice that it does not go through the centre of the Earth.

The geodetic latitude is the angle DBF.

GEOCENTRIC LATITUDE

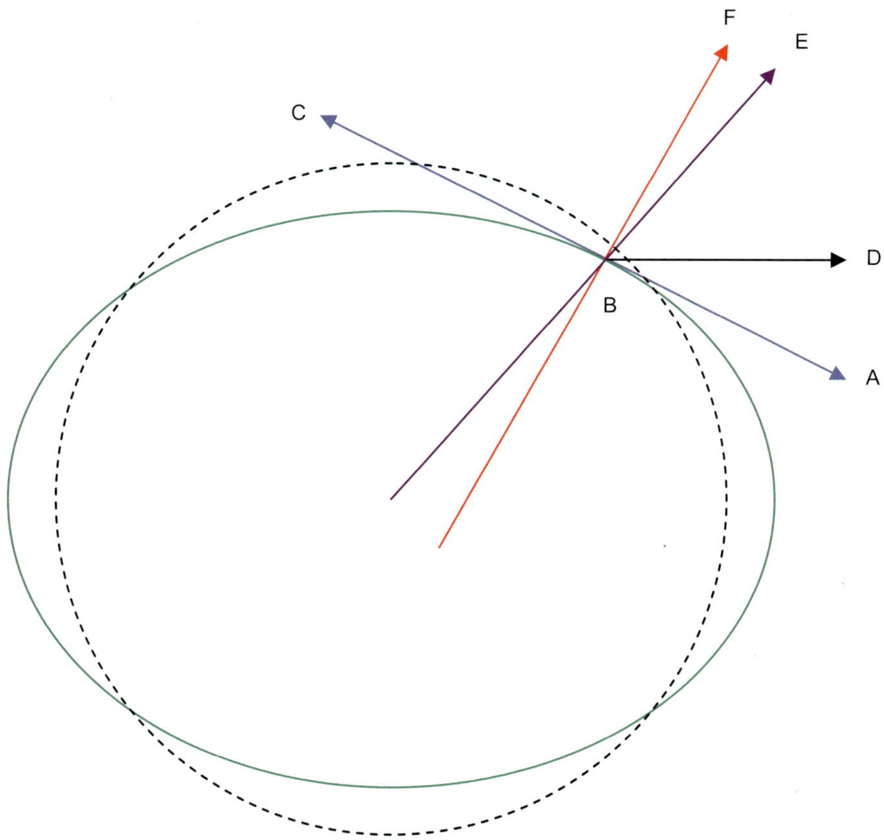

If a line is drawn from the centre of the Earth through B, the line BE is produced. The geocentric latitude is the angle DBE. This is clearly different from the geodetic latitude although the above diagram is very much exaggerated.

To construct a chart, a reduced Earth must be produced. The model is either ellipsoid or spherical. If it is spherical, the projected latitude is corrected by the difference between the geodetic and geocentric latitude. This difference is called the reduction in latitude which has:

- A maximum at latitude 45°
- A value of approximately 11.6 minutes

MAPS AND CHARTS ANSWERS

Maps and Charts Example 1
1 cm = 1 km = 100 000 cm
RF is 1:100 000

Maps and Charts Example 2
Chart Scale is 1:250 000
1 cm = 250 000 cm
10 cm = 2 500 000 cm = 25 km

Maps and Charts Example 3

STEP 1
100 nm = 100 x 72 960 inches
= 7 296 000 inches

STEP 2
Chart Scale is 1:400 000
CL = ED x RF
= 7 296 000 x $^1/_{400\ 000}$
=18.24 inches

Maps and Charts Example 4
150 nm = 10 944 000 inches
4 in = 10 944 000 inches
1 in = 2 736 000

RF is 1:2 736 000

Maps and Charts Example 5
1 in = 1 750 000 in
6 in = 10 500 000 in
10 500 000 x 2.54 = 26 670 000
26 670 000 ÷ 100 ÷ 1000 = 266.7 km

Maps and Charts Example 6

STEP 1
300 knots = 5 nm per minute
30 seconds = 2.5 nm
= 4.63 km

STEP 2
1 km = 4.75 cm
4.63 km = 4.75 x 4.63 = 21.99 cm

Maps and Charts Example 7
1 in = 3 600 000 in = 49.34 nm
91.38 km
5 in = 91.38 x 5 = 456.9 km

Maps and Charts Example 8
2.9 in represents 220 km
2.9 in = 7.366 cm
7.366 cm represents 220 km
1 cm = 29.87 km
RF is 1: 2 987 000

Maps and Charts Example 9

1 cm = 2 000 000 cm
28 cm = 56 000 000 cm
= 560 km
= 302 nm

40 min aircraft covers 302 nm
Groundspeed = 453 kt

Maps and Charts Example 10

1 cm = 4 000 000 cm = 40 km
= 40 x 3280 ft
= 131 200 ft = 24.85 sm

41.7 cm = 41.7 x 24.85 sm
= 1036

Chapter 10
Maps and Charts — Mercator

INTRODUCTION

The cylindrical projection can be imagined as being provided by a light source at the centre of the reduced Earth, which projects the meridians and parallels onto a cylinder wrapped around the Earth. When unwrapped:

- The Equator is represented by a straight line equal in length to that of the circumference of the reduced Earth (Standard Parallel).
- The meridians are represented by parallel straight lines.
- The parallels of latitude are straight lines parallel to the Equator. The distance between the parallels increases as the latitude increases, as shown in the diagram below.

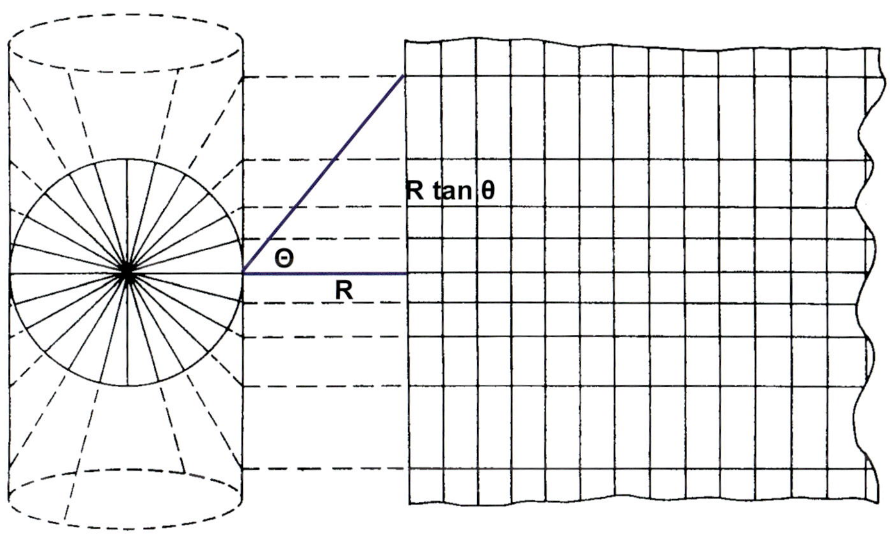

The parallels of latitude are drawn at distances from the Equator of R tan θ. This places a limit on the maximum usage of the chart, as the poles cannot be correctly represented.

The cylindrical projection is not conformal. This is because the rate of change of scale is different in a North-South direction than in an East-West direction. One of the properties of conformality is that scale should be the same in all directions, or the change of scale should occur at the same rate in all directions.

The Mercator chart is a specific kind of cylindrical projection that has been modified so the rate of change of scale is the same in the North-South direction as in the East-West direction. This means that the chart is non-perspective.

The chart discussed in this chapter is the direct Mercator chart. There are two other kinds of Mercator chart in the ATPL syllabus. These are the Transverse Mercator and the Oblique Mercator, which are discussed in a later chapter.

PROPERTIES OF THE MERCATOR CHART

Meridians	Straight parallel lines
Parallels	Straight parallel lines with spacing increasing toward the poles
Orthomorphic	Yes (after mathematical modelling)
Rhumb Line	Straight Line
Great Circle	A curve concave toward the Equator, except for the meridians and the Equator, which are straight lines
Convergence	Zero, as the meridians are parallel to each other. Chart convergence is correct at the Equator where the value is equal to convergence on the Earth.
Scale	Expands away from the Equator by the secant of the latitude
Limitations	70°N/S

SCALE

The projection is:

- Expanded in the East – West direction at high latitudes
- Expanded in the North – South direction away from the equator

To make the chart orthomorphic, mathematical modelling is required.

Once mathematical modelling is achieved, the scale is still only correct along the Equator where the cylinder touches the reduced Earth. At any other point on the chart, the scale is subject to expansion.

Another way of saying the scale is correct is by saying that the Scale Factor is 1:

SCALE FACTOR = CHART LENGTH ÷ REDUCED EARTH LENGTH

The length of the 90° line of latitude (i.e. the pole) is zero on the Earth and on the reduced Earth. So at the pole:

Scale Factor = Chart Length ÷ 0 = ∞ (infinity)

On a Mercator chart, the scale factor varies between 1 and infinity.

This expansion away from the Equator is constant and is proportional to the secant (1/cosine) of the latitude.

This gives the following formula:

SCALE AT LATITUDE = SCALE AT EQUATOR x SECANT LATITUDE

This formula can be further resolved to:

COS LAT A x SCALE DENOMINATOR LAT B = COS LAT B x SCALE DENOMINATOR LAT A

Note: The above derived formula is very important for the JAR exams.

Example	If the scale at the equator is 1:1 000 000, what is the scale at 60°N?
STEP 1	cos Equator x Scale Denominator 60N = cos 60N x Scale Denominator Equator
	1 x Scale 60N = ½ x 1 000 000
	1: 500 000

MEASUREMENT OF DISTANCE

The mid-latitude scale must be used because of the scale expansion away from the Equator.

USE OF CHART

The main use of the Mercator Chart is as a navigation plotting chart. In Equatorial regions, the projection is used as a topographical map. For small distances on either side of the Equator, the map scale is almost constant.

PLOTTING ON A MERCATOR CHART

In order to plot a position line on a chart, a fix from a radio aid is needed. As discussed in other parts of the course, radio waves follow the shortest path over the surface of the Earth. This shortest path is a great circle.

As described above, a great circle on a Mercator chart is a curve. Because curves cannot be plotted, the path must be converted to something that can be plotted — a straight line. A straight line on a Mercator chart is a rhumb line.

A previous chapter explained that the difference between a great circle and a rhumb line was half of convergence, which is called Conversion Angle.

The problem comes in knowing which way to apply conversion angle. The easiest way to solve this is by drawing a diagram representing the situation.

On a Mercator chart, the meridians are straight, parallels are straight, and the rhumb line is straight, so, considering a route in an East/West direction, start by drawing a letter **H**.

Example An aircraft obtains a magnetic bearing of 270° off an NDB. The variation at the aircraft position is 17W. The aircraft is in the Northern Hemisphere. What is the RL bearing to plot from the NDB position on the chart if the convergence between the aircraft and the NDB is 12°?

Step 1 The GC bearing to the NDB is 270°M – 17W = 253°T.

Calculate the conversion angle. This is half of the convergence = 6°.

Step 2 Draw the diagram. The GC to the NDB is 253°T; this puts the NDB to the west of the aircraft.

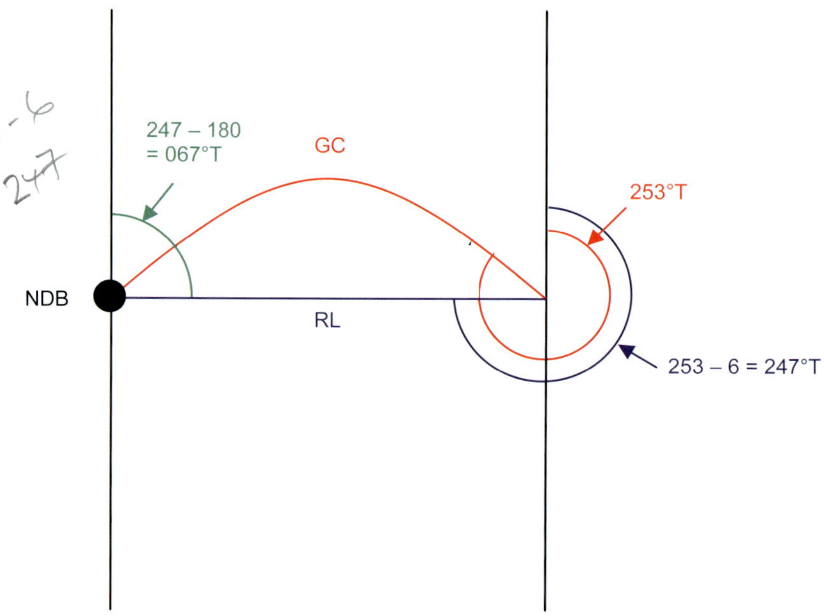

Step 3 In the diagram above, notice that the RL direction to the NDB is less than the GC direction.

The difference is the CA, calculated above as 6°.

The RL direction to the NDB is 253 – 6 = 247°T

To plot from the beacon, use the reciprocal of 247, which is 067°T

For the Southern Hemisphere

Step 1 Using the same figures again: the GC bearing to the NDB is 253°T, and the conversion angle is 6°.

Step 2 Draw the diagram. Again, the NDB is to the west of the aircraft.

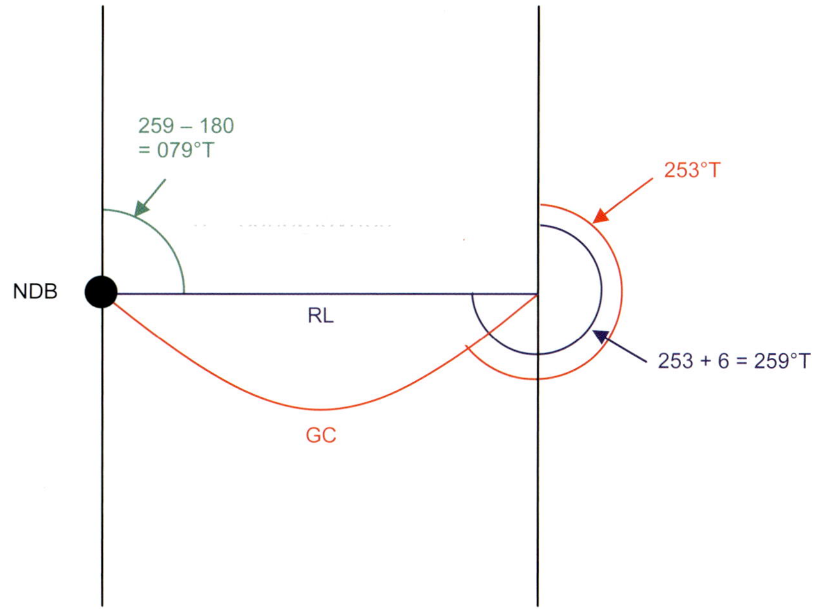

Step 3 In the diagram above, note that the RL direction to the NDB is greater than the GC direction, the opposite of the Northern Hemisphere case.

The RL direction to the NDB is 253 + 6 = 259°T.

To plot from the beacon, use the reciprocal of 259, which is 079°T.

Note: In both cases, the letter H is used to represent the situation, even though the direction is not directly East-West. In most of the questions, the directions used are very close to directly east or west. The H is an acceptable way to represent the problem. Some prefer to draw the rhumb line at an angle to more closely represent the situation.

The only difference in the two diagrams above is where the great circle is positioned. Remember, it is always closer to the nearer pole, so in the Northern Hemisphere it lies above (to the north of) the rhumb line, and in the Southern Hemisphere it lies below (to the south of) the rhumb line.

The examples above used the same information. In the Northern Hemisphere, with the beacon west of the aircraft, the conversion angle was added, and in the Southern Hemisphere it was subtracted. If the beacon were to the east of the aircraft, the situation would be reversed. That is why it is always better to draw a diagram than try to remember a rule. Errors are less likely with the diagram.

PLOTTING USING VORS

When using VORs for plotting, the situation is slightly different. As discussed elsewhere, a great circle's direction constantly changes throughout its length.

Take another look at the Southern Hemisphere question above. The RL direction from the beacon to the aircraft is as 079°T. The great circle direction is larger by the value of conversion angle. The great circle track from the beacon to the aircraft is 079 + 6 = 085°T. The reciprocal of this is 265°T. This does not match the great circle direction from the aircraft to the beacon, which was 259°T.

This proves the point about the great circle direction constantly changing. That is why, for the NDB, it was necessary to convert to a rhumb line before taking the reciprocal.

VOR equipment works a little differently from the NDB. The equipment tells which radial the aircraft is on, or the reciprocal of the radial. This is determined at the station, rather than in the aircraft.

For example, an RMI reading of 236°T to the station indicates that the aircraft is on the 056 radial. For VORs, take the reciprocal before applying conversion angle.

Example An aircraft obtains an RMI reading of 270° off a VOR. The variation at the aircraft position is 12°W. The variation at the station position is 17°W. The aircraft is in the Northern Hemisphere. What is the RL bearing to plot from the VOR position on the chart if the convergence between the aircraft and the VOR is 12°?

Step 1 The RMI reading is 270, so the aircraft is on the 090 radial (the reciprocal). This radial is the great circle from the station. Remember, radials are magnetic.

Step 2 Draw the diagram. The VOR is to the west of the aircraft.

Step 3 In the diagram below, note that the RL direction from the VOR is greater than the GC direction.

The RL direction is 090 + 6 = 096°M.

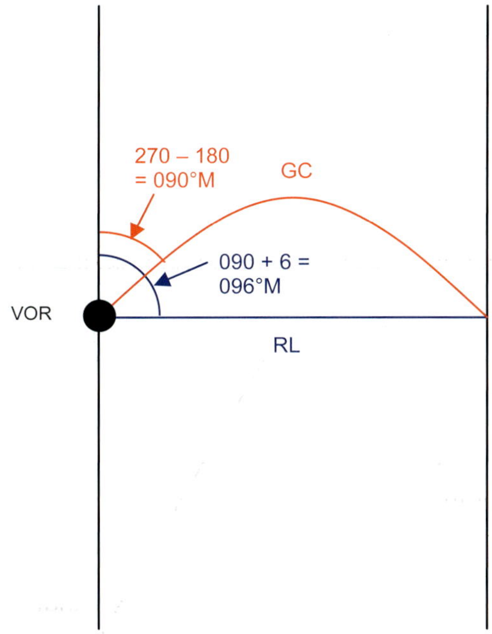

Step 4

Apply variation to get the true direction. Two values of variation have been given, one for the aircraft position and one for the VOR position. Whereas for an NDB, the aircraft variation is applied, use the station variation for a VOR.

So the true bearing to plot is 096 – 17 = 079°T.

SUMMARY OF PLOTTING

FOR AN NDB

1. Convert magnetic bearing to the beacon to a true bearing using the **aircraft** variation.
2. Apply conversion angle.
3. Take reciprocal to get RL from beacon.

FOR A VOR/VDF

1. Take reciprocal of RMI reading to get radial (magnetic).
2. Apply conversion angle.
3. Convert into a true bearing using the **station** variation.

MERCATOR PROBLEMS

Mercator Problem 1 On a Mercator, the distance between two meridians 1° apart is 3.58cm.

i. Express the scale at 40°N as a representative fraction.
ii. Where on the chart is the scale, 1:2 000 000?

Mercator Problem 2 The scale of a Mercator is 1:1 000 000 at 40°N.

i. What is the scale at the Equator?
ii. Explain whether it is possible for the scale to be 1:2 000 000 at any latitude.

Mercator Problem 3 The relative bearing of an NDB is 247° from an aircraft on a heading of 047°(T). If the change of longitude between the aircraft and the NDB is 12° and the mean latitude is 65°N, what bearing should be plotted on the Mercator?

Mercator Problem 4 The scale of a Mercator at 48°N is 1:4 000 000.
What is the spacing between two meridians 1° apart at 48°N?

Mercator Problem 5 With reference to a Mercator:

i. How does scale vary?
ii. Where is convergence correctly represented?
iii. Where on the chart would a straight line represent a great circle?

Mercator Problem 6 On a Mercator chart, at latitude 44°N, the measured distance between two fixes 10 minutes apart in time, along a track of 090°(T), is 1.63 inches. If the chart scale at 15°N is 1:3 000 000, what is the aircraft's speed in knots?

Mercator Problem 7 A Mercator extending from 008°W to 003°E has a scale of 1:1 000 000 at 56°N. What is the distance in inches between the limiting meridians?

Mercator Problem 8 When using a Mercator chart with a scale 1:4 000 000 at 58°N, a fix is plotted at position 4700N 00218E. Twenty minutes later, a second fix is obtained, indicating a track made good of 270°(T). These two fixes are 6cm apart.

i. What is mean groundspeed between fixes?
ii. Give the longitude of second fix.

ANSWERS TO MERCATOR PROBLEMS

Mercator Problem 1

i. Departure = Dlong x cos lat
60 x cos 40 = 45.96 nm
3.58 cm = 45.96 nm = 85.12 km
1 cm = 23.776 km = 2 377 595
Scale is 1: 2 377 595

ii. cos A x Scale Den B = cos B x Scale Den A
cos 40 x 2 000 000 = cos B x 2 377 595
cos B = 0.644
Lat = 50°

Mercator Problem 2

i. Scale E x cos 40 = 1 000 000 x cos E
Scale at the Equator is 1:1 305 407

ii. 1 305 407 x cos Lat = 2 000 000 x cos Equator
cos Lat = 2 000 000 ÷ 1 305 407 > 1
No

Mercator Problem 3

RB + Hdg = TB = 247 + 047 = 294°
The rhumb line must be plotted.
Convergence is Ch Long x Sin Lat = 10.87
CA = ½ convergence = 5.4°
GC – CA = RL
294 – 5.4 = RL = 288.6°
The reciprocal must be plotted from the beacon = 108.5°

Mercator Problem 4

60' @ 48° = 40.14 nm = 74.35 km
CD = $^{ED}/_{RF}$ = (74.35 x 100 000) ÷ 4 000 000 = 1.858 cm

Mercator Problem 5

i Expands away from the Equator
ii. The Equator
iii. The Equator and the Meridians

Mercator Problem 6

Scale Den 44N x cos 15 = Scale Den 15 x cos 44
Scale at 44 1: 2 234 146
1 inch = 2 234 146 inches = 30.62 nm
1.63 inches = 49.91 nm travelled in 10 minutes
Groundspeed = 300 knots

Mercator Problem 7

Dlong = 60 x 11 = 660' = 369 nm
1 inch = 1 000 000 = 13.7 nm
11° is represented by 369 ÷ 13.7 = 26.9"

Mercator Problem 8

i. Calculate the scale for 47°N
4 000 000 cos 47 = scale(47) cos 58
Scale (47) = 4 000 000 cos 47 ÷ cos 58 = 5 147 942
6 cm = ED ÷ 5 147 942
ED = 166.67 nm travelled in 20 minutes
Groundspeed 500 knots

ii. 166.67 = Dlong x cos 47
Dlong = 244.4'
4°04' of travel
New Longitude 001°46'W

Chapter 11
Maps and Charts — Lambert's Conformal

INTRODUCTION

The Mercator Chart discussed in the previous chapter can be used in its basic format from the Equator to 8° N/S. The Polar Stereographic Chart, which is discussed in the next chapter, is usable from 78° to 90°N/S.

Constant scale is defined as a scale change of no more than 1%. If a Scale Reduction Factor of 1% is allowed, this extends the range of these two projections to:

Mercator	0° to 11°N/S
Polar Stereographic	74° to 90°N/S

The remaining latitudes are covered by charts such as the Lambert's Conformal, which is a conical projection.

CONICAL PROJECTION

To picture the construction of a conical projection, imagine a cone placed over a reduced Earth, as in the diagram below.

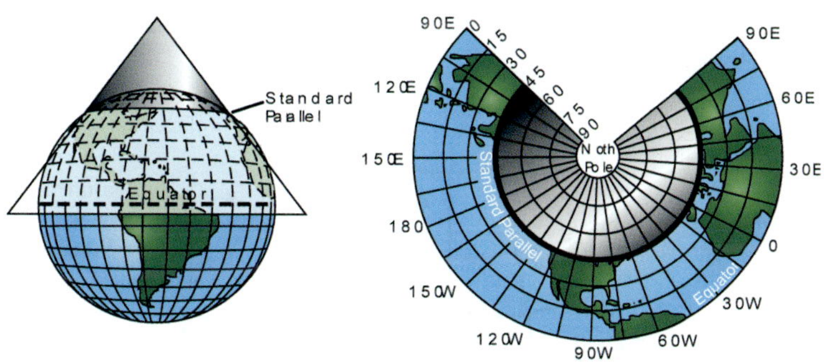

The cone is tangential along one parallel of latitude. This is called the Standard Parallel (SP). The imaginary light source is placed in the centre of the reduced Earth to display the graticule on the cone. The scale expands away from the standard parallel.

The unwrapped cone forms a segment, as shown above. In the example above, 260° represents 360° on the Earth.

The Standard Parallel controls the size of the segment.

$$\text{Size of the segment}/_{360} = \text{Sin SP}$$

Example: The segment size is 260. What is the Standard Parallel?

$$^{260}/_{360} = 0.722 = \text{Sin SP}$$
$$\text{SP} = 46.22°$$

The Lambert's Conformal Chart does not use one Standard Parallel, but two.

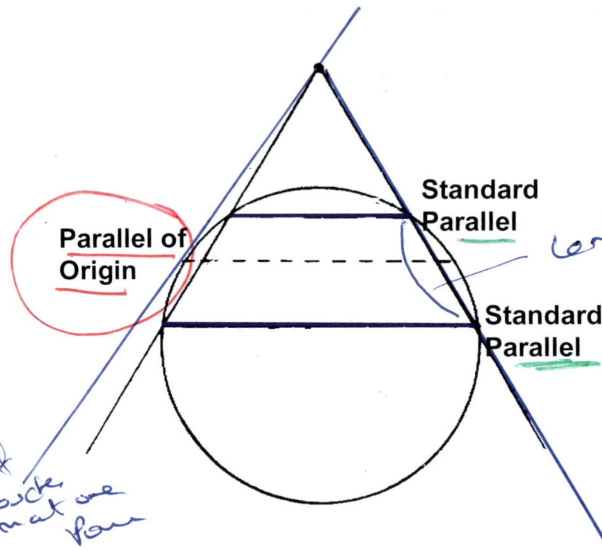

The Standard Parallels are split by a mean parallel - the Parallel of Origin.

The scale:

1. Is correct at the Standard Parallels
2. Expands away from the Standard Parallels
3. Contracts toward the Parallel of Origin
4. Is least at the Parallel of Origin

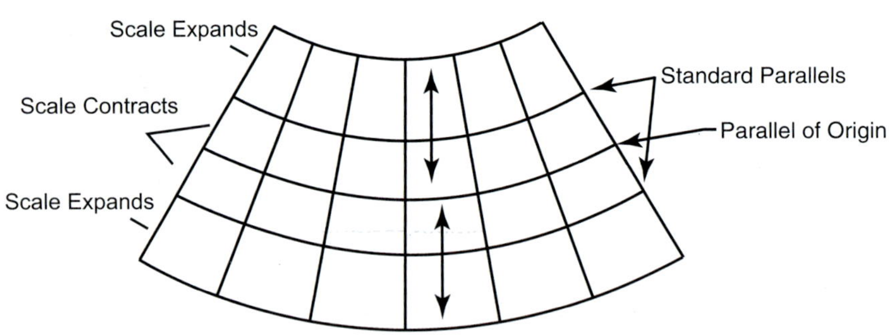

If the Standard Parallels are chosen correctly and the scale errors are minimal, the chart can be considered as constant scale.

$^{1}/_{6}$ RULE

The $^{1}/_{6}$ rule ensures that there is minimum scale variation over the coverage of the chart, and that it can be considered as a constant scale chart.

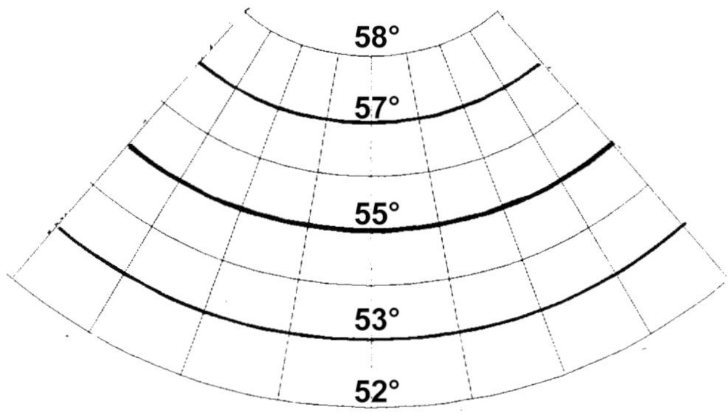

Where the Standard Parallels are 57° and 53°:

- $^{1}/_{6}$ of the chart is outside 57°
- $^{1}/_{6}$ of the chart is outside 53°
- The rest of the chart lies inside the two Standard Parallels

MERIDIANS AND PARALLELS

The meridians are depicted as straight lines converging toward the pole of projection.

The parallels of latitude are arcs of concentric circles concave toward the pole.

As described with Mercator charts, Earth convergence cannot be accurately represented on a flat piece of paper because it varies with the distance from some particular parallel. On a Lambert's Chart, as on a Mercator, the meridians are straight lines, so chart convergence is constant.

The value of convergence used on a Lambert's Chart can be calculated by the following formula:

CONVERGENCE = CH LONG X SIN OF THE PARALLEL OF ORIGIN

Earth convergence is calculated using the following formula:

CONVERGENCE = CH LONG X SIN LAT

This means that Earth convergence and chart convergence are only equal for positions that happen to be on the Parallel of Origin.

Away from the Parallel of Origin, the convergence is not an exact representation of Earth convergence. The chart coverage is generally quite small, and so any errors introduced are quite small.

CONSTANT OF THE CONE

This can also be referred to as the **convergence factor** or **cone convergence factor**. This may be abbreviated as CC or CCF. The constant of the cone is the ratio between the developed cone arc to the actual arc.

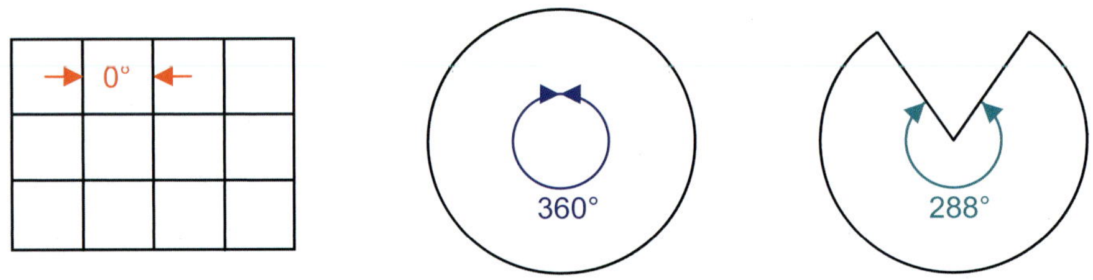

1 **2** **3**

1. For a cylindrical projection, the meridians do not converge, and the constant is zero.
2. For a Stereographic Projection, the actual arc is the same as the developed arc, and the constant is 1.
3. For the conic projection, the ratio is $^{288}/_{360} = 0.8$.

The constant of the cone is printed on the Lambert's Conformal Chart and can be used to calculate the convergence by using the following formula:

CONVERGENCE = CH LONG X CONSTANT OF THE CONE

It is already know that:

CONVERGENCE = CH LONG X SIN PARALLEL OF ORIGIN

This must mean that:

CONSTANT OF THE CONE = SIN PARALLEL OF ORIGIN

PROPERTIES OF THE LAMBERT'S CONFORMAL

Meridians	Straight lines converging toward the pole
Parallels	Concentric arcs concave toward the pole with nearly constant spacing
Orthomorphic	Yes
Great Circle	Great circles are a curve concave to the parallel of origin. Near the parallel of origin, they may be interpreted as a straight line. **Note:** Assume a straight line for JAR examinations, since charts over such a small range of latitudes produce a small chance of error.
Rhumb Line	Curves concave to the pole
Convergence	Correct only at the Parallel of Origin
Scale	Constant at the Standard Parallels

PLOTTING ON A LAMBERT'S CONFORMAL CHART

Assuming that a great circle is a straight line simplifies the plotting of bearings. There is no need to use the rhumb line as with the Mercator chart.

> **Note:** If conversion is necessary between a rhumb line and a great circle on a Lambert's Chart, use the same principle as for the Mercator chart, which uses the conversion angle.

VOR bearings are changed into a QTE (true bearing) and plotted directly from the station. As for a Mercator chart, use station variation since the VOR works on the principle of radials. VORs can be effectively ignored, as there is no convergence to be taken into account during plotting.

However, the ADF does pose a slight problem since the bearing is measured at the aircraft, but plotted at the station. Practical plotting is described in a later chapter. This chapter deals with the simple calculation of what is to be plotted. Since the aircraft and the station are most likely on different meridians, the convergence between the meridians must be taken into account.

Example An aircraft obtains an RMI reading of 065° off an NDB. The variation is 15°E at the aircraft position, and the convergence between the aircraft and the NDB is 18°. Assume Earth convergence and chart convergence are the same. The aircraft and NDB are in the Northern Hemisphere. What bearing would be plotted from the meridian passing through the NDB?

> **Note:** Convergence is given in this question but must be calculated in most Lambert's questions. Use one of the chart convergence formulae given earlier in the chapter, and use either the Parallel of Origin or the constant of the cone, depending on what information is given in the question.

STEP 1 Calculate the required information.
The GC bearing to the NDB is 065°M + 15°E = 080°T.

STEP 2 Draw a diagram.

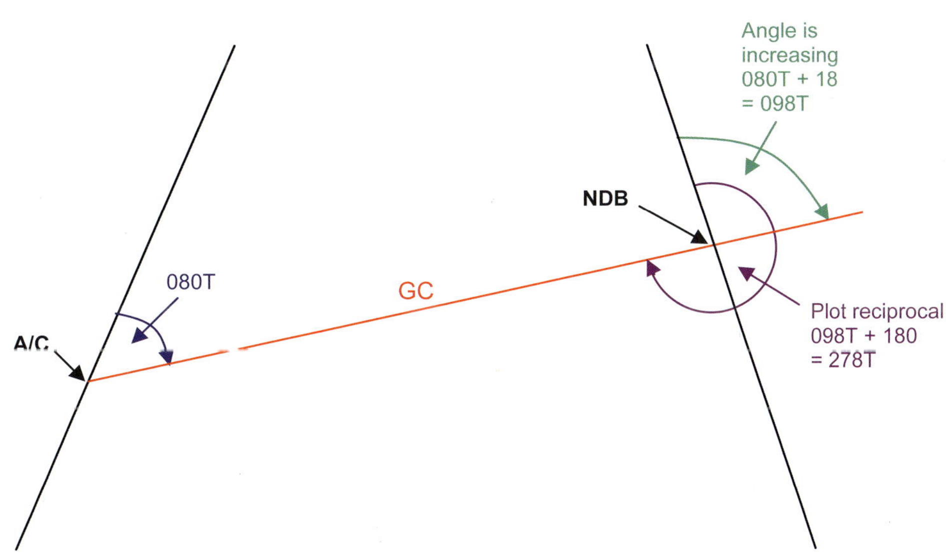

STEP 3 Remember that the GC changes direction by convergence.

It is clear that the bearing is increasing as it moves toward the NDB.

The direction of the GC at the NDB is:

080° + 18° = 098°T

The reciprocal of the bearing is plotted = 278°T.

For the Southern Hemisphere

STEP 1 Calculate the required information.

The GC bearing to the NDB is 065°M + 15°E = 080°T.

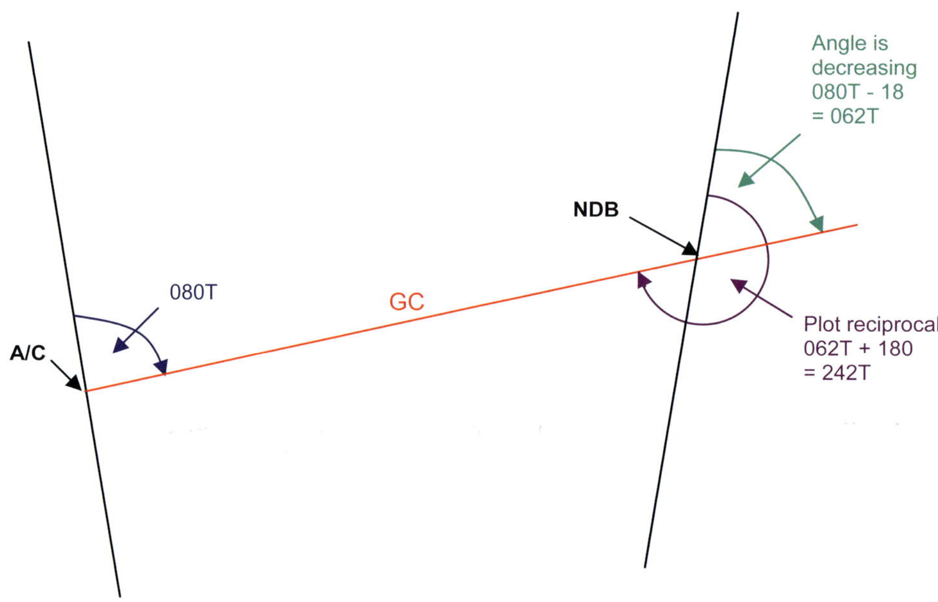

STEP 2 Draw the diagram.

STEP 3 Remember that the GC changes direction by convergence. It is clear that the bearing is decreasing as it moves toward the NDB.

The direction of the GC at the NDB is:
080° - 18° = 062°T

The reciprocal of the bearing is plotted = 242°T.

SUMMARY OF PLOTTING OF BEARINGS

Two examples were provided for plotting using an NDB – one in the Northern Hemisphere, one in the Southern Hemisphere. In both examples, the beacon was to the east of the aircraft. In the Northern Hemisphere example, convergence was added, while in the Southern Hemisphere example it was subtracted.

For a beacon to the west of the aircraft, it would have been the other way round.
In summary:

	Beacon to the east	**Beacon to the west**
Northern Hemisphere	Add convergence	Subtract convergence
Southern Hemisphere	Subtract convergence	Add convergence

LAMBERT'S PROBLEMS

Lambert's Problem 1

An aircraft heading 317°T has a RB of 291° to an NDB. The ChLong is 9° and the Mean Lat 61°S.

What would be plotted from the NDB on a Lambert's Chart with a Parallel of Origin of 48°S?

Lambert's Problem 2

On a Lambert's Chart with SPs 36°N and 60°N, a straight line joining A 50°00'N 030°00'W and B 40°00'N 060°00'W cuts the meridian at 045°W in the direction 065/245°T. What is the approximate great circle bearing of B from A?

Lambert's Problem 3

The convergence on a Lambert's Chart is 9.5° between positions 59°53'N 001°07'W and 63°28'N 010°56'E.

i. What is the constant of the cone?
ii. Calculate the Parallel of Origin.
iii. If one standard parallel is 37°, what is the expected latitude of the other Standard Parallel?

Lambert's Problem 4

A Lambert's Chart of scale 1:250 000 has SPs of 40°N and 62°N. The constant of the cone is .749. What is the parallel of origin?

Lambert's Problem 5

On a Lambert's Chart the distance along parallel 50°S between meridians 1° apart is 3.82 cm.

i. What is the scale at 50°S?
ii. What is the distance in cm along the meridian between 49°S and 51°S?

ANSWERS TO LAMBERT'S PROBLEMS

Lambert's Problem 1

Convergence = Ch long x Sin Parallel of Origin
= 9 x sin 48 = 6.68°
TB = RB + HDG
TB = 317° + 291° = 248°
Bearing at the beacon 248° + 6.68° = 254.68°
Plot the reciprocal 074.68°

Lambert's Problem 2

Convergence = 30 sin 48N = 22.3°
RL Track is 065/245
GC Track = RL Track + CA
= 245° + 11
Bearing A to B 256°

Lambert's Problem 3

i. Constant of the Cone = 9.5 ÷ 12.05 = .79
ii. Parallel of Origin = $\text{Sin}^{-1}.79$ = 52°
iii. SP difference between parallel of origin is 15°
Other SP 67°

Lambert's Problem 4

48.5°

Lambert's Problem 5

i. Departure = 60 cos 50 = 38.56 nm = 71.42 km
3.82 cm = 71.42 km
1 cm = 18.698 km = 1 869 805 cm
Scale 1: 1 869 805

ii Distance is 120 nm = 120 x 1.852 km = 222.24 km
Scale is 1 cm = 18.698 km
Distance is 222.24 km ÷ 18.69 = 11.89 cm

Chapter 12

Maps and Charts — Polar Stereographic

INTRODUCTION

For the Polar Stereographic Chart, the point of projection is directly opposite the point of tangency. It is not at the centre of the reduced Earth (If the point of projection is the centre of the reduced Earth, the chart is a Gnomonic).

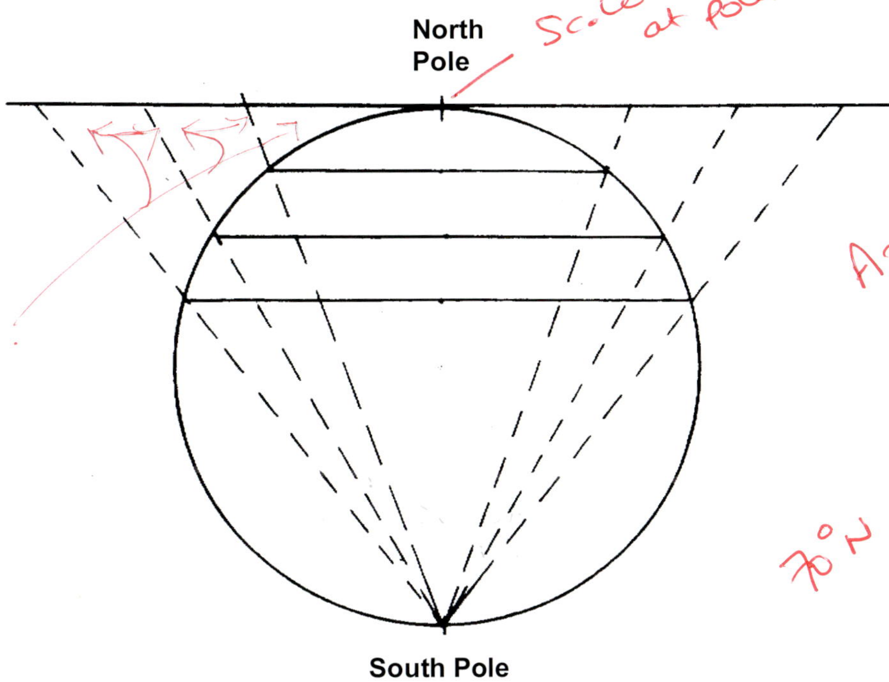

The above projection has the following properties (see diagram on the following page):

- Meridians appear as straight lines diverging from the Pole.
- Parallels of latitude are concentric circles. The spacing between the parallels increases with increasing distance from the pole at a rate of secant^2 (Co-Lat ÷ 2).
- Meridians and parallels cross at right angles.
- Chart scale is correct at the pole and increases away from it. The chart scale change is less than 1% above 78.5° latitude.
- The chart is not of constant scale. However, away from any point on the chart the scale is the same in all directions.
- The chart is conformal.
- A full hemisphere can be shown, so the Equator is projected as the edge of the chart.

SHAPES AND AREAS

Scale expansion causes both shapes and areas to be distorted away from the pole.

GREAT CIRCLE

A great circle, other than a meridian, is a curve concave to the pole. Near the pole the great circle can be considered a straight line.

RHUMB LINE

A rhumb line is a curve concave toward the pole.

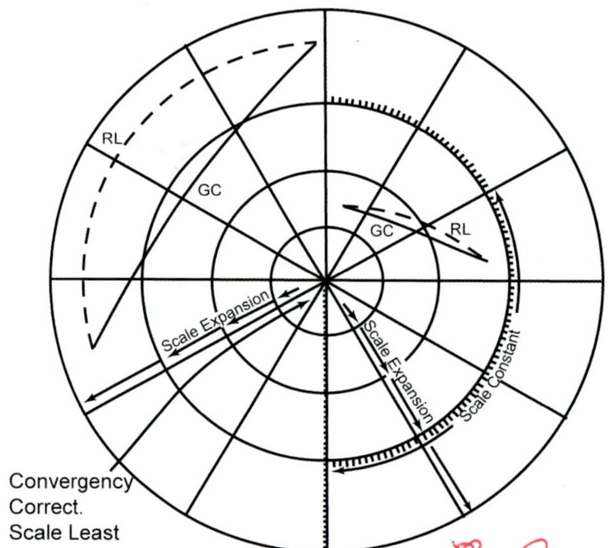

CONVERGENCE

The value of convergence is constant and equal to the change of longitude.

SCALE

The scale expands away from the Pole of Tangency at a rate of:

$$\mathbf{Sec^2\ (Co\text{-}Lat \div 2)}$$

Where: Co-Lat = 90 – Actual Latitude

USES OF THE POLAR STEREOGRAPHIC CHART

Normally, use is limited to latitudes greater than 65°. The problems incurred on the Polar Stereographic chart are based on the convergence being 1; for every 1° of longitude a straight line crosses, its direction changes by 1°.

GRID AND PLOTTING ON A POLAR CHART

Where a straight line is drawn on a Polar Stereographic chart, it roughly equates to a great circle. The direction of this line is changing, as stated above. To allow a constant straight line course direction, a grid is superimposed upon the Polar Stereographic chart normally aligned to the 0° meridian. This grid is printed because the use of true or magnetic references in polar regions is difficult because of the following:

- Magnetic variation changes rapidly over short distances
- The magnetic compass becomes unreliable at latitudes greater than 70°N
- The convergence of the meridians causes the course to change rapidly

Please note that other meridians may be used to reference the grid. The same principle applies.

Using the diagram below:

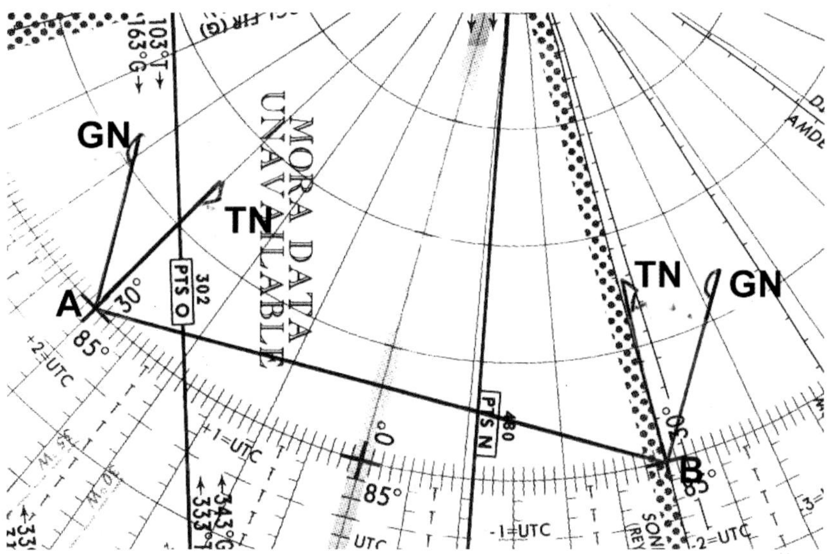

The direction of the datum meridian is grid north, and any course measured from this datum is known as grid direction. In the diagram above, the grid is aligned to the prime meridian.

A line is drawn between A (85°N 030°W) and B (85°N 030°E).

By inspection, the grid course equals the true course when the line passes through the 0° meridian. Both True North and Grid North are the same.

Grid Course 270°
True Course 270°

However, the true and grid course differ at both A and B.
By measurement, if transiting from B to A:

At B
Grid Course 270°
True Course 300°

At A
Grid Course 270°
True Course 240°

The angular difference between the two is convergence:

- Where True North is west of Grid North (B), there is westerly convergence
- Where True North is east of Grid North (A), there is easterly convergence

The angular difference between the Grid North and True North is 30°. The angular difference between the Reference Meridian (0°) and Point A or Point B is 030°.

Following a simple convention:

Convergence west – True best
Point B
Grid Course = True Course – 30°

Convergence east – True least
Point A
Grid Course = True Course + 30°

True Bearing = Grid Bearing **+ Longitude West** / **- Longitude East**

The longitude refers to whether True North is to the west or to the east of Grid North.

Where a magnetic direction is required, the convergence and variation must be added.

Example An aircraft is flying from A to B. The grid heading is 090°. Convergence is 15°E and Variation 15°E. What is the magnetic heading?

STEP 1 Find the true heading.
Grid Heading ± Conv = True Heading
090 – 15 = 075°

STEP 2 Find the magnetic heading.
True Heading ± Variation = Magnetic Heading
075 – 15 = 060°
Magnetic Heading = 060°

To do two calculations in this form can cause difficulties. To make the transformation from grid to magnetic easier, the convergence and variation can be combined to give grivation. In the example above:

Convergence + Variation = Grivation
15°E + 15°E = 30°E

The grivation is then applied to the grid heading to give the magnetic heading.

Polar Stereographic Example 1 Complete the following table:

	GRID	CONV	T	VAR	M	GRIV
1		45°E	200°	15°W		
2	119°		149°		139°	
3		30°E	315°	5°W		25°E
4	171°	45°W				71°W
5	204°		014°		359°	

AIRCRAFT HEADING

In the diagram below, the aircraft grid heading is given.

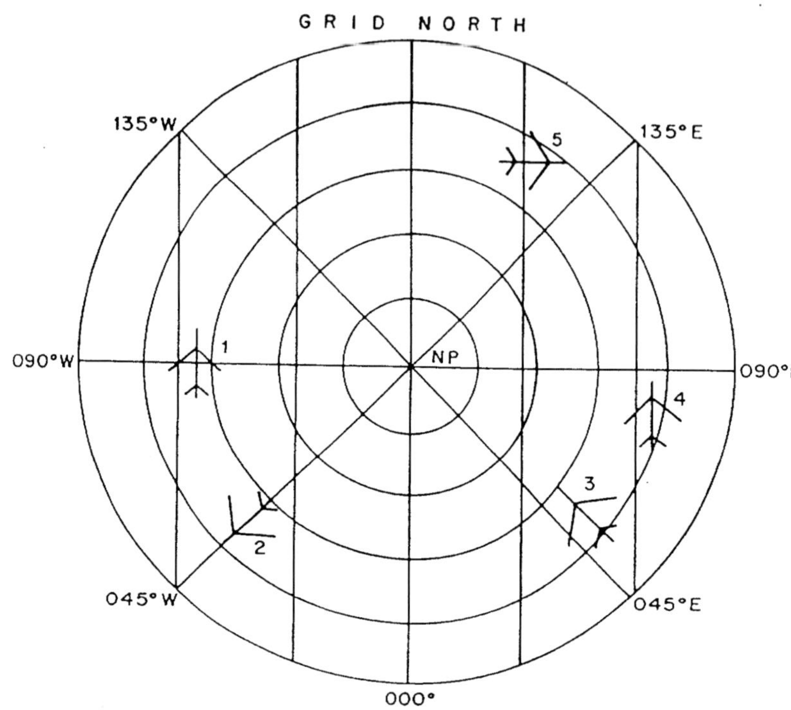

The Grid Headings are:

Aircraft 1	000°
Aircraft 2	225°
Aircraft 3	315°
Aircraft 4	000°
Aircraft 5	090°

The following are examples of the possible calculations to expect during the General Navigation examination. In the following questions, a convergence factor is given. This is because a grid can be superimposed on Lambert's Conformal Charts as well as Polar Stereographic charts. As stated in Example 1:

Grid Convergence = Ch Long x Convergence Factor

Example An aircraft is using a grid based on 20°W. What is the magnetic heading of an aircraft in position 50°E, given variation is 8°W and the convergence factor is 0.75? The grid heading of the aircraft is 224°.

STEP 1 Calculate the convergence.

Convergence = Convergence Factor x Ch Long

0.75 x 70

52½°W

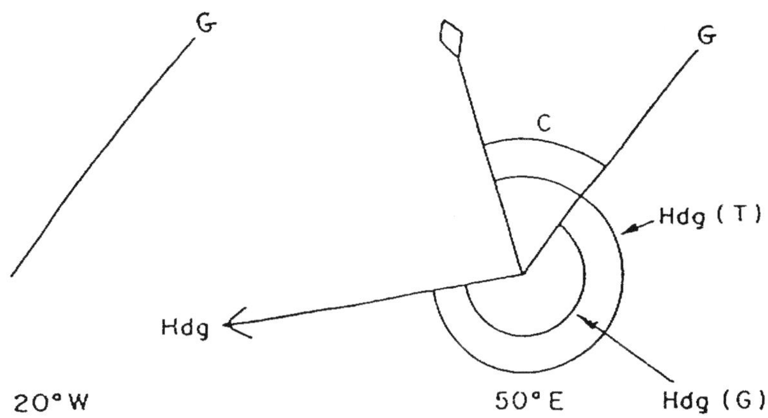

STEP 2 True Heading = Grid Heading + Convergence W

224° + 52½°

276½°T

STEP 3 Heading Magnetic

276½° + 8° = 284½°M

Example

An aircraft is in position 40°N 010°E on a magnetic heading of 150° and a grid heading of 170°. Variation is 10°W. What is the datum meridian of the grid?

STEP 1

Draw a diagram of the situation. Calculate true heading and the convergence.

True Heading = 150° – 10° = 140°T

Convergence = Grid Heading – True Heading

Convergence = 170° – 140° = 30°E (see diagram opposite)

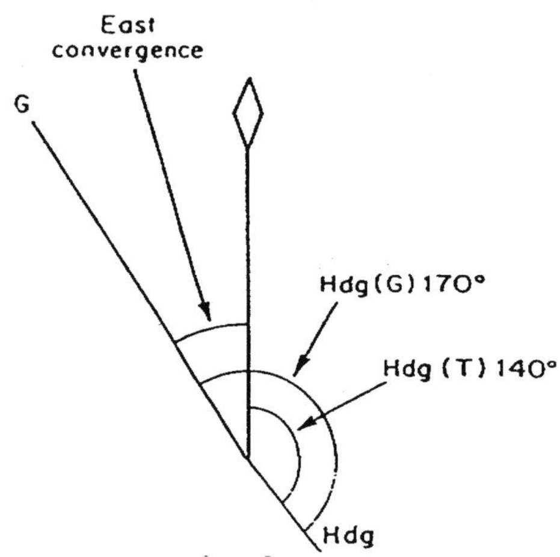

STEP 2

The datum is the aircraft position plus the Ch Long.

10°E + 30°E = 40°E

Example An aircraft using a north polar grid is steering 080°T and 140°G. What is the longitude?

STEP 1 Heading Grid = Heading True ± convergence

Heading Grid – True heading = Convergence
+ is Longitude W
- is Longitude E

140 – 80 = 60°W

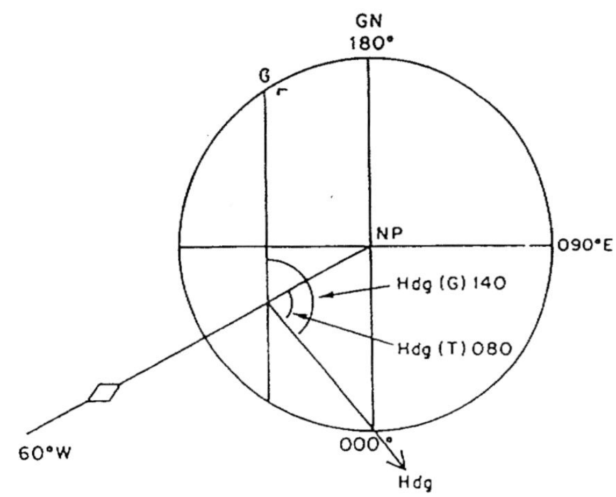

Example An aircraft is using a south polar grid in position 75°S 020°W. The grid heading is 210°. What is the true heading?

STEP 1 Heading True = Heading Grid + Longitude W
210 + 20 = 230°

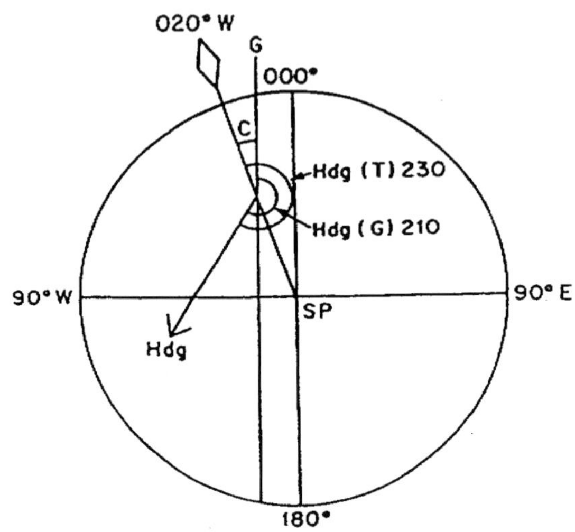

Polar Stereographic Example 2 An aircraft has a grid heading of 310° using a chart based on a grid datum of 40°W. If the variation is 10°E, and the heading 340°M, what is the aircraft longitude if the aircraft is in the Northern Hemisphere?

Polar Stereographic Example 3 The grid datum is 50°W. The aircraft is in position 50°N 020°W. The grid heading is 257° and the variation 8°W. What is the aircraft's magnetic heading?

ANSWERS TO POLAR STEREOGRAPHIC EXAMPLES

Polar Stereographic Example 1

	GRID	CONV	T	VAR	M	GRIV
1	**245°**	45°E	200°	15°W	**215°**	**30°E**
2	119°	**30°W**	149°	**10°E**	139°	**20°W**
3	**345°**	30°E	315°	5°W	**320°**	25°E
4	171°	45°W	**216°**	**26°W**	**242°**	71°W
5	204°	**170°W**	014°	**15°E**	359°	**155°W**

Polar Stereographic Example 2 0° E/W

Polar Stereographic Example 3 295°M

Chapter 13
Maps and Charts — Transverse and Oblique Mercator

INTRODUCTION

Both the Transverse Mercator and the Oblique Mercator are known as skew cylindricals. These projections do not use the Equator as the great circle of tangency. The Transverse Mercator uses any meridian as the great circle of tangency. Any great circle other than a meridian can serve as the circle of tangency for the Oblique Mercator.

TRANSVERSE MERCATOR

This projection is often used to map countries that have great North-South extent, but little East-West width (e.g. Chile).

The central meridian is a straight line, and all other meridians appear as curves.

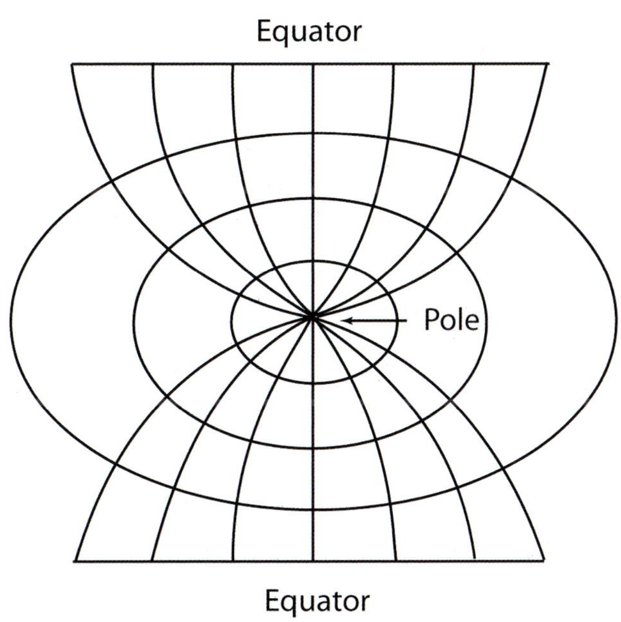

The Equator appears as a straight line. All other parallels are curves, as shown in the diagram above. A straight line drawn on this projection:

- Represents a great circle only when it is the central meridian or when it cuts the central meridian at right angles
- Represents a rhumb line only when it is the central meridian or the Equator

Rhumb lines are usually complex curves with the exceptions of the examples above.

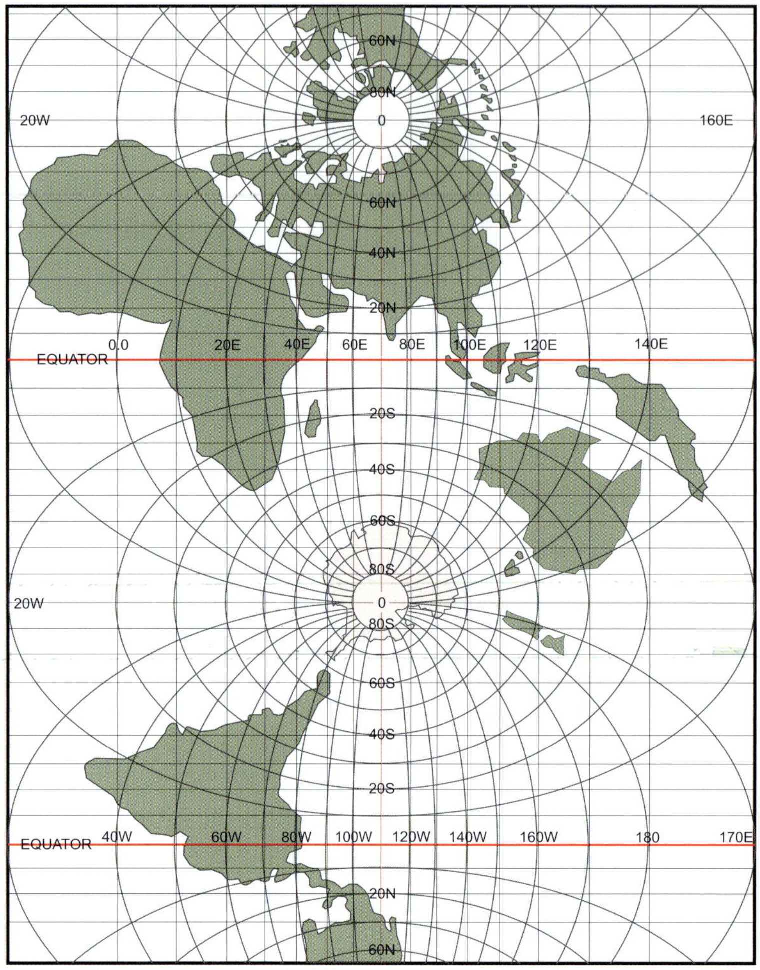

The chart scale is correct at the central meridian and increases with the great circle distance from the central meridian. If the meridian of tangency is chosen such that the total width projected is less than 960 nm wide, the scale change is not more than 1%. Other advantages are:

- Great circles are approximate straight lines
- There is little area distortion
- The latitude and longitude graticule appears regular in shape

Even though the chart is not constant scale, the scale variations are the same in all directions. Since the meridians and parallels intersect at right angles, the chart is orthomorphic. The scale expands away from the central meridian by the secant of the great circle distance.

Chart convergence is not constant and is correctly represented at the Equator and pole.

OBLIQUE MERCATOR

The Oblique Mercator is a skew projection that uses a great circle of tangency that is not a meridian. The only straight-line great circle is the meridian passing through the pole of the datum great circle. All other meridians are curves concave to the datum great circle.

The parallels of latitude are complex curves cutting the meridians at 90°.

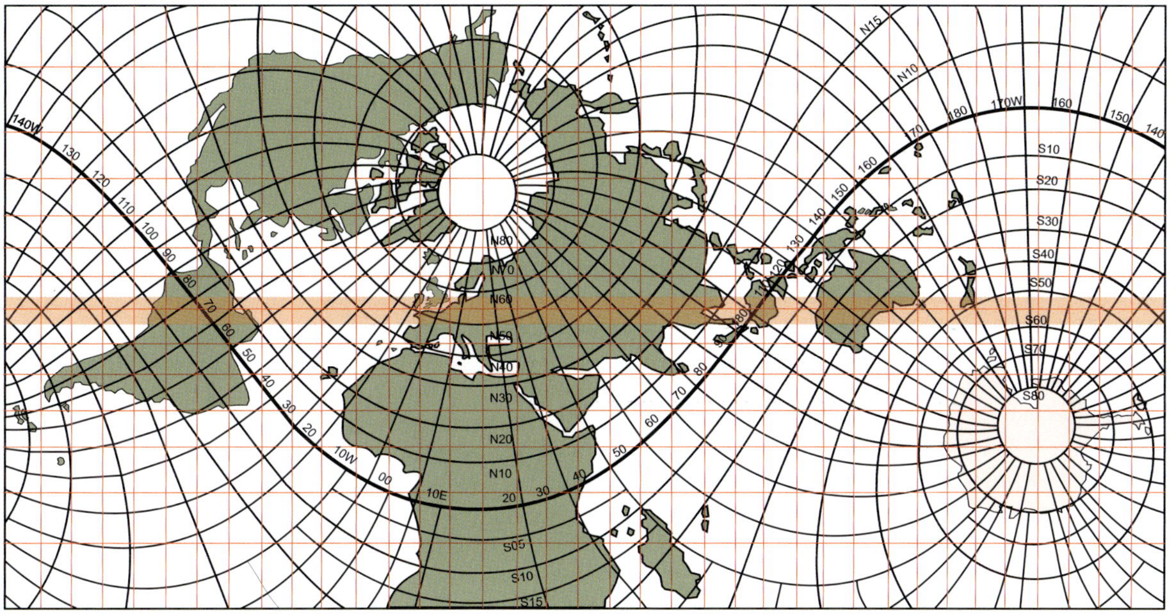

Great circles are curves concave to the datum great circle. Any great circle cutting the datum great circle at 90° is a straight line. In practice, assume any straight line near the datum great circle (and up to approximately 500 nm either side) is a great circle.

Rhumb lines are complex curves.

Within 700 nm of the datum great circle, assume convergence is correct. The scale is correct along the datum great circle. The scale varies with the secant of the great circle distance away from the datum great circle.

This chart is used for strip charts.

Chapter 14
Maps and Charts — Summary

MERCATOR

Origin of Projection	**Cylindrical** The cylinder touches the reduced Earth at the Equator Projection is from the centre of the sphere
Graticule	**Meridians** Parallel straight lines, equally spaced **Parallels of Latitude** Unequally-spaced parallel straight lines, with the spacing increasing away from the Equator
Scale	Correct at the Equator Expands away from the Equator as the secant of the latitude
Convergence	Correct at the Equator At all other latitudes, chart convergence is less than Earth convergence
Rhumb Line	Straight line
Great Circle	Curves convex to the nearer pole and concave to the Equator Equator and meridians are straight lines

LAMBERT'S CONFORMAL

Origin of Projection	**Conical** The cone touches the reduced Earth at the parallel of tangency Projection from the centre of the sphere
Graticule	**Meridians** Straight lines converge toward the pole of projection **Parallels of Latitude** Arcs of circles, nearly equally spaced, with their centre at the pole of projection
Scale	Correct at the standard parallels Expands outside the standard parallels and contracts between the standard parallels Is at a minimum at the parallel of origin
Convergence	Correct at the parallel of origin Chart convergence is equal to Ch Long x Sin Parallel of Origin
Rhumb Line	Curves concave to the pole of projection Meridians are straight lines
Great Circle	Curves concave to the parallel of origin Are closest to a straight line at the parallel of origin

POLAR STEREOGRAPHIC

Origin of Projection	**Azimuthal** The flat plate touches the reduced Earth at the pole Projection is from the opposite pole
Graticule	**Meridians** Straight lines radiating from the pole **Parallels of Latitude** Circles centred on the pole The spacing increases away from the pole The Equator can be projected
Scale	Correct at the pole Expands away from the pole as $\sec^2$ ½ Co Lat Scale is correct to within 1% to 78°N/S Scale is correct to within 3% to 70°N/S
Convergence	Correct at pole At all points on the chart, convergence equals Ch Long
Rhumb Line	Curves concave to the pole of projection Meridians are straight lines
Great Circle	Curves concave to the pole Meridians are straight lines Close to the pole may be considered a straight line for plotting purposes

TRANSVERSE MERCATOR

Origin of Projection	**Cylindrical** The cylinder touches the reduced Earth at the selected meridian
Graticule	**Meridians** The datum meridian, the Equator, and meridians at 90° to the datum meridian are straight lines Other meridians are complex curves **Parallels of Latitude** Ellipses, except the equator Close to the pole are nearly circular
Scale	Correct at the datum meridian Expands away from the datum meridian as secant of great circle distance from the datum meridian
Convergence	Correct at the Equator and poles
Rhumb Line	Complex curves. Datum meridian, meridians at 90° to the datum meridian are straight lines
Great Circle	Complex curves except the datum meridian Datum meridian, Equator, and the meridian at 90° to the datum meridian can be taken as straight lines Any straight line at a right angle to the datum meridian is a great circle

OBLIQUE MERCATOR

Origin of Projection	**Cylindrical** The cylinder touches the reduced Earth along a selected great circle route
Graticule	**Meridians** Curves concave to the datum great circle. The meridian passing through the pole of the datum great circle is a straight line **Parallels of Latitude** Complex curves cutting the meridians at 90°
Scale	Correct at the great circle of tangency Expands as secant of great circle distance from the great circle of tangency Within 500 nm of the great circle of tangency may be used as a constant scale chart
Convergence	Correct along the great circle of tangency, at the poles, and at the Equator
Rhumb Line	Complex curves
Great Circle	Complex curves Close to the great circle of tangency may be interpreted as a straight line

Chapter 15
Pilot Navigation Technique

INTRODUCTION

The basis of air navigation is the triangle of velocities explained previously. The use of the triangle to solve navigation problems in flight requires plotting charts, computers, and other navigation instruments that are normally denied to the pilot navigator. Pilots must use other navigation techniques to make observations of flight progress.

For the pilot navigator, flying the aeroplane and navigating it are concurrent activities. The predominance of one or the other at any instant of time is dictated by the immediate situation. Simplify this problem by logically approaching the navigation aspect and by making careful preparations. The navigational factors contributing to success are explored under the following headings:

- The Need for Accurate Flying
- Pre-Flight Planning
- Aircraft Performance
- Mental Dead Reckoning
- Chart Analysis and Chart Reading
- The Use of Radio Aids

THE NEED FOR ACCURATE FLYING

It is necessary that the highest possible standards of accuracy are maintained in respect to heading, airspeed, and altitude. Precise limits of each are not quoted here, but it is emphasised that skill in accurate flying can only be achieved by constant practice.

PRE-FLIGHT PLANNING

It is absolutely necessary to reduce the time spent on navigation in the air to a minimum. In this respect, thorough flight planning contributes to the success of any flight.

Flight planning should be carried out on a basis that requires the pilot to establish a position at the following intervals:

- Immediately after setting heading to provide a definite departure point and to establish a departure time on which to base ETA.
- At regular points along track to check the progress of the flight so that corrections for track error or time may be made.
- At a final point close to the destination so that final corrections may be made.

With chart preparation, there are only a few absolute rules:

Time/Distance Markers — The track line can either be calibrated in units of flight time or distance. If flight time is used, it can either be time elapsed or time to destination. Similarly, distance can be distance flown or distance to go. The choice between the two methods is a matter of personal opinion, but an advantage of the distance method is that it facilitates application of the 1 in 60 rule.

Track Error Lines — Lines drawn at angles of 5° or 10°, either side of track through departure point and destination, are most useful for quick estimation of track error and for estimating heading alterations.

Folding Charts — The chart should be folded so that complete track coverage is possible with the minimum number of page turns and without re-folding in flight. Charts should be numbered and arranged in order of use. It is also a good idea to have an emergency set of charts in an easily accessible spot to relieve any situation that might arise.

FLIGHT PLANNING SEQUENCE

A logical sequence is as follows:

- Review all information relevant to the flight, e.g. flight rules, navigation warnings, etc.
- Study the meteorological situation, and obtain wind velocities and temperatures required for planning.
- Select a flight planning chart and, if different, a set of charts for the route.
- Determine the route to be followed; consider the aim of the flight, flight rules, the meteorological situation, the availability of navigation aids, and any other factors involved.
- Draw in tracks, measure track angles and distances, and record them in the flight log.
- Determine safe altitudes, and decide on flight altitude or flight level, as applicable.
- From knowledge of aircraft performance, determine RAS for each flight stage. Enter RAS in log, and in conjunction with altitude and temperature, calculate TAS.
- Calculate headings to steer for each flight stage, and log them.
- Complete the log by the calculation of groundspeeds and fuels.
- Carry out a mental re-appraisal of the whole plan to check for obvious errors.
- Prepare the flight charts.
- Note positions of alternate airfields, and determine flight planning data from destination to alternates.

AIRCRAFT PERFORMANCE

With modern high-performance aircraft, flight planning choice may be restricted to the need to conform to operational limitations. This aspect of the subject is considered in Flight Planning.

MENTAL DEAD RECKONING

Mental DR is the mental calculation of the aeroplane's progress so that its position can be assessed, alterations to heading determined, and revisions of ETA calculated, as necessary.

ESTIMATION OF TRACK ERROR

As mentioned earlier, track error lines are useful for estimating alterations of heading quickly.

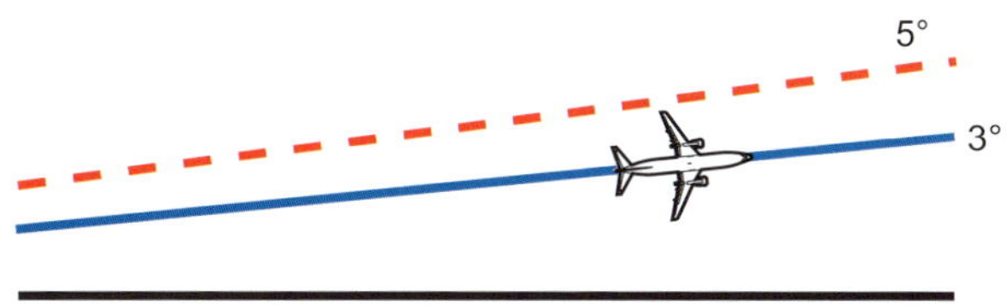

In the example above, the aeroplane position can be seen to be along the 3° line. The angle between planned track and track made good is 3°.

CORRECTION FOR TRACK ERROR

There are various geometric rules which can be used to correct for track error. Remember that all methods assume that the drift does not change after small alterations of heading:

- When track error is measured from the departure point, end-of-track heading should be altered toward the planned track by double the track error. When the planned track is regained, an appropriate alteration is made to parallel track.
- When track error is measured relative to the destination, it is usually sufficient to alter heading toward the destination by the amount of track-error.
- When track error is measured from both ends simultaneously, alteration should be made toward the destination by the sum of the two measured track errors.

THE 1 IN 60 RULE

The 1 in 60 rule is another method of correcting for track error and is based on the fact that one nautical mile subtends an angle of 1° at an approximate distance of 60 nm, so:

- 3 nm subtends 3° at 60 nm
- 5 nm subtends 5° at 60 nm

In applying the rule, the triangle relevant to the problem is identified, and the ratio of the long side 60 is established. This ratio may then be applied to the angle to reveal the length of the short side. Conversely, the ratio may be applied to the short side to determine the angle it subtends.

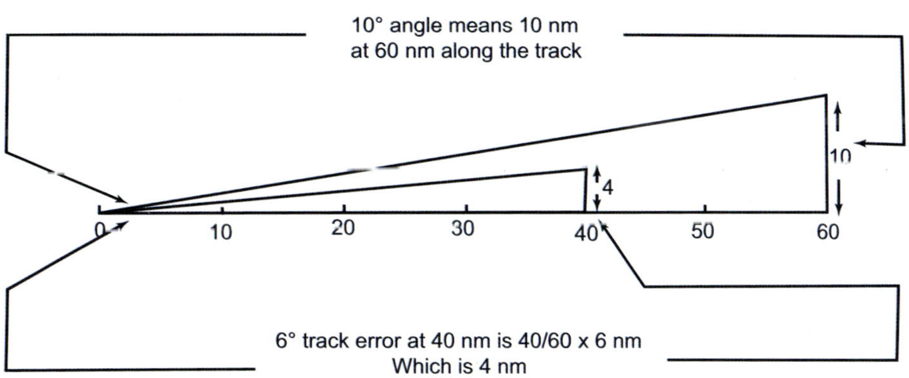

If the distance off track is known, the track error can be calculated. In the example below:

$$5 \text{ nm} = {}^{5}/_{30} \times 60 = 10°$$

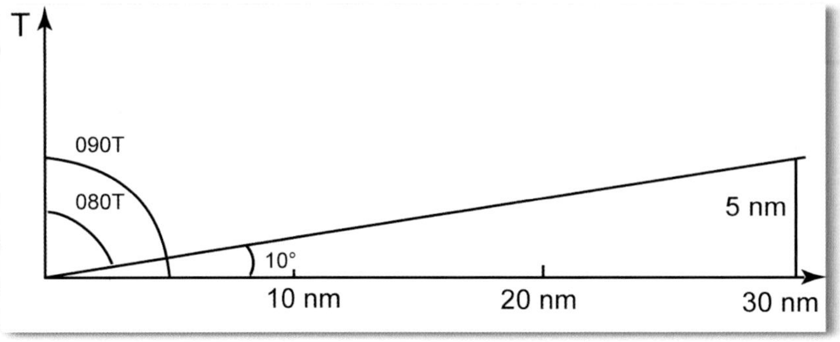

ESTIMATION OF TAS

An estimation of TAS can be obtained in the following ways:

- Two percent of the RAS is added for each 1000 ft of altitude. This is best done by multiplying 2 percent by the altitude figure and then applying the resultant percentage to the RAS.

Example	RAS	140 kt
	Altitude	4000 ft

2 x 4 = 8%
8% of 140 = 11 kt
TAS = 140 + 11 = 151 kt

- The RAS is divided by 60 and then multiplied by altitude in thousands of feet. The product is then added to RAS.

Example	RAS	140 kt
	Altitude	4000 ft

${}^{RAS}/_{60}$ x Alt = ${}^{140}/_{60}$ x 4 = 9 kt
TAS = 140 + 9 = 149 kt

Remember that both calculations are approximations.

CHART ANALYSIS AND CHART READING

Every pilot must be familiar with the general properties of various charts and with the conventional signs used for depicting the various ground features. The conventional signs are reproduced on the reverse side of most topographical charts, and those used commonly on ICAO charts are reproduced as an appendix to the MAP section of the Air Pilot. They are included at the end of this chapter and must be learnt.

CHART SCALE

Chart scale is the ratio of chart distance to Earth distance. The amount of detail which appears on a topographical chart depends upon the scale; the larger the scale, the more detail, and vice versa.

RELIEF

Elevation of the ground over which the aircraft flies is of vital importance. It can be a valuable feature in chart reading and a dangerous barrier to flight. Ground elevation is indicated on charts in one or more of the following ways:

Contours

Contours are lines joining points of equal elevation. The intervals at which contours are drawn depends on the scale of the chart. This interval is known as the vertical interval and is noted on the chart. The horizontal distance between successive contours is known as the horizontal equivalent. The vertical interval on ICAO charts is normally in feet, but on some charts may be in metres. It is therefore imperative that the units are checked.

Spot Heights

The highest point in a locality is marked by a dot with the elevation marked alongside. The highest spot height on some charts is given in a box. Spot heights are also given for the elevations of all airfields marked on the chart.

Layer Tinting

Contours are usually emphasised by colouring the area between adjacent contours. The shades of colour chosen normally become deeper with increase of height; on ICAO charts, the colours range from white through darker shades of yellow to brown.

Hachuring

Hachures are short tapered lines drawn on the chart radiating from peaks and high ground. A spot height usually appears. Hachures are used on topographical charts for incompletely surveyed areas, and also on some plotting charts on which physical detail is not provided.

Hill Shading

Hill shading is produced by assuming that a bright light is shining across the chart sheet so that shadows are cast by the high ground. Difficulty is caused when the shadow obliterates other detail. This method is not extensively used.

RELATIVE VALUES OF FEATURES

By knowing the amount of detail to be expected on charts of different scales and by knowing the conventional signs by which the detail is indicated, the chart reader is in a position to appreciate the relative values of the features seen on the ground. The beginner is sometimes confused by the amount of detail confronting the untrained eye. Pilots must learn to distinguish the more significant features and to remain undistracted by the irrelevant background. The following may help to indicate the type of features which are of value to the chart reader.

Coastlines

Coastlines are the most valuable, day or night. While it may be difficult to recognise a particular stretch of coast in an area merely by its appearance, a satisfactory degree of certainty can often be obtained by taking a bearing of its general direction. Study of any chart shows how difficult it is to find half a dozen two-mile stretches of coast similar in shape and bearing on the whole sheet.

Water Features

As with coastlines, water features show up well by day and by night. Large rivers, estuaries, canals, lakes, and reservoirs are the main water features, listed in order of importance. When using them, take into account the season of the year. Winter floods may cause considerable alteration in their shape, whilst in some parts of the world, rivers dry up altogether during the dry season.

Mountain and Hills

As an aircraft's height above the ground increases, the countryside below appears to flatten out. Nevertheless, the contours of prominent mountains frequently protrude above low-lying cloud and mist, and provide landmarks when all other features are obscured. In the case of low-level chart reading, contours assume great importance and even small hills are very helpful in fixing position.

Towns and Villages

Populated areas are not usually of a distinctive enough shape to be valuable by themselves, but when used in conjunction with other features, such as rivers, railways and coastlines that lie through or adjacent to them, they are usually easily identified. Large cities are useful in determining the general area of the aircraft's position, but accurate pinpointing must be done on other associated features.

Railways

The identification of a particular stretch of railway is often difficult in well-developed countries with many railways, particularly when the area of uncertainty is large. In the case of contact navigation, where the progress of the aircraft is continually followed on the chart, railways are very useful for position information. In countries with few railways, a railway line is a feature of high value. Traffic along railways, by day or night, assists considerably by making them more conspicuous.

Roads

As with railways, the value of roads depends on the extent to which the area has been developed. In the Sudan, for example, roads are of great value. In Great Britain, they are practically useless as landmarks, both because of their multiplicity and the difficulty often encountered in distinguishing between major and minor roads. The modern arterial road generally stands out well.

Woods

Woods make good landmarks, being clearly marked on charts, usually by green areas representing their shape and size. In heavily wooded or forested country, the shape of clearings becomes the most valuable feature. Exercise care when using woods to fix position since tree felling may have changed their shape since the area was surveyed.

PRINCIPLES OF CHART READING

Successful chart reading depends on four basic features:

- Knowledge of direction
- Knowledge of distance or time flown
- Identification of features
- Selection of landmarks

DIRECTION

The first step in chart reading is to orient the chart to match the general track of the aircraft. By doing so, the pilot navigator relates the direction of land features to their representation on the chart, which aids recognition.

DISTANCE

When the chart has been properly oriented, it becomes easier to compare distance between landmarks on the ground with their corresponding distances on the chart, facilitating the fixing of position.

ANTICIPATION OF LANDMARKS

During the flight planning stage, the relationship of easily recognisable features to the intended track should be noted and a time established at which the aircraft will be near them. Thus in flight, the chart reader is prepared to make a visual observation at a particular time, thereby avoiding undue diversion of attention from other aspects of flying the aircraft.

IDENTIFICATION OF FEATURES

Choose check features based on how easily they can be identified. They must be readily distinguishable from their surroundings. The conspicuousness of check features depends upon:

The Angle of Observation
At low levels, features are more easily recognised from their outline in elevation. As altitude is increased, the reverse is the case, and the plan outlines become more important.

Dimensions of the Feature
A feature which is long in one direction, but sharply defined in the other is best; the length makes the feature easier to see despite airframe restrictions to downward vision, and its shorter dimension permits accurate estimation of the aircraft's relation to the feature, either in tracking along it or in timing the movement of flight directly above it.

The Uniqueness of the Feature
To avoid ambiguity, the ideal feature should be unique in its particular outline in the vicinity.

Contrast and Colour
These properties play a large part in the identification of a particular feature. Chart reading is often complicated by seasonal variation, such as:

- The difference between deciduous woods in summer and winter
- The landscapes before and after extensive snow fall

Contrast and colour also play a part in identifying coastlines after a long sea crossing.

FIXING BY CHART READING

Chart reading techniques are largely dependent upon the weather and different techniques are evolved for:

- Conditions which permit continuous visual observation of the ground beneath.
- Conditions which limit visual observations of the ground to unpredicted intervals.

CHART READING IN CONTINUOUS CONDITIONS

By means of a time scale on the track, the pilot navigator should be prepared to look for a definite feature at a definite time. As a check on identification, additional ground detail surrounding the feature should be positively identified. Thus, when in continuous contact with the ground, read from chart to ground.

CHART READING AT UNPREDICTABLE INTERVALS

This technique is used when flying above or through broken cloud. First estimate a circle of uncertainty for the aircraft's position, based on a 10 percent error of the distance flown from the last known position. Then study the ground features passing underneath, noting outstanding features and the sequence in which they occur. Attempt to identify these features on the chart within the circle of DR error. Continue this procedure until obtaining some idea of the track flown. Thus, when seeking to establish position, read from ground to chart.

USE OF RADIO AIDS

When chart reading, the position of the aircraft is established relative to identifiable land features, and the information is interpreted by means of a chart. When using radio observations, the radio station takes the place of the landmark. Various different radio aids are available for air navigation.

ICAO CHART SYMBOLS

ICAO uses the following symbols on Aeronautical Charts. The General Navigation examination makes reference to them.

Symbol	**Meaning**	
Aerodromes		
	Civil Aerodrome - Land	
	Military Aerodrome - Land	
	Joint Civil and Military Aerodrome – Land	
	Where an anchor is inserted into the above symbols, the aerodrome is a water base	
	An Emergency Aerodrome and/or an Aerodrome with no facilities	
	Heliport	
	The runway pattern of the aerodrome may be shown instead of the aerodrome symbol	
LIVINGSTONE 357 L H 95	**Livingstone**	Name of Aerodrome
	357	Elevation given in the units of measurement selected for use on the chart
	L	Minimum Lighting – obstacles, boundary, or runway lights and lighted wind indicator or landing direction indicator
	H	Runway Hard Surfaced – Normally all weather
	95	Length of Longest Runway in hundreds of metres or feet
	-	A dash is used where L or H does not apply

Aerodrome Symbols For Approach Charts

Aerodromes affecting the traffic pattern on the aerodrome on which the procedure is based

The aerodrome on which the procedure is based

Radio Navigation Aids

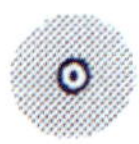

NDB

VOR

DME

VOR/DME

15 — Distance in kilometres (nautical miles) to the DME
KAV — Identification of the Radio Navigation Aid

Radial from and identification of the VOR

TACAN

VORTAC

Instrument Landing System

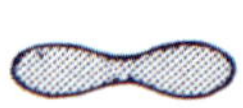

Radio Marker Beacon

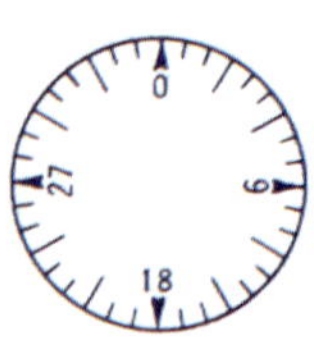

Compass Rose – Normally aligned to Magnetic North

Air Traffic Services

	Flight Information Region (FIR) Boundary
	Aerodrome Traffic Zone (ATZ)
	Control Area (CTA), Airway, or Controlled Route
  	(4 alternatives)
	Uncontrolled Route
	Advisory Airspace (ADA)
	Advisory Route (ADR)
	(4 alternatives)
	Control Zone (CTR)
	Scale Break
	Compulsory Reporting Point
	Non-compulsory Reporting Point
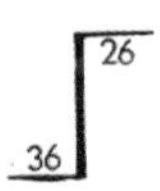	Change Over Point This is superimposed at right angles to the route
	Compulsory ATS/MET Reporting Point
	Non-compulsory ATS/MET Reporting Point
	Flyover Waypoint (WPT) Also used for the start and end point of a controlled turn
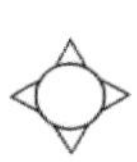	Fly By Waypoint

Airspace Restrictions

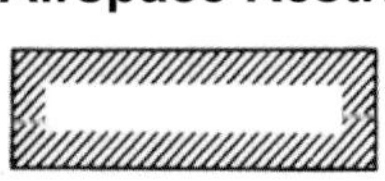	Restricted Airspace Prohibited, Restricted, or Danger Area
	Common Boundary of 2 Restricted Airspace Areas
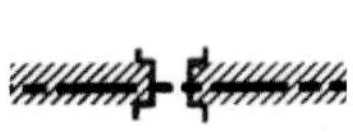	International Boundary Closed to the Passage of Aircraft Except Through an Air Corridor

Obstacles

	Obstacle	
	Lighted Obstacle	
	Group of Obstacles	
	Group of Lighted Obstacles	
	Exceptionally High Obstacle	For obstacles having a height of the order of 300 m (1000 ft) above terrain
	Exceptionally High Obstacle - Lighted	
	52 Elevation of the top of the obstacle (15) Height above specified datum	

Culture

Built-Up Areas

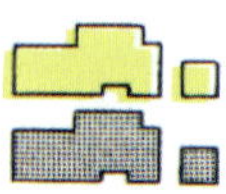	City or Large Town
	Town or Village (Dependent on size)
	Buildings

Highways and Roads

	Dual Highway
	Primary Road
	Secondary Road
	Trail
	Road Bridge
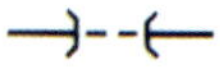	Road Tunnel

Railways

	Railroad – single track
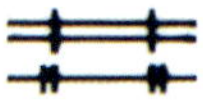	Railroad – two or more tracks
	Railroad under construction
	Railroad Bridge
	Railroad Tunnel
	Railroad Station

Topography

Contours

Lava Flow

Sand Area

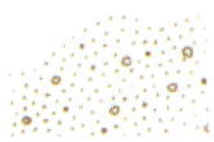

Gravel

Active Volcano

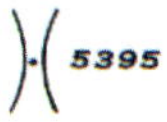

Mountain Pass

17456 Highest Elevation on Chart

.17456

.6397
.8975 Spot Elevation

.637c ± Spot Elevation – Of doubtful accuracy

Areas not surveyed for contour information, or relief data incomplete

Shore Line

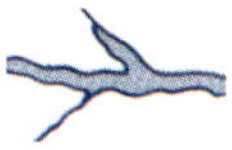

Large River

Small River

Canal

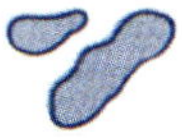

Lakes

Spring, Well or Water Hole

■ *Reservoir* Reservoir

Miscellaneous

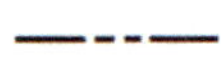

 International Boundary

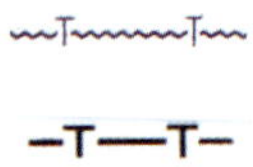 Telegraph or Telephone Line

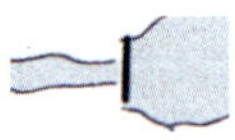 Dam

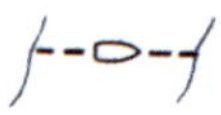 Ferry

 Oil or Gas Field

 Lookout Tower

 Fort

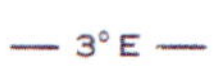

Isogonal

 Ocean Station Vessel

 Aeronautical Ground Light

 Lightship

Marine Light

Alt	Alternating
B	Blue
F	Fixed
Fl	Flashing
G	Green
Gp	Group
Occ	Occulting
R	Red
SEC	Sector
Sec	Second
(U)	Unwatched
W	White

Chapter 16
Relative Velocity

INTRODUCTION

Relative velocity is the apparent motion of a body relative to another. In the JAR FCL, three basic situations have to be addressed:

- Aircraft on the same or opposite tracks
- Aircraft on different tracks
- Aircraft starting from different positions

With all relative velocity problems, the calculation is easier after drawing a simple diagram.

AIRCRAFT ON THE SAME OR OPPOSITE TRACKS

In the simplest situation, aircraft on the same track are either closing or going away from each other.

Aircraft Closing

Speed 120 knots **Speed 250 knots**

Closing Speed is the sum of the two speeds

120 + 250 = 370 knots

Aircraft Opening

Speed 250 knots   Speed 120 knots

Opening Speed is the sum of the two speeds

120 + 250 = 370 knots

Overtaking

Speed 120 knots   Speed 250 knots

Overtaking Speed is the difference between the speeds of the aircraft

250 - 120 = 130 knots

CALCULATIONS

The calculations required break down into two areas:

- Meeting
- Overtaking

MEETING

Example The distance between Aerodrome A and Aerodrome B is 1000 nm. At 0900, Aircraft 1 leaves A for B at a groundspeed of 300 kt. Aircraft 2 leaves B for A at 0930, flying at a groundspeed of 400 kt.

- At what time will the aircraft pass each other?
- At what distance from A will the aircraft be?

STEP 1 Draw the position for 0930.

Aircraft 1 will travel 150 nm in 30 minutes

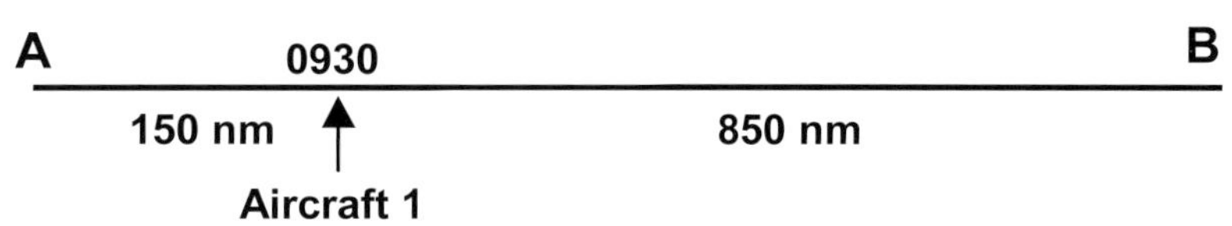

STEP 2 Calculate the closing speed of the aircraft

400 + 300 = 700 kt

Find time to travel 850 nm, the distance remaining between the 2 aircraft at 0930 at the closing speed of 700 kt.

850 nm @ 700 kt = 72½ minutes

Time of meeting is:

0930 + 72½ = 1042½

STEP 3 The distance from A is:

150 nm + 365 (72½ minutes @ 300 kt)

515 nm from A

OVERTAKING

Example 2 Aircraft 1 leaves point A at 1015, with a groundspeed of 250 kt.
Aircraft 2 leaves A at 1045, groundspeed 350 kt.

- At what time will Aircraft 2 overtake Aircraft 1?
- At what time will the aircraft be 30 nm apart?

STEP 1 Draw the position for 1045.
Aircraft 1 will travel 125 nm in 30 minutes.

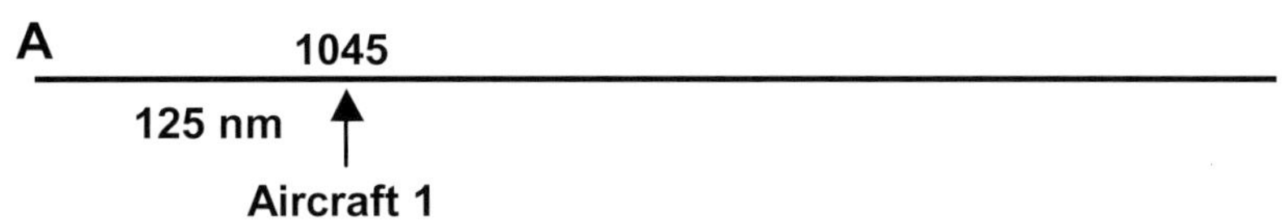

STEP 2 Calculate the closing speed.
350 – 250 = 100 kt

STEP 3 Aircraft 2 has 125 nm to close at a closing speed of 100 kt.
125 nm @ 100 kt = 75 minutes
Overtake time = 1200

STEP 4 To find where the aircraft are 30 nm apart:
Aircraft 2 would have 125 – 30 nm to close = 95 nm
95 nm @ 100 kt = 57 minutes
Time that the aircraft are 30 nm apart is 1142

Example 3 Aircraft 1 flying at a groundspeed of 360 kt is overtaking Aircraft 2. Aircraft 2 is 50 nm ahead of Aircraft 1. Aircraft 2 is overtaken in 25 minutes. What is the groundspeed of Aircraft 2?

STEP 1 Calculate the closing speed.
Distance to close is 50 nm.
Time to close is 25 minutes.
Closing speed is 120 kt

STEP 2 Groundspeed Aircraft 1 – Groundspeed 2 = Closing Speed
360 – 120 = 240 kt
Groundspeed Aircraft 1 = 240 kt

SPEED ADJUSTMENT

This style of calculation asks for the latest time and distance that an aircraft can reduce speed to meet an ETA at a beacon.

This is not strictly a relative velocity problem, as the calculation is for a single aircraft. To make the calculation simple, it is easier to calculate from a known distance.

Example An aircraft flying a groundspeed of 300 kt estimates Coventry at 1200. ATC tells the captain to delay arrival by 5 minutes. The planned reduction in groundspeed is to 240 kt. What is the latest time to reduce speed and at what distance from Coventry?

STEP 1 Choose a simple distance from Coventry.
300 nm @ 300 kt 60 minutes flying

STEP 2 Calculate the time it will take to fly 300 nm at 240 kt.
75 minutes

STEP 3 By reducing speed with 300 nm to go to Coventry, the aircraft would delay arrival by 15 minutes.

STEP 4 Using simple mathematics, the distance can be calculated for a 5 minute delay.
15 minutes delay is equivalent to 300 nm
1 minute delay is equivalent to 20 nm
5 minutes delay is equivalent to 100 nm

With more difficult figures use the formula:

$$\text{Distance} = \frac{\text{Delay x New Groundspeed x Old Groundspeed}}{\text{Difference in Groundspeed x 60}}$$

$$= (5 \times 300 \times 240) \div (60 \times 60)$$
$$= 100 \text{ nm}$$

Distance speed should be reduced is 100 nm from Coventry

STEP 5 Calculate the time the aircraft takes to fly the distance calculated in STEP 4.
100 nm @ 240 kt groundspeed = 25 minutes

STEP 6 Using the revised arrival time, calculate the time the speed reduction should be made.
1205 – 25 = 1140

DISTANCE BETWEEN BEACONS

Example Aircraft 2 flying a groundspeed of 360 kt reports at VOR A 5 minutes behind Aircraft 1, groundspeed 300 kt.

Aircraft 2 then reports overhead VOR B 3 minutes ahead of Aircraft 1.

What is the distance between VOR A and VOR B?

STEP 1 Always start this calculation using the faster aircraft.
When Aircraft 2 is overhead VOR A, Aircraft 1 is 5 minutes ahead.
5 minutes @ 300 kt = 25 nm

STEP 2 When Aircraft 2 is overhead VOR B, Aircraft 1 is 3 minutes behind.
3 minutes @ 300 kt = 15 nm

A1 is Aircraft 1

STEP 3 The total distance that Aircraft 2 has flown extra to Aircraft 1 is:
15 + 25 = 40 nm

STEP 4 Calculate the overtake speed.
360 – 300 = 60 kt

STEP 5 Calculate the time it takes to fly 40 nm using the overtake speed.
40 nm @ 60 kt is 40 minutes

STEP 6 Aircraft 2 will cover the total distance between VOR A and VOR B in the time calculated in STEP 5.
40 minutes @ 360 kt is 240 nm
Distance between VOR A and VOR B is 240 nm

GRAPHICAL SOLUTION FOR CALCULATING RELATIVE VELOCITY

The graphical solution to calculate the relative velocity is simple, but it can be time consuming.

Example Starting from the same point:
Aircraft 1 flies a track of 120° at 300 kt groundspeed.
Aircraft 2 flies a track of 180° at 200 kt groundspeed.
What is the relative velocity of 2 from 1?

STEP 1 Draw the vectors 120° and 180° from a point.

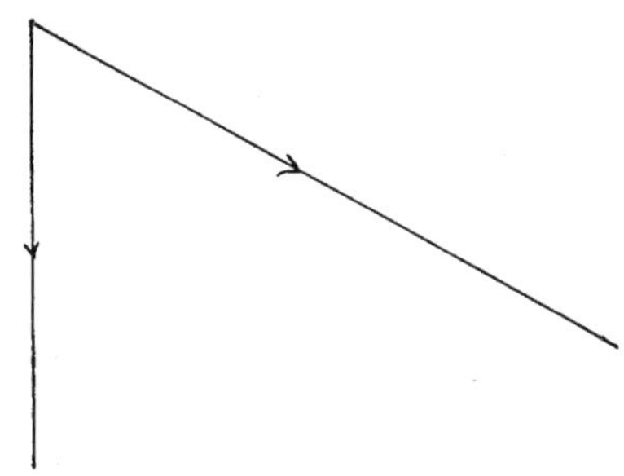

STEP 2 Choosing a suitable scale, mark off the distance along each vector equivalent to 300 kt groundspeed and 200 kt groundspeed.

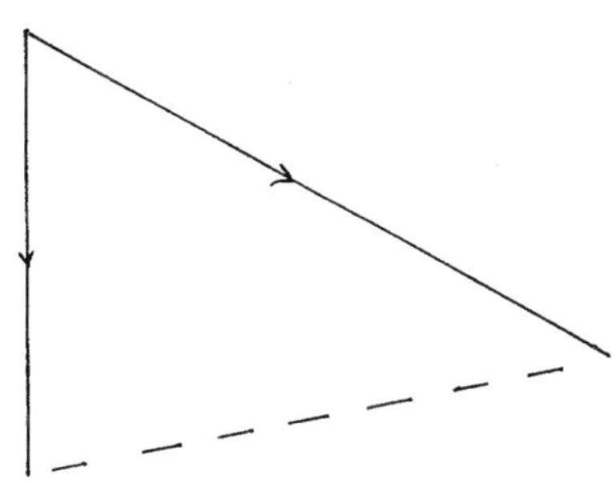

STEP 3 Draw in the vector between the range marks and measure the direction and length.
259/265

Chapter 17
Principles of Plotting

INTRODUCTION

Plotting is a process of recording information on a chart about the progress of an aircraft in flight in such a way as to enable the navigator to solve the triangle of velocities.

PLOTTING INSTRUMENTS

The necessary plotting instruments are:

- The protractor for the measurement and plotting of bearings
- Dividers for the measurement and laying off of distances
- Compasses for plotting DME position lines
- A straight edge
- The navigation computer

PLOTTING SYMBOLS

Conventional symbols are used in plotting, as illustrated below:

Symbol	**Meaning**
	Air Position
	DR Position
	Pinpoint
	Position Line Fix
	Position Line
	Transferred Position Line

In practice, there are two main forms of plot, the track plot and the air plot.

THE TRACK PLOT

The track plot is probably the simplest form of plotting. The position of the aircraft, as determined by fixes or as calculated from knowledge of the aircraft's track made good and groundspeed, is plotted at intervals on the chart. These positions are used to determine:

- Aircraft's progress
- To calculate future positions
- To calculate estimated time of arrival
- To calculate any corrections of heading that may be necessary

Typical Track plot

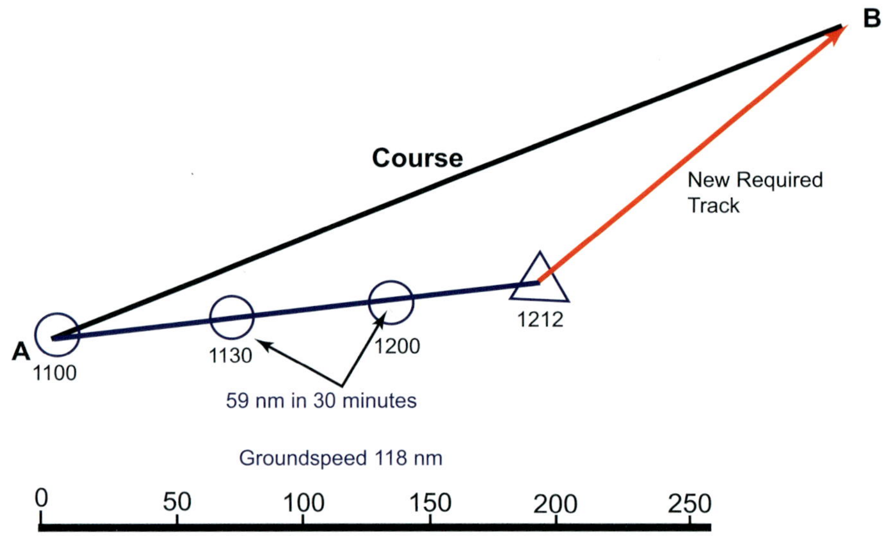

In the above trackplot, an aircraft plans a course between A and B.

1100 The aircraft leaves A

1130 A pinpoint is taken

1200 A second pinpoint is taken

From these pinpoints, the pilot can calculate:

- A track
- A groundspeed
- A wind velocity

At 1212, a DR position is plotted using the information above. This is a position the pilot navigator can calculate.

- The pinpoint at 1200 gives a definite position
- The track and the groundspeed are known
- Projecting the track for 12 minutes, at 1212 the aircraft will be at the DR position
- A new track required to B can be drawn

Calculating a wind velocity allows the pilot to work out a new heading and groundspeed to fly to B.

The time interval between fixes selected for the determination of track, groundspeed, and the wind velocity is critical. It must not be too short, and it must not be too long. In groundspeed:

- When the time interval is too short, measurement of fixing errors is magnified.
- When the time interval is too long, the groundspeed obtained becomes too much of an average.

The ideal time interval used in measurement of track and groundspeed should be at least 20 minutes and not more than 40 minutes.

THE AIR PLOT

One of the main disadvantages of the track plot is that the system is inflexible. Using the track plot, DR calculations of groundspeed and track are only possible when no alteration has been made in heading and TAS during the run between fixes. No such limitations occur when using the alternative method of plotting, called the air plot.

When keeping an air plot, the navigator lays off a vector representing the true heading and airspeed from the point of departure for the appropriate time of flight. Then estimate the position of the aircraft, neglecting wind effect (such a position is known as an air position). In the event that either heading or TAS is subsequently changed, it is possible to continue to plot vectors of heading and TAS to establish subsequent air positions of the aircraft for each time that a change takes place.

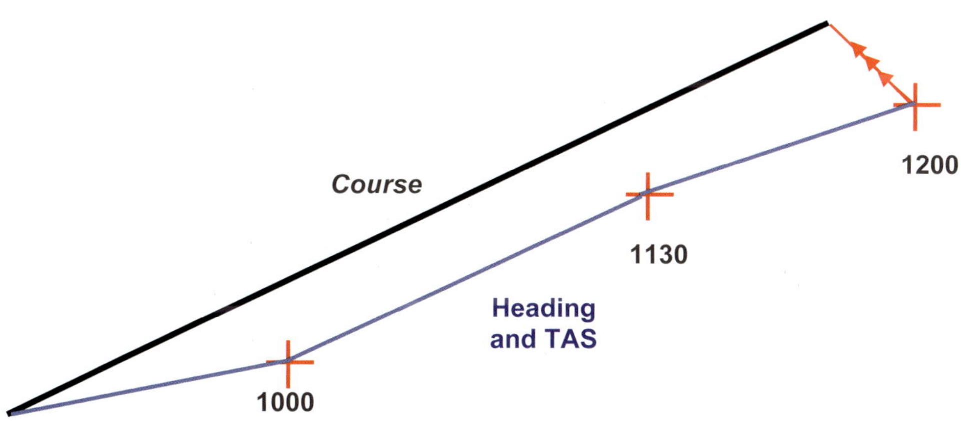

Eventually, when a fix is obtained, the navigator has both air position and ground position of the aircraft plotted for the same instant of time. The vector joining them gives the wind velocity for the appropriate period of time since the air plot was commenced. Wind velocity found by this method is known as an air plot wind velocity. Like the track and groundspeed wind velocity, there is an ideal interval of time over which it should be determined, and for similar reasons, this ideal interval is between 20 to 40 minutes.

In the above plot, the heading and TAS are plotted. Each time the aircraft changes heading, the new heading and TAS are plotted.

One of the greatest advantages of the air plot is that however often alterations of headings and airspeed are made, a record can be kept of the air position, which can be used to establish a DR position by plotting an appropriate amount of wind velocity from the air position.

RESTARTING THE AIR PLOT

To avoid having to draw very long vectors for wind velocity, which is both cumbersome and inaccurate, do not allow an air plot to run indefinitely, but restart it from fixes at convenient intervals. It is imperative that only accurate fixes are used for restarting an air plot, as any error in the initial fix is carried through the whole plot. Under no circumstances should an air plot be restarted from a DR position, as this only perpetuates any errors already present.

ESTABLISHMENT OF POSITION

The two methods of plotting, the track plot and the air plot, are described above. In each case, it is assumed that the ground position of the aircraft can be determined. This section is devoted to the methods of determining position.

DR POSITION

DR position, which is the calculated or deduced position of the aircraft, may be determined by either track plot or air plot.

TRACK PLOT METHOD

There are two methods of determining DR position by track plot.

Track is established by drawing the mean track through the fixes. The distance run between an optimum pair of fixes calculates groundspeed, and a future position of the aircraft is calculated.

Using Mean Track Made Good

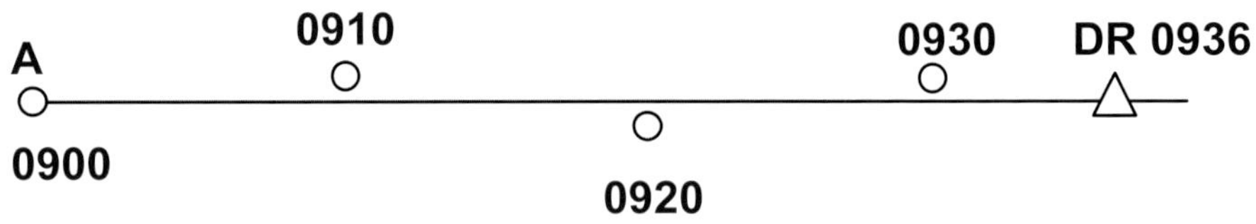

Having determined track and groundspeed from the application of known W/V to TAS and heading, the track is drawn in from the last known position. The distance covered since that position is laid off to give the new DR position.

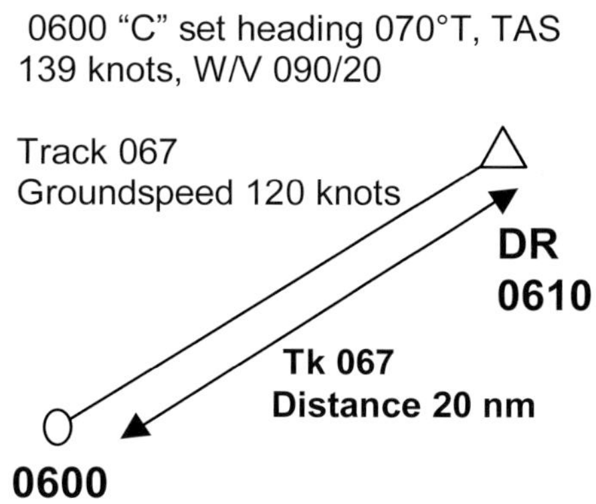

AIR PLOT METHOD

In this method, a full graphical record of headings and TAS is maintained. The DR position can then be determined for any time by applying the appropriate amount of wind velocity.

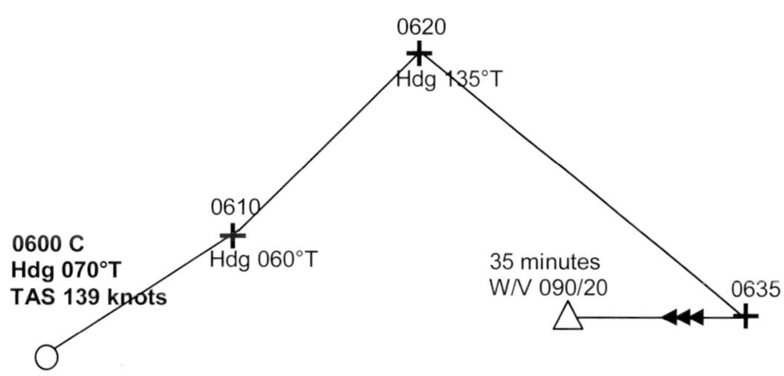

FIXING

Fixes are precise observations of the aircraft's position.

POSITION LINES

It is not always possible to determine the position of the aircraft precisely. When a definite fix is not obtainable, it is often possible to locate the aircraft along a line of position, which is a line along which the position of the aircraft is known to lie.

SOURCES OF POSITION LINES

Position lines may be obtained from the following sources:

Visual Visual position lines are bearings of the aircraft, to or from an object. They may be expressed as true bearings or relative bearings, depending upon the datum used.

ADF Position Lines ADF position lines are obtained using automatic direction-finding equipment, in conjunction with NDB beacons on the ground. An ADF position line is the GREAT CIRCLE bearing FROM the aircraft to the transmitter. It may be measured:

- Relative to the aircraft, in which case it is a RELATIVE BEARING (RBI)
- From magnetic north, in which case it is a MAGNETIC bearing (RMI)

Plotting complications may arise because the bearing is measured at the aircraft and plotted from the station. When plotting, the bearing must first be converted to a true bearing by applying the true heading to a relative bearing or by applying local variation at the aircraft's DR position to a magnetic bearing.

The procedure which follows depends upon the type of chart.

Mercator The true great circle bearing must be converted to a rhumb line bearing before taking the reciprocal to plot from the station.

Lambert The bearing to the station must be converted to a bearing from the station by the application of convergency.

Transfer of the aircraft meridian to the beacon meridian can apply the convergency.

For most plots, a Lambert's Chart is provided.

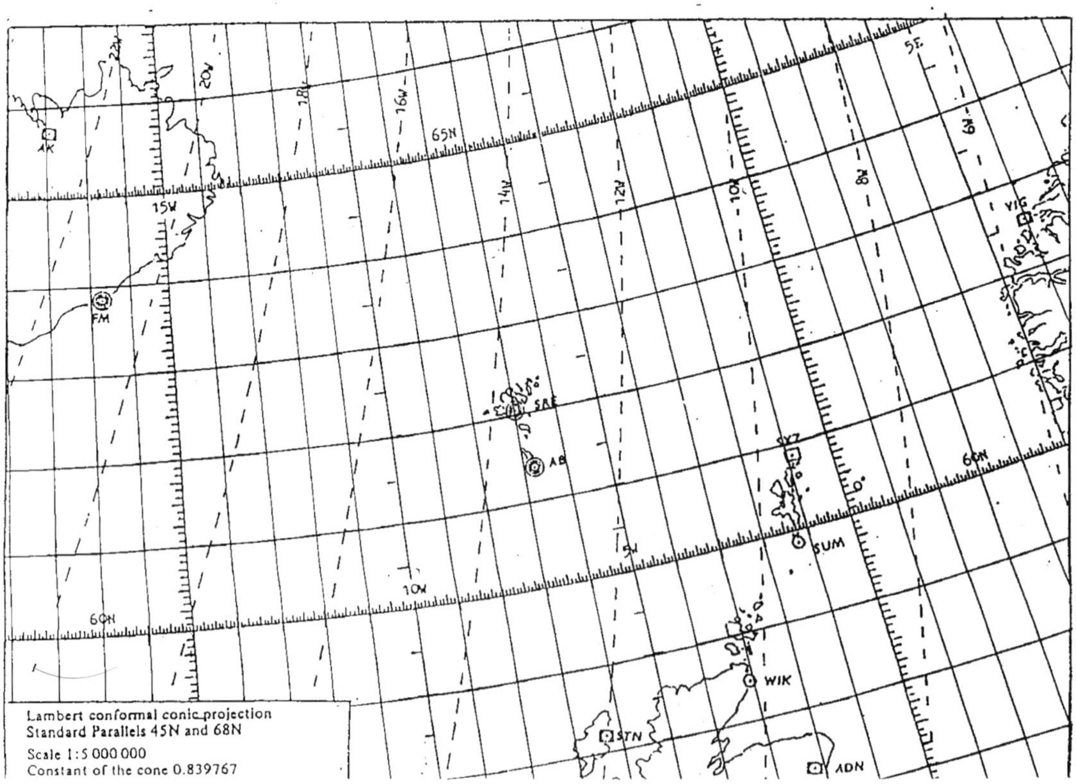

For simplicity, the number of the chart to be used is given in the example. The method of plotting is on a simple line diagram.

PLOTTING AN NDB POSITION LINE

An NDB position line is taken directly from the RMI or is given as a relative bearing.

Example Use Chart 1 at the end of the chapter. The RMI gives a magnetic bearing of 297° to the NDB AB. The assumed position is overhead SUM. Plot the NDB position line.

STEP 1 To plot the great circle, apply NDB position line convergence.

To apply the convergence, first transfer the assumed aircraft meridian to the AB meridian. Use the square protractor to make the transfer easy. Align the square grid in the centre of the protractor with the meridian nearest SUM.

Make sure the outer edge of the protractor goes through the beacon AB, as shown in the diagram below.

Draw a pencil line through AB. Use this meridian when plotting the bearing.

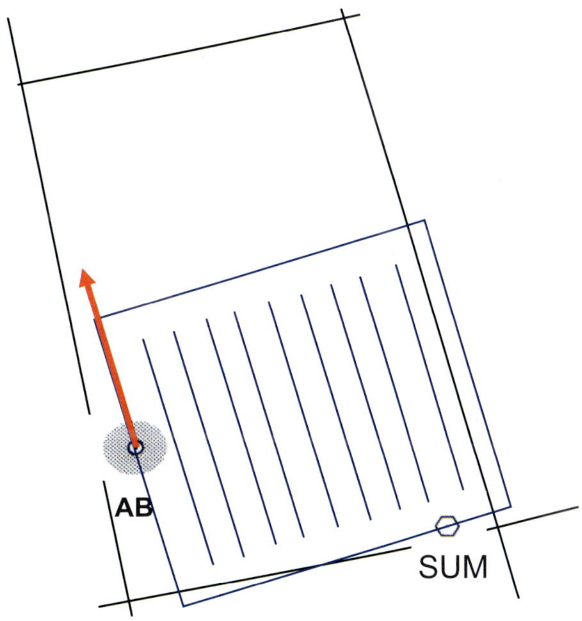

STEP 2 Apply the variation at the aircraft position using the pre-drawn isogonals. **Use 10 W.**

True Bearing is 297 – 10 = 287T

STEP 3 Plot the reciprocal 107° from the beacon AB using the transferred meridian.

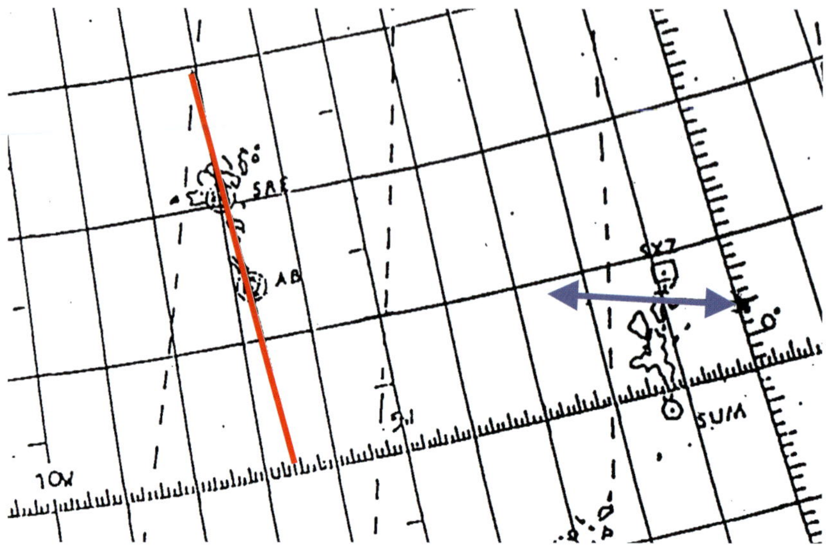

Plotting 1 Using the AB beacon, plot the following on Chart 1 provided at the end of this chapter:

RMI Bearing to the NDB	Assumed Position
1. 320°	5820N 00200W
2. 080°	6030N 01300W
3. 250°	6340N 00300E

VOR/VDF POSITION LINES

Certain ground VHF stations are equipped to provide DF facilities. The information may be either magnetic bearing TO (QDM) or FROM (QDR) the station. Alternatively, the bearing may be a true bearing FROM (QTE) the station. The bearing obtained must be converted to a QTE. If plotting on a Mercator chart, apply conversion angle.

VOR is a VHF navigation aid which provides QDM/QDR. The plotting considerations are identical with those of VDF.

Example Use Chart 2.
The pilot obtains a QDR from CJN of 345°.

STEP 1 Apply the variation at the VOR.
6W

STEP 2 Plot the true bearing.
345 – 6 = 339°

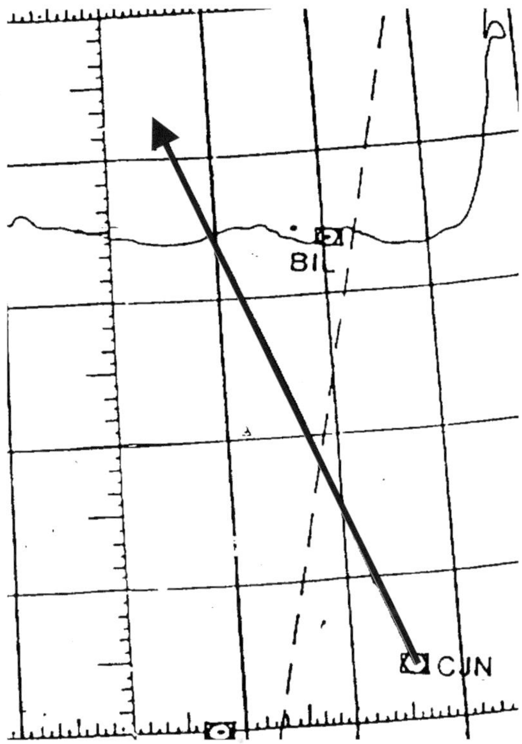

Plotting Example 2 Plot the following bearings:

VOR		Bearing
TOU	QDR	275°
QUV	QDR	305°
NTS	QDR	200°

The plot should meet at a single point, providing a three-position line fix.

DME POSITION LINES

Distance Measuring Equipment is a radio aid that permits the aircraft range to be measured from specific ground stations. The position line obtained is the arc of a circle centred on the position of the beacon. The distance measurement is the radius of that arc.

USES OF POSITION LINES

Position lines may be used for a variety of purposes:

- To check track made good
- To check groundspeed and/or ETA
- To obtain a fix, in combination with other position lines

CHECKING TRACK

A position line which is parallel or nearly parallel to track gives a good check on track. Bearings obtained from radio beacons along track are ideal for this purpose.

CHECKING GROUNDSPEED/ETA

For this purpose, a position line at right angles to track, or nearly so, is required. Where the distance from the last fix or similar position line can be measured, and the time interval is known, groundspeed can be determined and ETA checked. In the event that groundspeed measurement is not possible, ETA can still be checked using DR groundspeed.

FIXING BY POSITION LINES

Where two or more position lines are obtained simultaneously, the position of the aircraft must, by definition, be at their point of intersection. Where more than two are used, it is conceivable that because of small errors, the intersection may not be a single point.

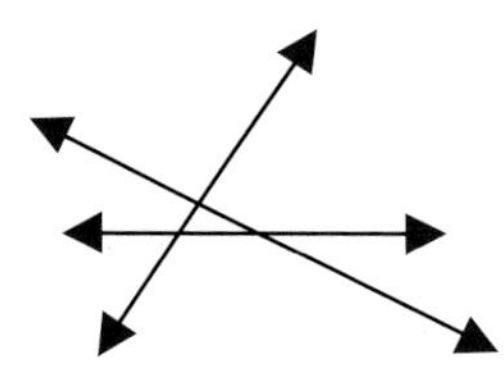

The small triangle is known as a **Cocked Hat**, and it is assumed the position of the aircraft is at the centre of the triangle. Normal practice is to use either two or three position lines, depending upon availability. Three position lines are preferable. When two position lines are used, the angle of cut between them should be as near 90° as possible. When three are used, the angle of cut should be 120°.

TRANSFERRING POSITION LINES

It is often impossible to obtain position lines simultaneously. However, provided that the DR track direction and groundspeed are known, it is possible to allow for the run of the aircraft in the time between two position lines on the chart, as shown below. Draw track direction so the position line cuts it; it is of little consequence where. Calculate the distance run at DR groundspeed and step off along track direction from the position line to be transferred. At the point obtained, draw a line parallel to the original position line. To indicate that it has been transferred, it carries two arrows at each end instead of one. Transfer procedure is to transfer the origin along track direction for the appropriate amount of time, then to draw the transferred position line directly. This is a good habit for two reasons:

- It is the only way that a circular position line can be transferred by the track and groundspeed method.
- It keeps the plotting area neater for any position line.

Note: On all the following plots, use a line of longitude to determine distances. Remember that 1° measured along a line of longitude is equal to 60 nm. This does not hold true for lines of latitude.

Example Use Chart 1 for this plot.

Start: Point A 6300N 00300W
Finish: Point B 6000N 00400E

Conditions:

TAS 500
Wind Velocity 190/50KT
Heading 134°T

Plot:

1215 Position A

1219 VIG RMI NDB 099

1228 SXZ RMI NDB 207

What is the aircraft position at 1228?

At 1228, what is the QDR from AB?

In this plot, assume that the aircraft is flying along track. For most plots, the pilot must work out the track made good, and plot it on the chart.

STEP 1 Calculate the aircraft groundspeed using the CRP-5. **475 kt**

STEP 2 Plot VIG RMI NDB 099.

The aircraft has travelled 32 nm. Mark off this distance on the chart. It places the aircraft near the 00200W meridian.

Transfer this meridian to VIG. The RMI gives a magnetic bearing. Apply the variation at the Aircraft meridian (10W).

This gives a bearing of 089T. Plot the reciprocal 269T.

STEP 3 Plot SXZ RMI NDB 207.

The aircraft has travelled approximately 103 nm, which places it near the Greenwich Meridian.

Transfer the Greenwich Meridian to SXZ.

With variation of 10W, plot a bearing of 017T.

STEP 4 To get the fix, transfer the position line of 1219.

Take the time between the fixes (9 minutes).

The distance the aircraft travels in this time is 71 nm. This is the distance that is to be transferred down track.

Mark 71 nm from the 1219 position line.

Using the square protractor, transfer the position line, as when transferring the meridian. This gives a fix.

6155N 00010W
Radial from AB 092M

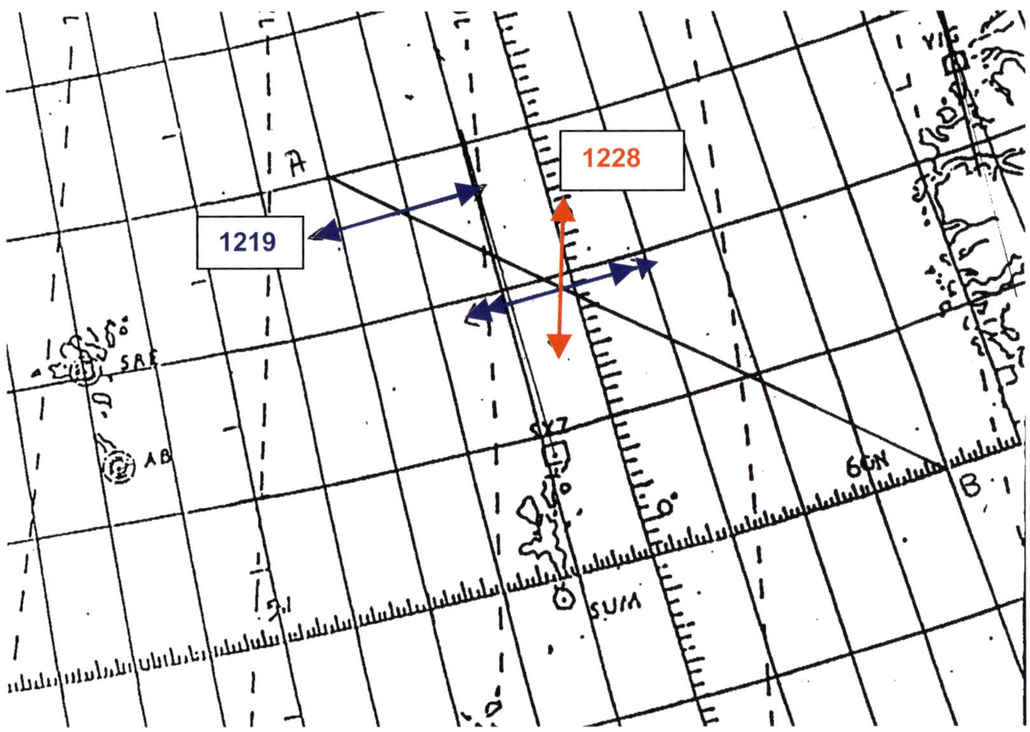

Example This plot involves the movement of a DME position line. Transfer of DME lines is slightly different. Instead of transferring the position line directly, the beacon is transferred.

Route: 326°M radial from SXZ

Conditions: Heading 324T
Drift 8 left
Groundspeed 425 kt

Plot:

1845 SRE DME 80 nm

1855 SRE DME 100 nm

STEP 1 Plot SRE DME 80 nm

STEP 2 Plot SRE DME 100 nm

STEP 3 Calculate the aircraft track: 8 left drift, heading 324T.
316T

STEP 4 From SRE, draw a track of 316T. The time between fixes is 10 minutes. The aircraft travels 71 nm (groundspeed 425 kt). Mark off 71 nm along the track.

STEP 5 From this point, plot 80 nm DME. Where the 1855 line and this line meet is the fix.

Note: The first position line need not be plotted if it is just being transferred.

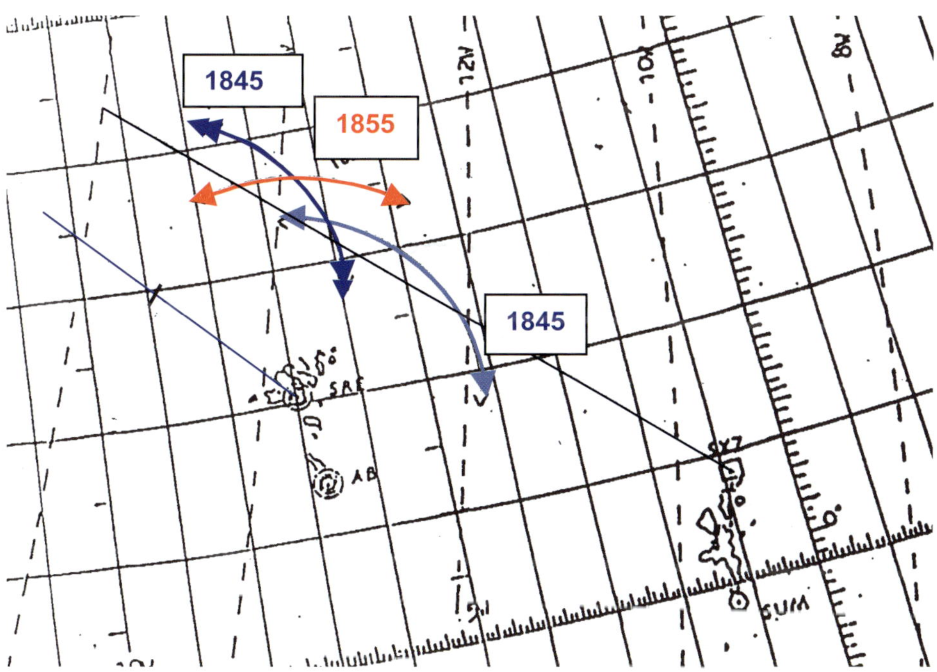

Plotting Example 3 (Use Chart 1)

0930 Position 6400N 00000E tracking 267°T, groundspeed 332 kt

0940 NDB SRE RMI 224°

0950 NDB SXZ RMI 164°

What is the aircraft position at 0950?

Plotting Example 4 (Use Chart 1)

1910 Overhead ADN VOR, heading 040°M Direct VIG

1934 SUM DME 60 nm

1935 Drift 1° right, groundspeed 310 kt

1955 VIG DME 165 nm

What is the aircraft position at 1955? (Note: Two positions can be plotted, but only one is possible because of the speed of the aircraft.)

Plotting Example 5 (Use Chart 3)

1510 Position 4300N 01200W, heading 180°M, TAS 300 kt, groundspeed 310 kt

1523 POR VOR 115 nm

1524 TAS 320 kt, drift 8° left

1540 POR VOR 115 nm

What is the position of the aircraft at 1540?

Plotting Example 6 (Use Chart 3)

2015 Position 3700N 01100W on a track direct to CAS VOR

2016 Groundspeed 240 kt

2024 RAB NDB RMI 138

2036 FAR NDB RMI 055

What is the radial from CSV VOR at 2036?

Plotting Example 7 (Use Chart 3)

2300 Position 4000N 01200W on a track direct to CAS VOR

2310 LIS VOR RMI 100° DME 150 nm

2311 Heading 130M, Wind velocity 060/80, TAS 270 kt

Heading (M) and ETA CSV is?

RADAR FIXING

When plotting a radar fix, use the relative bearing of the fix.

Example A fix is taken off an island that bears 20° left at 40 nm on the radar. The aircraft is heading 310°T. What is the bearing of the aircraft from the island?

STEP 1 Calculate the true bearing of the island from the aircraft.

Heading ± bearing = true bearing. If the bearing is left, subtract.

310 – 20 = 290 This is the bearing of the island from the aircraft.

STEP 2 Take the reciprocal to get the bearing of the aircraft from the island.

110°

CLIMB AND DESCENT

When planning a climb or descent, problems arise in the choice of wind velocity and in the determination of TAS, because at each different height, there is likely to be a different wind velocity and a different temperature. Consider the mean value of each selected for use during climb and descent.

CLIMB

The aircraft experiences many wind effects as it ascends through the various layers of the atmosphere. Use the mean of all the wind effects experienced by the aircraft for the wind velocity when flight planning a climb. In practice, the selection of this wind velocity depends upon whether the change of wind velocity with height is a regular or irregular change. It also depends upon whether the rate of climb of the aircraft is constant or whether it decreases with increase of height. Where the rate of climb is constant, and the winds vary regularly with increase of height, use wind at the mean height of the climb. Where the winds vary regularly, and the rate of climb falls off in the upper layers, a more accurate result is obtained by using the wind velocity at half the way up the climb.

In arriving at the mean equivalent, consider wind velocity at the time during which the aircraft is affected by various wind velocities, as each wind is proportionate to the time the aircraft spends in the band in which the wind velocity is operative. It is, therefore, necessary to calculate this time, and so arrive at the vector distance to be plotted.

DESCENT

As for the climb, the half-height wind velocity is used.

Chart 1

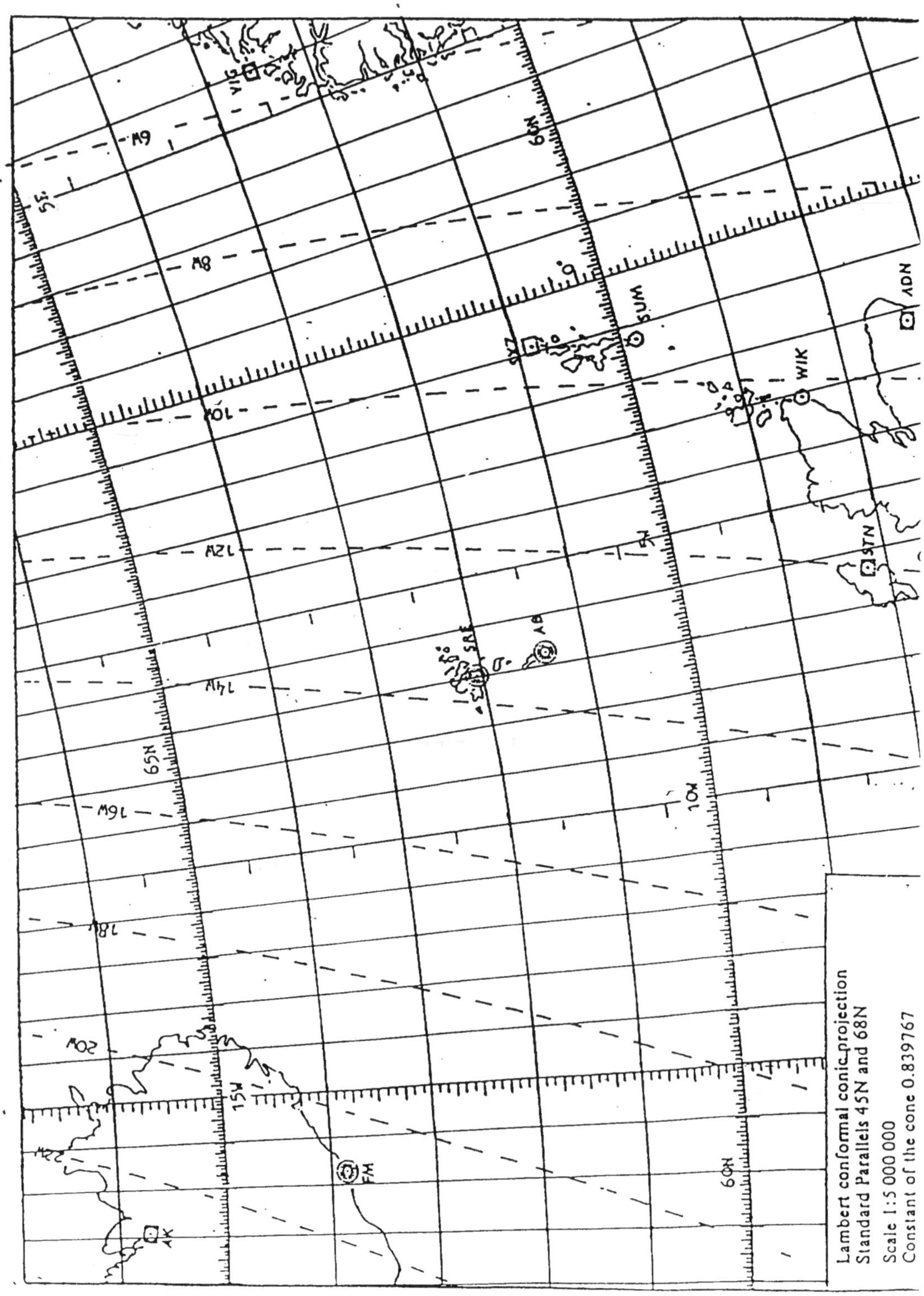

Chart 2

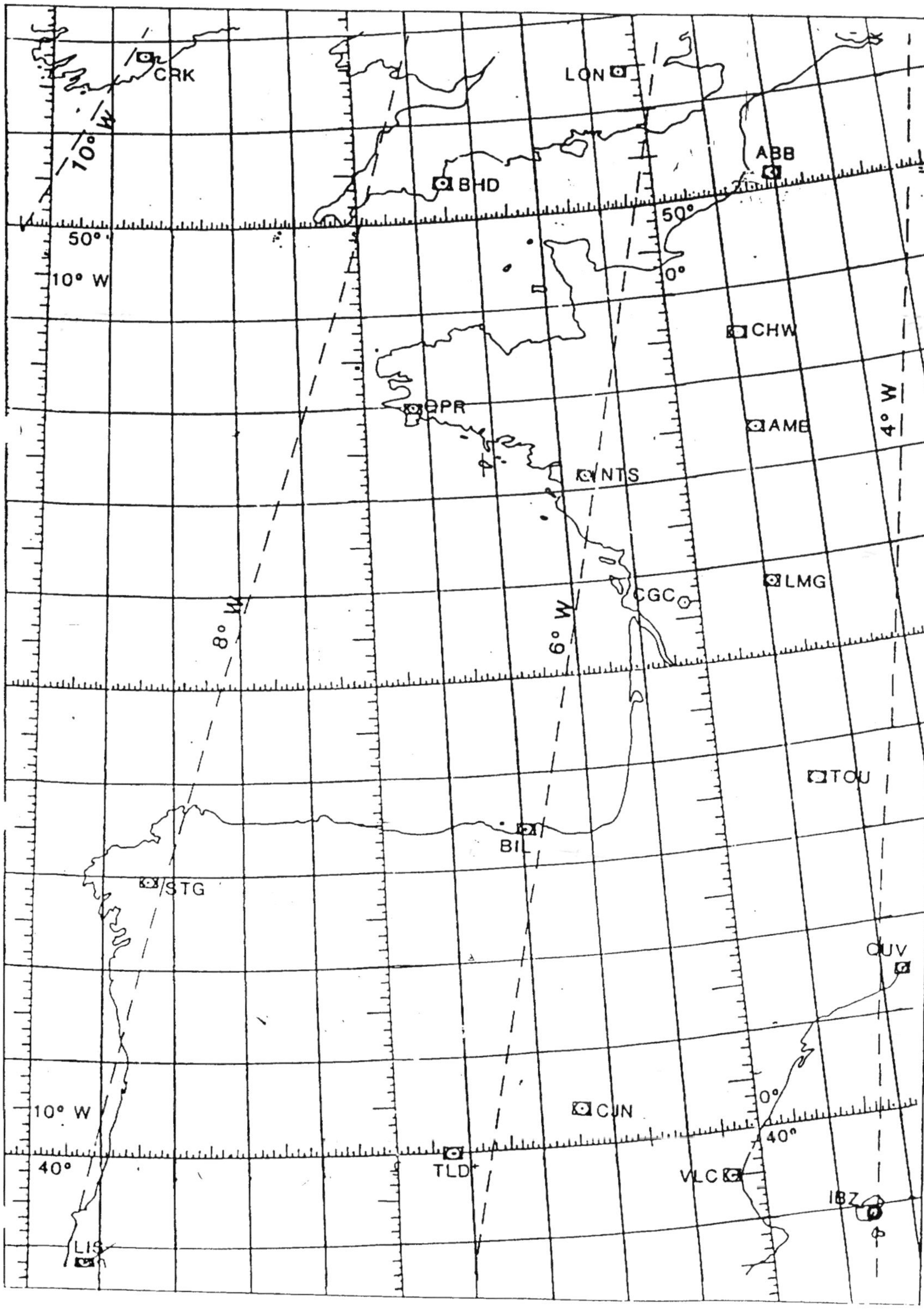
CRK
LON
ABB
BHD
10° W
50°
10° W
50°
0°
CHW
4° W
BPR
AMB
NTS
LMG
CGC
8° W
6° W
TOU
BIL
STG
OUV
CIN
10° W
0°
40°
40°
TLD
VLC
IBZ
LIS

Chart 3

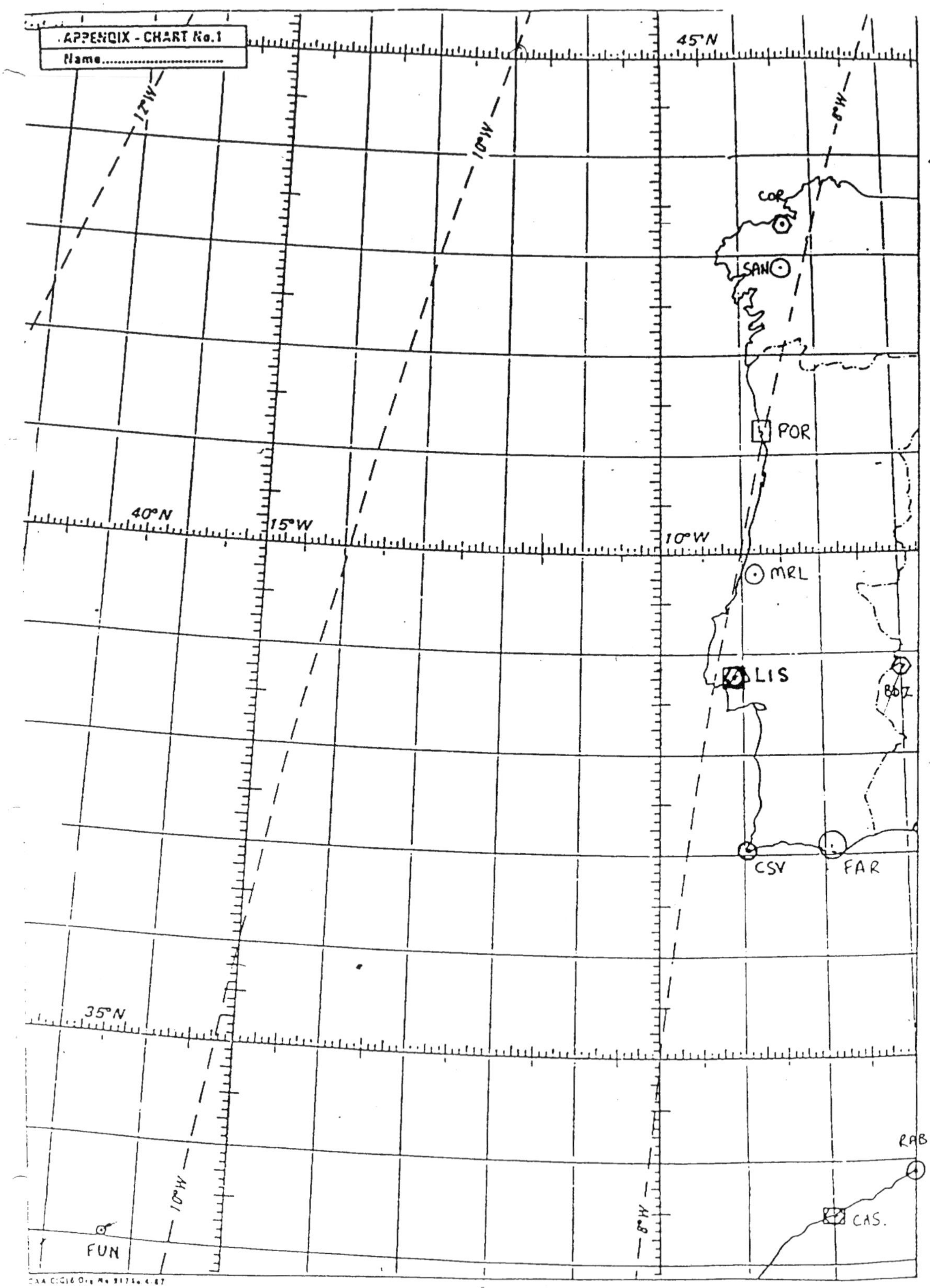
APPENDIX - CHART No.1
Name
45°N
40°N
35°N
15°W
10°W
12°W
10°W
8°W
COR
SAN
POR
MRL
LIS
BDZ
CSV
FAR
RAB
CAS.
FUN

ANSWERS TO PLOTTING QUESTIONS

Plotting Example 3	Position	6450N 00535W
Plotting Example 4	Position	6035N 00210E
Plotting Example 5	Position	4000N 01040W
Plotting Example 6	CSV Radial	218°M
Plotting Example 7	ETA CSV	0002
	Heading	116°M

Chapter 18
Time

INTRODUCTION

The word **time** is used to suggest both duration and a particular instant in that duration. Particular instants can be related to the rhythmic repetition of some recognisable patterns, such as the apparent motion of the heavenly bodies relative to the Earth. Duration of time can also be expressed as the function of these same repetitions.

THE UNIVERSE

The universe is a complex formation of clusters of galaxies. Individual galaxies are made up of hundreds of billions of stars, many of which have planets orbiting around them. Some of the planets, in turn, have moons in orbit around them. Our galaxy is called the Milky Way. People have named one of the stars in the Milky Way "Sol", and the planets and other objects orbiting Sol, including the Earth, are together called the solar system.

The main components of the solar system are:

- The sun
- Nine major planets
- Moons orbiting the major planets
- 2000 minor planets and asteroids

The sun is the central figure, about which all other elements rotate in elliptical orbits.

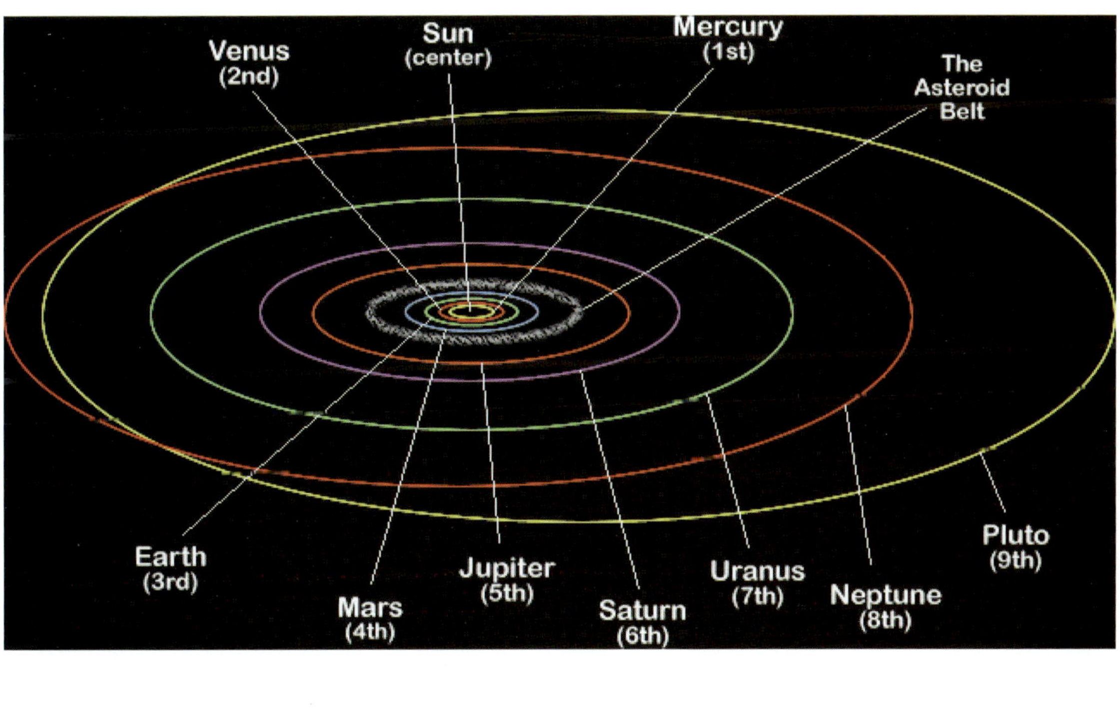

DEFINITION OF TIME

The motion of the Earth in its orbit round the sun, which results in apparent motion of the sun around the ecliptic, forms one main pattern. A year is defined as the time it takes for the Earth to complete one orbit of the sun. The uniform counter-clockwise rotation of the Earth about its own axis forms another pattern — one complete rotation defining a day. This rotation is defined as being in an easterly direction.

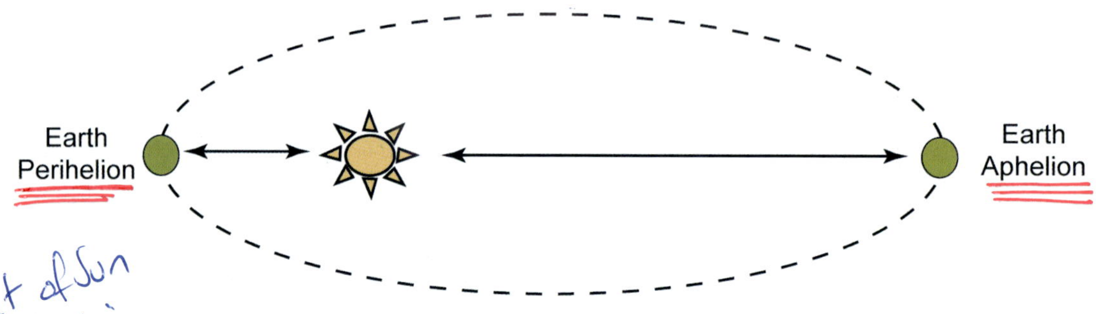

The Earth's Orbit

The Earth travels around the sun on a counter-clockwise elliptical orbit, as shown above, known as the ecliptic. The speed of orbit is not constant. The orbit is governed by Keppler's Laws of Planetary Motion, which state that:

- The orbit of each planet is an ellipse with the sun at one of the focii.
- The line joining the planet to the sun sweeps out an equal area in equal time. This is known as the **radius vector**.
- The square of the sidereal period of a planet is proportional to the cube of its mean distance from the sun.

PERIHELION

The Perihelion is where the sun is closest to the Earth:

- The sun is approximately 91.4 million miles from the Earth
- It occurs on 4 January
- The Earth's orbital speed is at its greatest

APHELION

The Earth is at its farthest point from the sun:

- The sun is approximately 94.6 million miles from the Earth
- It occurs on 3 July
- The Earth's orbital speed is at its lowest

The year and the day are the principal divisions of time because they depend upon astronomical phenomena. The lengths of the shorter divisions of time, the hour, the minute, and the second, are arbitrary sub-divisions of the day.

SEASONS OF THE YEAR

The North-South axis of the Earth is inclined at 66½° to the plane of the ecliptic. This means that the Earth is tilted by 23½° as it orbits the sun. The angle between the plane of the ecliptic and the plane of the Equator is 23½°. The parallel of latitude directly under the sun changes slowly. This causes the seasonal changes seen over the world.

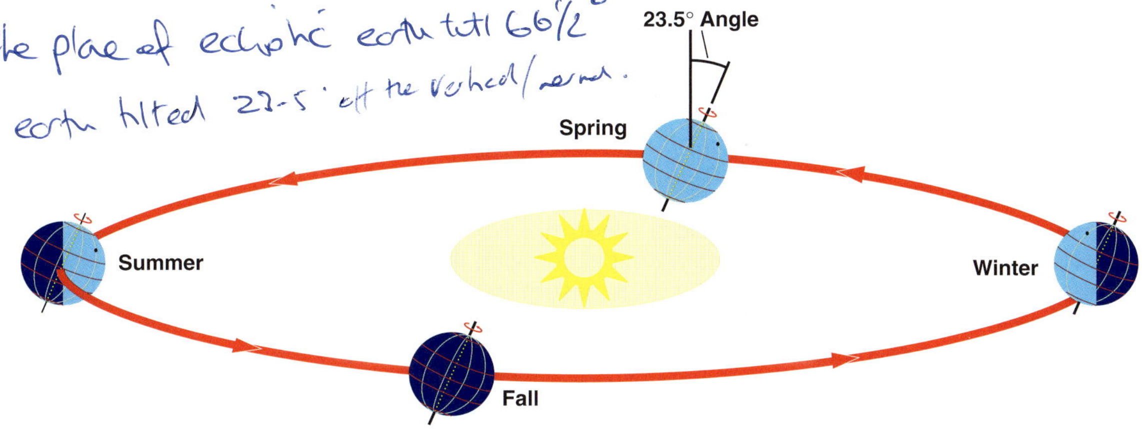

The Tilt of the Earth's Axis Causes the Seasons

The sun is at its most southerly point on 22 December. At this time it appears to be overhead the Tropic of Capricorn, at a latitude of 23½°S. This marks the Winter Solstice in the Northern Hemisphere, and the Summer Solstice in the Southern Hemisphere.

The sun is at its most northerly point on 21 June. At this time it is overhead the Tropic of Cancer, at a latitude of 23½°N. This marks the Summer Solstice in the Northern Hemisphere, and the Winter Solstice in the Southern Hemisphere.

The sun crosses the Equator from South to North on 21 March. This marks the Spring or Vernal Equinox in the Northern Hemisphere, and the Autumn Equinox in the Southern Hemisphere.

The sun crosses the Equator from North to South on 23 September. This marks the Autumn Equinox in the Northern Hemisphere, and the Spring or Vernal Equinox in the Southern Hemisphere.

THE DAY

Uniform motion of the Earth about its own axis results in an apparent uniform rotation of the celestial sphere about the Earth, so that heavenly bodies are continually crossing and re-crossing an observer's meridian in an East to West direction. A day is defined as the interval that elapses between two successive transits of a heavenly body across the same meridian.

Any heavenly body could be used as a timekeeper, but some are more convenient than others. The sun is not a perfect timekeeper because its apparent speed along the ecliptic varies. However, since the sun governs all life on Earth, it is used as the standard by which time is decided in everyday life.

THE APPARENT SOLAR DAY

The interval that elapses between two successive transits of the actual sun across the same meridian is an apparent solar day.

The time interval between two successive transits of the actual sun over the same meridian is more than 360° of the Earth's rotation because of the Earth's motion in its orbit around the sun. Furthermore, because of the varying speed of the Earth around its orbit, the amount above 360° of rotation is not constant.

THE MEAN SUN

Because of the problems outlined above, time as measured by the apparent or true sun does not increase at a uniform rate, and therefore, does not give a practical unit of measurement. To overcome this difficulty and still maintain connection with the true sun, an imaginary body called the mean sun is introduced. The mean sun is assumed to move along the celestial equator at a uniform speed around the Earth and to complete one revolution in the time it takes for the true sun to complete one revolution in the ecliptic.

THE MEAN SOLAR DAY

The time interval between two successive transits of the mean sun across the same meridian is called a mean solar day. In one mean solar day, the mean sun moves westward from the meridian and completes one circuit of 360° longitude in the 24 mean solar hours into which the day is divided. The rate of travel is 15° of longitude per mean solar hour. The mean solar hour (called an hour for short) is further divided into 60 minutes. These are then divided into 60 seconds.

THE CIVIL DAY

The civil day is the day that suffices for human affairs. It begins at midnight when the mean sun is on the observer's anti-meridian, and it ends at the next midnight.

It is divided into 24 mean solar hours.

THE YEAR

Two definitions can be used:

Sidereal Year The time the Earth takes to complete a full orbit of the sun measured against a distant star — 365 days, 5 hours, 48 minutes, 45 seconds. For ease, 365 days 6 hours is usually used.

Calendar Year Taken as 365 days, the calendar year is kept in step with the sidereal year by adding 1 day to the year each 4 years (Leap Year).

LOCAL MEAN TIME (LMT)

Local mean time is the time according to the mean sun. It obviously varies from one longitude to another since the mean sun can only be directly overhead at one meridian at one time. Difference of longitude between two places implies a difference of LMT between them. Since there is 24 hours change of time in 360° of rotation, simple calculation reveals that 15° change of longitude corresponds to one hour change of time, or 1° change of longitude corresponds to 4 minutes change of time. Other similar proportions can be derived, and a special table printed in the Air Almanac, an excerpt of which is shown below, facilitates conversion of arc to time. The table is split into columns of ° (degrees) and "hm" (hours and minutes). The table covers the time change from 0° to 359°. On the far right of the table, one column covers the arc to time for ' (minutes) of change of longitude. The corresponding timetable is labelled "ms" (minutes and seconds). This column covers 0' to 59'.

Conversion of Arc to Time													
°	h m	°	h m	°	h m	°	h m	°	h m	°	h m	'	m s
0	0 00	60	4 00	120								0	0 00
1	0 04	61	4 04	121								1	0 04
2	0 08	62	4 08	122								2	0 08
3	0 12	63	4 12	123								3	0 12
4	0 16	64	4 16	124								4	0 16

When the sun passes a particular meridian, it is 1200 hours LMT.

The table below shows the relationship of the Greenwich Meridian to other meridians when the time at Greenwich (0°E/W) is 1200 LMT.

Greenwich 1200 LMT

135°W	90°W	45°W	0°	45°E	90°E	135°E
0300	0600	0900	1200	1500	1800	2100

Where a meridian is:

- East of Greenwich, the time is later because the sun has already passed this meridian
- West of Greenwich, the time is earlier because the sun has yet to reach that meridian

The difference in LMT between two places can easily be calculated using the above. Remember:

- 15° is equivalent to 1 hour in LMT
- 1° is equivalent to 4 minutes
- 1' is equivalent to 4 seconds

Example What is the difference in LMT between London Heathrow (51°28N 000°27'W) and Kennedy International (New York) (40°38'N 073°46'W)?

STEP 1 Calculate the Ch Long between London and New York.
73°19'

STEP 2 Calculate the arc-to-time differences. This can be done by calculator or by looking at the arc-to-time tables. Remember 1° is equivalent to 4 minutes, and 1' is equivalent to 4 seconds.

73° is equivalent to 292 minutes

19' is equivalent to 76 seconds – 1 minute 16 seconds

Time difference LMT is 293 minutes 16 seconds

Remember New York is at an earlier time than London.

Example From the above example, if the time in London is 1200 LMT, what is the time in New York? The time difference is 4 hours, 53 minutes. Seconds are not normally included.

STEP 1	**London**	**1200 LMT**
	Time Difference	**- 0453**
	Time New York	**0707 LMT**

UNIVERSAL CO-ORDINATED TIME (UTC)

UTC is the LMT at the Greenwich meridian. It is more accurate than Greenwich Mean Time, as it is calculated against International Atomic Time. UTC is used by aviation as the reference time. The JAR examinations expect the student to be able to calculate UTC from LMT and vice versa.

CONVERSION OF LMT TO UTC

To convert LMT to UTC or vice versa, first convert the observer's longitude into time in accordance with the rules above. This time is then applied to the LMT to derive UTC or UTC to derive LMT. The relation between the two times is conveniently summarised as follows:

Longitude west	**UTC best**
Longitude east	**UTC least**

Example If the LMT in Goose Bay (060°W) is 1200, what is the UTC?

STEP 1 The arc to time for 60° is 4 hours

LMT Goose Bay	**1200**	
Arc to Time	**+ 0400**	**Longitude west UTC best**
	1600	

Example If the UTC in Munich (15°E) is 1200, what is the LMT?

STEP 1 The arc to time for 15° is 1 hours

UTC Munich	**1200**	
Arc to Time	**+ 0100**	**Longitude east UTC least**
	1300	

Longitude west UTC Best

Longitude East UTC least.

STANDARD TIME

It is clearly impractical for each and every place to keep the LMT applicable to its own meridian. For convenience, all places in the same territory, or part of the same territory, maintain a standard of time as mandated by the government responsible for that territory. In the Air Almanac, there is a list showing the factors necessary to convert LMT into standard time for territories throughout the world. Countries are listed alphabetically. Some countries such as Canada, Australia, and the United States are spread across a large change in longitude. One Standard Time is not sufficient, and it is necessary to enter the list with the area rather than the country. Standard time is split into three lists:

List 1 List 1 contains places where standard time is normally fast on UTC. (places east of Greenwich). The times listed should be:

- Added to UTC to give standard time
- Subtracted from standard time to give UTC

List 2 List 2 contains places which normally maintain UTC.

List 3 List 3 contains a list of places where standard time is slow on UTC. (place west of Greenwich). The times listed should be:

- Subtracted from UTC to give standard time
- Added to standard time to give UTC

With any calculation of UTC or standard time, use a methodical procedure to prevent mistakes.

INTERNATIONAL DATE LINE

An anomaly occurs at 180°W/E. Places east of Greenwich are ahead of UTC, places west behind UTC. The LMT at 180° is, therefore, 12 hours ahead or behind UTC, and there is a 24-hour time difference between two places separated by the Greenwich anti-meridian.

The local date must change when crossing 180°; this is called the International Date Line. The change of date depends upon whether the aircraft is travelling west or east:

- For an aircraft on a westerly track, a day must be added to the calendar.
    - The 14th becomes the 15th
- For an aircraft on an easterly track, a day must be subtracted from the calendar.
    - The 14th becomes the 13th

The International Date Line follows the 180° meridian, except where there are inhabited areas. A deviation may occur in these places.

Example The UTC and date are 2100, 3 January. What is the LMT at 71°30'W?

STEP 1	UTC	2100	3 January
	Arc to time	- 4 46	
	LMT	1614	3 January

Example LMT at 163°15'E is 0045, 14 March. What is the LMT and local date at 21°15'W?

STEP 1 When calculating the LMT at two different longitudes, calculate the UTC first.

LMT	0045	14 March
UTC	-1053	
UTC	1352	13 March

STEP 2 Use the UTC to calculate the LMT at 021°15'W.

UTC	1352	
21°15'W in time	- 0125	
LMT	1227	13 March

Example LMT at 003°27'E is 1816, 18 April. What is LMT at 165°32'E?

Example ST at Billund (Denmark) is 0645, 30 October:

What is the LMT at 127°30'E?
What is ST in Auckland (New Zealand)?
Use –1 hour for the ST calculation at Billund
Use +12 hours for the ST calculation at Auckland

ST Billund	0645	30 October
Convert to UTC	- 0100	
UTC	0545	30 October

UTC	0545	
127°30' in time	+ 0830	
	1415	30 October

UTC	0545	
ST New Zealand	+ 1200	
	1745	30 October

Time Example 2 LMT 179°50'W is 2300, 15 December, what is LMT at 179°50'E?

RISINGS, SETTINGS, AND TWILIGHT

TIMES OF VISIBLE SUNRISE AND SUNSET

It is sometimes necessary to be able to determine the times of visible sunrise and sunset, a phenomena which is said to occur when the sun's upper limb crosses the visible horizon. To facilitate these calculations, the times of sunrise and sunset for a range of latitudes from 60°S to 72°N are given in the Air Almanac. These times, which are given to the nearest minute, are the UTC of the phenomena at the Greenwich meridian, but they may be taken, without great error, to be the LMT of the phenomena at any other meridian.

The sunrise and sunset are tabulated for every third day in the format shown below.

SUNRISE			
	April		
Lat	2	5	8
°	h m	h m	h m
N 72	04 53	04 38	04 21
N70	05 01	47	04 33
N68	07	55	04 42

Example What is the LMT of sunrise at Perth (5626N 00322W) on 13 July?

STEP 1	LMT Sunrise	56°N	0331
	LMT Sunrise	58°N	0316
	Difference	2°	15 minutes
STEP 2	Difference	120'	900"
		26'	**195" (3 min 15 sec)**
STEP 3	LMT Sunrise	56°	0331
		+ 26'	-<u>0003 15"</u>
	LMT Sunrise	56°26'	0327 45"

TWILIGHT

There is a period of time before sunrise and after sunset when there is still sufficient illumination for normal daylight operations to continue. The duration of this period, which is known as the duration of civil twilight, is also tabulated in the Air Almanac in the same manner as the times of sunrise and sunset.

The period is split into three stages:

Civil Twilight	Occurs when the sun's centre is 6° below the horizon
Nautical Twilight	Occurs when the sun's centre is 12° below the horizon
Astronomical Twilight	Occurs when the sun's centre is 18° below the horizon. The moment of darkness.

For the JAR-FCL, pilots are only concerned with civil twilight. The times of civil twilight are given in the Air Almanac.

DURATION OF CIVIL TWILIGHT

Twilight begins when the sun's centre is at the appropriate depression below the horizon and lasts until sunrise. This can be calculated from the tables in the Air Almanac.

During the summer:

- When the sun's depression is less than 6°, civil twilight exists all night. The pole has the sun above the horizon continuously.
- When the sun's depression is greater than 6°, the pole has continuous darkness.

The tables in the Air Almanac are for an observer at sea level. At altitude, all phenomena occur either earlier in the morning or later in the evening.

THE FOLLOWING TABLES CAN BE FOUND ON THE NEXT SEVERAL PAGES:

STANDARD TIMES
SUNRISE, SUNSET, AND TWILIGHT TIMES
CONVERSION OF ARC TO TIME

A20

STANDARD TIMES (Corrected to June 1988)

LIST I—PLACES FAST ON UTC (mainly those EAST OF GREENWICH)

The times given below should be } *added* to UT to give Standard Time. *subtracted* from Standard Time to give UT.

Place	h	m
Admiralty Islands	10	
Afghanistan	04	30
Albania*	01	
Algeria	01	
Amirante Islands	04	
Andaman Islands	05	30
Angola	01	
Australia		
Australian Capital Territory*	10	
New South Wales [1]*	10	
Northern Territory	09	30
Queensland	10	
South Australia*	09	30
Tasmania*	10	
Victoria*	10	
Western Australia*	08	
Austria*	01	
Bahrain	03	
Balearic Islands*	01	
Banaba	11	30
Bangladesh	06	
Belgium*	01	
Benin (Dahomey)	01	
Bhutan	06	
Botswana, Republic of	02	
Brunei	08	
Bulgaria*	02	
Burma	06	30
Burundi	02	
Cameroon Republic	01	
Caroline Islands, Pala Islands	09	
Yal Islands, Truk Islands	10	
Ponapel	11	
Pingelap Islands, Kusaie	12	
Central African Republic	01	
Chad	01	
Chagos Archipelago [2]	05	
Chatham Islands*	12	45
China*	08	
Christmas Island, Indian Ocean	07	
Cocos Keeling Islands	06	30
Comoro Islands (Comoros)	03	
Congo Republic	01	
Corsica*	01	
Crete*	02	
Cyprus, Ercan*	02	
Larnaca*	02	
Czechoslovakia*	01	
Denmark*	01	
Djibouti	03	
Egypt, Arab Republic of*	02	
Equatorial Guinea, Republic of	01	
Ethiopia	03	
Fiji	12	
Finland*	02	
France	01	
Gabon	01	
Germany, East*	01	
West [3]*	01	
Gibraltar*	01	
Greece*	02	
Guam	10	
Holland (The Netherlands)*	01	
Hong Kong	08	
Hungary*	01	
India	05	30
Indonesia, Republic of		
Bangka, Billiton, Java, West and Middle Kalimantan, Madura, Sumatra	07	
Bali, Flores, South and East Kalimantan, Lombok, Sulawesi, Sumba, Sumbawa, Timor	08	
Aru, Irian Jaya, Kai, Moluccas, Tanimbar	09	
Iran	03	30
Iraq*	03	
Israel*	02	
Italy*	01	
Japan	09	
Jordan*	02	
Kampuchea, Democratic	07	
Kenya	03	
Kiribati Republic [4]	12	
Korea, North	09	
Republic of (South)*	09	
Kuril Islands	11	
Kuwait	03	
Laccadive Islands	05	30
Laos	07	
Lebanon*	02	
Lesotho	02	
Libya*	01	
Liechtenstein*	01	
Lord Howe Island*	10	30
Luxembourg*	01	

*Summer time may be kept in these countries.
[1] Except Broken Hill Area which keeps 09^h30^m.
[2] Except Diego Garcia which keeps 06^h.
[3] Including West Berlin.
[4] Except Kiritimati Island and the Phoenix Islands which keep 10^h and 11^h slow on UT.

STANDARD TIMES (Corrected to June 1988) A21

LIST I—(*Continued*).

	h	m
Macao	08	
Macias Nguema Biyogo Island (Fernando Póo)	01	
Madagascar, Democratic Republic of	03	
Malawi	02	
Malaysia		
Malaya, Sabah, Sarawak	08	
Maldives, Republic of The	05	
Malta*	01	
Mariana Islands	10	
Marshall Islands[1]	12	
Mauritius	04	
Monaco*	01	
Mongolia*	08	
Mozambique	02	
Namibia (South West Africa)	02	
Nauru	12	
Nepal	05	45
Netherlands, The*	01	
New Caledonia*	11	
New Zealand*	12	
Nicobar Islands	05	30
Niger	01	
Nigeria, Republic of	01	
Norfolk Island	11	30
Norway*	01	
Novaya Zemlya	03	
Okinawa	09	
Oman	04	
Pagalu (Annobon Islands)	01	
Pakistan	05	
Papua New Guinea	10	
Pescadores Islands	08	
Philippine Republic	08	
Poland*	01	
Qatar	03	
Réunion	04	
Romania*	02	
Rwanda	02	
Ryukyu Islands	09	
Sakhalin	11	
Santa Cruz Islands	11	
Sardinia*	01	
Saudi Arabia	03	
Schouten Islands	09	
Seychelles	04	
Sicily*	01	
Singapore	08	

	h	m
Socotra	03	
Solomon Islands	11	
Somalia Republic	03	
South Africa, Republic of	02	
South West Africa (Namibia)	02	
Spain*	01	
Spanish Possessions in North Africa (Ceuta, Melilla)*	01	
Spitsbergen (Svalbard)	01	
Sri Lanka	05	30
Sudan, Republic of	02	
Swaziland	02	
Sweden*	01	
Switzerland*	01	
Syria (Syrian Arab Republic)*	02	
Taiwan*	08	
Tanzania	03	
Thailand	07	
Tonga	13	
Tunisia*	01	
Turkey*	02	
Tuvalu	12	
Uganda	03	
Union of Soviet Socialist Republics[2]*		
Zone 1 Amderma, Arkhangelsk, Kiev, Leningrad, Moscow, Odessa	03	
Zone 2 Baku, Tbilsi, Volgogrnd	04	
Zone 3 Ashkabad, Novvy Port, Sverdlovsk	05	
Zone 4 Alma-Ata, Omsk, Tashkent	06	
Zone 5 Krasnoyarsk, Novosibirsk	07	
Zone 6 Irkutsk	08	
Zone 7 Tiksi, Yakutsk	09	
Zone 8 Khabarovsk, Okhotsk, Vladivostok	10	
Zone 9 Magadan, Sakhalin I.	11	
Zone 10 Anadyr, Petropaviovsk	12	
United Arab Emirates	04	
Vanuatu, Republic of*	11	
Vietnam, Socialist Republic of	07	
Wrangell Island	12	
Yemen	03	
Yugoslavia*	01	
Zaire		
Kinshasa, Mbandaka	01	
Haut-Zaire, Kasai, Kivu, Shaba	02	
Zambia, Republic of	02	
Zimbabwe	02	

*Summer time may be kept in these countries.

[1] Except the islands of Kwajalein and Eniwetok which keep a time 24^h slow on that of the rest of the islands.

[2] The boundaries between the zones are irregular; listed are towns in each zone.

A22 STANDARD TIMES (Corrected to June 1988)

LIST II—PLACES NORMALLY KEEPING UT

Ascension Island	Ghana	Irish Republic*	Morocco	Sierra Leone
Bourkina-Faso	Great Britain [1]	Ivory Coast	Portugal*	Togo Republic
Canary Islands*	Guinea Bissau	Liberia	Principe	Tristan da Cunha
Channel Islands [1]	Guinea Republic	Madeira*	St. Helena	
Faeroes*, The	Iceland	Mali	São Tomé	
Gambia	Ireland, Northern[1]	Mauritania	Senegal	

*Summer time may be kept in these countries.
[1] Summer time, one hour in advance of UT, is kept from March 25^d 01^h to October 28^d 01^h UT, subject to confirmation.

LIST III—PLACES SLOW ON UT (WEST OF GREENWICH)

The times given below should be { *subtracted* from UT to give Standard Time. / *added* to Standard Time to give UT. }

Place	h	m	Place	h	m
Argentina	03		Cape Verde Islands	01	
Austral Islands [1]	10		Cayman Islands	05	
Azores*	01		Chile*	04	
			Christmas Island, Pacific Ocean	10	
Bahamas*	05		Colombia	05	
Barbados	04		Cook Islands*	10	
Belize	06		Costa Rica	06	
Bermuda*	04		Cuba*	05	
Bolivia	04		Curaçao Island	04	
Brazil, eastern [2]*	03				
Territory of Acre*	05		Dominican Republic	04	
western*	04				
British Antarctic Territory [3]	03		Easter Island (I. de Pascua)*	06	
			Ecuador	05	
Canada					
Alberta*	07		Falkland Islands*	04	
British Columbia*	08		Fanning Island	10	
Labrador*	04		Fernando de Noronha Island*	02	
Manitoba*	06		French Guiana	03	
New Brunswick*	04				
Newfoundland*	03	30	Galápagos Islands	06	
Northwest Territories*			Greenland [4], Scoresby Sound*	01	
east of long. W.68°	04		Angmagssalik and west coast*	03	
long. W.68° to W.85°	05		Thule area	04	
long. W.85° to W.102°	06		Grenada	04	
west of long. W.102°	07		Guadeloupe	04	
Nova Scotia*	04		Guatemala	06	
Ontario*, east of long. W.90°	05		Guyana, Republic of	03	
west of long. W.90°	06				
Prince Edward Island*	04		Haiti*	05	
Quebec*, east of long. W.63°	04		Honduras	06	
west of long. W.63°	05				
Saskatchewan*			Jamaica	05	
east of long. W.106°	06		Jan Mayen Island	01	
west of long. W.106°	07		Johnston Island	10	
Yukon*	08		Juan Fernandez Islands*	04	

*Summer time may be kept in these countries.
[1] This is the legal standard time, but local mean time is generally used.
[2] Including all the coast and Brasilia.
[3] Except South Georgia which keeps 02^h.
[4] Danmarkshavn keeps UT.

STANDARD TIMES (Corrected to June 1988) A23

LIST III—*(Continued)*

	h	m
Leeward Islands	04	
Marquesas Islands	09	30
Martinique	04	
Mexico[1]	06	
Midway Islands	11	
Nicaragua	06	
Niue	11	
Panama, Republic of	05	
Paraguay*	04	
Peru	05	
Pitcairn Island	08	30
Puerto Rico	04	
St. Pierre and Miquelon	03	
Salvador, El	06	
Samoa	11	
Society Islands	10	
South Georgia	02	
Surinam	03	
Tobago	04	
Trindade Island*, South Atlantic	02	
Trinidad	04	
Tuamotu Archipelago	10	
Tubuai Islands	10	
Turks and Caicos Islands*	05	
United States of America		
Alabama[2]	06	
Alaska[2], east of long. W.169°30′	09	
Aleutian Is., west of W.169°30′	10	
Arizona	07	
Arkansas[2]	06	
California[2]	08	
Colorado[2]	07	
Connecticut[2]	05	
Delaware[2]	05	
District of Columbia[2]	05	
Florida[2,3]	05	
Georgia[2]	05	
Hawaii[2]	10	
Idaho[2,3]	07	
Illinois[2]	06	
Indiana[3]	05	
Iowa[2]	06	
Kansas[2,3]	06	
Kentucky[2], eastern part	05	
western part	06	
Louisiana[2]	06	
Maine[2]	05	
Maryland[2]	05	
Massachusetts[2]	05	
Michigan[2,3]	05	
Minnesota[2]	06	
Mississippi[2]	06	
Missouri[2]	06	
Montana[2]	07	
Nebraska[2,3]	06	
Nevada[2]	08	
New Hampshire[2]	05	
New Jersey[2]	05	
New Mexico[2]	07	
New York[2]	05	
North Carolina[2]	05	
North Dakota[2,3]	06	
Ohio[2]	05	
Oklahoma[2]	06	
Oregon[2,3]	08	
Pennsylvania[2]	05	
Rhode Island[2]	05	
South Carolina[2]	05	
South Dakota[2], eastern part	06	
western part	07	
Tennessee[2,3]	06	
Texas[2,3]	06	
Utah[2]	07	
Vermont[2]	05	
Virginia[2]	05	
Washington[2]	08	
Washington, D.C.[2]	05	
West Virginia[2]	05	
Wisconsin[2]	06	
Wyoming[2]	07	
Uruguay*	03	
Venezuela	04	
Virgin Islands	04	
Windward Islands	04	

*Summer time may be kept in these countries.

[1] Except the states of Sonora, Sinaloa, Nayarit and the Southern District of Lower California, which keep 07^h, and the Northern District of Lower California, which keeps 08^{h}*.

[2] Summer (daylight-saving) time, one hour fast on the time given, is kept in these states from the first Sunday in April to the last Sunday in October, changing at 02^h00^m local clock time.

[3] This applies to the greater portion of the state.

A130

SUNRISE

Lat.	Dec.	January										February					
	30	2	5	8	11	14	17	20	23	26	29	1	4	7	10	13	16
°	h m	h m	h m	h m	h m	h m	h m	h m	h m	h m	h m	h m	h m	h m	h m	h m	h m
N 72	—	—	—	—	—	—	—	—	—	11 51	11 00	10 31	10 07	09 46	09 27	09 08	08 51
70	—	—	—	—	—	—	11 53	11 09	10 44	10 23	10 05	09 48	09 32	09 16	09 01	08 46	31
68	—	—	11 32	11 11	10 55	10 40	10 25	10 12	09 58	09 45	09 32	09 19	09 07	08 54	08 41	28	16
66	10 31	10 26	10 20	10 13	10 05	09 57	09 48	09 38	29	09 19	09 08	08 58	08 47	36	26	15	08 04
64	09 51	09 49	09 45	09 40	09 35	29	22	09 14	09 06	08 58	08 50	41	32	22	13	08 03	07 53
62	24	22	19	09 16	09 12	09 07	09 01	08 55	08 49	42	34	27	19	10	08 02	07 53	44
N 60	09 03	09 02	09 00	08 57	08 54	08 50	08 45	08 40	08 34	08 28	08 22	08 15	08 08	08 00	07 53	07 45	07 37
58	08 46	08 45	08 44	42	39	35	31	27	22	17	11	08 05	07 58	07 52	45	37	30
56	32	31	30	28	26	23	19	15	11	08 06	08 01	07 56	50	44	38	31	24
54	19	19	18	16	14	12	09	08 06	08 02	07 57	07 53	48	42	37	31	25	19
52	08 08	08 08	08 07	08 06	08 04	08 02	08 00	07 57	07 53	49	45	41	36	31	25	20	14
N 50	07 58	07 58	07 58	07 57	07 56	07 54	07 51	07 49	07 46	07 42	07 38	07 34	07 30	07 25	07 20	07 15	07 10
45	38	38	38	38	37	35	34	32	29	27	24	20	17	13	09	07 05	07 00
40	22	22	22	22	21	21	19	18	16	14	12	07 09	07 06	07 03	07 00	06 56	06 52
35	07 08	07 08	07 08	07 08	07 08	07 08	07 07	07 06	07 05	07 03	07 01	06 59	06 57	06 54	06 52	49	46
30	06 55	06 56	06 57	06 57	06 57	06 57	06 56	06 56	06 55	06 54	06 52	51	49	47	45	42	40
N 20	06 34	06 35	06 36	06 37	06 37	06 38	06 38	06 38	06 38	06 37	06 36	06 36	06 35	06 33	06 32	06 31	06 29
N 10	06 16	17	18	19	20	21	22	22	22	23	23	22	22	22	21	20	20
0	05 59	06 00	06 02	06 03	06 04	06 05	06 06	06 07	06 08	06 09	06 10	06 10	06 10	06 11	11	11	11
S 10	41	05 43	05 45	05 46	05 48	05 49	05 51	05 52	05 54	05 55	05 56	05 57	05 59	05 59	06 00	06 01	06 02
20	23	24	26	28	30	32	34	36	38	40	42	44	45	47	05 49	05 50	05 52
S 30	05 01	05 03	05 05	05 07	05 10	05 12	05 15	05 18	05 20	05 23	05 26	05 28	05 31	05 33	05 36	05 38	05 41
35	04 48	04 50	04 52	04 55	04 58	05 01	05 03	05 07	05 10	13	16	19	22	25	28	31	34
40	33	35	38	41	44	04 47	04 50	04 54	04 57	05 01	05 05	05 08	12	16	20	23	27
45	04 15	04 18	04 21	24	27	31	35	39	43	04 47	04 52	04 56	05 00	05 05	05 09	14	18
50	03 53	03 56	03 59	04 03	04 07	11	16	20	25	30	36	41	04 46	04 51	04 57	05 02	07
S 52	03 42	03 45	03 49	03 53	03 57	04 02	04 07	04 12	04 17	04 22	04 28	04 34	04 39	04 45	04 51	04 57	05 02
54	30	33	37	41	46	03 51	03 56	04 02	04 08	14	20	26	32	38	45	51	04 57
56	16	20	24	28	33	39	45	03 51	03 57	04 04	04 10	17	24	30	37	44	51
58	03 00	03 04	03 08	03 13	19	25	31	38	45	03 52	03 59	04 07	14	22	29	37	44
S 60	02 40	02 44	02 49	02 55	03 01	03 08	03 15	03 23	03 31	03 39	03 47	03 55	04 03	04 12	04 20	04 28	04 36

SUNSET

Lat.	Dec.	January										February					
	30	2	5	8	11	14	17	20	23	26	29	1	4	7	10	13	16
°	h m	h m	h m	h m	h m	h m	h m	h m	h m	h m	h m	h m	h m	h m	h m	h m	h m
N 72	—	—	—	—	—	—	—	—	—	12 36	13 27	13 57	14 22	14 44	15 03	15 22	15 39
70	—	—	—	—	—	—	12 30	13 14	13 41	14 03	14 22	14 40	14 58	15 14	29	15 44	15 59
68	—	—	12 38	13 02	13 21	13 38	13 55	14 11	14 26	14 41	14 55	15 09	15 22	36	15 49	16 01	16 14
66	13 34	13 41	13 50	14 00	14 10	14 21	14 32	14 44	14 56	15 07	15 19	30	42	15 53	16 04	15	26
64	14 14	14 19	14 25	33	14 41	14 49	14 59	15 08	15 18	27	37	15 47	15 57	16 07	17	27	36
62	14 41	14 45	14 51	14 57	15 04	15 11	15 19	27	35	44	15 52	16 01	16 10	19	28	36	45
N 60	15 02	15 06	15 11	15 16	15 22	15 29	15 36	15 43	15 50	15 58	16 05	16 13	16 21	16 29	16 37	16 45	16 52
58	19	23	27	32	37	43	15 49	15 56	16 02	16 09	16	23	30	38	45	52	16 59
56	34	37	41	45	15 50	15 55	16 01	16 07	13	19	26	32	39	45	52	16 58	17 05
54	46	15 49	15 53	15 57	16 02	16 06	12	17	22	28	34	40	46	52	16 58	17 04	10
52	15 57	16 00	16 03	16 07	11	16	21	26	31	36	42	47	53	16 58	17 04	09	15
N 50	16 07	16 09	16 13	16 16	16 20	16 25	16 29	16 34	16 38	16 43	16 48	16 53	16 59	17 04	17 09	17 14	17 19
45	27	30	33	36	39	43	16 47	16 50	16 55	16 59	17 03	17 07	17 12	16	20	24	29
40	44	16 46	16 49	16 51	16 54	16 58	17 01	17 04	17 08	17 11	15	19	22	26	29	33	36
35	16 58	17 00	17 02	17 05	17 07	17 10	13	16	19	22	25	28	31	35	37	40	43
30	17 10	12	14	16	19	21	24	27	29	32	34	37	39	42	44	47	17 49
N 20	17 31	17 32	17 34	17 36	17 38	17 40	17 42	17 44	17 46	17 48	17 50	17 52	17 54	17 55	17 57	17 58	18 00
N 10	17 49	17 51	17 52	17 54	17 55	17 57	17 58	18 00	18 01	18 03	18 04	18 05	18 06	18 07	18 07	18 08	09
0	18 06	18 08	18 09	18 10	18 11	18 13	18 14	15	15	16	17	17	17	18	18	18	18
S 10	24	25	26	27	28	29	29	29	30	30	30	30	29	29	28	27	26
20	18 42	18 43	18 44	18 45	18 45	18 46	18 46	18 46	18 45	18 45	18 44	43	42	41	39	38	36
S 30	19 04	19 05	19 05	19 06	19 06	19 05	19 05	19 04	19 03	19 02	19 00	18 59	18 57	18 55	18 52	18 50	18 47
35	17	17	18	18	17	17	16	15	13	12	10	19 08	19 05	19 03	19 00	18 57	18 53
40	32	32	32	32	31	30	29	27	26	23	21	18	15	12	08	19 05	19 01
45	19 50	19 50	19 49	19 49	19 48	19 46	19 44	19 42	40	37	34	30	27	23	18	14	09
50	20 12	20 12	20 11	20 10	20 08	20 06	20 03	20 01	19 57	19 54	50	45	41	36	31	25	20
S 52	20 22	20 22	20 21	20 20	20 18	20 15	20 12	20 09	20 06	20 01	19 57	19 52	19 47	19 42	19 36	19 31	19 25
54	34	34	33	31	29	26	23	19	15	10	20 05	20 00	19 55	49	43	36	30
56	20 48	20 48	20 46	44	41	38	34	30	25	20	15	09	20 03	19 56	50	43	36
58	21 05	21 04	21 02	20 59	20 56	20 52	20 47	43	37	31	25	19	12	20 05	19 58	50	43
S 60	21 25	21 23	21 20	21 17	21 13	21 08	21 03	20 58	20 51	20 45	20 38	20 30	20 23	20 15	20 07	19 59	19 50

MORNING CIVIL TWILIGHT

A131

Lat.	Dec.	January										February					
	30	2	5	8	11	14	17	20	23	26	29	1	4	7	10	13	16
°	h m	h m	h m	h m	h m	h m	h m	h m	h m	h m	h m	h m	h m	h m	h m	h m	h m
N 72	10 49	10 40	10 31	10 20	10 09	09 57	09 45	09 32	09 20	09 07	08 54	08 40	08 27	08 13	08 00	07 46	07 32
70	09 52	09 48	09 43	09 37	09 30	09 22	09 13	09 03	08 54	08 43	33	21	08 10	07 59	07 47	35	23
68	09 19	09 16	09 12	09 08	09 02	08 56	08 49	08 42	34	25	16	08 07	07 57	47	36	26	15
66	08 54	08 52	08 50	08 46	08 42	37	31	25	18	08 10	08 03	07 54	46	37	27	18	08
64	35	33	31	29	25	21	16	08 11	08 05	07 58	07 51	44	36	28	20	11	07 02
62	19	18	16	14	08 11	08 08	08 03	07 59	07 54	48	42	35	28	21	13	06	06 57
N 60	08 06	08 05	08 04	08 02	07 59	07 56	07 53	07 49	07 44	07 39	07 33	07 27	07 21	07 15	07 08	07 00	06 53
58	07 55	07 54	07 53	07 51	49	46	43	40	36	31	26	21	15	09	07 03	06 56	49
56	44	44	43	42	40	38	35	32	28	24	19	15	09	07 04	06 58	52	45
54	36	35	35	34	32	30	28	25	21	18	14	09	07 04	06 59	54	48	42
52	27	28	27	26	25	23	21	18	15	12	08	07 04	06 59	55	50	45	39
N 50	07 20	07 20	07 20	07 19	07 18	07 17	07 15	07 12	07 10	07 07	07 03	06 59	06 55	06 51	06 46	06 41	06 36
45	07 04	07 05	07 05	07 04	07 04	07 03	07 01	06 59	06 57	06 55	06 52	49	46	42	38	34	30
40	06 51	06 52	06 52	06 52	06 51	06 51	06 50	48	47	45	43	40	38	35	32	28	24
35	39	40	41	41	41	40	40	39	38	36	35	33	30	28	25	23	20
30	29	30	30	31	31	31	31	30	29	28	27	25	24	22	20	17	15
N 20	06 10	06 11	06 12	06 13	06 14	06 14	06 14	06 14	06 14	06 14	06 13	06 13	06 12	06 11	06 09	06 08	06 06
N 10	05 53	05 54	05 55	05 57	05 57	05 58	05 59	06 00	06 00	06 01	06 01	06 01	06 00	06 00	06 00	05 59	05 58
0	36	38	39	40	42	43	44	05 45	05 46	05 47	05 48	05 48	05 49	05 49	05 49	50	50
S 10	05 18	20	22	23	25	27	28	30	31	33	34	35	37	38	39	39	40
20	04 58	05 00	05 02	05 04	05 06	05 08	05 10	05 12	05 14	05 17	19	20	22	24	26	28	29
S 30	04 33	04 35	04 38	04 40	04 43	04 45	04 48	04 51	04 54	04 57	05 00	05 02	05 05	05 08	05 11	05 13	05 16
35	18	21	23	26	29	32	35	38	41	45	04 48	04 51	04 55	04 58	05 01	05 05	05 08
40	04 00	04 03	04 06	04 09	04 12	04 15	19	23	27	30	34	38	42	46	04 50	04 54	04 58
45	03 38	03 41	03 44	03 47	03 51	03 55	04 00	04 04	04 09	04 13	04 18	23	28	32	37	42	46
50	03 09	03 12	16	20	24	29	03 34	03 40	03 45	03 51	03 57	04 03	09	15	20	26	32
S 52	02 54	02 57	03 01	03 06	03 11	03 16	03 22	03 28	03 34	03 40	03 47	03 53	04 00	04 06	04 12	04 19	04 25
54	36	40	02 45	02 50	02 55	03 01	03 08	03 14	21	28	35	42	03 49	03 56	04 03	10	17
56	02 14	02 19	02 24	30	36	02 43	02 50	02 58	03 06	03 14	22	29	37	45	03 53	04 01	04 09
58	01 46	01 51	01 57	02 04	02 12	02 21	29	38	02 47	02 56	03 05	03 15	24	33	41	03 50	03 59
S 60	00 59	01 08	01 17	01 27	01 39	01 50	02 01	02 13	02 24	02 35	02 46	02 57	03 27	03 18	03 28	03 37	03 47

EVENING CIVIL TWILIGHT

Lat.	Dec.	January										February					
	30	2	5	8	11	14	17	20	23	26	29	1	4	7	10	13	16
°	h m	h m	h m	h m	h m	h m	h m	h m	h m	h m	h m	h m	h m	h m	h m	h m	h m
N 72	13 17	13 27	13 40	13 53	14 07	14 21	14 36	14 50	15 05	15 19	15 34	15 48	16 02	16 16	16 30	16 44	16 58
70	14 13	14 19	14 27	14 36	14 46	14 57	15 08	15 19	31	15 43	15 55	16 07	19	31	43	16 55	17 07
68	14 47	14 52	14 58	15 05	15 13	15 22	31	41	15 50	16 01	16 11	21	32	43	16 54	17 04	15
66	15 11	15 15	15 21	27	34	41	15 49	15 58	16 06	15	24	34	43	16 53	17 02	12	22
64	30	34	39	44	15 50	15 57	16 04	16 12	19	27	36	44	16 52	17 01	10	18	27
62	46	15 49	15 54	15 59	16 04	16 10	17	23	30	38	45	16 53	17 01	08	16	24	32
N 60	15 59	16 02	16 06	16 11	16 16	16 22	16 27	16 34	16 40	16 47	16 53	17 00	17 08	17 15	17 22	17 29	17 36
58	16 11	14	17	22	26	31	37	42	48	16 54	17 01	07	14	20	27	34	40
56	21	24	27	31	36	41	45	51	16 56	17 02	07	13	19	25	31	38	44
54	30	33	36	40	44	48	16 53	16 58	17 03	08	13	19	24	30	36	41	47
52	38	41	44	47	51	16 55	17 00	17 04	09	14	19	24	29	34	39	45	50
N 50	16 45	16 48	16 51	16 54	16 58	17 02	17 06	17 10	17 15	17 19	17 24	17 28	17 33	17 38	17 43	17 48	17 53
45	17 01	17 03	17 06	17 09	17 12	16	19	23	27	31	34	38	42	47	51	17 55	17 59
40	14	17	19	22	24	27	30	34	37	40	44	47	51	17 54	17 57	18 01	18 04
35	26	28	30	32	35	38	41	43	46	49	17 52	17 55	17 58	18 01	18 03	06	09
30	36	38	40	17 42	17 45	17 47	17 50	17 52	17 55	17 57	18 00	18 02	18 04	07	09	11	14
N 20	17 55	17 56	17 58	18 00	18 02	18 04	18 06	18 08	18 10	18 11	18 13	18 15	18 16	18 18	18 19	18 21	18 22
N 10	18 12	18 13	18 15	16	18	19	21	22	23	25	26	27	28	28	29	30	30
0	29	30	32	33	34	35	36	37	37	38	38	39	39	39	39	39	39
S 10	18 47	18 48	18 49	18 50	18 51	18 51	18 52	18 52	18 52	18 52	18 52	18 52	18 51	18 51	18 50	18 49	48
20	19 07	19 08	19 09	19 09	19 09	19 10	19 10	19 09	19 09	19 08	19 07	19 06	19 05	19 04	19 02	19 00	18 59
S 30	19 32	19 32	19 33	19 33	19 33	19 32	19 31	19 30	19 29	19 28	19 26	19 24	19 22	19 20	19 17	19 15	19 12
35	19 46	19 47	19 47	19 47	19 47	19 46	19 45	43	42	40	38	35	33	30	27	23	20
40	20 03	20 05	20 05	20 04	20 03	20 02	20 00	19 59	19 56	19 54	19 51	19 48	45	41	37	33	29
45	27	27	26	25	24	22	20	20 17	20 14	20 11	20 07	20 04	19 59	19 55	19 50	19 46	41
50	20 56	20 55	20 54	20 53	20 51	20 48	45	41	37	33	28	23	20 18	20 12	20 07	20 01	19 55
S 52	21 11	21 10	21 08	21 06	21 04	21 00	20 57	20 53	20 48	20 43	20 38	20 33	20 27	20 21	20 15	20 08	20 02
54	28	27	25	22	19	15	21 11	21 06	21 01	20 56	20 50	43	37	30	23	16	09
56	21 50	21 48	21 45	21 42	21 38	33	28	22	16	21 10	21 03	20 56	20 49	41	33	26	18
58	22 18	22 16	22 12	22 07	22 01	21 55	21 49	21 42	34	26	19	21 10	21 02	20 54	45	36	28
S 60	23 04	22 58	22 51	22 43	22 34	22 25	22 16	22 06	21 57	21 47	21 38	21 28	21 18	21 08	20 58	20 49	20 39

A132

SUNRISE

Lat.	February					March										Apr.
	16	19	22	25	28	3	6	9	12	15	18	21	24	27	30	2
°	h m	h m	h m	h m	h m	h m	h m	h m	h m	h m	h m	h m	h m	h m	h m	h m
N 72	08 51	08 33	08 17	08 01	07 45	07 29	07 13	06 58	06 42	06 27	06 11	05 56	05 41	05 25	05 09	04 53
70	31	17	08 02	07 48	34	20	06	53	39	25	11	57	43	29	15	05 01
68	16	08 03	07 51	38	26	13	07 01	48	36	23	11	58	45	33	20	07
66	08 04	07 53	41	30	19	07	06 56	45	33	22	10	05 59	47	36	24	13
64	07 53	43	33	23	13	07 02	52	42	31	21	10	06 00	49	38	28	17
62	44	35	26	17	08	06 58	48	39	29	20	10	00	50	41	31	21
N 60	07 37	07 28	07 20	07 11	07 03	06 54	06 45	06 36	06 27	06 18	06 09	06 00	05 51	05 42	05 33	05 24
58	30	22	15	07	06 59	51	43	34	26	17	09	01	52	44	35	27
56	24	17	10	07 03	55	48	40	32	25	17	09	01	53	45	37	29
54	19	12	06	06 59	52	45	38	31	24	16	09	01	54	46	39	32
52	14	08	07 02	56	49	43	36	29	22	15	09	02	55	48	41	34
N 50	07 10	07 04	06 58	06 53	06 47	06 40	06 34	06 28	06 21	06 15	06 08	06 02	05 55	05 49	05 42	05 36
45	07 00	06 56	51	46	41	35	30	25	19	14	08	02	57	51	46	40
40	06 52	48	44	40	36	31	27	22	17	12	08	03	58	53	48	43
35	46	42	39	35	31	28	24	20	16	11	07	03	05 59	55	51	46
30	40	37	34	31	28	24	21	18	14	11	07	03	06 00	56	53	49
N 20	06 29	06 27	06 25	06 23	06 21	06 19	06 16	06 14	06 11	06 09	06 06	06 04	06 01	05 58	05 56	05 53
N 10	20	19	17	16	15	13	12	11	09	07	06	04	02	06 01	05 59	05 57
0	11	11	10	10	09	09	08	07	07	06	05	04	03	02	06 01	06 01
S 10	06 02	06 02	06 03	06 03	06 03	06 04	06 04	04	04	04	04	04	04	04	04	04
20	05 52	05 53	05 55	05 56	05 57	05 58	05 59	06 00	06 01	02	03	04	05	06	06	07
S 30	05 41	05 43	05 45	05 48	05 50	05 52	05 54	05 56	05 58	06 00	06 02	06 04	06 05	06 07	06 09	06 11
35	34	37	40	43	46	48	51	53	56	05 59	01	04	06	08	11	13
40	27	30	34	37	41	44	47	51	54	57	06 00	03	06	09	12	16
45	18	22	27	31	35	39	43	47	51	55	05 59	03	07	11	14	18
50	07	13	18	23	28	33	38	43	48	53	58	03	07	12	17	21
S 52	05 02	05 08	05 14	05 19	05 25	05 31	05 36	05 41	05 47	05 52	05 57	06 02	06 08	06 13	06 18	06 23
54	04 57	05 03	09	15	21	27	33	39	45	51	57	02	08	13	19	25
56	51	04 58	05 04	11	18	24	31	37	43	50	56	02	08	14	20	26
58	44	51	04 59	06	13	20	27	34	41	48	55	02	08	15	22	28
S 60	04 36	04 45	04 53	05 01	05 08	05 16	05 24	05 31	05 39	05 46	05 54	06 01	06 09	06 16	06 23	06 30

SUNSET

Lat.	February					March										Apr.
	16	19	22	25	28	3	6	9	12	15	18	21	24	27	30	2
°	h m	h m	h m	h m	h m	h m	h m	h m	h m	h m	h m	h m	h m	h m	h m	h m
N 72	15 39	15 56	16 12	16 28	16 43	16 57	17 12	17 26	17 40	17 54	18 08	18 22	18 35	18 49	19 03	19 17
70	15 59	16 13	27	40	16 53	17 06	19	31	44	56	08	20	32	45	18 57	09
68	16 14	26	38	50	17 01	13	24	35	46	57	08	19	30	41	52	19 03
66	26	37	47	16 58	08	19	29	39	49	17 59	08	18	28	38	47	18 57
64	36	46	16 56	17 05	14	23	33	42	51	18 00	09	17	26	35	44	53
62	45	16 54	17 02	11	19	28	36	44	52	01	09	17	25	33	41	49
N 60	16 52	17 00	17 08	17 16	17 24	17 31	17 39	17 46	17 54	18 01	18 09	18 16	18 23	18 30	18 38	18 45
58	16 59	06	13	20	27	34	41	48	55	02	09	15	22	29	35	42
56	17 05	12	18	25	31	37	44	50	56	03	09	15	21	27	33	39
54	10	16	22	28	34	40	46	52	57	03	09	14	20	26	31	37
52	15	21	26	32	37	42	48	53	17 58	04	09	14	19	24	30	35
N 50	17 19	17 24	17 29	17 35	17 40	17 45	17 50	17 55	18 00	18 04	18 09	18 14	18 19	18 23	18 28	18 33
45	29	33	37	41	45	49	54	17 58	01	05	09	13	17	21	25	28
40	36	40	43	47	50	53	17 57	18 00	03	06	09	12	16	19	22	25
35	43	46	49	52	54	17 57	18 00	02	05	07	10	12	14	17	19	22
30	17 49	17 52	17 54	17 56	17 58	18 00	02	04	06	08	10	12	14	15	17	19
N 20	18 00	18 01	18 02	18 03	18 05	18 06	18 07	18 08	18 09	18 10	18 10	18 11	18 12	18 13	18 14	18 14
N 10	09	09	10	10	10	11	11	11	11	11	11	11	11	11	11	10
0	18	17	17	17	16	15	15	14	13	12	11	11	10	09	08	07
S 10	26	25	24	23	22	20	19	17	16	14	12	10	09	07	05	03
20	36	34	32	30	28	26	23	21	18	16	13	10	08	05	03	18 00
S 30	18 47	18 44	18 41	18 38	18 35	18 32	18 28	18 25	18 21	18 18	18 14	18 10	18 07	18 03	18 00	17 56
35	18 53	50	47	43	39	35	31	27	23	19	15	11	06	02	17 58	54
40	19 01	18 57	18 53	48	44	39	35	30	25	20	16	11	06	01	56	51
45	09	19 05	19 00	18 55	49	44	39	33	28	22	17	11	05	18 00	54	49
50	20	14	08	19 02	56	50	44	37	31	24	18	11	05	17 58	52	45
S 52	19 25	19 18	19 12	19 06	18 59	18 53	18 46	18 39	18 32	18 25	18 18	18 11	18 04	17 57	17 51	17 44
54	30	23	16	10	19 03	55	48	41	34	26	19	11	04	57	49	42
56	36	29	21	14	06	18 59	51	43	35	27	19	12	04	56	48	40
58	43	35	27	19	11	19 02	54	46	37	29	20	12	03	55	46	38
S 60	19 50	19 42	19 33	19 24	19 15	19 06	18 57	18 48	18 39	18 30	18 21	18 12	18 03	17 54	17 45	17 36

MORNING CIVIL TWILIGHT

A133

Lat.	February					March										Apr.
	16	19	22	25	28	3	6	9	12	15	18	21	24	27	30	2
°	h m	h m	h m	h m	h m	h m	h m	h m	h m	h m	h m	h m	h m	h m	h m	h m
N 72	07 32	07 18	07 04	06 50	06 35	06 20	06 06	05 51	05 35	05 20	05 04	04 48	04 31	04 14	03 57	03 38
70	23	10	06 58	45	32	19	05	52	38	24	10	04 56	41	26	04 11	03 55
68	15	07 04	52	41	29	17	05	53	41	28	15	05 02	49	36	22	04 08
66	08	06 58	48	37	27	16	05	54	42	31	19	08	04 56	44	31	19
64	07 02	53	44	34	25	15	05	54	44	33	23	12	05 01	50	39	27
62	06 57	49	41	32	23	14	04	55	45	36	26	16	06	04 56	45	35
N 60	06 53	06 45	06 38	06 29	06 21	06 13	06 04	05 55	05 46	05 37	05 28	05 19	05 10	05 00	04 51	04 41
58	49	42	35	27	19	12	04	55	47	39	30	22	13	04	04 56	47
56	45	39	32	25	18	10	03	55	48	40	32	24	16	08	05 00	51
54	42	36	30	23	17	10	03	55	48	41	33	26	18	11	03	56
52	39	34	28	22	15	09	02	56	49	42	35	28	21	14	07	04 59
N 50	06 36	06 31	06 25	06 20	06 14	06 08	06 02	05 56	05 49	05 43	05 36	05 30	05 23	05 16	05 10	05 03
45	30	25	21	16	11	06	06 01	55	50	44	39	33	27	22	16	10
40	24	21	17	13	08	04	05 59	55	50	46	41	36	31	26	21	16
35	20	16	13	10	06	02	58	54	50	46	42	38	34	29	25	21
30	15	12	10	07	06 04	06 00	57	54	50	47	43	39	36	32	28	25
N 20	06 06	06 05	06 03	06 01	05 59	05 56	05 54	05 52	05 49	05 47	05 44	05 42	05 39	05 37	05 34	05 31
N 10	05 58	05 57	05 56	05 55	54	53	51	50	48	46	45	43	41	40	38	36
0	50	49	49	49	48	48	47	47	46	45	44	43	42	42	41	40
S 10	40	41	41	42	42	42	43	43	43	43	43	43	43	43	43	43
20	29	31	32	34	35	36	37	38	39	40	41	42	43	44	44	45
S 30	05 16	05 18	05 21	05 23	05 26	05 28	05 30	05 32	05 34	05 36	05 38	05 40	05 42	05 44	05 45	05 47
35	05 08	11	14	17	20	23	25	28	31	33	36	38	41	43	45	48
40	04 58	05 02	05 06	09	13	16	20	23	26	30	33	36	39	42	45	48
45	46	04 51	04 56	05 00	05 05	09	13	18	22	26	30	34	38	41	45	49
50	32	38	43	04 49	04 54	05 00	05	10	15	21	25	30	35	40	44	49
S 52	04 25	04 31	04 38	04 44	04 50	04 55	05 01	05 07	05 12	05 18	05 23	05 29	05 34	05 39	05 44	05 49
54	17	24	31	38	44	51	04 57	05 03	09	15	21	27	32	38	44	49
56	04 09	16	24	31	38	45	52	04 59	05	12	18	25	31	37	43	49
58	03 59	04 07	15	23	31	39	47	54	05 01	08	15	22	29	36	42	49
S 60	03 47	03 56	04 06	04 15	04 23	04 32	04 40	04 48	04 57	05 04	05 12	05 20	05 27	05 34	05 42	05 49

EVENING CIVIL TWILIGHT

Lat.	February					March										Apr.
	16	19	22	25	28	3	6	9	12	15	18	21	24	27	30	2
°	h m	h m	h m	h m	h m	h m	h m	h m	h m	h m	h m	h m	h m	h m	h m	h m
N 72	16 58	17 12	17 26	17 39	17 53	18 06	18 20	18 34	18 48	19 02	19 16	19 30	19 45	20 01	20 17	20 34
70	17 07	20	32	44	56	08	20	32	44	18 57	09	22	35	19 48	20 02	16
68	15	26	37	47	17 58	09	20	31	42	53	04	15	27	38	19 50	20 03
66	22	31	41	51	18 00	10	20	30	40	50	19 00	10	20	30	41	19 52
64	27	36	45	54	02	11	20	29	38	47	18 56	05	14	24	33	43
62	32	40	48	56	04	12	20	28	36	45	53	19 01	09	18	26	35
N 60	17 36	17 44	17 51	17 59	18 06	18 13	18 21	18 28	18 35	18 43	18 50	18 58	19 05	19 13	19 21	19 29
58	40	47	54	18 01	07	14	21	28	34	41	48	55	19 02	09	16	23
56	44	50	56	02	09	15	21	27	33	40	46	52	18 58	05	11	17
54	47	53	17 58	04	10	16	21	27	33	38	44	50	56	19 01	07	13
52	50	55	18 01	06	11	16	22	27	32	37	43	48	53	18 58	04	09
N 50	17 53	17 58	18 02	18 07	18 12	18 17	18 22	18 27	18 31	18 36	18 41	18 46	18 51	18 56	19 01	19 06
45	17 59	18 03	07	11	15	19	23	27	31	35	38	42	46	50	18 54	18 58
40	18 04	08	11	14	17	21	24	27	30	33	36	40	43	46	49	52
35	09	12	15	17	20	22	25	27	30	32	35	37	40	42	45	47
30	14	16	18	20	22	24	26	28	30	32	34	36	37	39	41	43
N 20	18 22	18 23	18 25	18 26	18 27	18 28	18 29	18 30	18 31	18 32	18 32	18 33	18 34	18 35	18 36	18 37
N 10	30	31	31	31	32	32	32	32	32	32	32	32	32	32	32	32
0	39	38	38	37	37	36	36	35	34	33	32	31	30	30	29	28
S 10	48	47	46	44	43	41	40	38	37	35	33	32	30	28	26	25
20	18 59	18 57	18 55	18 52	50	48	45	43	40	38	35	32	30	27	25	22
S 30	19 12	19 09	19 06	19 03	18 59	18 56	18 52	18 49	18 45	18 42	18 38	18 34	18 31	18 27	18 23	18 20
35	20	16	13	09	19 05	19 01	18 57	53	49	44	40	36	32	27	23	19
40	29	25	21	16	12	07	19 02	18 57	52	48	43	38	33	28	23	18
45	41	36	30	25	20	14	08	19 03	18 57	51	46	40	34	29	23	18
50	19 55	49	42	36	30	23	17	10	19 03	57	50	43	37	30	24	17
S 52	20 02	19 55	19 48	19 41	19 34	19 27	19 20	19 13	19 06	18 59	18 52	18 45	18 38	18 31	18 24	18 17
54	09	20 02	19 55	47	40	32	24	17	09	19 02	54	47	39	32	24	17
56	18	10	20 02	19 54	46	38	29	21	13	05	18 57	49	41	33	25	17
58	28	19	10	20 01	19 52	44	35	26	17	08	19 00	51	42	34	26	17
S 60	20 39	20 29	20 19	20 10	20 00	19 50	19 41	19 31	19 22	19 12	19 03	18 54	18 44	18 35	18 26	18 17

A134

SUNRISE

Lat.	April 2	April 5	April 8	April 11	April 14	April 17	April 20	April 23	April 26	April 29	May 2	May 5	May 8	May 11	May 14	May 17
°	h m	h m	h m	h m	h m	h m	h m	h m	h m	h m	h m	h m	h m	h m	h m	h m
N 72	04 53	04 38	04 21	04 05	03 48	03 30	03 12	02 54	02 34	02 12	01 48	01 19	00 36	▭	▭	▭
70	05 01	47	33	18	04 03	03 49	33	03 18	03 02	02 45	02 28	02 10	01 50	01 27	00 59	▭
68	07	04 55	42	29	16	04 03	03 50	36	23	03 09	02 55	02 41	02 26	02 11	01 55	01 38
66	13	05 01	49	38	26	14	04 03	03 51	39	27	03 16	03 04	02 52	02 40	02 28	02 16
64	17	06	04 56	45	35	24	13	04 03	03 52	42	32	22	03 12	03 02	02 52	02 42
62	21	11	05 01	52	42	32	23	13	04 04	03 54	45	36	27	19	03 11	03 02
N 60	05 24	05 15	05 06	04 57	04 48	04 39	04 30	04 22	04 13	04 05	03 57	03 49	03 41	03 33	03 26	03 19
58	27	18	10	05 02	53	45	37	29	22	14	04 07	03 59	03 52	45	39	33
56	29	22	14	06	04 58	51	43	36	29	22	15	04 08	04 02	03 56	03 50	44
54	32	24	17	10	05 03	04 56	49	42	35	29	23	17	11	04 05	04 00	03 55
52	34	27	20	13	07	05 00	54	47	41	35	29	24	18	13	08	04 04
N 50	05 36	05 29	05 23	05 17	05 10	05 04	04 58	04 52	04 47	04 41	04 36	04 30	04 25	04 21	04 16	04 12
45	40	34	29	23	18	13	05 08	05 03	04 58	04 53	04 49	44	40	36	33	29
40	43	39	34	29	25	20	16	11	05 07	05 03	05 00	04 56	04 52	04 49	46	43
35	46	42	38	34	30	26	22	19	15	12	09	05 06	05 03	05 00	04 58	04 55
30	49	45	42	38	35	32	28	25	22	19	17	14	12	10	05 08	05 06
N 20	05 53	05 51	05 48	05 46	05 43	05 41	05 38	05 36	05 34	05 32	05 30	05 29	05 27	05 26	05 25	05 23
N 10	05 57	05 55	54	52	50	49	47	46	45	44	43	42	41	40	39	39
0	06 01	06 00	05 59	05 58	05 57	05 56	05 56	05 55	05 55	05 54	05 54	05 53	05 53	05 53	05 53	05 53
S 10	04	04	06 04	06 04	06 04	06 04	06 04	06 04	06 04	06 04	06 05	06 05	06 05	06 06	06 06	06 07
20	07	08	09	09	10	11	12	13	14	15	16	17	18	19	20	22
S 30	06 11	06 13	06 14	06 16	06 18	06 20	06 22	06 24	06 25	06 27	06 29	06 31	06 33	06 35	06 37	06 39
35	13	16	18	20	23	25	27	30	32	34	37	39	41	44	46	06 48
40	16	19	22	25	28	30	33	36	39	42	45	48	06 51	06 54	06 57	07 00
45	18	22	26	29	33	37	41	44	48	06 52	06 55	06 59	07 02	07 06	07 09	13
50	21	26	31	35	40	45	49	54	06 58	07 03	07 07	07 12	16	20	25	29
S 52	06 23	06 28	06 33	06 38	06 43	06 48	06 53	06 58	07 03	07 08	07 13	07 18	07 23	07 27	07 32	07 36
54	25	30	36	41	46	52	06 57	07 03	08	14	19	24	29	35	40	44
56	26	32	38	44	50	06 56	07 02	08	14	20	26	32	37	43	48	07 54
58	28	35	41	48	54	07 01	08	14	21	27	33	40	46	07 52	07 58	08 04
S 60	06 30	06 37	06 45	06 52	06 59	07 06	07 13	07 21	07 28	07 35	07 42	07 49	07 56	08 03	08 10	08 16

SUNSET

Lat.	April 2	April 5	April 8	April 11	April 14	April 17	April 20	April 23	April 26	April 29	May 2	May 5	May 8	May 11	May 14	May 17
°	h m	h m	h m	h m	h m	h m	h m	h m	h m	h m	h m	h m	h m	h m	h m	h m
N 72	19 17	19 32	19 46	20 01	20 17	20 33	20 50	21 08	21 27	21 49	22 13	22 44	23 52	▭	▭	▭
70	09	22	35	19 48	20 01	14	28	20 43	20 58	21 14	21 31	21 49	22 09	22 33	23 04	▭
68	19 03	14	25	36	19 48	20 00	20 12	24	36	20 49	21 03	21 16	21 31	21 46	22 02	22 20
66	18 57	07	17	27	38	19 48	19 58	20 09	19	30	20 41	20 53	21 04	21 16	21 28	21 40
64	53	19 02	11	20	29	38	47	19 56	20 06	15	25	34	20 44	20 54	21 03	21 13
62	49	18 57	05	13	21	29	38	46	19 54	20 03	20 11	19	28	36	20 44	20 52
N 60	18 45	18 52	19 00	19 07	19 14	19 22	19 29	19 37	19 44	19 52	19 59	20 07	20 14	20 21	20 28	20 35
58	42	49	18 55	19 02	09	15	22	29	36	42	49	19 56	20 02	20 09	15	21
56	39	45	51	18 58	19 04	10	16	22	28	34	40	46	19 52	19 58	20 04	20 09
54	37	42	48	54	18 59	05	10	16	22	27	33	38	43	49	19 54	19 59
52	35	40	45	50	55	19 00	05	11	16	21	26	31	36	40	45	50
N 50	18 33	18 37	18 42	18 47	18 51	18 56	19 01	19 06	19 10	19 15	19 19	19 24	19 29	19 33	19 37	19 41
45	28	32	36	40	44	47	18 51	18 55	18 59	19 02	19 06	19 10	13	17	21	24
40	25	28	31	34	37	40	43	46	49	18 52	18 55	18 58	19 01	19 04	19 07	19 10
35	22	24	27	29	31	34	36	38	41	43	46	48	18 51	18 53	18 55	18 58
30	19	21	23	24	26	28	30	32	34	36	38	40	42	43	45	47
N 20	18 14	18 15	18 16	18 17	18 18	18 19	18 20	18 21	18 22	18 23	18 24	18 25	18 26	18 27	18 28	18 30
N 10	10	10	10	10	10	11	11	11	11	11	12	12	13	13	14	14
0	07	06	05	18 04	18 04	18 03	18 02	18 02	18 01	18 01	18 00	18 00	18 00	18 00	18 00	18 00
S 10	03	18 02	18 00	17 59	17 57	17 56	17 54	17 53	17 52	17 50	17 49	17 48	17 48	17 47	17 46	17 46
20	18 00	17 58	17 55	53	50	48	46	43	41	40	38	36	35	33	32	31
S 30	17 56	17 53	17 49	17 46	17 42	17 39	17 36	17 33	17 30	17 27	17 24	17 22	17 20	17 18	17 16	17 14
35	54	50	46	42	38	34	30	27	23	20	17	14	11	17 08	17 06	17 04
40	51	47	42	37	33	28	24	20	16	12	17 08	17 05	17 01	16 58	16 56	16 53
45	49	43	38	32	27	22	17	12	17 07	17 02	16 58	16 54	16 50	46	43	40
50	45	39	32	26	20	14	08	17 02	16 57	16 51	46	41	36	32	27	23
S 52	17 44	17 37	17 30	17 23	17 17	17 10	17 04	16 58	16 52	16 46	16 40	16 35	16 30	16 25	16 20	16 16
54	42	35	27	20	13	06	17 00	53	47	40	34	28	23	17	12	16 08
56	40	32	25	17	10	17 02	16 55	48	41	34	27	21	15	09	16 04	15 58
58	38	30	22	13	05	16 57	50	42	34	27	20	13	16 06	16 00	15 54	48
S 60	17 36	17 27	17 18	17 09	17 01	16 52	16 43	16 35	16 27	16 19	16 11	16 03	15 56	15 49	15 42	15 36

MORNING CIVIL TWILIGHT

Lat.	April 2	5	8	11	14	17	20	23	26	29	May 2	5	8	11	14	17
°	h m	h m	h m	h m	h m	h m	h m	h m	h m	h m	h m	h m	h m	h m	h m	h m
N 72	03 38	03 19	02 59	02 36	02 12	01 43	01 04	////	////	////	////	////	////	▭	▭	▭
70	03 55	39	03 21	03 04	02 45	02 24	02 01	01 35	01 00	////	////	////	////	////	////	////
68	04 08	03 54	39	24	03 08	02 51	34	02 15	01 55	01 31	01 01	////	////	////	////	////
66	19	04 06	03 53	40	26	03 12	02 58	02 43	02 27	02 10	01 52	01 32	01 08	00 33	////	////
64	27	16	04 04	03 52	41	28	03 16	03 03	02 50	37	02 23	02 08	01 53	01 37	01 18	00 57
62	35	24	14	04 03	03 52	41	30	19	03 08	02 57	02 45	34	02 22	02 10	01 57	01 45
N 60	04 41	04 32	04 22	04 12	04 02	03 53	03 43	03 33	03 23	03 13	03 03	02 54	02 44	02 34	02 24	02 14
58	47	38	29	20	11	04 02	03 53	44	36	27	18	03 09	03 01	02 53	02 44	36
56	51	43	35	27	19	10	04 02	03 54	46	38	30	23	15	03 08	03 01	02 54
54	56	48	40	33	25	18	10	04 03	03 55	48	41	34	28	21	15	03 09
52	04 59	52	45	38	31	24	17	10	04 04	03 57	51	44	38	32	27	21
N 50	05 03	04 56	04 50	04 43	04 36	04 30	04 23	04 17	04 11	04 05	03 59	03 53	03 48	03 42	03 37	03 32
45	10	05 05	04 59	04 53	48	42	37	31	26	21	04 16	04 12	04 07	04 03	03 59	03 55
40	16	11	05 06	05 01	04 57	04 52	47	43	39	34	30	26	23	19	04 16	04 13
35	21	17	12	08	05 04	05 00	04 56	04 52	49	45	42	38	35	32	30	27
30	25	21	18	14	10	07	05 04	05 00	04 57	04 54	04 51	04 49	04 46	04 44	04 42	04 39
N 20	05 31	05 29	05 26	05 23	05 21	05 18	05 16	05 14	05 12	05 09	05 07	05 06	05 04	05 02	05 01	05 00
N 10	36	34	32	31	29	27	26	24	23	22	21	20	19	18	17	16
0	40	39	38	37	36	35	34	34	33	33	32	32	31	31	31	31
S 10	43	43	43	42	42	42	42	42	42	43	43	43	43	44	44	44
20	45	46	47	47	48	49	50	51	05 51	05 52	05 53	05 54	05 55	05 56	05 57	05 58
S 30	05 47	05 49	05 51	05 52	05 54	05 56	05 57	05 59	06 01	06 03	06 04	06 06	06 08	06 10	06 11	06 13
35	48	50	52	55	05 57	05 59	06 01	06 04	06	08	10	13	15	17	19	21
40	48	51	54	05 57	06 00	06 03	06	09	11	14	17	20	23	25	28	30
45	49	52	56	06 00	03	07	11	14	18	21	25	28	31	34	38	41
50	49	54	58	03	07	12	16	20	25	29	33	37	41	45	49	53
S 52	05 49	05 54	05 59	06 04	06 09	06 14	06 18	06 23	06 28	06 32	06 37	06 41	06 46	06 50	06 54	06 58
54	49	55	06 00	05	11	16	21	26	31	36	41	46	51	06 55	07 00	07 04
56	49	55	01	07	12	18	24	29	35	40	46	51	06 56	07 01	06	11
58	49	55	02	08	14	21	27	33	39	45	51	06 56	07 02	08	13	18
S 60	05 49	05 56	06 03	06 10	06 17	06 23	06 30	06 37	06 43	06 50	06 56	07 03	07 09	07 15	07 21	07 26

EVENING CIVIL TWILIGHT

Lat.	April 2	5	8	11	14	17	20	23	26	29	May 2	5	8	11	14	17
°	h m	h m	h m	h m	h m	h m	h m	h m	h m	h m	h m	h m	h m	h m	h m	h m
N 72	20 34	20 52	21 11	21 32	21 57	22 27	23 11	////	////	////	////	////	////	▭	▭	▭
70	16	31	20 47	21 03	21 21	21 41	22 04	22 31	23 11	////	////	////	////	////	////	▭
68	20 03	16	29	20 43	20 57	21 12	21 29	21 47	22 07	22 32	23 05	////	////	////	////	////
66	19 52	20 03	14	26	38	20 51	21 04	21 18	21 33	21 50	22 07	22 28	22 54	23 41	////	////
64	43	19 53	20 03	13	23	34	20 45	20 57	21 09	22	21 35	21 49	22 04	22 21	22 40	23 05
62	35	44	19 53	20 02	11	20	30	40	20 50	21 01	21 12	23	21 34	21 46	21 59	22 12
N 60	19 29	19 36	19 44	19 52	20 01	20 09	20 18	20 26	20 35	20 44	20 53	21 03	21 12	21 22	21 31	21 41
58	23	30	37	44	19 52	19 59	20 07	15	22	30	38	20 46	20 54	21 02	21 10	18
56	17	24	31	37	44	51	19 57	20 04	11	18	25	32	39	20 47	20 53	21 00
54	13	19	25	31	37	43	49	19 56	20 02	20 08	14	21	27	33	39	20 45
52	09	15	20	25	31	37	42	48	19 53	19 59	20 05	10	16	22	27	32
N 50	19 06	19 10	19 15	19 20	19 26	19 31	19 36	19 41	19 46	19 51	19 56	20 01	20 07	20 12	20 16	20 21
45	18 58	19 02	19 06	10	14	18	22	26	30	35	39	19 43	19 47	19 51	19 55	19 58
40	52	18 56	18 59	19 02	19 05	08	11	15	18	21	25	28	31	34	37	41
35	47	50	52	18 55	18 57	19 00	19 02	19 05	19 08	10	13	16	18	21	23	26
30	43	45	47	49	51	18 53	18 55	18 57	18 59	19 01	19 03	19 05	19 07	19 09	19 11	19 13
N 20	18 37	18 37	18 38	18 39	18 40	18 41	18 42	18 43	18 44	18 46	18 47	18 48	18 49	18 51	18 52	18 53
N 10	32	32	32	32	32	32	32	32	33	33	33	34	35	35	36	37
0	28	27	26	25	25	24	23	23	23	22	22	22	22	22	22	22
S 10	25	23	21	20	18	17	16	14	13	12	11	18 10	18 09	18 09	18 08	18 08
20	22	19	17	15	12	10	08	18 06	18 04	18 02	18 00	17 59	17 57	17 56	17 55	17 54
S 30	18 20	18 16	18 13	18 10	18 06	18 03	18 00	17 57	17 54	17 52	17 49	17 47	17 45	17 43	17 41	17 39
35	19	15	11	07	03	18 00	17 56	53	49	46	43	40	38	35	33	31
40	18	14	09	04	18 00	17 56	51	48	44	40	37	33	30	27	24	22
45	18	12	07	18 02	17 56	52	47	42	37	33	29	25	21	18	15	12
50	17	11	05	17 59	53	47	41	36	30	25	20	16	11	07	17 03	17 00
S 52	18 17	18 11	18 04	17 57	17 51	17 45	17 39	17 33	17 27	17 22	17 16	17 11	17 07	17 02	16 58	16 54
54	17	10	03	56	49	43	36	30	24	18	12	07	17 01	16 57	52	48
56	17	10	02	55	47	40	33	26	20	14	07	17 02	16 56	51	46	41
58	17	09	01	53	45	38	30	23	16	09	17 02	16 56	50	44	39	34
S 60	18 17	18 09	18 00	17 51	17 43	17 35	17 27	17 19	17 11	17 04	16 57	16 50	16 43	16 37	16 31	16 26

A136

SUNRISE

Lat.	May					June										July
	17	20	23	26	29	1	4	7	10	13	16	19	22	25	28	1
°	h m	h m	h m	h m	h m	h m	h m	h m	h m	h m	h m	h m	h m	h m	h m	h m
N 72	▭	▭	▭	▭	▭	▭	▭	▭	▭	▭	▭	▭	▭	▭	▭	▭
70	▭	▭	▭	▭	▭	▭	▭	▭	▭	▭	▭	▭	▭	▭	▭	▭
68	01 38	01 20	00 58	00 25	▭	▭	▭	▭	▭	▭	▭	▭	▭	▭	▭	▭
66	02 16	02 04	01 52	01 39	01 27	01 14	01 01	00 47	00 31	▭	▭	▭	▭	▭	▭	00 13
64	02 42	33	02 24	02 15	02 07	01 59	01 52	01 45	01 40	01 36	01 33	01 31	01 31	01 32	01 35	01 40
62	03 02	02 55	02 47	02 40	34	02 28	02 23	02 18	02 14	02 12	02 10	02 09	02 09	02 10	02 13	02 16
N 60	03 19	03 12	03 06	03 00	02 55	02 50	02 46	02 42	02 39	02 37	02 36	02 36	02 36	02 37	02 39	02 42
58	33	27	21	16	03 12	03 08	03 04	03 01	02 59	02 57	02 56	02 56	02 56	02 57	02 59	03 01
56	44	39	34	30	26	23	20	17	03 15	03 14	03 13	03 13	03 13	03 14	03 16	18
54	03 55	03 50	46	42	38	35	33	30	29	28	27	27	27	28	30	32
52	04 04	04 00	03 56	03 52	49	46	44	42	41	40	39	39	40	41	42	44
N 50	04 12	04 08	04 05	04 02	03 59	03 56	03 54	03 52	03 51	03 50	03 50	03 50	03 51	03 51	03 53	03 54
45	29	26	23	21	04 19	04 17	04 15	04 14	04 13	04 13	04 13	04 13	04 13	04 14	04 15	04 17
40	43	41	39	37	35	33	32	31	31	30	30	31	31	32	33	34
35	04 55	04 53	04 51	04 50	04 48	47	46	46	45	45	45	46	46	04 47	04 48	04 49
30	05 06	05 04	05 03	05 01	05 00	04 59	04 59	04 58	04 58	04 58	04 58	04 59	04 59	05 00	05 01	05 02
N 20	05 23	05 22	05 22	05 21	05 20	05 20	05 20	05 20	05 20	05 20	05 20	05 21	05 22	05 22	05 23	05 24
N 10	39	38	38	38	38	38	38	38	38	39	39	40	40	41	42	05 43
0	05 53	05 53	05 53	05 53	05 54	05 54	05 55	05 55	05 56	05 56	05 57	05 57	05 58	05 59	05 59	06 00
S 10	06 07	06 07	06 08	06 09	06 10	06 10	06 11	06 12	06 13	06 13	06 14	06 15	06 16	06 16	06 17	17
20	22	23	24	25	26	28	29	30	31	32	33	33	34	35	35	35
S 30	06 39	06 40	06 42	06 44	06 46	06 47	06 49	06 50	06 52	06 53	06 54	06 55	06 55	06 56	06 56	06 56
35	06 48	06 51	06 53	06 55	06 57	06 59	07 01	07 02	07 04	07 05	07 06	07 07	07 08	07 08	07 09	07 08
40	07 00	07 02	07 05	07 07	07 10	07 12	14	16	17	19	20	21	22	22	23	23
45	13	16	19	22	25	27	30	32	34	36	37	38	07 39	07 39	07 39	39
50	29	33	36	40	43	46	49	07 52	07 54	07 56	07 58	07 59	08 00	08 00	08 00	07 59
S 52	07 36	07 40	07 45	07 48	07 52	07 55	07 59	08 01	08 04	08 06	08 08	08 09	08 10	08 10	08 10	08 09
54	44	49	07 54	07 58	08 02	08 06	08 09	12	15	17	19	20	21	21	21	20
56	07 54	07 59	08 04	08 08	13	17	21	24	27	29	31	33	33	34	33	33
58	08 04	08 10	16	21	26	30	34	38	41	08 44	08 46	08 47	08 48	08 48	08 48	08 47
S 60	08 16	08 23	08 29	08 35	08 40	08 46	08 50	08 54	08 58	09 01	09 03	09 05	09 06	09 06	09 05	09 04

SUNSET

Lat.	May					June										July
	17	20	23	26	29	1	4	7	10	13	16	19	22	25	28	1
°	h m	h m	h m	h m	h m	h m	h m	h m	h m	h m	h m	h m	h m	h m	h m	h m
N 72	▭	▭	▭	▭	▭	▭	▭	▭	▭	▭	▭	▭	▭	▭	▭	▭
70	▭	▭	▭	▭	▭	▭	▭	▭	▭	▭	▭	▭	▭	▭	▭	▭
68	22 20	22 39	23 03	▭	▭	▭	▭	▭	▭	▭	▭	▭	▭	▭	▭	▭
66	21 40	21 52	22 05	22 18	22 31	22 45	22 59	23 15	23 33	▭	▭	▭	▭	▭	▭	23 44
64	21 13	22	21 32	21-41	21 50	21 58	22 06	22 14	22 20	22 25	22 29	22 32	22 32	22 32	22 29	22 26
62	20 52	21 00	21 08	21 15	22	29	21 35	21 40	21 45	21 49	21 51	21 53	21 54	21 54	21 53	21 50
N 60	20 35	20 42	20 49	20 55	21 01	21 07	21 12	21 16	21 20	21 23	21 25	21 27	21 28	21 28	21 27	21 25
58	21	27	33	39	20 44	20 49	20 53	20 57	21 00	21 03	21 05	21 06	21 07	21 07	21 07	21 05
56	20 09	15	20	25	29	34	38	41	20 44	20 46	20 48	20 50	20 50	20 51	20 50	20 49
54	19 59	20 04	20 08	13	17	21	24	27	30	32	34	35	36	36	36	35
52	50	19 54	19 58	20 02	20 06	10	13	16	18	20	22	23	24	24	24	23
N 50	19 41	19 45	19 49	19 53	19 57	20 00	20 03	20 05	20 08	20 10	20 11	20 12	20 13	20 13	20 13	20 12
45	24	27	30	33	36	19 39	19 41	19 44	19 46	19 47	19 49	19 50	19 50	19 51	19 51	19 50
40	19 10	12	15	18	20	22	24	26	28	29	31	32	32	33	33	33
35	18 58	19 00	19 02	19 04	19 06	19 08	19 10	19 12	13	15	16	17	17	18	18	18
30	47	18 49	18 51	18 53	18 55	18 56	18 58	18 59	19 00	19 02	19 03	19 03	19 04	19 05	19 05	19 05
N 20	18 30	18 31	18 32	18 33	18 34	18 36	18 37	18 38	18 39	18 40	18 41	18 41	18 42	18 43	18 43	18 43
N 10	14	15	16	16	17	18	19	19	20	21	22	22	23	24	24	25
0	18 00	18 00	18 00	18 01	18 01	18 01	18 02	18 02	18 03	18 03	18 04	18 05	18 05	18 06	18 07	18 07
S 10	17 46	17 45	17 45	17 45	17 45	17 45	17 45	17 46	17 46	17 46	17 47	17 47	17 48	17 49	17 49	17 50
20	31	30	29	28	28	28	28	28	28	28	28	29	30	30	31	32
S 30	17 14	17 12	17 11	17 10	17 09	17 08	17 07	17 07	17 07	17 07	17 07	17 08	17 08	17 09	17 10	17 11
35	17 04	17 02	17 00	16 59	16 57	16 56	16 56	16 55	16 55	16 55	16 55	16 55	16 56	16 57	16 58	16 59
40	16 53	16 50	16 48	46	45	43	42	41	41	41	41	41	42	42	44	45
45	40	37	34	32	30	28	27	25	25	24	24	24	25	26	27	28
50	23	20	17	14	11	09	16 07	16 05	16 04	16 04	16 03	16 03	16 04	16 05	16 06	16 08
S 52	16 16	16 12	16 08	16 05	16 02	16 00	15 57	15 56	15 55	15 54	15 53	15 53	15 54	15 55	15 56	15 58
54	16 08	16 03	15 59	15 56	15 52	15 49	47	45	44	43	42	42	43	44	45	47
56	15 58	15 53	49	45	41	38	35	33	31	30	30	30	30	31	33	35
58	48	42	37	33	29	25	22	19	17	15 16	15 15	15 15	15 16	15 17	18	21
S 60	15 36	15 29	15 24	15 18	15 14	15 09	15 06	15 03	15 00	14 59	14 58	14 57	14 58	14 59	15 01	15 04

MORNING CIVIL TWILIGHT A137

Lat.	May					June										July
	17	20	23	26	29	1	4	7	10	13	16	19	22	25	28	1
°	h m	h m	h m	h m	h m	h m	h m	h m	h m	h m	h m	h m	h m	h m	h m	h m
N 72	▭	▭	▭	▭	▭	▭	▭	▭	▭	▭	▭	▭	▭	▭	▭	▭
70	////	▭	▭	▭	▭	▭	▭	▭	▭	▭	▭	▭	▭	▭	▭	▭
68	////	////	////	////	▭	▭	▭	▭	▭	▭	▭	▭	▭	▭	▭	▭
66	////	////	////	////	////	////	////	////	////	▭	▭	▭	▭	▭	▭	////
64	00 57	00 23	////	////	////	////	////	////	////	////	////	////	////	////	////	////
62	01 45	01 31	01 17	01 01	00 42	00 10	////	////	////	////	////	////	////	////	////	////
N 60	02 14	02 05	01 55	01 45	01 36	01 27	01 19	01 11	01 03	00 57	00 52	00 49	00 49	00 51	00 55	01 02
58	36	29	02 21	02 14	02 07	02 01	01 55	01 50	01 46	01 43	01 41	01 40	01 40	01 42	01 44	01 48
56	02 54	02 47	41	35	30	25	02 21	02 17	02 14	02 12	02 11	02 10	02 10	02 12	02 14	02 16
54	03 09	03 03	02 58	02 53	02 48	02 44	41	38	36	34	33	32	33	34	36	38
52	21	16	03 12	03 07	03 03	03 00	02 57	02 55	02 53	02 51	02 51	02 50	02 51	02 52	02 53	02 56
N 50	03 32	03 28	03 24	03 20	03 17	03 13	03 11	03 09	03 07	03 06	03 06	03 06	03 06	03 07	03 08	03 10
45	03 55	03 51	03 48	03 45	03 43	03 41	03 39	37	36	35	35	35	36	37	03 38	03 39
40	04 13	04 10	04 07	04 05	04 03	04 01	04 00	03 59	03 58	03 58	03 58	03 58	03 58	03 59	04 00	04 02
35	27	25	23	21	19	18	17	04 16	04 16	04 16	04 16	04 16	04 17	04 17	18	20
30	04 39	38	36	35	33	32	32	31	31	31	31	31	32	33	34	35
N 20	05 00	04 59	04 58	04 57	04 56	04 56	04 55	04 55	04 55	04 55	04 56	04 56	04 57	04 58	04 59	04 59
N 10	16	05 16	05 15	05 15	05 15	05 15	05 15	05 15	05 15	05 16	05 16	05 17	05 17	05 18	05 19	05 20
0	31	31	31	31	31	32	32	33	33	34	34	35	36	36	37	38
S 10	44	45	05 46	05 46	05 47	05 48	05 48	05 49	05 50	05 51	05 51	05 52	05 53	05 53	05 54	05 54
20	05 58	05 59	06 01	06 02	06 03	06 04	06 05	06 06	06 07	06 08	06 09	06 09	06 10	06 11	06 11	06 11
S 30	06 13	06 15	06 17	06 18	06 20	06 21	06 23	06 24	06 25	06 26	06 27	06 28	06 29	06 30	06 30	06 30
35	21	23	25	27	29	31	33	34	36	37	38	39	40	40	40	41
40	30	33	35	38	40	42	44	46	06 47	06 48	06 50	06 51	06 51	06 52	06 52	06 52
45	41	44	06 47	06 49	06 52	06 54	06 57	06 59	07 00	07 02	07 03	07 04	07 05	07 05	07 06	07 05
50	53	06 56	07 00	07 03	07 06	07 09	07 11	07 14	16	18	19	20	21	21	21	21
S 52	06 58	07 02	07 06	07 09	07 13	07 16	07 19	07 21	07 23	07 25	07 27	07 28	07 29	07 29	07 29	07 29
54	07 04	08	13	16	20	23	26	29	31	33	35	36	37	37	37	37
56	11	15	20	24	28	31	35	37	40	42	44	45	46	46	46	46
58	18	23	28	32	37	41	44	47	07 50	07 52	07 54	07 55	07 56	07 57	07 56	07 56
S 60	07 26	07 32	07 37	07 42	07 47	07 51	07 55	07 58	08 01	08 04	08 06	08 07	08 08	08 08	08 08	08 07

EVENING CIVIL TWILIGHT

Lat.	May					June										July
	17	20	23	26	29	1	4	7	10	13	16	19	22	25	28	1
°	h m	h m	h m	h m	h m	h m	h m	h m	h m	h m	h m	h m	h m	h m	h m	h m
N 72	▭	▭	▭	▭	▭	▭	▭	▭	▭	▭	▭	▭	▭	▭	▭	▭
70	▭	▭	▭	▭	▭	▭	▭	▭	▭	▭	▭	▭	▭	▭	▭	▭
68	////	////	////	▭	▭	▭	▭	▭	▭	▭	▭	▭	▭	▭	▭	▭
66	////	////	////	////	////	////	////	////	////	▭	▭	▭	▭	▭	▭	////
64	23 05	////	////	////	////	////	////	////	////	////	////	////	////	////	////	////
62	22 12	22 26	22 41	22 58	23 20	////	////	////	////	////	////	////	////	////	////	////
N 60	21 41	21 51	22 01	22 11	22 21	22 31	22 40	22 49	22 57	23 04	23 10	23 13	23 14	23 13	23 09	23 03
58	18	26	21 34	21 42	21 49	21 56	22 02	22 08	22 13	22 17	22 20	22 22	22 23	22 23	22 21	22 19
56	21 00	21 07	21 14	20	26	32	21 37	21 41	21 45	21 48	21 51	21 52	21 53	21 53	21 52	21 50
54	20 45	20 51	20 57	21 02	21 07	21 12	17	20	24	26	29	30	31	31	30	29
52	32	38	43	20 47	20 52	20 56	21 00	21 03	21 06	21 09	21 11	21 12	21 13	21 13	21 12	21 11
N 50	20 21	20 26	20 30	20 35	20 39	20 43	20 46	20 49	20 52	20 54	20 56	20 57	20 58	20 58	20 57	20 57
45	19 58	20 02	20 06	20 09	20 12	20 15	20 18	20 21	23	25	26	27	28	28	28	28
40	41	19 44	19 46	19 49	19 52	19 54	19 57	19 59	20 01	20 02	20 03	20 04	20 05	20 06	20 06	20 05
35	26	28	31	33	35	38	39	41	19 43	19 44	19 45	19 46	19 47	19 47	19 48	19 47
30	19 13	19 16	19 18	19 20	19 21	23	25	26	28	29	30	31	32	32	32	32
N 20	18 53	18 55	18 56	18 57	18 59	19 00	19 01	19 02	19 03	19 04	19 05	19 06	19 07	19 07	19 08	19 08
N 10	37	37	38	39	40	18 41	18 41	18 42	18 43	18 44	18 45	18 45	18 46	18 47	18 47	18 48
0	22	22	22	23	23	24	24	25	25	26	27	27	28	29	29	30
S 10	18 08	18 08	18 07	18 07	18 07	18 08	18 08	18 08	18 09	18 09	18 10	18 10	18 11	18 11	18 12	18 13
20	17 54	17 53	17 53	17 52	17 52	17 51	17 51	17 51	17 52	17 52	17 52	17 53	17 53	17 54	17 55	17 56
S 30	17 39	17 38	17 37	17 35	17 35	17 34	17 33	17 33	17 33	17 33	17 34	17 34	17 35	17 35	17 36	17 37
35	31	29	28	26	25	24	24	23	23	23	23	23	24	25	26	27
40	22	20	18	16	15	13	12	17 12	17 11	17 11	17 11	17 12	17 12	17 13	14	15
45	12	17 09	17 06	17 04	17 02	17 01	17 00	16 59	16 58	16 58	16 58	16 58	16 59	16 59	17 01	17 02
50	17 00	16 56	16 53	16 51	16 48	16 46	16 45	43	42	42	42	42	43	44	16 45	16 46
S 52	16 54	16 50	16 47	16 44	16 42	16 39	16 38	16 36	16 35	16 35	16 34	16 34	16 35	16 36	16 37	16 39
54	48	44	40	37	34	32	30	28	27	26	26	26	27	28	29	31
56	41	37	33	30	26	24	21	20	18	17	17	17	18	19	20	22
58	34	29	25	21	17	14	12	16 10	16 08	16 07	16 07	16 07	16 07	16 09	16 10	12
S 60	16 26	16 20	16 16	16 11	16 07	16 04	16 01	15 59	15 57	15 56	15 55	15 55	15 56	15 57	15 58	16 01

A138

SUNRISE

Lat.	June	July											August				
	28	1	4	7	10	13	16	19	22	25	28	31	3	6	9	12	15
°	h m	h m	h m	h m	h m	h m	h m	h m	h m	h m	h m	h m	h m	h m	h m	h m	h m
N 72	▭	▭	▭	▭	▭	▭	▭	▭	▭	▭	▭	▭	▭	00 49	01 30	01 58	02 21
70	▭	▭	▭	▭	▭	▭	▭	▭	▭	▭	00 21	01 11	01 39	02 01	02 20	02 37	02 54
68	▭	▭	▭	▭	▭	▭	▭	00 39	01 10	01 32	01 50	02 07	02 22	02 37	02 51	03 04	03 17
66	▭	00 13	00 38	00 55	01 10	01 24	01 37	01 50	02 03	02 15	02 27	02 39	02 51	03 03	03 14	25	36
64	01 35	01 40	01 46	01 52	02 00	02 08	02 17	02 26	35	02 44	02 54	03 03	03 13	22	32	41	03 50
62	02 13	02 16	02 20	02 25	31	37	02 44	02 51	02 58	03 06	03 14	22	30	38	46	03 54	04 02
N 60	02 39	02 42	02 45	02 49	02 54	02 59	03 04	03 10	03 17	03 23	03 30	03 37	03 44	03 51	03 58	04 06	04 13
58	02 59	03 01	03 04	03 08	03 12	03 16	21	26	32	38	44	03 50	03 56	04 02	04 09	15	22
56	03 16	18	20	23	27	31	35	40	45	03 50	03 55	04 01	04 06	12	18	24	30
54	30	32	34	37	40	44	48	03 52	03 56	04 01	04 06	11	16	21	26	31	37
52	42	44	46	49	03 52	03 55	03 58	04 02	04 06	10	15	19	24	29	33	38	43
N 50	03 53	03 54	03 57	03 59	04 02	04 05	04 08	04 11	04 15	04 19	04 23	04 27	04 31	04 35	04 40	04 44	04 49
45	04 15	04 17	04 18	04 20	23	25	28	31	34	37	40	43	47	04 50	04 54	04 57	05 01
40	33	34	36	38	40	42	44	46	04 49	04 51	04 54	04 57	04 59	05 02	05 05	05 08	11
35	04 48	04 49	04 51	04 52	04 54	04 56	04 57	04 59	05 01	05 04	05 06	05 08	05 10	13	15	17	19
30	05 01	05 02	05 03	05 05	05 06	05 08	05 09	05 11	13	14	16	18	20	22	23	25	27
N 20	05 23	05 24	05 25	05 26	05 27	05 28	05 29	05 30	05 31	05 33	05 34	05 35	05 36	05 37	05 38	05 39	05 40
N 10	42	05 43	05 43	05 44	05 45	05 46	05 46	05 47	05 48	05 48	05 49	05 49	05 50	05 50	05 50	05 51	05 51
0	05 59	06 00	06 01	06 01	06 02	06 02	06 02	06 02	06 03	06 03	06 03	06 03	06 03	06 02	06 02	06 02	06 01
S 10	06 17	17	18	18	18	18	18	18	18	17	17	16	15	15	14	12	11
20	35	35	36	36	36	35	35	34	34	33	32	30	29	27	26	24	22
S 30	06 56	06 56	06 56	06 56	06 56	06 55	06 54	06 53	06 52	06 50	06 48	06 46	06 44	06 42	06 40	06 37	06 34
35	07 09	07 08	07 08	07 08	07 07	07 06	07 05	07 04	07 02	07 00	06 58	06 56	06 53	06 50	47	44	41
40	23	23	22	22	21	19	18	16	14	12	07 09	07 06	07 03	07 00	06 56	06 53	49
45	07 39	39	39	38	36	35	33	31	28	25	22	19	15	11	07 07	07 03	06 58
50	08 00	07 59	07 59	07 57	07 56	07 54	07 51	48	45	42	38	34	29	25	20	14	07 09
S 52	08 10	08 09	08 08	08 07	08 05	08 03	08 00	07 57	07 53	07 49	07 45	07 41	07 36	07 31	07 25	07 20	07 14
54	21	20	19	17	15	13	09	08 06	08 02	07 58	07 53	48	43	38	32	26	20
56	33	33	31	29	27	24	20	16	12	08 07	08 02	07 57	07 51	45	39	33	26
58	08 48	08 47	08 45	43	40	37	33	28	24	18	13	08 07	08 01	07 54	47	40	33
S 60	09 05	09 04	09 02	08 59	08 56	08 52	08 48	08 43	08 37	08 31	08 25	08 18	08 11	08 04	07 56	07 49	07 41

SUNSET

Lat.	June	July											August				
	28	1	4	7	10	13	16	19	22	25	28	31	3	6	9	12	15
°	h m	h m	h m	h m	h m	h m	h m	h m	h m	h m	h m	h m	h m	h m	h m	h m	h m
N 72	▭	▭	▭	▭	▭	▭	▭	▭	▭	▭	▭	▭	▭	23 08	22 33	22 06	21 43
70	▭	▭	▭	▭	▭	▭	▭	▭	▭	▭	23 29	22 52	22 27	22 06	21 46	21 29	21 12
68	▭	▭	▭	▭	▭	▭	▭	23 22	22 56	22 35	22 18	22 01	21 46	21 31	21 17	21 03	20 49
66	▭	23 44	23 25	23 10	22 56	22 43	22 31	22 18	22 06	21 54	21 42	21 30	21 18	21 07	20 55	20 43	31
64	22 29	22 26	22 21	22 15	22 08	22 01	21 53	21 44	21 36	26	21 17	21 07	20 57	20 47	37	27	17
62	21 53	21 50	21 47	21 43	21 38	21 33	27	20	21 13	21 05	20 57	20 49	41	32	23	14	20 05
N 60	21 27	21 25	21 23	21 20	21 16	21 11	21 06	21 01	20 55	20 48	20 41	20 34	20 27	20 19	20 11	20 03	19 55
58	21 07	21 05	21 03	21 01	20 58	20 54	20 50	20 45	39	34	28	21	15	20 08	20 01	19 53	46
56	20 50	20 49	20 47	20 45	43	39	36	31	27	22	16	10	20 04	19 58	19 52	45	38
54	36	35	34	32	30	27	23	20	15	11	20 06	20 01	19 55	50	44	38	31
52	24	23	22	20	18	16	13	09	20 06	20 02	19 57	19 52	47	42	37	31	25
N 50	20 13	20 12	20 11	20 10	20 08	20 06	20 03	20 00	19 57	19 53	19 49	19 45	19 40	19 35	19 30	19 25	19 19
45	19 51	19 50	19 50	19 49	19 47	19 46	19 43	19 41	38	35	32	29	25	21	17	12	19 07
40	33	33	32	32	30	29	27	26	23	21	18	15	12	19 09	19 05	19 01	18 57
35	18	18	18	17	16	15	14	13	11	19 09	19 07	19 04	19 02	18 59	18 56	18 52	49
30	19 05	19 05	19 05	19 05	19 04	19 03	19 02	19 01	19 00	18 58	18 56	18 54	18 52	50	47	44	42
N 20	18 43	18 43	18 43	18 43	18 43	18 43	18 43	18 42	18 41	18 40	18 39	18 38	18 36	18 35	18 33	18 31	18 29
N 10	24	25	25	25	26	26	26	25	25	24	24	23	22	21	20	19	18
0	18 07	18 07	18 08	18 08	18 09	18 09	18 10	18 10	18 10	18 10	18 10	18 10	18 10	18 09	18 09	18 08	18 08
S 10	17 49	17 50	17 51	17 52	17 52	17 53	17 54	17 54	17 55	17 56	17 56	17 56	17 57	17 57	17 58	17 58	17 58
20	31	32	33	34	35	36	37	38	39	40	41	43	44	45	45	46	47
S 30	17 10	17 11	17 12	17 14	17 15	17 16	17 18	17 20	17 21	17 23	17 25	17 27	17 29	17 30	17 32	17 34	17 35
35	16 58	16 59	17 00	17 02	17 03	17 05	17 07	17 09	17 11	13	15	17	20	22	24	26	28
40	44	45	16 46	16 48	16 50	16 52	16 54	16 57	16 59	17 02	17 04	17 07	17 10	12	15	18	21
45	27	28	30	32	34	37	39	42	45	16 48	16 51	16 55	16 58	17 01	17 05	17 08	12
50	16 06	16 08	10	13	15	18	21	25	28	32	36	40	44	16 48	16 52	16 56	17 01
S 52	15 56	15 58	16 00	16 03	16 06	16 09	16 12	16 16	16 20	16 24	16 28	16 33	16 37	16 42	16 46	16 51	16 56
54	45	47	15 50	15 52	15 56	15 59	16 03	16 07	11	15	20	25	30	35	40	45	50
56	33	35	38	41	44	48	15 52	15 56	16 01	16 06	11	16	22	27	33	38	44
58	18	21	23	27	31	35	39	44	15 50	15 55	16 01	16 07	12	18	25	31	37
S 60	15 01	15 04	15 07	15 10	15 15	15 20	15 25	15 30	15 36	15 42	15 49	15 55	16 02	16 09	16 15	16 22	16 29

MORNING CIVIL TWILIGHT

A139

Lat.	June 28	July 1	July 4	July 7	July 10	July 13	July 16	July 19	July 22	July 25	July 28	July 31	August 3	August 6	August 9	August 12	August 15
°	h m	h m	h m	h m	h m	h m	h m	h m	h m	h m	h m	h m	h m	h m	h m	h m	h m
N 72	▭	▭	▭	▭	▭	▭	▭	▭	▭	▭	▭	▭	▭	////	////	////	////
70	▭	▭	▭	▭	▭	▭	▭	▭	▭	▭	////	////	////	////	////	////	////
68	▭	▭	▭	▭	▭	▭	▭	////	////	////	////	////	////	////	////	01 10	01 39
66	▭	////	////	////	////	////	////	////	////	////	////	////	00 45	01 19	01 42	02 01	02 18
64	////	////	////	////	////	////	////	////	////	00 36	01 08	01 30	01 48	02 04	02 18	32	02 45
62	////	////	////	////	////	00 24	00 53	01 12	01 28	01 43	01 56	02 09	02 21	32	02 44	02 54	03 05
N 60	00 55	01 02	01 09	01 18	01 27	01 36	01 46	01 56	02 06	02 16	02 25	02 35	02 45	02 54	03 03	03 12	03 21
58	01 44	01 48	01 52	01 57	02 03	02 10	02 17	02 24	32	39	02 47	02 55	03 03	03 11	19	27	35
56	02 14	02 16	02 20	02 24	29	34	39	02 45	02 52	02 58	03 05	03 12	19	25	32	39	46
54	36	38	41	02 44	02 48	02 53	02 58	03 03	03 08	03 14	20	26	32	38	44	50	03 56
52	02 53	02 56	02 58	03 01	03 05	03 09	03 13	17	22	27	32	37	43	48	03 54	03 59	04 05
N 50	03 08	03 10	03 13	03 15	03 19	03 22	03 26	03 30	03 34	03 39	03 43	03 48	03 53	03 58	04 03	04 08	04 13
45	03 38	03 39	03 41	03 44	03 46	03 49	03 52	03 55	03 59	04 02	04 06	04 09	04 13	04 17	21	25	29
40	04 00	04 02	04 03	04 05	04 07	04 10	04 12	04 15	04 17	20	23	26	29	32	36	39	42
35	18	20	21	23	25	26	29	31	33	35	38	40	43	45	48	04 50	04 53
30	34	35	04 36	04 37	04 39	04 41	04 42	04 44	04 46	04 48	04 50	04 52	04 54	04 56	04 58	05 00	05 02
N 20	04 59	04 59	05 00	05 01	05 03	05 04	05 05	05 06	05 08	05 09	05 10	05 11	05 12	05 14	05 15	05 16	05 17
N 10	05 19	05 20	20	21	22	23	24	24	25	26	27	27	28	28	28	29	29
0	37	38	38	39	39	40	40	40	41	41	41	41	41	41	41	40	40
S 10	05 54	05 54	05 55	05 55	05 55	05 56	05 56	05 56	05 55	05 55	05 55	05 54	05 53	05 53	05 52	05 51	50
20	06 11	06 11	06 12	06 12	06 12	06 12	06 11	06 11	06 10	06 09	06 08	06 07	06 06	06 04	06 03	06 01	05 59
S 30	06 30	06 30	06 30	06 30	06 30	06 29	06 28	06 27	06 26	06 25	06 23	06 21	06 19	06 17	06 15	06 12	06 09
35	40	41	40	40	39	39	38	36	35	33	31	29	26	24	21	18	15
40	06 52	06 52	06 52	06 51	06 50	06 49	06 48	46	45	42	40	37	34	31	28	25	21
45	07 06	07 05	07 05	07 04	07 03	07 02	07 00	06 58	06 56	06 53	06 50	47	43	40	36	32	27
50	21	21	21	19	18	16	14	07 12	07 09	07 05	07 02	06 58	54	50	45	40	35
S 52	07 29	07 29	07 28	07 27	07 25	07 23	07 21	07 18	07 15	07 11	07 07	07 03	06 59	06 54	06 49	06 44	06 39
54	37	37	36	34	32	30	28	25	21	17	13	09	07 04	06 59	54	48	42
56	46	46	44	43	41	38	36	32	28	24	20	15	10	07 04	06 59	53	47
58	07 56	07 56	07 54	07 53	07 50	48	44	41	36	32	27	22	16	10	07 04	06 58	51
S 60	08 08	08 07	08 06	08 04	08 01	07 58	07 54	07 50	07 45	07 41	07 35	07 29	07 23	07 17	07 10	07 03	06 56

EVENING CIVIL TWILIGHT

Lat.	June 28	July 1	July 4	July 7	July 10	July 13	July 16	July 19	July 22	July 25	July 28	July 31	August 3	August 6	August 9	August 12	August 15
°	h m	h m	h m	h m	h m	h m	h m	h m	h m	h m	h m	h m	h m	h m	h m	h m	h m
N 72	▭	▭	▭	▭	▭	▭	▭	▭	▭	▭	▭	▭	▭	////	////	////	////
70	▭	▭	▭	▭	▭	▭	▭	▭	▭	▭	////	////	////	////	////	////	23 51
68	▭	▭	▭	▭	▭	▭	▭	////	////	////	////	////	////	////	23 32	22 50	22 23
66	▭	////	////	////	////	////	////	////	////	////	////	////	23 15	22 46	22 23	22 04	21 47
64	////	////	////	////	////	////	////	////	////	23 24	22 57	22 37	22 20	22 04	21 49	21 35	21
62	////	////	////	////	////	23 36	23 12	22 55	22 40	22 26	22 13	22 01	21 48	21 36	25	21 13	21 02
N 60	23 09	23 03	22 57	22 49	22 41	22 32	22 23	22 14	22 04	21 55	21 45	21 35	21 25	21 16	21 06	20 56	20 46
58	22 21	22 19	22 15	22 11	22 05	22 00	21 53	21 46	21 39	31	23	21 15	21 07	20 59	20 50	42	33
56	21 52	21 50	21 48	21 44	21 41	21 36	31	25	19	21 13	21 06	20 59	20 52	45	37	29	21
54	30	29	27	24	21	17	21 13	21 08	21 03	20 58	20 52	46	39	33	26	19	11
52	21 12	21 11	21 10	21 08	21 05	21 02	20 58	20 54	20 49	45	39	34	28	22	16	10	20 03
N 50	20 57	20 57	20 55	20 53	20 51	20 48	20 45	20 42	20 38	20 33	20 29	20 24	20 18	20 13	20 07	20 01	19 55
45	28	28	27	25	24	22	20 19	20 17	20 13	20 10	20 06	20 02	19 58	19 54	19 49	19 44	39
40	20 06	20 05	20 05	20 04	20 03	20 01	19 59	19 57	19 55	19 52	19 49	19 46	42	39	35	31	26
35	19 48	19 47	19 47	19 47	19 46	19 44	43	41	39	37	35	32	29	26	23	19	16
30	32	32	32	32	31	30	29	28	26	25	23	20	18	19 15	19 13	19 10	19 07
N 20	19 08	19 08	19 08	19 08	19 08	19 07	19 07	19 00	19 05	19 04	19 03	19 01	19 00	18 58	18 56	18 54	18 52
N 10	18 47	18 48	18 48	18 48	18 48	18 48	18 48	18 48	18 47	18 47	18 46	18 45	18 45	43	42	41	40
0	29	30	30	31	31	31	32	32	32	32	32	32	31	31	30	30	29
S 10	18 12	18 13	18 14	18 14	18 15	16	16	17	17	18	18	19	19	19	19	19	19
20	17 55	17 56	17 57	17 58	17 59	18 00	18 01	18 02	18 03	18 04	18 05	18 06	18 07	18 07	18 08	18 09	10
S 30	17 36	17 37	17 38	17 40	17 41	17 42	17 44	17 45	17 47	17 49	17 50	17 52	17 54	17 55	17 57	17 58	18 00
35	26	27	28	30	31	33	35	36	38	40	42	44	46	48	50	52	17 54
40	14	15	17	18	20	22	24	26	29	31	33	36	38	41	43	46	49
45	17 01	17 02	17 04	17 05	17 08	17 10	17 12	15	17	20	23	26	29	32	36	39	42
50	16 45	16 46	16 48	16 50	16 53	16 55	16 58	17 01	17 04	08	11	15	19	23	26	30	34
S 52	16 37	16 39	16 41	16 43	16 46	16 49	16 52	16 55	16 59	17 02	17 06	17 10	17 14	17 18	17 22	17 27	17 31
54	29	31	33	35	38	41	45	48	52	16 56	17 00	17 04	09	13	18	23	27
56	20	22	24	27	30	33	37	41	45	49	16 54	16 58	17 03	08	13	18	23
58	16 10	12	14	17	21	24	28	32	37	42	46	52	16 57	17 02	08	13	19
S 60	15 58	16 01	16 03	16 06	16 10	16 14	16 18	16 23	16 28	16 33	16 38	16 44	16 50	16 56	17 02	17 08	17 14

A140 SUNRISE

Lat.	August						September										Oct.
	15	18	21	24	27	30	2	5	8	11	14	17	20	23	26	29	2
°	h m	h m	h m	h m	h m	h m	h m	h m	h m	h m	h m	h m	h m	h m	h m	h m	h m
N 72	02 21	02 41	02 59	03 17	03 33	03 49	04 04	04 18	04 33	04 47	05 00	05 14	05 27	05 41	05 54	06 08	06 21
70	02 54	03 09	03 23	38	03 51	04 04	17	30	42	04 54	06	18	30	42	54	06	18
68	03 17	30	42	03 54	04 05	17	28	39	50	05 01	11	22	32	43	54	04	15
66	36	46	03 57	04 07	17	27	37	47	04 56	06	15	25	34	44	53	03	12
64	03 50	03 59	04 09	18	27	35	44	53	05 02	10	19	27	36	44	53	02	10
62	04 02	04 11	19	27	35	43	51	04 59	06	14	22	30	37	45	53	06 01	08
N 60	04 13	04 20	04 27	04 34	04 42	04 49	04 56	05 03	05 10	05 17	05 24	05 31	05 38	05 45	05 52	05 59	06 07
58	22	28	35	41	48	54	05 01	07	14	20	27	33	39	46	52	59	05
56	30	36	41	47	53	04 59	05	11	17	23	28	34	40	46	52	58	04
54	37	42	47	53	04 58	05 04	09	14	20	25	30	36	41	46	52	57	03
52	43	48	53	04 58	05 03	07	12	17	22	27	32	37	42	47	52	57	02
N 50	04 49	04 53	04 58	05 02	05 07	05 11	05 16	05 20	05 24	05 29	05 33	05 38	05 42	05 47	05 51	05 56	06 01
45	05 01	05 04	05 08	12	15	19	22	26	29	33	37	40	44	48	51	55	05 58
40	11	14	17	20	22	25	28	31	34	37	39	42	45	48	51	54	57
35	19	22	24	26	28	31	33	35	37	39	42	44	46	48	50	53	55
30	27	29	30	32	34	35	37	39	40	42	44	45	47	48	50	52	54
N 20	05 40	05 41	05 41	05 42	05 43	05 44	05 44	05 45	05 46	05 46	05 47	05 48	05 48	05 49	05 50	05 50	05 51
N 10	05 51	05 51	05 51	51	51	51	51	51	50	50	50	50	49	49	49	49	49
0	06 01	06 01	06 00	05 59	05 58	05 57	05 56	05 55	54	53	52	51	50	49	48	47	46
S 10	11	10	09	06 07	06 06	06 04	06 02	06 00	05 59	05 57	55	53	51	49	47	46	44
20	22	20	18	15	13	11	08	05	06 03	06 00	05 57	55	52	49	47	44	41
S 30	06 34	06 31	06 28	06 25	06 22	06 18	06 15	06 11	06 08	06 04	06 00	05 57	05 53	05 49	05 45	05 42	05 38
35	41	38	34	30	26	23	19	14	10	06	02	57	53	49	44	40	36
40	49	45	41	36	32	27	23	18	13	08	03	05 59	54	49	44	39	34
45	06 58	06 53	49	43	38	33	28	22	17	11	05	06 00	54	48	43	37	31
50	07 09	07 03	06 58	52	46	40	33	27	21	14	08	01	54	48	41	35	28
S 52	07 14	07 08	07 02	06 56	06 49	06 43	06 36	06 29	06 22	06 16	06 09	06 02	05 55	05 48	05 41	05 34	05 27
54	20	13	07	07 00	53	46	39	32	25	17	10	02	55	47	40	33	25
56	26	19	12	05	06 57	50	42	35	27	19	11	03	55	47	39	31	23
58	33	25	18	10	07 02	54	46	38	29	21	12	04	55	47	38	30	21
S 60	07 41	07 33	07 24	07 16	07 07	06 59	06 50	06 41	06 32	06 23	06 14	06 05	05 56	05 47	05 37	05 28	05 19

SUNSET

Lat.	August						September										Oct.
	15	18	21	24	27	30	2	5	8	11	14	17	20	23	26	29	2
°	h m	h m	h m	h m	h m	h m	h m	h m	h m	h m	h m	h m	h m	h m	h m	h m	h m
N 72	21 43	21 22	21 03	20 44	20 27	20 10	19 53	19 36	19 20	19 04	18 49	18 33	18 18	18 02	17 47	17 31	17 16
70	21 12	20 55	20 40	24	20 09	19 54	40	26	11	18 57	43	29	15	01	47	34	20
68	20 49	35	22	20 09	19 55	42	30	17	19 04	51	38	26	13	01	48	35	23
66	31	20	20 08	19 56	44	33	21	09	18 58	46	35	23	11	18 00	48	37	26
64	17	20 06	19 56	46	35	25	14	19 03	53	42	31	21	10	17 59	49	38	28
62	20 05	19 56	46	37	27	17	08	18 58	48	38	29	19	09	59	49	39	30
N 60	19 55	19 46	19 38	19 29	19 20	19 11	19 02	18 53	18 44	18 35	18 26	18 17	18 08	17 58	17 49	17 40	17 31
58	46	38	30	22	14	06	18 57	49	41	32	24	15	07	58	50	41	33
56	38	31	24	16	09	19 01	53	45	38	30	22	14	06	58	50	42	34
54	31	25	18	11	19 04	18 57	49	42	35	27	20	12	05	58	50	43	35
52	25	19	12	06	18 59	53	46	39	32	25	18	11	04	57	50	43	36
N 50	19 19	19 14	19 08	19 02	18 56	18 49	18 43	18 37	18 30	18 24	18 17	18 10	18 04	17 57	17 51	17 44	17 38
45	19 07	19 03	18 58	18 52	47	42	36	31	25	20	14	08	03	57	51	46	40
40	18 57	18 53	49	45	40	36	31	26	21	16	11	06	01	56	51	47	42
35	49	46	42	38	34	30	26	22	18	13	09	05	01	56	52	48	43
30	42	39	35	32	29	25	22	18	15	11	07	04	18 00	56	52	49	45
N 20	18 29	18 27	18 25	18 22	18 20	18 17	18 15	18 12	18 10	18 07	18 04	18 01	17 59	17 56	17 53	17 50	17 48
N 10	18	17	15	14	12	10	09	07	05	03	18 01	18 00	58	56	54	52	50
0	18 08	18 07	18 06	18 06	18 05	18 04	18 03	18 02	18 01	18 00	17 59	17 58	57	56	55	54	53
S 10	17 58	17 58	17 58	17 58	17 58	17 58	17 58	17 57	17 57	17 57	57	56	56	56	56	55	55
20	47	48	49	50	50	51	52	52	53	54	54	55	55	56	57	17 57	17 58
S 30	17 35	17 37	17 39	17 40	17 42	17 44	17 45	17 47	17 48	17 50	17 52	17 53	17 55	17 56	17 58	18 00	18 02
35	28	31	33	35	37	39	42	44	46	48	50	52	55	57	17 59	01	04
40	21	23	26	29	32	35	37	40	43	46	49	51	54	57	18 00	03	06
45	12	15	19	22	26	29	33	36	40	43	47	50	54	58	01	05	09
50	17 01	05	09	14	18	23	27	31	36	40	45	49	54	58	03	07	12
S 52	16 56	17 00	17 05	17 10	17 15	17 20	17 24	17 29	17 34	17 39	17 44	17 49	17 53	17 58	18 03	18 08	18 13
54	50	16 55	17 01	06	11	16	21	27	32	37	43	48	53	59	04	10	15
56	44	50	16 55	17 01	07	13	18	24	30	36	41	47	53	59	05	11	17
58	37	43	50	16 56	17 02	09	15	21	27	34	40	46	53	17 59	06	12	19
S 60	16 29	16 36	16 43	16 50	16 57	17 04	17 11	17 18	17 25	17 32	17 39	17 46	17 53	18 00	18 07	18 14	18 21

MORNING CIVIL TWILIGHT

A141

Lat.	August						September										Oct.
	15	18	21	24	27	30	2	5	8	11	14	17	20	23	26	29	2
°	h m	h m	h m	h m	h m	h m	h m	h m	h m	h m	h m	h m	h m	h m	h m	h m	h m
N 72	////	////	////	01 07	01 44	02 12	02 35	02 55	03 14	03 31	03 47	04 03	04 18	04 32	04 46	05 00	05 14
70	////	01 06	01 40	02 05	02 26	02 45	03 02	03 18	33	03 48	04 01	15	28	40	53	05	17
68	01 39	02 02	02 21	02 38	02 54	03 08	22	36	03 48	04 01	13	24	36	47	04 58	09	19
66	02 18	34	02 48	03 02	03 14	27	38	03 50	04 01	11	22	32	42	52	05 02	12	21
64	02 45	02 57	03 08	20	31	41	03 51	04 01	11	20	30	39	48	04 57	06	14	23
62	03 05	03 15	25	35	44	03 53	04 02	11	19	28	36	44	52	05 01	09	16	24
N 60	03 21	03 30	03 38	03 47	03 55	04 03	04 13	04 19	04 27	04 34	04 42	04 49	04 57	05 04	05 11	05 18	05 25
58	35	42	03 50	03 57	04 05	12	19	26	33	40	47	53	05 00	07	13	20	26
56	46	03 53	04 00	04 06	13	19	26	32	38	45	51	04 57	03	09	15	21	27
54	03 56	04 02	08	14	20	26	32	37	43	49	54	05 00	06	11	17	22	27
52	04 05	10	16	21	26	32	37	42	47	53	04 58	03	08	13	18	23	28
N 50	04 13	04 18	04 22	04 27	04 32	04 37	04 42	04 47	04 51	04 56	05 01	05 05	05 10	05 15	05 19	05 24	05 29
45	29	33	37	41	44	48	04 52	04 56	05 00	05 03	07	11	15	18	22	26	29
40	42	45	48	04 51	04 54	04 57	05 00	05 03	06	09	12	15	18	21	24	27	30
35	04 53	04 55	04 58	05 00	05 02	05 05	07	09	12	14	16	18	21	23	25	27	30
30	05 02	05 04	05 06	07	09	11	13	15	16	18	20	21	23	25	26	28	30
N 20	05 17	05 18	05 19	05 20	05 21	05 21	05 22	05 23	05 24	05 24	05 25	05 26	05 26	05 27	05 28	05 28	05 29
N 10	29	29	29	30	30	30	29	29	29	29	29	29	28	28	28	28	28
0	40	39	39	38	37	36	35	35	34	33	32	31	30	29	28	27	25
S 10	50	48	47	46	44	43	41	39	38	36	34	32	30	28	26	25	23
20	05 59	05 57	05 55	05 53	51	48	46	43	41	38	35	33	30	27	24	22	19
S 30	06 09	06 07	06 04	06 01	05 57	05 54	05 51	05 47	05 44	05 40	05 36	05 33	05 29	05 25	05 21	05 18	05 14
35	15	12	08	05	06 01	05 57	53	49	45	41	37	32	28	24	19	15	11
40	21	17	13	09	04	06 00	55	51	46	41	36	32	27	22	17	12	07
45	27	23	18	14	09	03	05 58	53	47	42	36	31	25	19	13	07	05 02
50	35	30	24	19	13	07	06 01	55	48	42	35	29	22	16	09	02	04 56
S 52	06 39	06 33	06 27	06 21	06 15	06 09	06 02	05 56	05 49	05 42	05 35	05 28	05 21	05 14	05 07	05 00	04 53
54	42	36	30	24	17	10	03	56	49	42	35	27	20	12	05	04 57	49
56	47	40	33	26	19	12	05	57	50	42	34	26	18	10	05 02	54	46
58	51	44	37	29	22	14	06	58	50	42	33	25	16	08	04 59	50	42
S 60	06 56	06 48	06 41	06 33	06 25	06 16	06 08	05 59	05 50	05 42	05 33	05 24	05 14	05 05	04 56	04 46	04 37

EVENING CIVIL TWILIGHT

Lat.	August						September										Oct.
	15	18	21	24	27	30	2	5	8	11	14	17	20	23	26	29	2
°	h m	h m	h m	h m	h m	h m	h m	h m	h m	h m	h m	h m	h m	h m	h m	h m	h m
N 72	////	////	////	22 45	22 11	21 44	21 20	20 58	20 38	20 19	20 01	19 44	19 27	19 10	18 54	18 38	18 23
70	23 51	22 50	22 19	21 54	21 32	21 12	20 54	36	19	20 03	19 47	32	17	19 03	48	34	20
68	22 23	22 01	21 41	23	21 06	20 50	34	19	20 04	19 50	36	23	09	18 56	43	31	18
66	21 47	21 31	21 15	21 00	20 46	32	19	20 06	19 53	40	27	15	19 03	51	39	28	16
64	21	21 08	20 55	20 43	30	18	20 06	19 55	43	32	20	09	18 58	47	36	25	15
62	21 02	20 50	39	28	17	20 07	19 56	45	35	24	14	19 04	53	43	33	23	14
N 60	20 46	20 36	20 26	20 16	20 07	19 57	19 47	19 37	19 28	19 18	19 08	18 59	18 50	18 40	18 31	18 22	18 13
58	33	24	15	20 06	19 57	48	39	30	22	13	19 04	55	46	38	29	20	12
56	21	13	20 05	19 57	49	41	32	24	16	08	18 59	51	43	35	27	19	11
54	11	20 04	19 57	49	42	34	26	19	11	03	56	48	40	33	25	18	10
52	20 03	19 56	49	42	35	28	21	14	07	19 00	52	45	38	31	24	17	10
N 50	19 55	19 49	19 43	19 36	19 30	19 23	19 16	19 10	19 03	18 56	18 50	18 43	18 36	18 29	18 23	18 16	18 10
45	39	34	29	23	18	12	19 07	19 01	18 55	49	43	38	32	26	20	15	09
40	26	22	18	13	08	19 03	18 59	18 54	49	44	39	34	28	23	18	13	09
35	16	12	08	19 04	19 00	18 56	52	48	43	39	35	30	26	21	17	13	09
30	19 07	19 04	19 00	18 57	18 53	50	46	43	39	35	31	27	24	20	16	12	09
N 20	18 52	18 50	18 47	18 45	18 43	18 40	18 37	18 34	18 32	18 29	18 26	18 23	18 21	18 18	18 15	18 12	18 10
N 10	40	38	37	35	33	32	30	28	26	24	22	21	19	17	15	13	11
0	29	29	28	27	26	25	24	23	22	21	20	19	18	16	15	14	13
S 10	19	19	19	19	19	19	19	18	18	18	18	17	17	17	17	17	16
20	10	11	11	12	13	13	14	14	15	16	16	17	18	18	19	20	20
S 30	18 00	18 02	18 03	18 05	18 06	18 08	18 09	18 11	18 12	18 14	18 16	18 17	18 19	18 20	18 22	18 24	18 26
35	17 54	17 57	17 59	18 01	18 03	05	07	09	11	13	16	18	20	22	24	27	29
40	49	51	54	17 57	17 59	18 02	05	07	10	13	16	18	21	24	27	30	33
45	42	45	49	52	55	17 59	18 02	06	09	13	16	20	23	27	31	34	38
50	34	39	43	47	51	55	17 59	04	08	12	17	21	26	31	35	40	45
S 52	17 31	17 36	17 40	17 45	17 49	17 54	17 58	18 03	18 08	18 12	18 17	18 22	18 27	18 32	18 37	18 42	18 47
54	27	32	37	42	47	52	57	02	07	13	18	23	29	34	40	45	51
56	23	29	34	39	45	50	56	01	07	13	18	24	30	36	42	48	55
58	19	25	31	37	42	48	54	01	07	13	19	26	32	39	45	52	18 59
S 60	17 14	17 21	17 27	17 33	17 40	17 46	17 53	18 00	18 06	18 13	18 20	18 27	18 34	18 41	18 49	18 56	19 04

A142

SUNRISE

Lat.	October										November						
	2	5	8	11	14	17	20	23	26	29	1	4	7	10	13	16	19
°	h m	h m	h m	h m	h m	h m	h m	h m	h m	h m	h m	h m	h m	h m	h m	h m	h m
N 72	06 21	06 35	06 49	07 03	07 17	07 32	07 47	08 03	08 19	08 36	08 54	09 13	09 34	09 58	10 27	11 14	▬
70	18	30	42	06 54	07 07	20	33	07 46	08 00	08 14	28	08 44	08 59	09 16	09 34	09 53	10 14
68	15	26	36	47	06 58	10	21	33	07 44	07 56	08 09	21	34	08 48	09 01	09 15	09 30
66	12	22	32	41	51	07 01	11	22	32	43	07 53	08 04	15	27	08 38	08 49	09 01
64	10	19	28	36	45	06 54	07 03	13	22	31	41	07 50	08 00	08 10	19	29	08 39
62	08	16	24	32	40	48	06 57	07 05	13	22	30	39	07 47	07 56	08 04	08 13	21
N 60	06 07	06 14	06 21	06 28	06 36	06 43	06 50	06 58	07 06	07 13	07 21	07 29	07 36	07 44	07 52	07 59	08 07
58	05	12	18	25	32	38	45	52	06 59	06	13	20	27	34	41	48	07 54
56	04	10	16	22	28	34	41	47	53	07 00	06	12	19	25	31	37	43
54	03	08	14	19	25	31	36	42	48	06 54	07 00	07 05	11	17	23	29	34
52	02	07	12	17	22	27	33	38	43	49	06 54	06 59	07 05	10	16	21	26
N 50	06 01	06 05	06 10	06 15	06 19	06 24	06 29	06 34	06 39	06 44	06 49	06 54	06 59	07 04	07 09	07 14	07 18
45	05 58	02	06	10	14	18	22	26	30	34	38	42	46	06 50	06 54	06 58	07 02
40	57	06 00	06 03	06	09	12	15	18	22	25	28	32	35	39	42	46	06 49
35	55	05 57	05 59	06 02	04	07	10	12	15	18	21	23	26	29	32	35	38
30	54	55	57	05 59	06 01	06 03	06 05	06 07	06 09	11	13	16	18	20	23	25	28
N 20	05 51	05 52	05 52	05 53	05 54	05 55	05 56	05 57	05 59	06 00	06 01	06 03	06 04	06 06	06 07	06 09	06 11
N 10	49	48	48	48	48	48	49	49	49	05 50	05 50	05 51	05 52	05 53	05 54	05 55	05 56
0	46	45	44	44	43	42	42	41	41	40	40	40	40	40	41	41	42
S 10	44	42	40	39	37	36	34	33	32	31	30	29	29	28	28	28	28
20	41	38	36	33	31	29	26	24	22	20	19	17	16	05 15	05 14	05 13	05 12
S 30	05 38	05 34	05 31	05 27	05 24	05 20	05 17	05 14	05 11	05 08	05 06	05 03	05 01	04 59	04 57	04 56	04 54
35	36	32	28	24	19	16	12	08	05 05	05 01	04 58	04 55	04 53	50	48	46	44
40	34	29	24	19	15	10	05 06	05 02	04 57	04 54	50	46	43	40	37	34	32
45	31	26	20	15	09	05 04	04 59	04 54	49	44	40	35	31	27	24	21	18
50	28	22	15	09	05 02	04 56	50	44	38	33	27	22	17	13	08	04 04	04 00
S 52	05 27	05 20	05 13	05 06	04 59	04 53	04 46	04 40	04 34	04 28	04 22	04 16	04 11	04 05	04 01	03 56	03 52
54	25	18	10	03	56	49	42	35	28	22	15	09	04 03	03 58	03 52	48	43
56	23	15	08	05 00	52	44	37	30	22	15	08	04 02	03 55	49	43	38	32
58	21	13	05	04 56	48	40	32	24	16	08	04 00	03 53	46	39	33	26	21
S 60	05 19	05 10	05 01	04 52	04 43	04 34	04 25	04 17	04 08	04 00	03 51	03 43	03 35	03 28	03 20	03 13	03 06

SUNSET

Lat.	October										November						
	2	5	8	11	14	17	20	23	26	29	1	4	7	10	13	16	19
°	h m	h m	h m	h m	h m	h m	h m	h m	h m	h m	h m	h m	h m	h m	h m	h m	h m
N 72	17 16	17 01	16 45	16 30	16 14	15 58	15 41	15 25	15 08	14 50	14 32	14 13	13 52	13 28	13 00	12 14	▬
70	20	06	52	38	24	16 10	15 56	42	27	15 13	14 58	14 42	14 27	14 11	13 54	13 35	13 15
68	23	10	16 58	45	33	20	16 08	15 55	43	30	15 17	15 05	14 52	14 39	14 26	14 13	14 00
66	26	14	17 03	51	40	29	17	16 06	15 55	44	33	22	15 11	15 00	14 50	14 39	29
64	28	17	07	16 56	46	36	25	15	16 05	15 55	45	36	26	17	15 08	15 00	14 51
62	30	20	10	17 01	51	42	32	23	14	16 05	15 56	48	39	31	23	16	15 09
N 60	17 31	17 22	17 13	17 04	16 56	16 47	16 38	16 30	16 22	16 13	16 06	15 58	15 51	15 43	15 36	15 30	15 23
58	33	25	16	08	17 00	52	44	36	28	21	13	16 06	16 00	15 53	47	41	36
56	34	26	18	11	03	56	48	41	34	27	21	14	08	16 02	15 56	15 51	46
54	35	28	21	14	06	16 59	53	46	39	33	27	21	15	10	16 05	16 00	15 56
52	36	29	23	16	09	17 03	16 56	50	44	38	33	27	22	17	12	08	16 04
N 50	17 38	17 31	17 25	17 18	17 12	17 06	17 00	16 54	16 49	16 43	16 38	16 33	16 28	16 23	16 19	16 15	16 12
45	40	34	29	23	18	13	08	17 03	16 58	16 53	49	45	41	37	34	31	28
40	42	37	32	27	23	18	14	10	17 06	17 02	16 58	16 55	16 52	49	46	44	41
35	43	39	35	31	27	23	20	16	13	09	17 06	17 04	17 01	16 59	16 56	16 54	16 53
30	45	41	38	34	31	28	25	22	19	16	14	11	09	17 07	17 05	17 04	17 03
N 20	17 48	17 45	17 43	17 40	17 38	17 36	17 33	17 31	17 29	17 28	17 26	17 24	17 23	17 22	17 21	17 20	17 20
N 10	50	49	47	45	44	42	41	40	39	38	37	36	35	35	35	35	35
0	53	52	51	50	49	49	48	48	47	47	47	47	47	17 47	17 48	17 48	17 49
S 10	55	55	17 55	17 55	17 55	17 55	17 56	17 56	17 57	17 57	17 58	17 58	17 59	18 00	18 01	18 02	18 03
20	17 58	17 59	18 00	18 01	18 02	18 03	18 04	18 05	18 06	18 07	18 09	18 10	18 12	14	15	17	19
S 30	18 02	18 03	18 05	18 07	18 09	18 11	18 13	18 15	18 17	18 20	18 22	18 24	18 27	18 29	18 32	18 34	18 37
35	04	06	09	11	13	16	19	21	24	27	30	32	35	38	41	44	47
40	06	09	12	15	18	21	25	28	31	35	38	42	45	18 49	18 52	18 56	18 59
45	09	12	16	20	24	28	32	36	40	44	18 48	18 53	18 57	19 01	19 05	19 10	19 14
50	12	17	21	26	31	36	41	46	51	18 56	19 01	19 06	19 11	16	21	26	31
S 52	18 13	18 18	18 24	18 29	18 34	18 39	18 45	18 50	18 56	19 01	19 07	19 12	19 18	19 24	19 29	19 34	19 40
54	15	21	26	32	37	43	49	18 55	19 01	07	13	19	25	31	37	43	19 49
56	17	23	29	35	41	48	18 54	19 01	07	14	20	27	34	40	47	19 53	20 00
58	19	25	32	39	46	53	19 00	07	14	21	28	36	43	19 50	19 58	20 05	12
S 60	18 21	18 28	18 36	18 43	18 51	18 58	19 06	19 14	19 22	19 30	19 38	19 46	19 54	20 02	20 10	20 18	20 26

MORNING CIVIL TWILIGHT

A143

Lat.	October										November						
	2	5	8	11	14	17	20	23	26	29	1	4	7	10	13	16	19
°	h m	h m	h m	h m	h m	h m	h m	h m	h m	h m	h m	h m	h m	h m	h m	h m	h m
N 72	05 14	05 27	05 41	05 54	06 07	06 20	06 34	06 47	07 00	07 14	07 27	07 41	07 54	08 08	08 23	08 37	08 51
70	17	29	41	52	04	16	27	39	06 51	07 03	14	26	38	07 50	08 02	08 14	25
68	19	30	41	51	06 01	12	22	33	43	06 54	07 04	14	25	35	07 46	07 56	08 06
66	21	31	40	50	05 59	09	18	27	37	46	06 55	07 05	14	23	32	41	07 50
64	23	32	40	49	57	06	14	23	31	40	48	06 56	07 05	13	21	29	37
62	24	32	40	48	55	03	11	18	26	34	41	49	06 57	07 04	12	19	26
N 60	05 25	05 33	05 40	05 47	05 54	06 01	06 08	06 15	06 22	06 29	06 36	06 43	06 50	06 57	07 03	07 10	07 16
58	26	33	39	46	52	05 59	05	12	18	24	31	37	44	50	06 56	07 02	08
56	27	33	39	45	51	57	03	09	15	20	26	32	38	44	49	06 55	07 01
54	27	33	38	44	49	55	06 00	06	11	17	22	28	33	38	44	49	06 54
52	28	33	38	43	48	53	05 58	03	08	13	18	23	28	33	38	43	48
N 50	05 29	05 33	05 38	05 42	05 47	05 51	05 56	06 01	06 06	06 10	06 15	06 20	06 24	06 29	06 33	06 38	06 42
45	29	33	37	40	44	48	52	05 56	05 59	06 03	07	11	15	19	23	26	30
40	30	33	35	38	41	44	48	51	54	05 57	06 00	06 04	07	10	13	17	20
35	30	32	34	37	39	42	44	47	49	52	05 54	05 57	06 00	06 02	06 05	08	11
30	30	31	33	35	37	39	41	43	45	47	49	51	05 53	05 55	05 58	06 00	06 02
N 20	05 29	05 30	05 30	05 31	05 32	05 33	05 34	05 35	05 36	05 37	05 39	05 40	05 41	05 43	05 44	05 46	05 48
N 10	28	27	27	27	27	27	28	28	28	28	29	29	30	31	32	33	34
0	25	25	24	23	22	21	21	20	19	19	19	19	18	19	19	19	20
S 10	23	21	19	18	16	14	13	11	10	05 09	05 08	05 07	05 07	05 06	05 06	05 05	05 05
20	19	16	14	11	05 08	05 06	05 04	05 02	05 00	04 58	04 56	04 54	04 53	04 51	04 50	04 49	04 48
S 30	05 14	05 10	05 07	05 03	04 59	04 56	04 53	04 49	04 46	04 43	04 41	04 38	04 36	04 33	04 31	04 30	04 28
35	11	06	05 02	04 58	54	50	46	42	38	35	31	28	25	22	20	18	16
40	07	05 02	04 57	52	47	42	38	33	29	25	21	17	04 13	04 10	04 07	04 04	04 01
45	05 02	04 56	50	44	39	33	28	23	18	04 12	04 08	04 03	03 59	03 54	03 50	03 47	03 43
50	04 56	49	42	36	29	22	16	10	04 03	03 57	03 51	03 46	40	35	30	25	21
S 52	04 53	04 45	04 38	04 31	04 24	04 17	04 10	04 03	03 57	03 50	03 44	03 37	03 31	03 25	03 20	03 14	03 09
54	49	42	34	26	19	11	04 04	03 56	49	42	35	28	21	14	03 08	03 02	02 57
56	46	38	29	21	13	04 05	03 57	48	41	33	25	17	03 10	03 02	02 55	02 48	42
58	42	33	24	15	04 06	03 57	48	40	31	22	13	03 05	02 56	02 48	39	31	24
S 60	04 37	04 27	04 18	04 08	03 58	03 49	03 39	03 29	03 19	03 09	03 00	02 50	02 40	02 30	02 21	02 11	02 01

EVENING CIVIL TWILIGHT

Lat.	October										November						
	2	5	8	11	14	17	20	23	26	29	1	4	7	10	13	16	19
°	h m	h m	h m	h m	h m	h m	h m	h m	h m	h m	h m	h m	h m	h m	h m	h m	h m
N 72	18 23	18 08	17 53	17 38	17 23	17 09	16 55	16 40	16 26	16 12	15 59	15 45	15 31	15 18	15 05	14 51	14 38
70	20	07	53	40	27	14	17 01	48	36	24	16 12	16 00	15 48	37	26	15 15	15 04
68	18	06	53	41	29	18	06	16 55	44	33	22	11	16 01	15 51	42	33	24
66	16	05	54	43	32	21	11	17 00	50	40	31	21	12	16 04	15 55	47	40
64	15	04	54	44	34	24	15	05	16 56	47	38	30	22	14	16 06	15 59	15 53
62	14	04	54	45	36	27	18	09	17 01	53	45	37	30	23	16	16 10	16 04
N 60	18 13	18 04	17 55	17 46	17 38	17 29	17 21	17 13	17 05	16 58	16 50	16 43	16 37	16 30	16 24	16 19	16 13
58	12	03	55	47	39	32	24	16	09	17 02	16 56	49	43	37	32	27	22
56	11	03	56	48	41	33	26	19	13	06	17 00	54	49	43	38	34	29
54	10	03	56	49	42	35	29	22	16	10	04	16 59	54	49	44	40	36
52	10	03	56	50	43	37	31	25	19	14	08	17 03	16 58	54	50	46	42
N 50	18 10	18 03	17 57	17 51	17 45	17 39	17 33	17 27	17 22	17 17	17 12	17 07	17 03	16 58	16 55	16 51	16 48
45	09	03	58	53	47	42	37	33	28	24	20	16	12	17 09	17 05	17 03	17 00
40	09	04	17 59	55	50	46	42	38	34	30	27	23	20	17	15	12	10
35	09	04	18 00	56	53	49	45	42	39	35	33	30	27	25	23	21	20
30	09	05	02	17 58	17 55	52	49	46	43	41	38	36	34	32	31	29	28
N 20	18 10	18 07	18 05	18 02	18 00	17 58	17 55	17 53	17 52	17 50	17 49	17 47	17 46	17 45	17 44	17 44	17 43
N 10	11	10	08	06	05	18 03	18 02	18 01	18 00	17 59	17 58	17 58	17 57	17 57	17 57	17 57	17 57
0	13	13	12	11	10	10	09	09	09	18 09	18 09	18 09	18 09	18 09	18 10	18 10	18 11
S 10	16	16	16	16	17	17	17	18	18	19	20	20	21	22	23	24	26
20	20	21	22	23	24	25	26	28	29	30	32	33	35	37	39	18 41	18 43
S 30	18 26	18 27	18 29	18 31	18 33	18 36	18 38	18 40	18 42	18 45	18 47	18 50	18 52	18 55	18 58	19 00	19 03
35	29	32	34	37	39	42	45	48	18 50	18 53	18 57	19 00	19 03	19 06	19 09	12	16
40	33	36	39	43	46	49	18 53	18 56	19 00	19 04	19 07	11	15	19	23	27	30
45	38	42	46	50	18 54	18 58	19 03	19 07	12	16	21	25	30	35	19 39	19 44	19 48
50	43	49	54	18 59	19 05	19 10	15	21	26	32	37	43	49	19 54	20 00	20 06	20 11
S 52	18 47	18 53	18 58	19 04	19 09	19 15	19 21	19 27	19 33	19 39	19 45	19 51	19 58	20 04	20 10	20 17	20 23
54	51	18 57	19 03	09	15	21	27	34	41	47	19 54	20 01	20 08	15	22	29	36
56	55	19 01	08	14	21	28	35	42	49	19 57	20 04	12	20	28	35	20 43	20 51
58	18 59	06	13	20	28	36	43	19 51	19 59	20 08	16	25	33	20 42	20 51	21 00	21 09
S 60	19 04	19 12	19 19	19 28	19 36	19 44	19 53	20 02	20 11	20 20	20 30	20 40	20 50	21 00	21 11	21 21	21 32

A144

SUNRISE

Lat.	November 19	22	25	28	December 1	4	7	10	13	16	19	22	25	28	31	Jan. 3
°	h m	h m	h m	h m	h m	h m	h m	h m	h m	h m	h m	h m	h m	h m	h m	h m
N 72	—	—	—	—	—	—	—	—	—	—	—	—	—	—	—	—
70	10 14	10 40	11 19	—	—	—	—	—	—	—	—	—	—	—	—	—
68	09 30	09 45	10 00	10 16	10 33	10 52	11 14	—	—	—	—	—	—	—	—	—
66	09 01	09 12	09 23	09 34	09 45	09 55	10 05	10 14	10 22	10 28	10 32	10 35	10 35	10 33	10 30	10 25
64	08 39	08 48	08 57	09 06	09 15	09 23	09 30	09 36	09 42	09 47	09 50	09 52	09 53	09 52	09 51	09 48
62	21	29	37	08 45	08 52	08 59	09 05	09 10	09 15	09 19	22	24	24	24	23	22
N 60	08 07	08 14	08 21	08 28	08 34	08 40	08 45	08 50	08 54	08 58	09 00	09 02	09 03	09 03	09 03	09 01
58	07 54	08 01	08 07	13	19	24	29	33	37	40	08 43	08 45	08 46	08 46	08 46	08 45
56	43	07 49	07 55	08 01	08 06	08 11	15	19	23	26	28	30	31	32	32	31
54	34	40	45	07 50	07 55	07 59	08 03	08 07	08 10	13	15	17	19	19	19	19
52	26	31	36	40	45	49	07 53	07 56	07 59	08 02	08 04	08 06	08 07	08 08	08 08	08 08
N 50	07 18	07 23	07 28	07 32	07 36	07 40	07 43	07 47	07 50	07 52	07 54	07 56	07 57	07 58	07 59	07 58
45	07 02	07 06	07 10	07 14	17	21	24	27	29	32	34	35	37	38	38	38
40	06 49	06 53	06 56	06 59	07 02	07 05	07 08	07 10	07 13	15	17	18	20	21	22	22
35	38	41	44	46	06 49	06 52	06 54	06 57	06 59	07 01	07 03	07 04	07 06	07 07	07 08	07 08
30	28	30	33	35	38	40	43	45	47	06 49	06 50	06 52	06 53	06 54	06 55	06 56
N 20	06 11	06 13	06 15	06 16	06 18	06 20	06 22	06 24	06 26	06 28	06 29	06 31	06 32	06 33	06 35	06 36
N 10	05 56	05 57	05 58	06 00	06 01	06 03	06 04	06 06	06 07	06 09	06 10	06 12	06 13	06 15	06 16	17
0	42	42	43	05 44	05 45	05 46	05 48	05 49	05 50	05 52	05 53	05 55	05 56	05 58	05 59	06 01
S 10	28	28	28	28	29	30	31	32	33	34	35	37	39	40	42	05 43
20	05 12	05 12	05 11	05 11	05 12	05 12	05 13	05 13	05 14	05 15	05 17	05 18	05 20	05 21	23	25
S 30	04 54	04 53	04 52	04 52	04 51	04 51	04 51	04 52	04 52	04 53	04 55	04 56	04 58	04 59	05 01	05 03
35	44	42	41	40	39	39	39	39	40	41	42	43	45	46	04 48	04 51
40	32	30	28	27	26	25	25	25	25	26	27	28	29	31	34	36
45	18	04 15	04 13	04 11	04 09	04 08	04 07	04 07	04 07	04 08	04 08	04 10	04 11	04 13	04 16	04 19
50	04 00	03 57	03 54	03 51	03 49	03 47	03 46	03 45	03 45	03 45	03 46	03 47	03 49	03 51	03 54	03 57
S 52	03 52	03 48	03 45	03 42	03 39	03 37	03 36	03 35	03 34	03 34	03 35	03 36	03 38	03 40	03 43	03 46
54	43	39	35	31	29	26	24	23	22	22	23	24	26	28	31	34
56	32	28	23	19	16	03 13	03 11	03 09	03 09	03 08	03 09	03 10	03 12	03 14	17	21
58	21	15	03 10	03 06	03 02	02 58	02 55	02 53	02 52	02 52	02 52	02 53	02 55	02 57	03 01	03 05
S 60	03 06	03 00	02 54	02 49	02 44	02 40	02 37	02 34	02 32	02 31	02 31	02 32	02 34	02 37	02 41	02 45

SUNSET

Lat.	November 19	22	25	28	December 1	4	7	10	13	16	19	22	25	28	31	Jan. 3
°	h m	h m	h m	h m	h m	h m	h m	h m	h m	h m	h m	h m	h m	h m	h m	h m
N 72	—	—	—	—	—	—	—	—	—	—	—	—	—	—	—	—
70	13 15	12 51	12 13	—	—	—	—	—	—	—	—	—	—	—	—	—
68	14 00	13 47	13 33	13 19	13 04	12 47	12 27	—	—	—	—	—	—	—	—	—
66	29	14 19	14 10	14 01	13 52	13 44	13 37	13 30	13 26	13 22	13 21	13 21	13 24	13 29	13 35	13 43
64	14 51	14 43	36	29	14 22	14 17	14 12	14 08	14 05	14 04	14 03	14 04	14 06	14 10	14 15	14 21
62	15 09	15 02	14 56	14 50	14 45	14 41	37	34	32	31	32	33	35	38	14 42	14 47
N 60	15 23	15 18	15 12	15 08	15 03	15 00	14 57	14 55	14 54	14 53	14 53	14 55	14 57	14 59	15 03	15 07
58	36	31	26	22	19	16	15 13	15 12	15 11	15 10	15 11	15 12	15 14	15 17	20	24
56	46	42	38	35	32	29	27	26	25	25	26	27	29	31	34	38
54	15 56	15 52	48	45	43	41	39	38	38	38	39	40	42	44	47	15 50
52	16 04	16 01	15 58	15 55	15 53	15 51	50	49	48	49	49	15 51	15 52	15 55	15 58	16 01
N 50	16 12	16 09	16 06	16 03	16 01	16 00	15 59	15 58	15 58	15 58	15 59	16 01	16 02	16 05	16 07	16 10
45	28	26	24	22	21	20	16 19	16 19	16 19	16 19	16 20	21	23	25	28	30
40	41	39	38	37	36	35	35	35	35	36	37	38	40	42	44	16 47
35	16 53	16 51	16 50	16 49	16 49	16 48	16 48	16 48	16 49	16 50	16 51	16 52	16 54	16 56	16 58	17 00
30	17 03	17 01	17 01	17 00	17 00	17 00	17 00	17 01	17 01	17 02	17 04	17 05	17 07	17 09	17 10	13
N 20	17 20	17 19	17 19	17 19	17 19	17 20	17 20	17 21	17 22	17 23	17 25	17 26	17 28	17 29	17 31	17 33
N 10	35	35	35	36	37	37	38	39	41	42	17 43	17 45	17 46	17 48	17 50	17 51
0	17 49	17 50	17 51	17 52	17 53	17 54	17 55	17 56	17 58	17 59	18 01	18 02	18 04	18 05	18 07	18 08
S 10	18 03	18 05	18 06	18 07	18 09	18 10	18 12	18 14	18 15	18 17	18	20	21	23	24	25
20	19	21	23	25	26	28	30	32	34	36	37	18 39	18 40	18 41	18 43	18 44
S 30	18 37	18 39	18 42	18 44	18 47	18 49	18 51	18 54	18 56	18 58	18 59	19 01	19 02	19 03	19 04	19 05
35	47	18 50	18 53	18 56	18 59	19 02	19 04	19 06	19 09	19 11	19 12	14	15	16	17	18
40	18 59	19 03	19 06	19 09	19 13	16	18	21	23	26	27	29	30	31	32	32
45	19 14	18	22	25	29	32	36	19 39	19 41	19 44	19 45	19 47	19 48	19 49	19 50	19 50
50	31	36	41	45	50	19 54	19 57	20 01	20 03	20 06	20 08	20 10	20 11	20 12	20 12	20 11
S 52	19 40	19 45	19 50	19 55	19 59	20 04	20 07	20 11	20 14	20 17	20 19	20 21	20 22	20 22	20 22	20 22
54	19 49	19 55	20 00	20 05	20 10	15	19	23	26	29	31	33	34	34	34	34
56	20 00	20 06	12	18	23	28	33	37	40	20 43	20 45	20 47	20 48	20 49	20 48	20 47
58	12	19	25	32	38	20 43	20 48	20 53	20 57	21 00	21 02	21 04	21 05	21 05	21 05	21 03
S 60	20 26	20 34	20 41	20 48	20 55	21 01	21 07	21 12	21 17	21 20	21 23	21 25	21 25	21 25	21 24	21 22

MORNING CIVIL TWILIGHT A145

Lat.	November				December											Jan.
	19	22	25	28	1	4	7	10	13	16	19	22	25	28	31	3
°	h m	h m	h m	h m	h m	h m	h m	h m	h m	h m	h m	h m	h m	h m	h m	h m
N 72	08 51	09 05	09 20	09 34	09 48	10 02	10 15	10 27	10 38	10 48	10 54	10 57	10 57	10 53	10 46	10 38
70	25	08 37	08 48	08 59	09 09	09 19	09 28	09 36	09 43	09 48	09 52	09 54	09 55	09 54	09 51	09 47
68	08 06	08 15	25	34	08 42	08 50	08 57	09 04	09 09	09 14	09 17	09 19	09 20	09 20	09 18	09 15
66	07 50	07 58	08 06	08 14	22	29	35	08 40	08 45	08 49	08 52	08 54	08 55	08 55	08 54	08 52
64	37	44	07 52	07 59	08 05	08 11	17	22	26	29	32	34	35	35	34	33
62	26	33	39	45	07 51	07 57	08 02	08 06	08 10	13	16	18	19	19	19	18
N 60	07 16	07 23	07 29	07 34	07 40	07 45	07 49	07 53	07 57	08 00	08 02	08 04	08 05	08 06	08 06	08 05
58	08	14	19	24	29	34	38	42	45	07 48	07 51	07 52	07 54	07 54	07 54	07 54
56	07 01	07 06	11	16	21	25	29	32	36	38	40	42	43	44	44	44
54	06 54	06 59	07 04	08	13	17	20	24	27	29	32	33	35	35	36	35
52	48	53	06 57	07 01	07 05	09	13	16	19	21	23	25	26	27	28	27
N 50	06 42	06 47	06 51	06 55	06 59	07 02	07 06	07 09	07 11	07 14	07 16	07 18	07 19	07 20	07 20	07 20
45	30	34	38	41	44	06 47	06 50	06 53	06 56	06 58	07 00	07 02	07 03	07 04	07 05	07 05
40	20	23	26	29	32	35	38	40	42	44	06 46	06 48	06 49	06 50	06 51	06 52
35	11	13	16	19	21	24	26	29	31	33	34	36	38	39	40	40
30	06 02	06 05	06 07	06 10	06 12	06 14	06 16	18	20	22	24	26	27	28	29	30
N 20	05 48	05 49	05 51	05 53	05 55	05 56	05 58	06 00	06 02	06 04	06 05	06 07	06 08	06 09	06 11	06 12
N 10	34	35	36	37	39	40	42	05 43	05 45	05 46	05 48	05 49	05 51	05 52	05 54	05 55
0	20	20	21	22	23	24	25	26	28	29	31	32	34	35	37	38
S 10	05 05	05 05	05 05	05 06	05 06	05 07	05 08	05 09	05 10	05 11	05 13	05 14	05 16	05 17	05 19	20
20	04 48	04 48	04 48	04 47	04 47	04 48	04 48	04 49	04 50	04 51	04 52	04 53	04 55	04 57	04 59	05 00
S 30	04 28	04 27	04 26	04 25	04 24	04 24	04 24	04 25	04 25	04 26	04 27	04 28	04 30	04 32	04 34	04 36
35	16	04 14	04 12	04 11	04 10	04 10	04 10	04 10	04 10	04 11	04 12	04 13	04 15	04 17	19	21
40	04 01	03 59	03 57	03 55	03 54	03 53	03 52	03 52	03 52	03 53	03 54	03 55	03 57	03 59	04 01	04 04
45	03 43	40	38	35	33	32	31	30	30	30	31	32	34	36	03 39	03 42
50	21	17	13	03 10	03 07	03 04	03 03	03 01	03 01	03 01	03 01	03 03	03 04	03 07	03 10	03 13
S 52	03 09	03 05	03 00	02 57	02 53	02 51	02 49	02 47	02 46	02 46	02 46	02 47	02 49	02 52	02 55	02 58
54	02 57	02 51	02 46	42	38	35	32	30	29	28	28	29	31	34	37	41
56	42	35	30	24	02 20	02 15	02 12	02 09	02 07	02 06	02 06	02 07	02 09	02 12	02 16	02 20
58	24	02 16	02 09	02 02	01 56	01 50	01 46	01 42	01 39	01 37	01 36	01 37	01 39	01 42	01 47	01 53
S 60	02 01	01 52	01 42	01 33	01 24	01 16	01 07	00 59	00 53	00 49	00 47	00 47	00 49	00 54	01 01	01 10

EVENING CIVIL TWILIGHT

Lat.	November				December											Jan.
	19	22	25	28	1	4	7	10	13	16	19	22	25	28	31	3
°	h m	h m	h m	h m	h m	h m	h m	h m	h m	h m	h m	h m	h m	h m	h m	h m
N 72	14 38	14 26	14 13	14 01	13 49	13 37	13 27	13 17	13 09	13 02	12 59	12 59	13 02	13 09	13 19	13 31
70	15 04	14 54	14 45	14 36	14 28	14 20	14 14	14 08	14 04	14 02	14 01	14 02	14 04	14 09	14 14	14 21
68	24	15 16	15 08	15 01	14 55	14 49	14 44	14 41	14 38	14 36	14 36	14 37	14 39	14 43	14 47	14 53
66	40	33	26	20	15 15	15 11	15 07	15 04	15 02	15 01	15 01	15 03	15 05	15 08	15 12	15 17
64	15 53	47	41	36	32	28	25	23	21	21	21	22	24	27	31	35
62	16 04	15 58	15 54	15 49	46	42	40	38	37	37	37	39	41	43	15 46	15 51
N 60	16 13	16 09	16 04	16 01	15 57	15 55	15 53	15 51	15 50	15 50	15 51	15 52	15 54	15 57	16 00	16 03
58	22	17	14	10	16 08	16 05	16 04	16 02	16 02	16 02	16 03	16 04	16 06	16 08	11	15
56	29	26	22	19	17	15	13	13	12	12	13	14	16	19	21	25
54	36	33	30	27	25	23	22	21	21	21	22	24	25	28	30	33
52	42	39	36	34	32	31	30	29	29	29	30	32	34	36	39	41
N 50	16 48	16 45	16 43	16 41	16 39	16 38	16 37	16 36	16 37	16 37	16 38	16 39	16 41	16 43	16 46	16 48
45	17 00	16 58	16 56	16 55	16 53	16 53	16 52	16 52	16 52	16 53	16 54	16 55	16 57	16 59	17 01	17 04
40	10	17 09	17 07	17 06	17 06	17 05	17 05	17 05	17 06	17 06	17 08	17 09	17 11	17 13	15	17
35	20	18	17	17	16	16	16	17	17	18	19	21	22	24	26	28
30	28	27	27	26	26	26	26	27	28	29	30	31	33	35	37	39
N 20	17 43	17 43	17 43	17 43	17 43	17 44	17 45	17 45	17 46	17 48	17 49	17 50	17 52	17 53	17 55	17 57
N 10	17 57	17 57	17 58	17 58	17 59	18 00	18 01	18 02	18 03	18 05	18 06	18 08	18 09	18 11	18 12	18 14
0	18 11	18 12	18 13	18 14	18 15	16	17	19	20	22	23	25	26	28	29	30
S 10	26	27	29	30	32	33	35	37	38	18 40	18 41	18 43	18 44	18 46	18 47	18 48
20	18 43	18 45	18 47	18 49	18 51	18 53	18 55	18 57	18 58	19 00	19 02	19 03	19 05	19 06	19 07	19 08
S 30	19 03	19 06	19 09	19 11	19 14	19 16	19 19	19 21	19 23	19 25	19 27	19 28	19 30	19 31	19 32	19 32
35	16	19	22	25	28	31	33	36	38	40	19 42	19 44	19 45	19 46	19 47	19 47
40	30	34	38	19 41	19 45	19 48	19 51	19 54	19 56	19 58	20 00	20 02	20 03	20 04	20 05	20 05
45	19 48	19 53	19 57	20 01	20 05	20 09	20 12	20 16	20 18	20 21	23	25	26	26	27	27
50	20 11	20 17	20 22	27	32	37	41	44	20 48	20 50	20 53	20 54	20 55	20 56	20 56	20 55
S 52	20 23	20 29	20 35	20 40	20 45	20 50	20 55	20 59	21 03	21 06	21 08	21 10	21 11	21 11	21 11	21 10
54	36	42	20 49	20 55	21 01	21 07	21 12	21 16	20	23	26	27	28	29	28	27
56	20 51	20 58	21 06	21 13	20	26	32	21 37	21 42	21 45	21 48	21 50	21 51	21 50	21 49	21 47
58	21 09	21 18	27	21 36	21 44	21 51	21 59	22 05	22 10	22 15	22 18	22 20	22 20	22 20	22 18	22 15
S 60	21 32	21 43	21 55	22 06	22 17	22 27	22 39	22 48	22 57	23 04	23 08	23 10	23 09	23 07	23 03	22 56

Ar66 CONVERSION OF ARC TO TIME

°	h m	°	h m	°	h m	°	h m	°	h m	°	h m	′	m s
0	0 00	60	4 00	120	8 00	180	12 00	240	16 00	300	20 00	0	0 00
1	0 04	61	4 04	121	8 04	181	12 04	241	16 04	301	20 04	1	0 04
2	0 08	62	4 08	122	8 08	182	12 08	242	16 08	302	20 08	2	0 08
3	0 12	63	4 12	123	8 12	183	12 12	243	16 12	303	20 12	3	0 12
4	0 16	64	4 16	124	8 16	184	12 16	244	16 16	304	20 16	4	0 16
5	0 20	65	4 20	125	8 20	185	12 20	245	16 20	305	20 20	5	0 20
6	0 24	66	4 24	126	8 24	186	12 24	246	16 24	306	20 24	6	0 24
7	0 28	67	4 28	127	8 28	187	12 28	247	16 28	307	20 28	7	0 28
8	0 32	68	4 32	128	8 32	188	12 32	248	16 32	308	20 32	8	0 32
9	0 36	69	4 36	129	8 36	189	12 36	249	16 36	309	20 36	9	0 36
10	0 40	70	4 40	130	8 40	190	12 40	250	16 40	310	20 40	10	0 40
11	0 44	71	4 44	131	8 44	191	12 44	251	16 44	311	20 44	11	0 44
12	0 48	72	4 48	132	8 48	192	12 48	252	16 48	312	20 48	12	0 48
13	0 52	73	4 52	133	8 52	193	12 52	253	16 52	313	20 52	13	0 52
14	0 56	74	4 56	134	8 56	194	12 56	254	16 56	314	20 56	14	0 56
15	1 00	75	5 00	135	9 00	195	13 00	255	17 00	315	21 00	15	1 00
16	1 04	76	5 04	136	9 04	196	13 04	256	17 04	316	21 04	16	1 04
17	1 08	77	5 08	137	9 08	197	13 08	257	17 08	317	21 08	17	1 08
18	1 12	78	5 12	138	9 12	198	13 12	258	17 12	318	21 12	18	1 12
19	1 16	79	5 16	139	9 16	199	13 16	259	17 16	319	21 16	19	1 16
20	1 20	80	5 20	140	9 20	200	13 20	260	17 20	320	21 20	20	1 20
21	1 24	81	5 24	141	9 24	201	13 24	261	17 24	321	21 24	21	1 24
22	1 28	82	5 28	142	9 28	202	13 28	262	17 28	322	21 28	22	1 28
23	1 32	83	5 32	143	9 32	203	13 32	263	17 32	323	21 32	23	1 32
24	1 36	84	5 36	144	9 36	204	13 36	264	17 36	324	21 36	24	1 36
25	1 40	85	5 40	145	9 40	205	13 40	265	17 40	325	21 40	25	1 40
26	1 44	86	5 44	146	9 44	206	13 44	266	17 44	326	21 44	26	1 44
27	1 48	87	5 48	147	9 48	207	13 48	267	17 48	327	21 48	27	1 48
28	1 52	88	5 52	148	9 52	208	13 52	268	17 52	328	21 52	28	1 52
29	1 56	89	5 56	149	9 56	209	13 56	269	17 56	329	21 56	29	1 56
30	2 00	90	6 00	150	10 00	210	14 00	270	18 00	330	22 00	30	2 00
31	2 04	91	6 04	151	10 04	211	14 04	271	18 04	331	22 04	31	2 04
32	2 08	92	6 08	152	10 08	212	14 08	272	18 08	332	22 08	32	2 08
33	2 12	93	6 12	153	10 12	213	14 12	273	18 12	333	22 12	33	2 12
34	2 16	94	6 16	154	10 16	214	14 16	274	18 16	334	22 16	34	2 16
35	2 20	95	6 20	155	10 20	215	14 20	275	18 20	335	22 20	35	2 20
36	2 24	96	6 24	156	10 24	216	14 24	276	18 24	336	22 24	36	2 24
37	2 28	97	6 28	157	10 28	217	14 28	277	18 28	337	22 28	37	2 28
38	2 32	98	6 32	158	10 32	218	14 32	278	18 32	338	22 32	38	2 32
39	2 36	99	6 36	159	10 36	219	14 36	279	18 36	339	22 36	39	2 36
40	2 40	100	6 40	160	10 40	220	14 40	280	18 40	340	22 40	40	2 40
41	2 44	101	6 44	161	10 44	221	14 44	281	18 44	341	22 44	41	2 44
42	2 48	102	6 48	162	10 48	222	14 48	282	18 48	342	22 48	42	2 48
43	2 52	103	6 52	163	10 52	223	14 52	283	18 52	343	22 52	43	2 52
44	2 56	104	6 56	164	10 56	224	14 56	284	18 56	344	22 56	44	2 56
45	3 00	105	7 00	165	11 00	225	15 00	285	19 00	345	23 00	45	3 00
46	3 04	106	7 04	166	11 04	226	15 04	286	19 04	346	23 04	46	3 04
47	3 08	107	7 08	167	11 08	227	15 08	287	19 08	347	23 08	47	3 08
48	3 12	108	7 12	168	11 12	228	15 12	288	19 12	348	23 12	48	3 12
49	3 16	109	7 16	169	11 16	229	15 16	289	19 16	349	23 16	49	3 16
50	3 20	110	7 20	170	11 20	230	15 20	290	19 20	350	23 20	50	3 20
51	3 24	111	7 24	171	11 24	231	15 24	291	19 24	351	23 24	51	3 24
52	3 28	112	7 28	172	11 28	232	15 28	292	19 28	352	23 28	52	3 28
53	3 32	113	7 32	173	11 32	233	15 32	293	19 32	353	23 32	53	3 32
54	3 36	114	7 36	174	11 36	234	15 36	294	19 36	354	23 36	54	3 36
55	3 40	115	7 40	175	11 40	235	15 40	295	19 40	355	23 40	55	3 40
56	3 44	116	7 44	176	11 44	236	15 44	296	19 44	356	23 44	56	3 44
57	3 48	117	7 48	177	11 48	237	15 48	297	19 48	357	23 48	57	3 48
58	3 52	118	7 52	178	11 52	238	15 52	298	19 52	358	23 52	58	3 52
59	3 56	119	7 56	179	11 56	239	15 56	299	19 56	359	23 56	59	3 56

The above table is for converting expressions in arc to their equivalent in time; its main use in this Almanac is for the conversion of longitude for application to L.M.T. (*added* if *west*, *subtracted* if *east*) to give UT or vice versa, particularly in the case of sunrise, sunset, etc.

ANSWERS TO TIME PROBLEMS

Time Example 1 LMT at 0327E is 1816, 18 April. What is LMT at 165°32'E?

LMT	1816	18 April
Convert to UTC	- 0014	
UTC	1802	18 April
165°33' in time	+ 1102	
	2904	
	- 2400	
	0504	19 April

Time Example 2 LMT 179°50'W is 2300, 15 December, what is LMT at 179°50'E?

LMT 179°50'W	2300	15 December
Convert to UTC	+ 1159	
	3459	
	- 2400	
UTC	1059	16 December
179°50' in time	+ 1159	
LMT	2258	16 December

Chapter 19
Point of Equal Time, Point of Safe Return, and Radius of Action

INTRODUCTION

When flight planning, a pilot must be aware of the actions necessary in an emergency. This includes the decision whether to:

- ➢ Return to the airport of departure
- ➢ Continue to the destination
- ➢ Fly to an alternate

This chapter shows how to calculate both the Point of Equal Time (Critical Point) and the Point of Safe Return (Point of No Return).

POINT OF EQUAL TIME

The Point of Equal Time (PET) is the point between two aerodromes from which it would take the same time to fly to either aerodrome.

For the still air case, the Point of Equal Time would be halfway between the two aerodromes. This is not likely, so the PET is seldom halfway between the two aerodromes. The calculation of the PET is based on a ratio of the groundspeed to the destination and groundspeed back to base. The TAS used for the calculation depends upon whether the aircraft is to fly with:

- ➢ All engines operating
- ➢ One-engine inoperative

PET FORMULA

The PET is based on the statement that the time to destination is equal to the time to return to the aerodrome of departure.

Certain assumptions have to be made for the calculation:

D is the total distance between airfields
X is the distance from the PET back to A
D-X is the distance to the destination (B)
H is the groundspeed home
O is the groundspeed to B

Time = Distance ÷ Groundspeed

PET is the point where time to destination is equal to the time to return to aerodrome of departure.

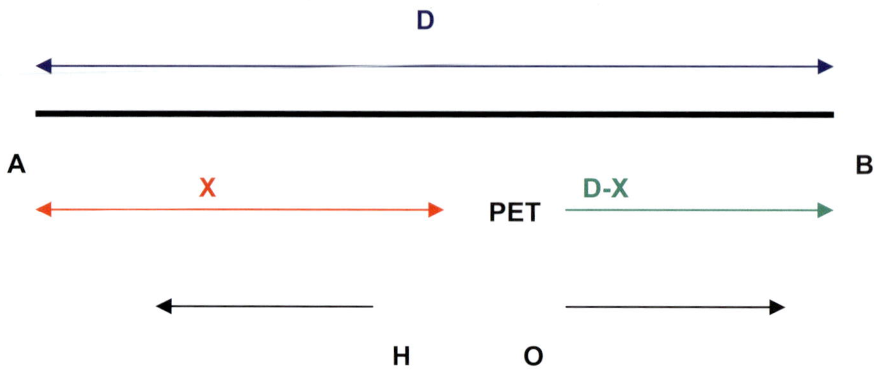

Time to destination = $\frac{D-X}{O}$

Time to return = $\frac{X}{H}$

$$\frac{X}{H} - \frac{D-X}{O}$$

$$\mathbf{X = \frac{DH}{O + H}}$$

X defines the distance of the PET from the departure.

Example Assume that points A and B are 600 nm apart.
TAS is 300 kt.
Calculate the PET for the three conditions:

- Still air
- 50 knot headwind
- 50 knot tailwind

In the still air condition, the PET must be halfway along the route.
300 nm

In the 50 knot headwind case:
H = 350 kt
O = 250 kt
$X = \frac{600 \times 350}{250 + 350} =$ **350 nm**

In the 50 knot tailwind case:
H = 250 kt
O = 350 kt
$X = \frac{600 \times 250}{350 + 250} =$ **250 nm**

To check that the calculation is correct, check the time it takes to go to B or return to A.
In both cases, the time is 1 hour.

The wind effect moves the PET into wind.

PET Example 1	A – B	1240 nm
	TAS	340 kt
	Wind Component	+20 kt outbound
PET Example 2	A – B	2700 nm
	TAS	450 kt
	Wind Component	+50 kt outbound
PET Example 3	A – B	1400 nm
	TAS	270 kt
	Wind Component	+40 kt outbound
PET Example 4	A – B	1120 nm
	TAS	210 kt
	Wind Component	-35 kt outbound

ENGINE FAILURE PET

In most jet aircraft, the loss of a power unit causes **drift down**—the aircraft descends to a pressure altitude that the power can sustain. There is now a decision to be made as to whether the aircraft continues or returns.

Example	**Using Example 2**	
	A – B	2700 nm
	TAS	450 kt
	Wind Component	+50 kt outbound
	PET from A	**1200 nm**
	Time	**2 hours 24 minutes**

Consider the case of an engine failure: the TAS is most likely to be lower.
Assume a TAS of 360 knots. Use the same conditions as for Example 2.

H = 310 kt
O = 410 kt
$X = \frac{2700 \times 310}{410 + 310} = 1162$ nm

PET from A **1162 nm**

With one engine inoperative, the wind has more effect, and the PET is removed further from mid-point than in the all-engines-operative case.

The aeroplane flies with all engines operating until the engine failure. The reduced speed is used only to establish the one-engine-inoperative PET.

Therefore, the time to the PET is the all-engines groundspeed out.

A – B	1162 nm
GS	500 kt
Time	**2 Hours, 15 Minutes**

PET Example 5

A – B	2254 nm
Wind Component	-25 kt outbound
4 Engine TAS	475 kt
3 Engine TAS	440 kt

Calculate the distance and time from A to the one-engine-out PET.

PET Example 6

A – B	1260 nm
Wind Velocity	020/35 kt
Course	040°T
4 Engine TAS	480 kt
3 Engine TAS	435 kt

Calculate the distance and time from A to the one-engine-out PET.

PET Example 7

A – B	1700 nm
Wind Velocity	240/45 kt
Course	030°T
4 Engine TAS	480 kt
3 Engine TAS	370 kt

Calculate the distance and time from A to the one-engine-out PET.

MULTI-LEG PET

Unfortunately, most routes involve more than one leg, and multi-route calculations need to be made. Consider the route below.

TWO-LEG PET

An aircraft is operating on the following route. What is the PET for one engine inoperative?

Route	Distance	Course	Wind Velocity
A – B	1025 nm	210	270/40
B – C	998 nm	330	280/20

4 Engine TAS	380 kt
3 Engine TAS	350 kt

STEP 1 Determine the groundspeed for:

B – C	334 kt
B – A	368 kt

STEP 2 Determine the times:

B – C	179 minutes
B – A	167 minutes

STEP 3 Because the time B – C is greater than the time B – A, the PET must be along B – C. To find the PET, the time of return must be equal to the time to travel to the destination.

Find the point along B – C (call this Point X) where the time to C is equal to the time B – A (167 minutes). This leaves a distance from which to calculate the PET.

Groundspeed	334 knots
Point X	930 nm from C

STEP 4 The PET must lie between B and X. Distance BX is
998 – 930 = 68 nm

STEP 5 Using the PET formula, calculate the PET for the 68 nm leg B – X.
A return groundspeed is needed for X – B = 365 kt

$$\frac{68 \times 365}{334 + 365} = 35 \text{ nm from B}$$

A – PET is 1060 nm

STEP 6 To calculate the time to the PET, calculate the four-engine time to B.
The calculate the four-engine time to the PET using the 35 nm calculated above:

A – B	**4 Engine**	**172 min**
B – PET	**4 Engine**	**6 min**
A – PET		**178 min**

THREE-LEG PET

Consider the route below. Calculate the one-engine-inoperative PET using the figures below:

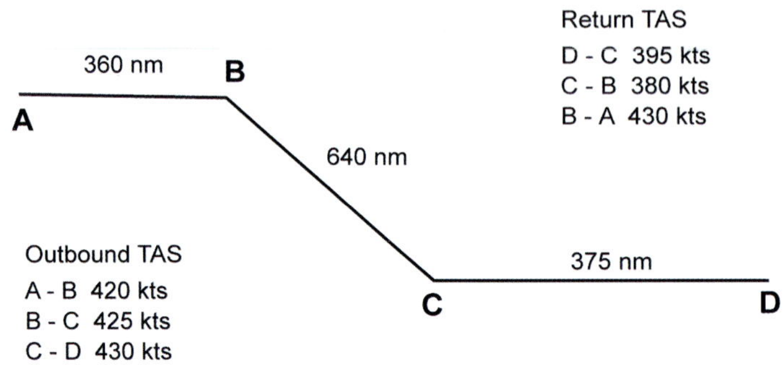

Outbound

Route	TAS	Wind Component	Groundspeed	Distance	Time
A – B	420	+30	450	360	48
B – C	425	+55	480	640	80
C – D	430	+20	450	375	50

Return

Route	TAS	Wind Component	Groundspeed	Distance	Time
D – C	395	-20	375	375	60
C – B	380	-60	320	640	120
B – A	425	-25	400	360	54

STEP 1 By inspection of the times, it is obvious that the PET lies between B and C. Add all the outbound times together and halve them.

178 minutes total, therefore **89 minutes.**

This would put the aircraft along leg B – C.

STEP 2 To fly from B – A takes 54 minutes.

To fly from C – D takes 50 minutes.

If the times were equal, the normal PET formula could be used to calculate a PET between B – C. The times must be equalised. This is done by working out how far the aircraft travels (54 – 50) in 4 minutes along the outbound leg.

Groundspeed 480 kt
Distance 32 nm

STEP 3 This gives the same time for the outbound leg as the inbound.

STEP 4 Now establish a PET for a revised distance of 608 nm (640 – 32).

$$\frac{608 \times 320}{320 + 480} = 243 \text{ nm}$$

which makes the PET 243 nm from B.

PET Example 8 Using the following data, calculate the distance and time to the one-engine-inoperative PET for the following route:

4 Engine TAS 200 kt
3 Engine TAS 160 kt

Route	Course	Distance	Wind Velocity
A – B	115	170	180/20
B – C	178	110	230/30
C – D	129	147	250/15

PET Example 9 Using the following data, calculate the distance and time to the all-engines-operative PET for the following route:

TAS 175 kt

Route	TAS	Wind Component	Distance
A – B	175	-5 kt	450
B – C	175	-15 kt	430

PET Example 10 Using the following data, calculate the distance and time to the all-engines-operative PET for the following route:
4 Engine TAS 250 kt

Route	Distance	Wind Component
A – B	252	-20
B – C	502	-5
C – D	310	+10

POINT OF SAFE RETURN

This is also known as the point of no return. The Point of Safe Return (PSR) is the point furthest from the airfield of departure that an aircraft can fly and still return to base within its safe endurance.

The term safe endurance should not be confused with the term total endurance.

Total Endurance	The time an aircraft can remain airborne.
Safe Endurance	The time an aircraft can fly without using the reserves of fuel that are required.

The distance to the PSR equals the distance from the PSR back to the aerodrome of departure.

Let:

E	Safe endurance
T	Time to the PSR
E – T	Time to return to the aerodrome of departure
O	Groundspeed to the PSR
H	Groundspeed on return to the aerodrome of departure

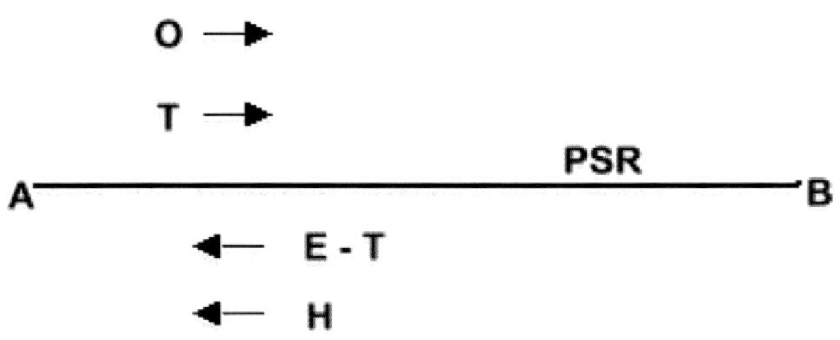

Time to the PSR	T x O
Time to return to the aerodrome of departure	(E – T) x H
	(E – T) x H = T x O

$$\mathbf{T = \frac{EH}{O + H}}$$

SINGLE-LEG PSR

Given the following data, calculate the time and distance to the PSR:

TAS	220 kt
Wind Component	+45 kt
Safe Endurance	6 hours

$$T = \frac{360 \times 175}{175 + 265} = 143 \text{ min} = 632 \text{ nm}$$

PSR Example 1 Calculate the PSR, given the following data:

A – B	800 nm
TAS	175 kt
Wind Component Outbound	-15 kt
Safe Endurance	5 hours

PSR Example 2 Calculate the PSR, given the following data:

Fuel Available, excluding Reserve	21 240 lb
Fuel Consumption	3730 lb/hr
TAS Outbound	275 kt
TAS for Return Leg	285 kt
Wind Component Outbound	-35 kt

PSR Example 3 Calculate the PSR, given the following data:

A – B	2200 nm
TAS	455 kt
Wind Component Outbound	-15 kt
Safe Endurance	6½ hours

MULTI-LEG PSR

Using the same principle as above, calculate the multi-leg PSR. Use the route below;

Route	Distance	Groundspeed		Time	
		Out	In	Out	In
A – B	300 nm	315 kt	440 kt	57 min	41 min
B – C	250 nm	375 kt	455 kt	40 min	33 min
C – D	350 nm	310 kt	375 kt	68 min	56 min

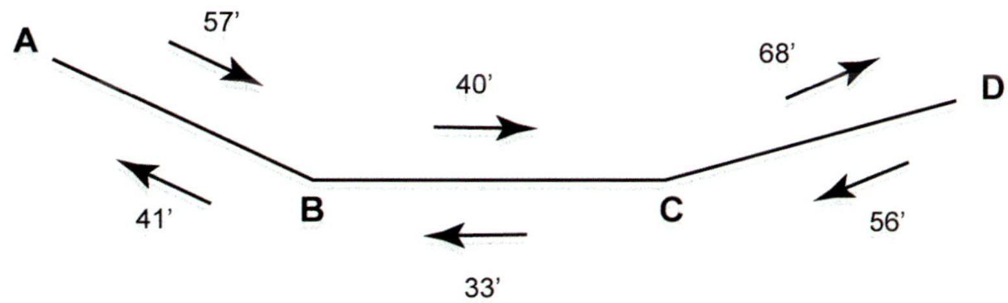

Safe Endurance is 210 minutes.

STEP 1 Determine on which leg the PSR will be by inspection

Time A – B	57 min	Time B – C	40 min
Time B – A	41 min	Time C – B	33 min
	98 min		73 min
Total Time	171 min		

The Safe Endurance is 210 min

PSR must be on leg C to D

STEP 2 Remaining endurance is 39 min

Calculate the PSR for C – D, using 39 min as the safe endurance.

$$T = \frac{39 \times 375}{310 + 375} = 21 \text{ min from C}$$

PSR Example 4 Calculate the time and distance to the PSR from A:

Route	Distance	TAS	Wind Component
A – B	520	200	-20
B – C	480	200	+6

Safe Endurance 6 hours 10 minutes

PSR Example 5 Calculate the time and distance to the PSR from A:

Route	Distance	TAS	Wind Component
A – B	410	250	-35
B – C	360	250	-25
C – D	200	250	-30

Safe Endurance 6 hours 10 minutes

PSR WITH VARIABLE FUEL FLOW

So far, the PSR has been given as a time. In the formula below, the data is based upon the total fuel resolved into kg/nm.

Let:

D	Distance to the PSR
F	Fuel available for the PSR
FO	Fuel consumption out to the PSR (kg/nm)
FH	Fuel consumption home from the PSR (kg/nm)

The fuel used to get to the PSR plus the fuel used to get home from the PSR must equal the total fuel available (less reserves).

$$(d \times FO) + (d \times FH) = F$$

$$\mathbf{d = F \div (FO + FH)}$$

Example Given the following data, calculate the time to the PSR.

TAS	310 kt
Wind Component	+30 kt
Fuel Available	39 500 kg
Fuel Flow Out	6250 kg/hr
Fuel Flow Home	5300 kg/hr

STEP 1 Calculate the groundspeed out and the groundspeed home.

Groundspeed Out 340 kt

Groundspeed Home 280 kt

STEP 2 Calculate the kg/nm for leg out and leg home.

FO = 6250 ÷ 340 = 18.4 kg/nm

FH = 5300 ÷ 280 = 18.9 kg/nm

STEP 3 Calculate the time to the PSR.

Distance = 39 500 ÷ (18.4 + 18.9)

= 1059 nm

Time = 187 min

PSR Example 6 Given the following data, calculate the distance and time to the PSR.

TAS Out	474 kt
Wind Component Out	-50 kt
Fuel Flow Out	11 500 lb/hr
TAS Home	466 kt
Wind Component Home	+70 kt
Fuel Flow Home	10 300 lb/hr
Flight Plan Fuel	82 000 lb
Reserves	12 000 lb

PSR Example 7 Given the following data, calculate the distance and time to the PSR.

Leg Distance	1190 nm
TAS Out	210 kt
Wind Component Out	-30 kt
Fuel Flow Out	2400 kg/hr
TAS Home	210 kt
Wind Component Home	+30 kt
Fuel Flow Home	2000 kg/hr
Flight Plan Fuel	20 500 kg
Reserves	6000 kg

MULTI-LEG PSR WITH VARIABLE FUEL FLOW

In the previous multi-leg case, time out and time home were calculated on consecutive legs. In the variable fuel case, replace these figures by fuel out and fuel home and compare the total fuel burn.

Example Find the distance and time to the PSR from A. Given:

Route	Distance	TAS	Wind Component Out	Wind Component Home
A – B	270	480	-30	+35
B – C	340	480	-50	+55

Fuel Flow Out 11 900 kg/hr
Fuel Flow Home 11 650 kg/hr
Fuel Available 20 000 kg

STEP 1 Calculate the fuel A – B and B – A:

Time for Leg A – B **36.1 min**
Time for Leg B – A **31.5 min**

Fuel Used A – B **7160 kg**
Fuel Used B – A **6116 kg**
Fuel **13 276 kg**

STEP 2 Calculate the fuel remaining:

20 000 – 13 276 = 6724 kg

STEP 3 The PSR is on B – C.

FO = 11 900 ÷ 430 = 27.7 kg/nm
FH = 11 650 ÷ 535 = 21.8 kg/nm

STEP 4 Calculate the distance for the PSR:

D = 6724 ÷ (27.7 + 21.8)
D = 136 nm

The above distance is from B.

Total distance from A is **406 nm.**

STEP 5 Calculate the time to the PSR:

Time A – B **36.1 min**
Time B – PSR **18.2 min**
Time to PSR **54 min**

PSR Example 8 Given the following route, calculate the distance and time to the PSR, assuming that the aircraft returns to A on 3 engines:

Route	Course	Distance	Wind Velocity
A – B	042	606	260/110
B – C	064	417	280/80
C – D	011	61	290/50

TAS 4 Engine	410 kt
TAS 3 Engine	350 kt
4 Engine Fuel Flow	3000 kg/hr
3 Engine Fuel Flow	2800 kg/hr
Fuel Available	12 900 kg

RADIUS OF ACTION

The radius of action can be defined as the distance to the furthest point from departure that an aircraft can fly, carry out a given task, and return to its airfield of departure within the safe endurance.

The formula for radius of action is derived from the PSR formula, and is:

$$\text{Radius of action} = \frac{E \times O \times H}{(O + H)}$$

Where: E is the safe endurance minus time on task.

PET & PSR ANSWERS

PET Example 1	PET from A	584 nm
	Time	1 hour 37 minutes
PET Example 2	PET from A	1200 nm
	Time	2 hours 24 minutes
PET Example 3	PET from A	596 nm
	Time	1 hour 55 minutes
PET Example 4	PET from A	653 nm
	Time	3 hours 44 minutes
PET Example 5	PET from A	1191 nm
	Time	2 hours 39 minutes
PET Example 6	PET from A	679 nm
	Time	1 hour 32 minutes
PET Example 7	PET from A	760 nm
	Time	1 hour 28 minutes
PET Example 8	PET from A	221 nm
	Time	1 hour 11 minutes
PET Example 9	PET from A	488 nm
	Time	3 hours 14 minutes
PET Example 10	PET from A	540 nm
	Time	2 hour 16 minutes
PSR Example 1	PSR from A	163 minutes
	Distance	435 nm
PSR Example 2	PSR from A	195 minutes
	Distance	781 nm
PSR Example 3	PSR from A	201 minutes
	Distance	1477 nm
PSR Example 4	PSR from A	200 minutes
	Distance	611 nm
PSR Example 5	PSR from A	208 minutes
	Distance	760 nm

PSR Example 6	Distance	1510 nm
	Time	213 minutes
PSR Example 7	Distance	669 nm
	Time	223 minutes
PSR Example 8	Distance	765 nm
	Time	94 minutes

Chapter 20
Aircraft Magnetism

PRINCIPLES OF MAGNETISM

Direct-reading magnetic compasses were among the first of the airborne flight instruments introduced into aircraft. The primary function of the direct-reading compass was to show the direction in which the fore-and-aft axis of an aircraft was pointing (heading) with reference to the Earth's local magnetic meridian. However, the direct-reading magnetic compass has now been overtaken as a heading reference instrument by the gyro-magnetic compass and flight director systems. The direct-reading compass is now relegated to the standby role, although its carriage in all types of aircraft is still a mandatory requirement of Joint Airworthiness Requirements (JAR).

The operating principles of direct-reading compasses are based on the fundamentals of magnetism. They are also based on the reaction between the magnetic field of a suitably-suspended magnetic element and the magnetic field surrounding the Earth. It is useful for the student to have a basic understanding of the fundamentals before proceeding further.

MAGNETIC PROPERTIES

The three principle properties of a simple, permanent bar magnet are:

- It attracts other pieces of iron and steel.

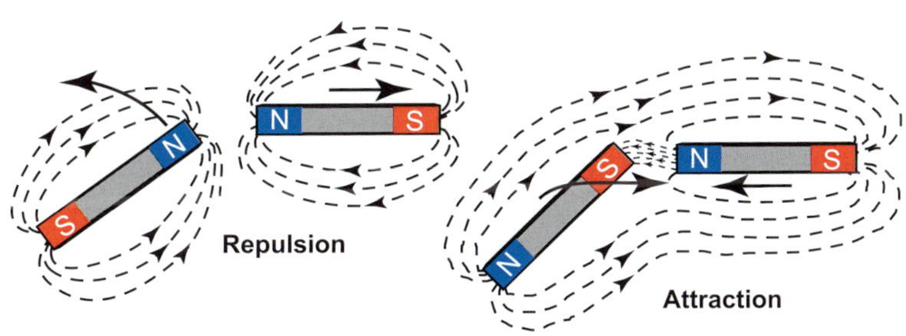

- Its power of attraction is concentrated at each end of the bar.

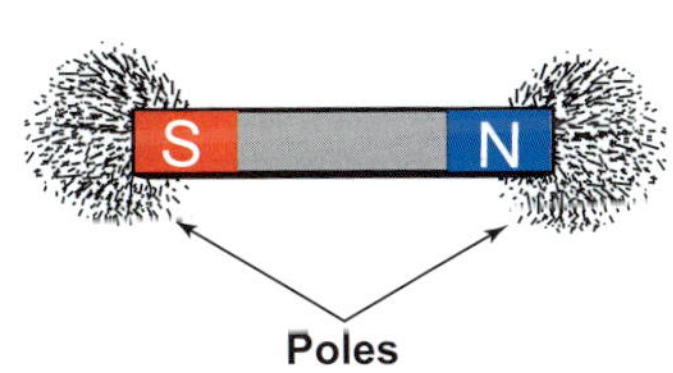

- When suspended so as to move horizontally, it always comes to rest in an approximately north-south direction.

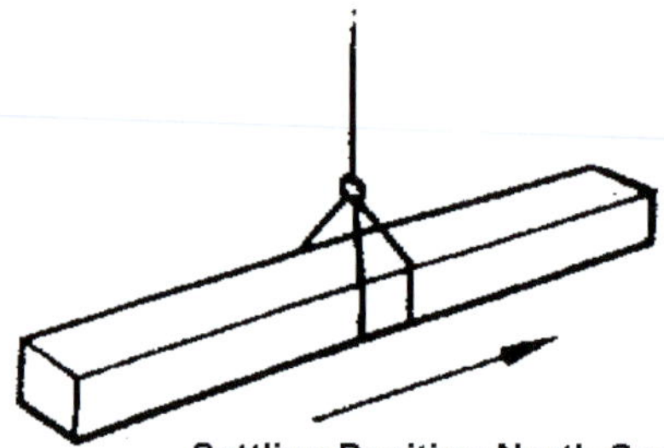

The second and third properties are related to the poles of a magnet. The end which seeks north is called the north or red pole, and the end which seeks south is called the south or blue pole.

When two such magnets are brought together so that both north or both south poles face each other, a force is felt between the magnets which keeps them apart, as shown in the diagram on Page 1. However, if one magnet is turned round so that a north pole faces a south pole, a force is also created between the magnets, but it pulls them together. Thus:

- Like poles repel.
- Unlike poles attract.

This is a fundamental law of magnetism. The force of attraction or repulsion between the two magnets varies inversely as the square of the distance between them.

A magnetic field is the region in which the force exerted by a magnet can be detected. This field has a magnetic flux which may be represented in direction and intensity by lines of flux. The direction of the lines of flux outside a magnet are from the north to the south pole. The lines are continuous, and do not cross one another so that, within the magnet, flow is from the south pole to the north pole. If two magnetic fields are brought close together, the lines of flux do not cross one another, but together form a distorted field consisting of closed loops.

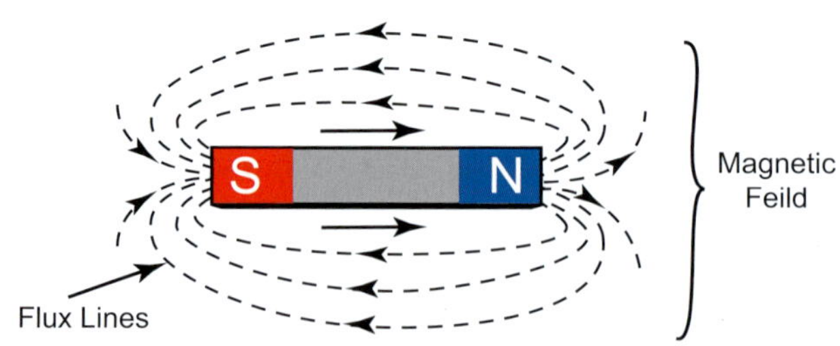

Magnetic flux is established more easily in some materials than in others. All materials, whether magnetic or not, have a property called reluctance which resists the establishment of magnetic flux and equates to the resistance found in an electric circuit.

MAGNETIC MOMENT

The magnetic moment of a magnet is the tendency for it to turn or be turned by another magnet. It is a requirement of aircraft compass design that the strength of the moment is such that the magnetic detection system rapidly responds to the directive force of a magnetic field.

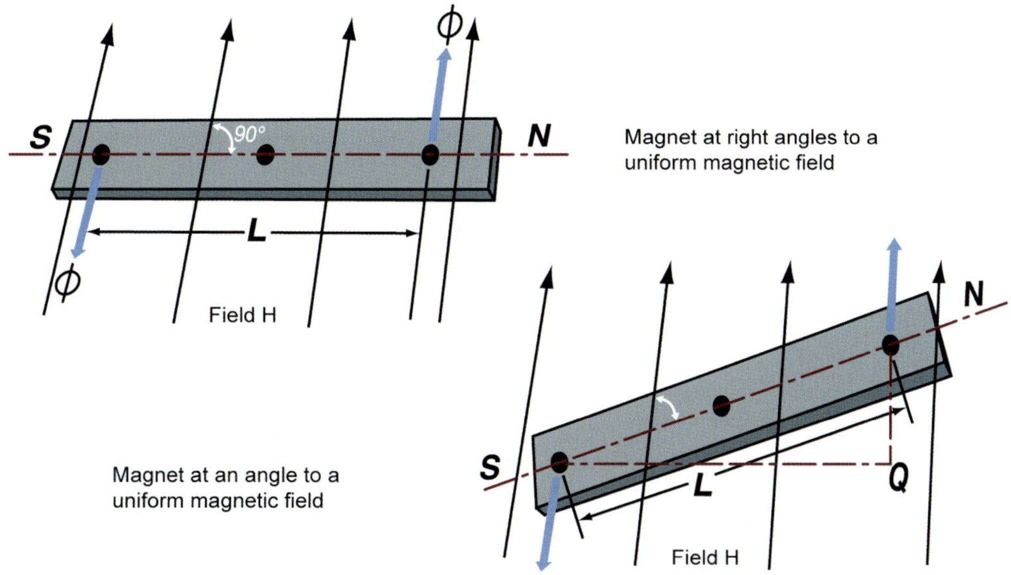

In the diagram above, a pivoted magnet of pole strength **S** and magnetic axis **L** is positioned at right angles to a uniform magnetic field **H**. In this situation, the field is distorted in order to pass through the magnet. In resisting the distortion, the field tries to pull the magnet round until it is correctly aligned with the field. As the forces applied to the magnet act in opposite directions, the magnet's moment works as a couple, swinging the magnet into line with the magnetic field:

M = S (pole strength) x L (length of magnetic axis)

From the above, it is evident that the greater the pole strength and the longer the magnetic moment, the greater the magnet's tendency to align itself quickly with the applied field and the greater the force it exerts upon the surrounding field or upon any magnetic material in its vicinity.

MAGNET IN A DEFLECTING FIELD

The diagram below shows a magnet situated in a uniform magnetic field of strength H_1 and subject to a uniform deflecting field of strength H_2 acting at right angles to H_1.

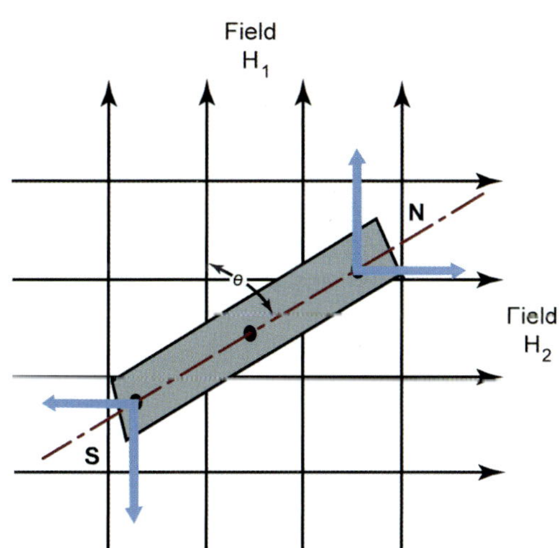

Assuming the magnet is at an angle θ to field H_1, the torque due to H_1 is magnetic moment (m).

$$m \times H_1 \times \sin\theta \text{ or } m\,H_1 \sin\theta$$

The torque due to H_2 is

$$m\, H_1 \cos\theta$$

Thus, for the magnet to be in equilibrium

$$m\, H_1 \sin\theta = m\, H_2 \cos\theta$$

and therefore the strength of the deflecting field H_2

$$H_1 \tan\theta.$$

PERIOD OF A SUSPENDED MAGNET

If a suspended magnet is deflected from its position of rest in a magnetic field, the magnet is immediately subject to a couple urging the magnet to resume its original position. When the deflecting influence is removed, the magnet swings back, and if undamped, the system oscillates about its equilibrium position before coming to rest. The time it takes for the magnet to swing from one extremity of oscillation to the other and back again is known as the **period of the magnet**.

As the magnet comes to rest, the amplitude of the oscillations gradually decreases, but the period remains the same and cannot be altered by adjusting amplitude. The period of a magnet depends upon its shape and size or mass (factors which effect the moment of inertia), its magnetic moment, and the strength of the field in which it is oscillating. The period growing longer as the magnet's mass is increased and becomes shorter as the field strength increases.

HARD IRON AND SOFT IRON

Hard and **soft** are terms used to describe various magnetic materials according how easy they are magnetised. Metals such as cobalt and tungsten steels are of the hard type since they are difficult to magnetise, but once in a magnetised state, they retain the magnetism for a considerable length of time. This long term magnetic state is known as **permanent magnetism**. Hard iron has **coercive force**. Coercive force is how much the magnet resists magnetisation or, if already magnetised, of resists demagnetisation. Metals which are easily magnetised, such as silicon or iron, and which generally lose their magnetised state once the magnetising force is removed, are known as **soft iron**. These terms are also used to describe the magnetic effects occurring in aircraft.

TERRESTRIAL MAGNETISM

The planet Earth is surrounded by a weak magnetic field which culminates in two internal magnetic poles situated near the north and south geographic poles. This is illustrated in the fact that a magnet, freely suspended at various locations within the Earth's magnetic field, settles in a definite direction which varies with the location relative to true north. A plane passing through the magnet and the centre of the Earth would trace an imaginary line on the Earth's surface called a **magnetic meridian**, as shown on the next page.

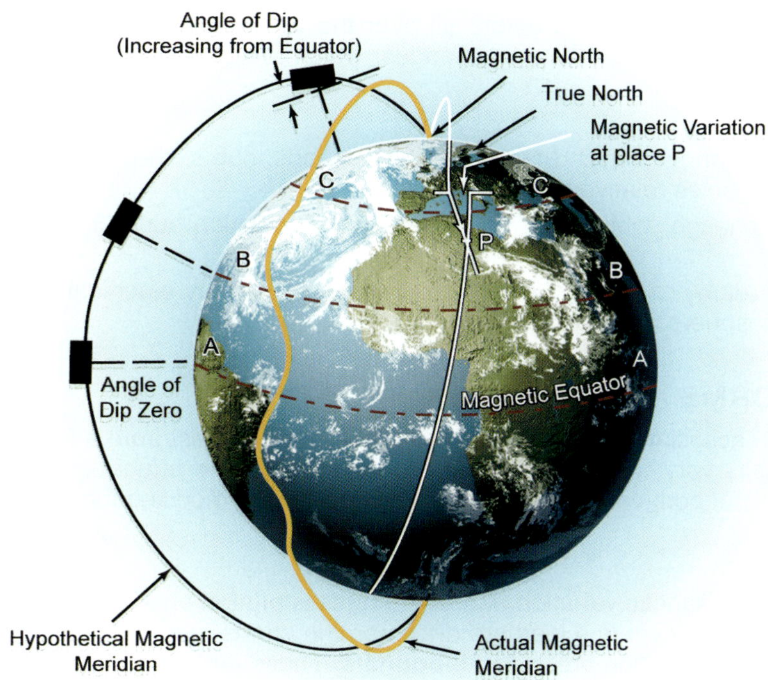

It would appear that the Earth's magnetic field is similar to that which would be expected if a short, but very powerful bar magnet were located at the centre of the planet. This partly explains why the magnetic poles cover relatively large geographic areas, due to the lines of force spreading out. It also provides for the lines of force to be horizontal in the vicinity of the Equator. However, the precise origin of the field is not known, but for purpose of explanation, the bar magnet analogy is most useful in visualising the general form of the Earth's magnetic field.

The Earth's magnetic field differs from that of an ordinary magnet in many respects. Its points of maximum intensity are not at the magnetic poles, as they are in a bar magnet, but occur as four other positions, known as magnetic foci, two of which are near the magnetic poles. Also, the magnetic poles are continually changing position by a small amount, and at any point on the Earth's surface, the field is not constant, as it is subject to changes, both periodic and irregular.

MAGNETIC VARIATION

Just as meridians and parallels are constructed with reference to the geographic poles, so magnetic meridians and parallels may be plotted with reference to the magnetic poles. If a map were prepared showing both true and magnetic meridians, it would be clear that the meridians intersect each other at angles varying from 0° to 180° at different points on the Earth's surface. The horizontal angle contained between the geographic and magnetic meridians at any place when looking north is known as magnetic variation.

When the direction of the magnetic meridian inclines to the left of the true meridian, the variation is said to be west; inclination to the right of the true meridian is said to be variation east. Variation can change from 0° in areas where the magnetic meridians run parallel to a maximum of 180° in places located between the true and magnetic north poles.

At some locations on Earth, where the ferrous nature of the rock disturbs the Earth's magnetic field, magnetic anomalies occur, which may cause large changes in the value of variation over very short distances. While variation differs all over the world, it does not maintain a constant value in any one place, and the following changes, which are not constant in themselves, may occur:

- Secular changes, which occur over long periods, due to the changing position of the magnetic poles relative to the true poles
- Annual change, which is a small seasonal fluctuation super-imposed on a secular change
- Diurnal (daily) changes, which appear to be caused by electrical currents flowing in the atmosphere as a result of solar heating

MAGNETIC STORMS

Magnetic storms are associated with sunspot activity. These may last from a few hours to several days, with an intensity varying from very small to very great. The effect on aircraft compasses varies with intensity, but both variation and local values of H are modified for as long as the storm lasts.

Information regarding magnetic variation and its changes is printed on special charts of the world, which are issued every few years. Lines are drawn on the charts, and those joining places which have the same value of variation are called **Isogonals**. Those drawn through places which have zero variation are known as **Agonic** lines.

MAGNETIC DIP

As stated earlier, a freely-suspended magnetic needle settles in a definite direction at any point on the Earth's surface, aligning itself with the magnetic meridian. However, it does not lie parallel to the Earth's surface at all points, because the Earth's lines of magnetic flux (force) are not horizontal. The lines of force emerge vertically from the north magnetic pole, bend over to parallel the Earth's surface, and descend vertically at the south magnetic pole. If, therefore, a magnetic needle is transported along a meridian from north to south:

At the start	The red end is pointing down
Near the magnetic equator	The needle is horizontal
At the South Pole	The blue end points down

The angle that lines of force make with the Earth's surface at any given place is called the **angle of dip**. Dip varies from:

- 0° at the magnetic equator
- Virtually 90° at the magnetic poles

Dip is conventionally positive when the red end of a freely-suspended magnetic needle is below the horizontal and negative when the blue end dips below the horizontal.

The angle of dip at all locations undergoes changes similar to those described for variation and is also shown on charts of the world. Lines known as Isoclinals join places on these charts having the same value of magnetic dip, while one which joins places having zero dip is known as an **Aclinic** line.

EARTH'S TOTAL MAGNETIC FORCE

When a magnetic needle freely suspended in the Earth's field comes to rest, it does so under the influence of the total force of the Earth's magnetic field. The value of this total force at a given place is not easy to measure. Therefore, the total force is usually resolved into a horizontal component termed **H** and a vertical component termed **Z**. If the value of dip angle (θ) for the particular location is known, the total force can readily be calculated.

It is valuable to know about horizontal component (H) and vertical component (Z), as both are responsible for magnetisation of ferrous metal parts of the aircraft (both hard and soft iron) that lie in their respective planes. Both components may be responsible for providing a deflecting or deviating force around the aircraft's compass position. In order for the compass to provide a worthwhile heading reference, the deviating force must be determined and corrections calibrated. The relationship between dip, horizontal, vertical, and total force is shown below.

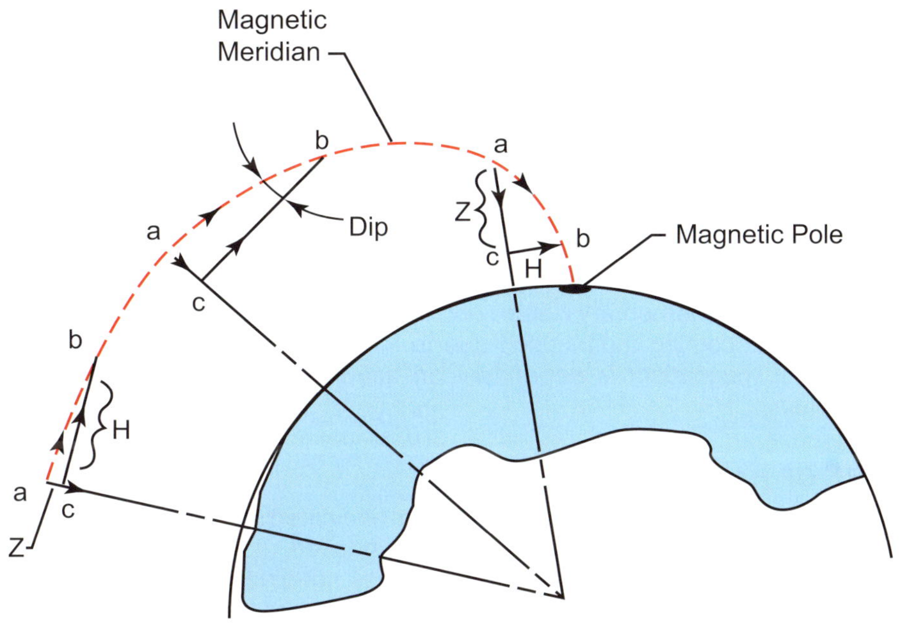

The figure shows that H is of maximum value at the magnetic equator and decreases in value toward the poles. Conversely Z is zero at the magnetic equator and, together with the value of dip, increases toward the poles.

AIRCRAFT MAGNETISM

A challenge to the designers of aircraft compasses since the early days of aviation is that aircraft are magnetised in various degrees and that a direct-reading compass must be located where the pilot can readily see it, namely the cockpit area, where it is surrounded by magnetic material and electrical circuits. Such magnetic influence provides a deviation force to the Earth's magnetic field, which causes a compass needle to be deflected away from the local magnetic meridian. Fortunately, the deviation caused by aircraft magnetism can be analysed and resolved into components acting along the aircraft's major axes. This allows errors, or deviations, resulting from aircraft magnetism to be minimised.

TYPES OF AIRCRAFT MAGNETISM

Essentially, there are two types of aircraft magnetism which can be divided in the same way that magnetic materials are classified, according to their ability to be magnetised.

HARD IRON MAGNETISM

This is of a permanent nature and is due to the presence of iron or steel parts used in the aircraft structure, power plants, and other equipment. The Earth's magnetic field influences the molecular structure of ferrous parts of the aircraft during construction while it is lying on one heading for a long period. Hammering and working of the materials also plays a part in molecular alignment and magnetisation of component parts.

SOFT IRON MAGNETISM

Soft iron magnetism is of a temporary nature and is caused by metallic parts of the aircraft which are magnetically soft becoming magnetised due to induction by the Earth's magnetic field. The effect of this type of magnetism is dependent on heading and attitude of the aircraft and its geographical location.

COMPONENTS OF HARD IRON MAGNETISM

The various components which cause deviation are indicated by letters, those for permanent, hard iron magnetism being capitals, and those for induced, soft iron magnetism being small letters. Positive deviations (those deflecting the compass needle to the right) are termed easterly, while negative deviations (deflection of the needle to the left) are termed westerly.

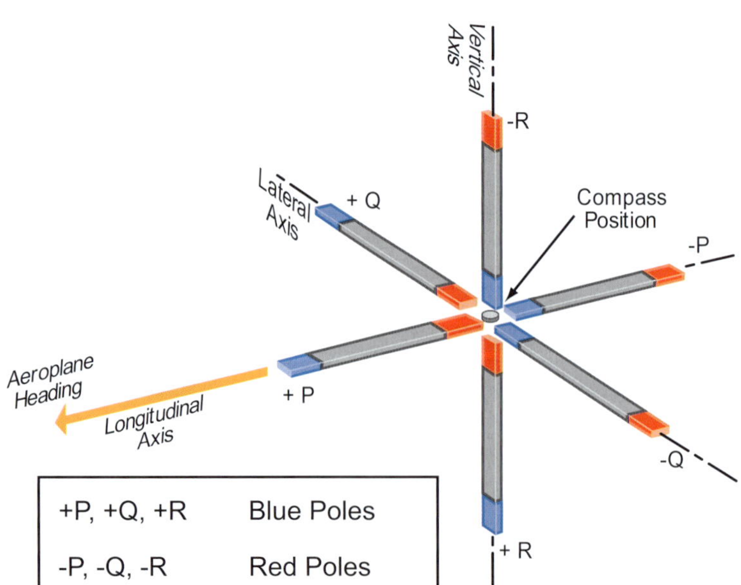

The total effect of hard iron magnetism at the compass position is likened to a number of bar magnets lying longitudinally, laterally, and vertically about the compass position. To analyse the effect of hard iron, the imaginary bar magnets are annotated as component P, component Q and component R. The components do not vary in strength with change of heading or latitude, but may vary with time due to a weakening of the magnetism in the aircraft. From the diagram above, it should be clear that when the blue poles of the imaginary magnets are forward of, to starboard of, and beneath the compass position, the components are positive, and when poles are in the opposite direction, they are negative.

When an aircraft is heading north, the imaginary magnet due to component P, together with the compass needle, is in alignment with the aircraft's fore-and-aft axis and Earth's component H, thus P adds or subtracts to the directive force H and does not cause any deviation. If the aircraft is turned through 360°, as it commences the turn (ignoring compass pivot friction, liquid swirl, etc.), the magnet system remains attracted to the Earth's component H. However, component P, which is still acting in the aircraft's fore-and-aft axis, causes the compass needle to align itself in the resultant position between the directive force H and the deflecting force P, making the needle point so many degrees east or west of north, depending on the polarity of P. The deviation increases during the turn, being a maximum on east and west and zero on north and south. Deviation resulting from a positive P is shown in the diagram below.

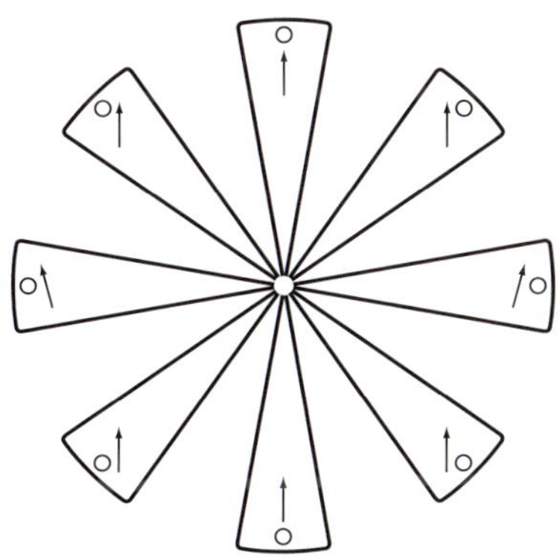

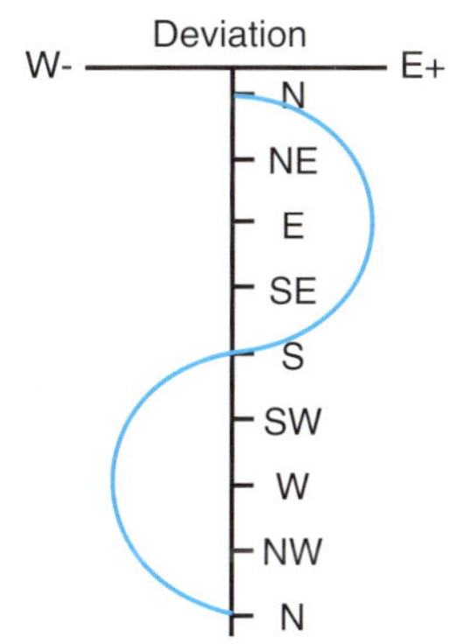

Hdg (M)	**Deviation**
N	No deviation; directive force increased
NE	Easterly deviation
E	Maximum Easterly deviation
SE	Easterly deviation
S	No deviation; directive force decreased
SW	Westerly deviation
W	Maximum Westerly deviation
NW	Westerly Deviation

This is a sine curve with P proportional to sine Hdg (M), thus:

$$\text{Deviation} = P \text{ sine Hdg (M)}.$$

Component Q produces a similar effect, but since it acts along the aircraft's lateral axis (wing tip to wingtip), deviation resulting from Q is at a maximum on north and south and zero on east and west when the component is aligned with the directive force H. Deviations resulting from a negative Q (blue pole starboard of compass position) are shown below.

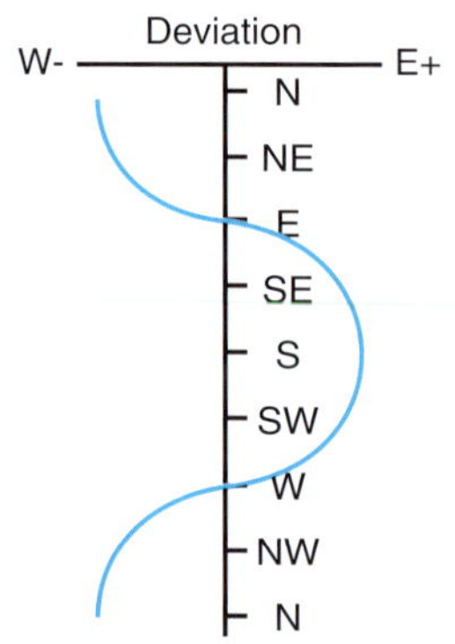

This is a cosine curve with Q proportional to cosine Hdg (M), thus:

Deviation = Q cos Hdg (M).

Component R acts in the vertical, and when the aircraft is in level flight, has no effect on the compass system. If, however, the aircraft flies with its longitudinal or lateral axis other than horizontal, component R is out of the vertical, and a horizontal vector of the component affects the compass system.

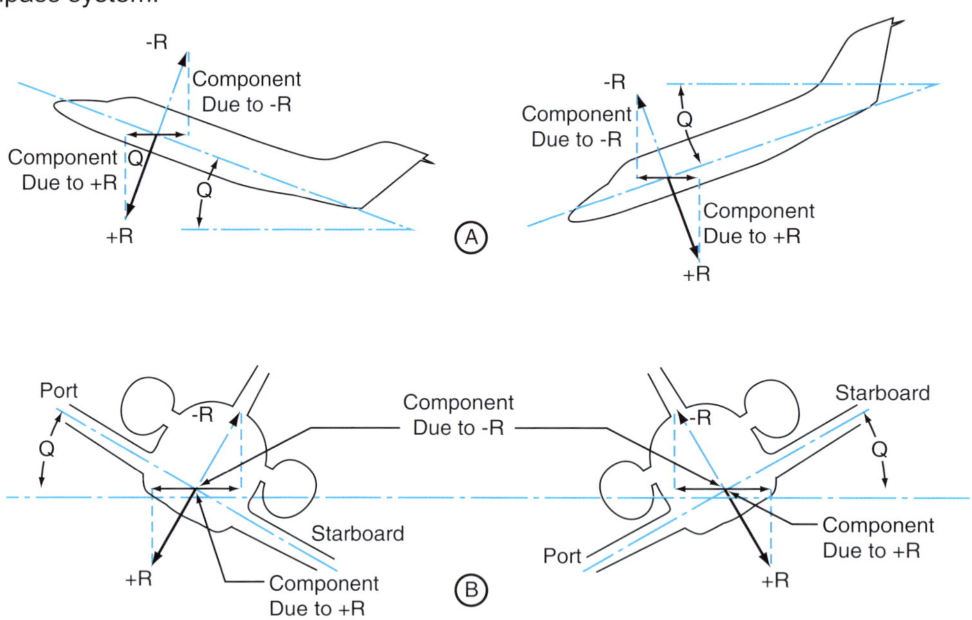

The diagrams above demonstrate the effect of this and show that an element of R would affect components P and Q. A similar situation occurs when a tail-wheel aircraft is on the ground. The value of R varies, but because the angles of climb or dive for most aircraft are normally small, any deviation resulting from component R is correspondingly small. Other errors affecting direct-reading compasses due to turns and accelerations, are such as to make errors due to R of no practical significance, while the circuitry of remote-indicating compasses is such that turn errors are virtually eliminated and the effect of component P is negligible.

COMPONENTS OF SOFT IRON MAGNETISM

Soft iron magnetism affecting the compass may be considered as originating from soft iron rods adjacent to the compass position in which magnetism is induced by the Earth's magnetic field. Although the field has two components, H and Z, in order to analyse the effect of soft iron, H must be split into two horizontal components, X and Y, which together with Z, can be related to the three principal axes of the aircraft.

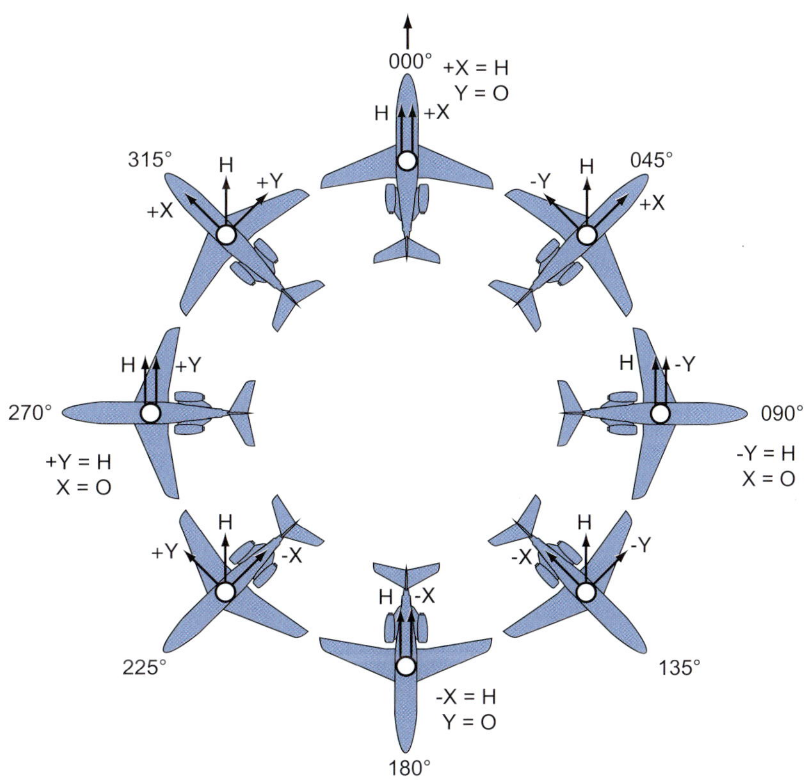

The diagram above shows how the polarities and strengths of X and Y change with change of aircraft heading as the aircraft turns relative to the direction of component H. Component Z acts vertically through the compass and does not effect the directional properties of the magnet system.

When an aircraft is moved to a new geographic location, all three components of soft iron magnetism change due to the change in the Earth's field strength and direction at the new location. However, the sign of Z changes only if the aircraft moves to the other magnetic hemisphere.

Recall that magnetic induction due to soft iron is visualised as soft iron rods disposed about the compass position, and that soft iron components are indicated conventionally by small letters **a** to **k**, which are then related to the Earth field components X, Y, and Z. Of the soft iron components, cZ and fZ are significant, as they do not change polarity with change of heading, and they act in the same manner as hard iron components P and Q, respectively. Pairs of vertical soft iron rods positioned fore and aft and athwart the compass position can represent cZ and fZ. In the Northern Hemisphere (magnetic), the lower of each rod would be induced with red magnetism. This is represented in the diagram below:

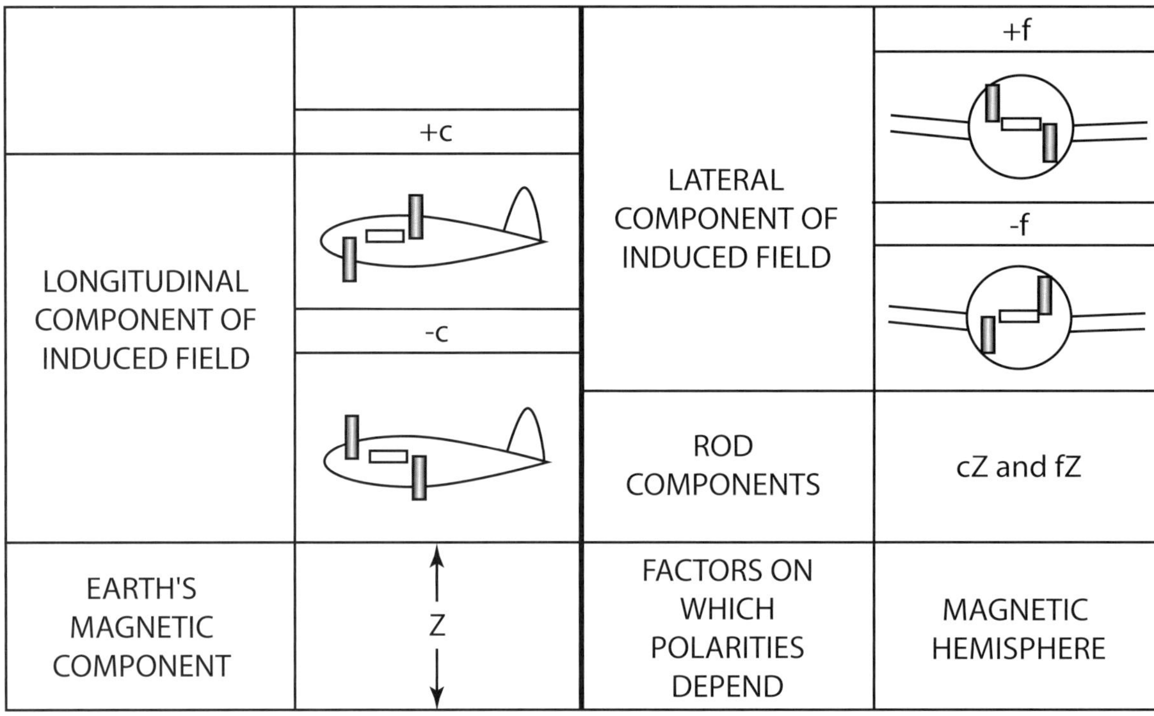

DETERMINATION OF DEVIATION CO-EFFICIENTS

Before taking action to minimise the effect of hard iron and soft iron magnetism on an aircraft's compass, the deviations caused by the components of aircraft magnetism on various headings must be determined. The values of such deviations are analysed into **co-efficients of deviation**.

There are five co-efficients of deviation, named A, B, C, D and E; of these D and E, are soft iron and will not be studied, leaving:

Co-efficient A which is usually constant on all headings and results from misalignment of the compass

Co-efficient B which results from deviations caused by hard iron P and soft iron cZ, with deviation maximum on east and west

Co-efficient C which results from deviations caused by hard iron Q and soft iron a, with maximum deviation on north and south

Taking each of the three co-efficients in turn:

Co-efficient A is calculated by taking the algebraic sum of the deviations on a number of equally-spaced compass headings and dividing the sum by the number of observations made. Usually readings are taken on the four cardinal and four quadrantal headings:

$$\text{Co-efficient A} = \frac{\text{Deviation on N + NE + E + SE + S + SW + W + NW}}{8}$$

Co-efficient B represents the resultant deviation due to the presence, either together or separately, of hard iron component P and soft iron component cZ. Calculate co-efficient B by taking half the algebraic difference between deviations on compass heading east and west:

$$\text{Co-efficient B} = \frac{\text{Deviation on east - Deviation on west}}{2}$$

This may also be expressed for any heading as:
Deviation = B x sin (heading)

Co-efficient C represents the resultant deviation due to the presence, either together or separately, of hard iron component Q and soft iron component a. Calculate co-efficient C by taking half the algebraic difference between deviations on compass heading north and south:

$$\text{Coefficient C} = \frac{\text{Deviation on north - Deviation on south}}{2}$$

Co-efficient C may also be expressed (for any heading) as:
Deviation = C x cosine (heading)

Accepting the above, the total deviation on an uncorrected compass for any given direction of aircraft heading (compass) may be expressed as:

$$\text{Total deviation} = A + B \sin \text{Hdg} + C \cos \text{Hdg}$$

In order to determine by what amount compass readings are affected by aircraft hard and soft iron magnetism, a special calibration procedure, known as **compass swinging**, is carried out so that deviations may be determined, co-efficients calculated, and the deviations compensated.

Before reviewing the mechanics of the compass swing, there are certain occasions or events which require that the instrument should be swung. These are:

- On acceptance of a new aircraft from manufacture
- When a new compass is fitted
- Periodically
- After a major inspection
- Following a change of magnetic material in the aircraft
- If the aircraft is moved permanently or semi-permanently to another airfield involving a large change of magnetic latitude
- Following a lightning strike or prolonged flying in heavy static
- After standing on one heading for more than four weeks
- When carrying ferrous (magnetic) freight
- Whenever specified in the maintenance schedule
- For issue of a C of A
- At any time when the compass or residual deviation recorded on the compass card is in doubt

JOINT AIRWORTHINESS REQUIREMENTS (JAR) LIMITS

JAR 25 for large aeroplanes requires that a placard showing the calibration of the magnetic direction indicator (compass) in level flight with engines running must be installed on or near the instrument. The placard (compass residual deviation card) must show each calibration reading in terms of magnetic heading of the aircraft in not greater than 45° steps. Further, the compass after compensation may not have deviation in normal level flight greater than 10° on any heading.

The distance between a compass and any item of equipment containing magnetic material shall be such that the equipment does not cause a change of deviation exceeding 1°, nor shall the combined effect of all such equipment exceed 2 percent. The same ruling shall apply to installed electrical equipment and associated wiring when such equipment is powered up.

Change in deviation caused by movement of the flight or undercarriage controls shall not exceed 1°.

The effect of the aeroplane's permanent and induced magnetism, as given by co-efficients B and C with associated soft iron components, shall not exceed:

Coefficient	Direct Reading Compass	Remote Reading Compass
B	15°	5°
C	15°	5°

Note 1: After correction, the greatest deviation on any heading shall be 3° for direct reading compasses and 1° for remote indicating compasses.

Note 2: Emergency standby compasses and non-mandatory compasses need not fully comply, but evidence of satisfactory installation is required.

COMPASS SWING

The term compass swing has already been mentioned, as well as the occasions when a swing is necessary. Although there are a number of methods by which a swing may be achieved, the usual method involves an engineer with a landing or datum compass, mounted on a tripod well in front or, in some circumstances, behind the aircraft, so that accurate sightings can be made along the fore-and-aft line. Calibration is normally in the hands of an experienced compass adjuster, with a pilot only being called on occasionally to drive the aeroplane. The procedure is split into two phases, correcting and check swing:

- Ensure compass is serviceable.
- Ensure all equipment not carried in flight is removed from the aircraft.
- Ensure all equipment carried in flight is correctly stowed.
- Take the aircraft to swing site (at least 50 m from other aircraft and 100 m from a hangar).
- Ensure flying controls are in normal flying position, engines running, radios and electrical circuits on.
- Position aircraft on a heading of south (M) and note deviation (difference between datum compass and aircraft compass reading).
- Position aircraft on a heading of west (M) and note deviation.
- Position aircraft on a heading of north (M) and note deviation. Calculate co-efficient C, and apply it direct to compass reading. If applicable, set required corrected heading on compass grid ring or set heading pointer.
- Place the compass corrector key in the micro-adjuster box using the winder which is across (at 90°) to compass needle. Turn the key until the compass needle shows corrected heading. Remove key.
- Position aircraft on a heading of east (M) and note deviation. Calculate co-efficient B, and correct for B in the same manner as for co-efficient C.
- The correcting swing is now complete.
- Carry out a check swing on eight headings, starting on southeast (M), noting deviation on each heading.
- Calculate co-efficient A on completion of check swing, and apply to compass reading. Set required corrected heading on compass grid ring or set heading pointer. Loosen compass, or, for remote indicating instrument, the detector head retaining screws, and rotate until compass needle indicates correct heading. Re-tighten retaining screws.
- Having applied A algebraically to all deviations found during the check swing, plot the residual (remaining) deviations, and make out a compass deviation card for placing in the aircraft.

Compass Swing – Example

Correcting Swing

<table>
<tr><th></th><th>Datum Compass Heading (M)</th><th>Aircraft Compass Heading (C)</th><th>Deviation</th><th></th></tr>
<tr><td>S</td><td>182</td><td>180</td><td>+2</td><td></td></tr>
<tr><td>W</td><td>274</td><td>270</td><td>+4</td><td></td></tr>
<tr><td>N</td><td>000</td><td>354</td><td>+6</td><td></td></tr>
<tr><td colspan="4">Co-efficient C = $\frac{+6 - (+2)}{2} = +2$</td><td>Make compass read 356</td></tr>
<tr><td>E</td><td>090</td><td>090</td><td>0</td><td></td></tr>
<tr><td colspan="4">Co-efficient B = $\frac{0 - (+4)}{2} = -2$</td><td>Make compass read 088</td></tr>
</table>

Datum Compass	Aircraft Compass	Deviation	Residual Deviation Following A
136	131	+5	+2
183	181	+2	-1
225	221	+4	+1
270	268	+2	-1
313	308	+5	+2
000	358	+2	-1
047	044	+3	0
092	090	+3	-1

Co-efficient A = 25 ÷ 8 = +3

Finally, a deviation card is produced showing residual deviations against headings (M) and placed in the aircraft adjacent to the compass position.

DEVIATION COMPENSATION DEVICES

With the compass swing complete, co-efficients B, C, and A are known, but now the co-efficients must be applied to correct or offset the compass needle by an amount in degrees equivalent to deviation.

MECHANICAL COMPENSATION

The majority of mechanical deviation compensation devices consist of two pairs of magnets, each pair being fitted into a bevel gear assembly made of non-magnetic material. The gears are mounted one above the other, so that in the neutral position one pair of magnets is parallel to the aircraft's fore-and-aft plane for correction of co-efficient C, while the other pair lies athwartships to correct for co-efficient B. By use of the compass correction key, a small bevel pinion may be turned, rotating one pair of bevel gears.

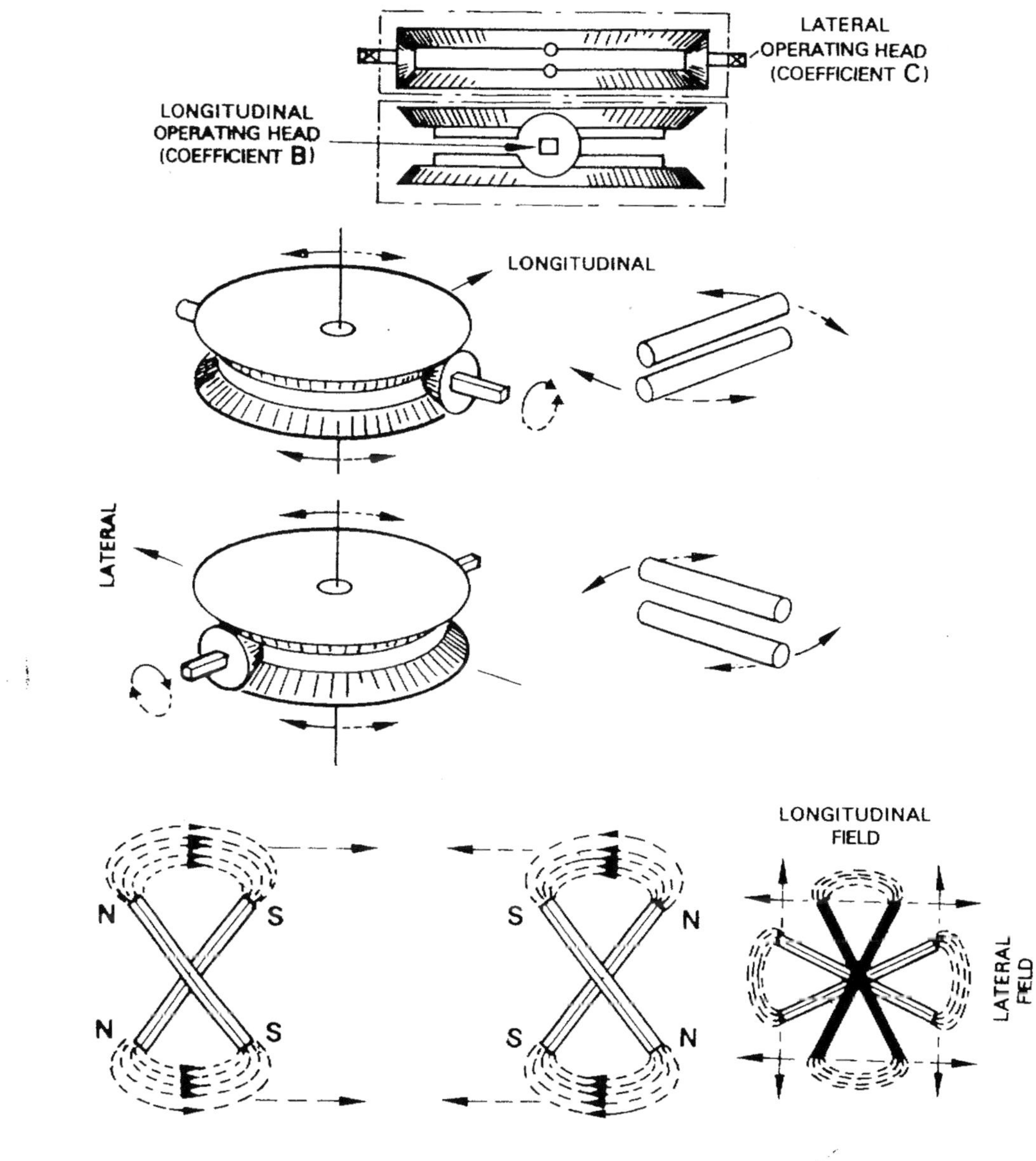

The pairs of magnets are made to open, creating a magnetic field between the poles to deflect the compass needle and correct for co-efficient B or C, depending which pair of magnets are used. The micro-adjuster unit is normally mounted above the needle assembly in the compass.

ELECTRICAL COMPENSATION

The exact design and construction of the electro-magnetic compensator depends on the compass manufacturer. However, they all follow a similar concept whereby two variable potentiometers are connected to the coils of the flux detector unit. The potentiometers correspond to the co-efficient B and C magnets of a mechanical compensator and, when moved with respect to calibrated dials, they insert very small DC signals into the flux detector coils. The magnetic fields produced by the signals are sufficient to oppose those causing deviations and accordingly modify the output from the detector head via the synchronous transmission link to drive the gyro, and thus the compass heading indicator, to show corrected readings.

Chapter 21
Aircraft Magnetism — Compasses

DIRECT-READING MAGNETIC COMPASS

The basis of the direct-reading magnetic compass is simply a magnetic needle, which points to the northern end of the Earth's magnetic field. It is installed in an instrument of dimensions and weight that make it suitable for use in aircraft.

It is mandatory, through the articles of JAR 25, for modern civil transport aircraft to carry a direct-reading, non-stabilised magnetic compass as a standby direction indicator.

PRINCIPLE OF OPERATION

For a direct-reading compass to function efficiently, its magnetic element must:

- Lie horizontal, thereby sensing only the horizontal or directive component of the Earth's field.
- Be sensitive, in order to operate effectively down to low values of H.
- Be aperiodic, or dead-beat, to minimise oscillation of the sensitive element about a new heading following a turn.

HORIZONTALITY

Horizontality is obtained by making the magnet system pendulous. This is achieved by mounting the magnets close together, below the needle pivot. When the system is tilted by the Earth's vertical force Z, the C of G moves out from below the pivot, away from the nearer Earth pole, thereby introducing a righting force upon the magnet system and reducing the effect of Z. The compass needle takes up a position along the resultant of the two forces: H, and reduced effect of Z. In temperate latitudes, the final inclination of the needle is approximately 2° to 3° to the horizontal, but the tilt increases such that, by about 70° north or south (where the magnetic force is less than 6 micro-Teslas), the compass is virtually useless. It is stressed that the displacement of the C of G is a function of the system's pendulosity, it is not a mechanical adjustment. It works, therefore, in either hemisphere without further adjustment.

SENSITIVITY

Sensitivity is achieved by increasing the pole strengths of the magnets used, so that the needle remains firmly aligned with the local magnetic meridian. Sensitivity is aided by keeping pivot friction to a minimum by using an iridium-tipped pivot moving in a sapphire cup. Filling the compass bowl with a liquid, which also serves to lubricate the pivot, reduces the effective weight of the magnet system.

APERIODICITY

If a suspended magnet is deflected from its position of rest and then released, it tends to oscillate around the correct direction for some time before stabilising. This is obviously undesirable, as it could, at worst, lead to the pilot chasing the needle. Ideally, the compass needle should come to rest without oscillation. In attempting to achieve aperiodicity:

- The compass bowl is filled with methyl alcohol or a silicone fluid, and damping filaments are fitted to the magnet system.

- The buoyancy of the fluid reduces the apparent weight of the system, and the weight is concentrated as close to the pivot as possible to further reduce the turning moment.

- The liquids used in the compass bowl must be transparent, have a wide temperature range, a low viscosity, high resistance to corrosion, and should be free from any tendency toward discoloration in use. One disadvantage of using a liquid in the compass bowl is that, in a prolonged turn, it turns with the aircraft, taking the magnet system with it and affecting compass readings. To offset the effect of liquid swirl, a good clearance is provided between damping wires and the side of the compass bowl. However, liquid swirl does delay the immediate settling of the system on a new compass heading.

- Although the liquid in the compass bowl has a wide temperature range, it expands and contracts with variation of temperature. It is, therefore, necessary for all direct-reading compasses to be fitted with some form of expansion chamber, thus ensuring that the liquid neither bursts a seal, or contracts, leaving vacuum bubbles.

"E" TYPE COMPASS DESCRIPTION

The majority of the standby compasses in use today are of the card type shown below.

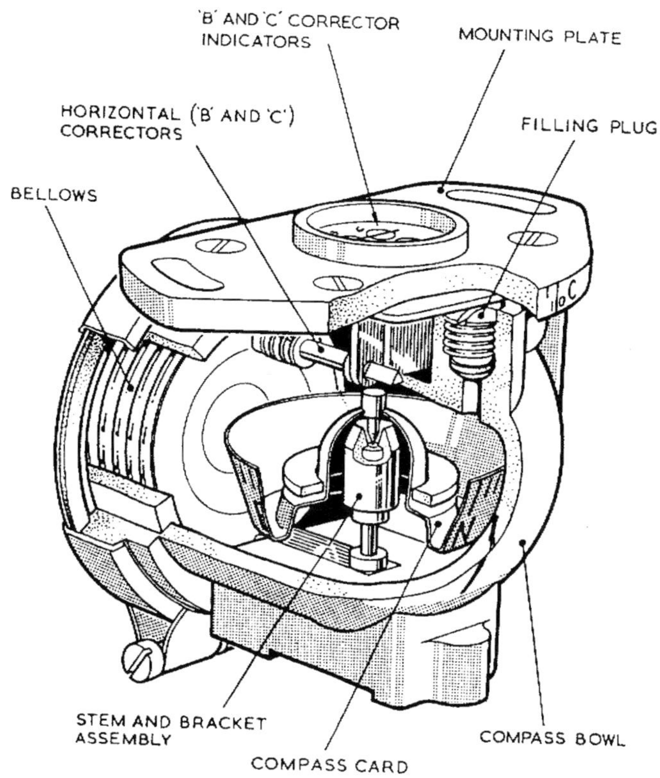

These compasses have a single circular cobalt steel magnet, which is attached to the compass card. The assembly is mounted close to the inner face of the bowl, thereby minimising errors in observation due to parallax. The card is graduated every 10°, with intermediate indications being estimated. Heading observations are made against a lubber line on the inner face of the bowl. The diagram below shows a cutaway version of the magnet and pivot assembly.

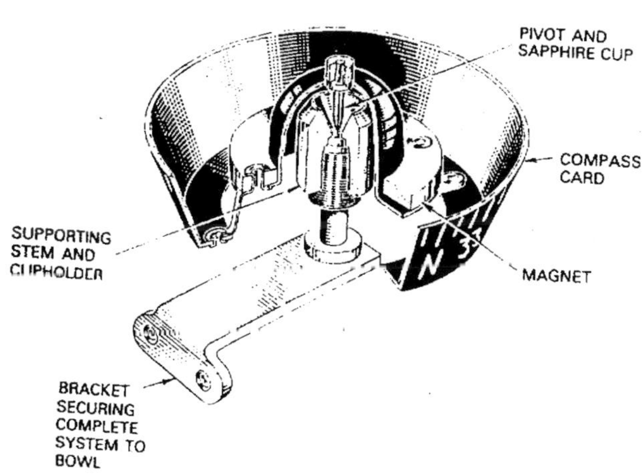

Suspension of the system is by means of the usual iridium-tipped pivot revolving in a sapphire cup. The bowl is moulded in plastic and painted on the outside with black enamel, except for a small area at the front through which the vertical card can be seen. This part of the bowl is so moulded that it has a magnifying effect on the compass card. The damping liquid is silicone fluid, and the bellows-type expansion chamber located at the rear of the bowl compensates for changes in liquid volume due to temperature variation. The effects of deviation co-efficient B and C are compensated for by permanent magnet corrector assemblies secured to the compass mounting plate.

SERVICEABILITY TESTS – DIRECT-READING COMPASS

- Check liquid is free from bubbles, discoloration, and sediment.
- Examine all parts for luminosity.
- Test for pivot friction by deflecting the magnet system through 10° to 15° each way; note the readings on return — should be within 2° of each other.
- Periodically test for damping by deflecting the system through 90°, holding for 30 seconds to allow liquid to settle, and timing the return through 85°. Maximum and minimum times are laid down in the manufacturer's instrument manual, usually about 6.5 to 8.5 seconds.

ACCELERATION AND TURNING ERRORS

In the search for accuracy of an indicating system, it is often found that the methods used to counter an undesirable error under one set of circumstances create other errors under different circumstances. This is precisely what happens when the compass system is made pendulous to counteract the effect of dip by displacing the C of G to make the instrument effective over a greater latitude band. Unfortunately, having done this, any manoeuvre which introduces a component of aircraft acceleration either east or west from the aircraft's magnetic meridian produces a torque about the magnet system's vertical axis, causing it to rotate in azimuth to a false meridian.

There are two main elements resulting from these accelerations, namely **Acceleration Error** and **Turning Error**. Before examining these more closely, consider what would happen to a plain pendulum, freely suspended in the aircraft fuselage. If a constant direction and speed were maintained, the pendulum would remain at rest. However, if the aircraft turns, accelerates or decelerates, the pendulum is displaced from the true vertical, because inertia causes the centre of gravity to lag behind the pendulum pivot, thus moving it from its normal position directly below the point of suspension. Since turns themselves are accelerations toward the centre of the turn and, whether correctly or incorrectly banked, always cause a pendulum to adopt a false vertical, it may be stated that, in broad terms, any accelerations or decelerations of the aircraft cause the C of G of a pendulum to be deflected from its normal position vertically below the point of suspension.

From the above, it is apparent that a magnet system, constructed and pendulously suspended to counteract the effect of dip, behaves in a similar manner to a pendulum — any acceleration or deceleration in flight resulting in a displacement of the C of G of the system from its normal position. A torque is established about the vertical axis of the compass, unless the compass is on the magnetic Equator, where the Earth field vertical component Z is zero.

ACCELERATION ERROR

The force applied by an aircraft when accelerating or decelerating on a fixed heading is applied to the magnet system at the pivot, which is the magnet's only connection with the remainder of the instrument. The reaction to the force must be equal and opposite and must act through the C of G, which is below and offset from the pivot (except at the magnetic equator). The two forces thus constitute a couple which, dependent on heading, cause the magnet system to change the angle of dip or to rotate in azimuth.

The figure below shows the forces affecting a compass needle when an aircraft accelerates on a northerly heading. Since both the pivot (P) and C of G are in the plane of the local magnetic meridian, the reactive force R causes the northern or poleward end of the system to dip further, thus increasing the angle of dip without any needle rotation.

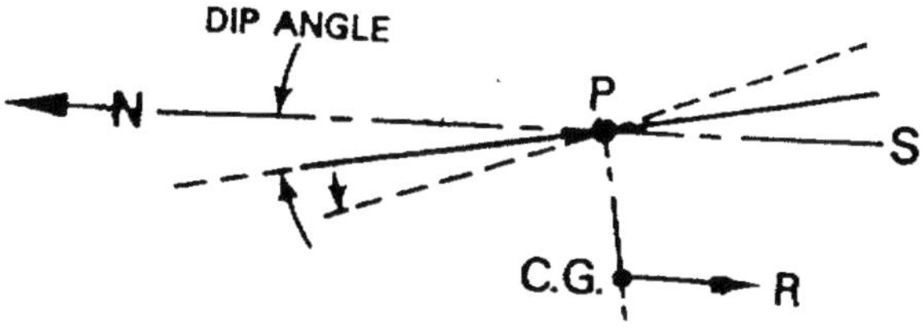

Acceleration on northerly heading

Conversely, when the aircraft decelerates on north, the reaction tilts the needle down at the south end. The opposite of these reactions are observed when accelerating/decelerating on north along the meridian in the Southern Hemisphere.

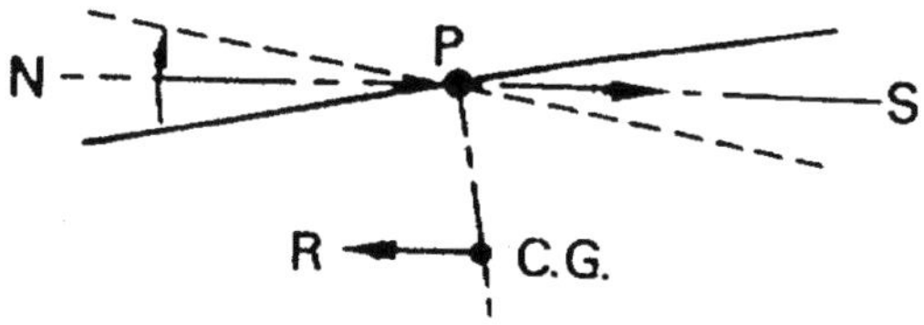

Deceleration on northerly heading

When an aircraft flying in either hemisphere changes speed on headings other than north or south, the change results in azimuth rotation of the magnet system, and hence there are errors in heading indication.

When an aircraft flying in the northern hemisphere accelerates on an easterly heading, as shown below, the accelerating force acts through the pivot P, and, unless the value of Z is zero, the reaction R acts through the C of G. The two forces now form a couple, turning the needle in a clockwise direction.

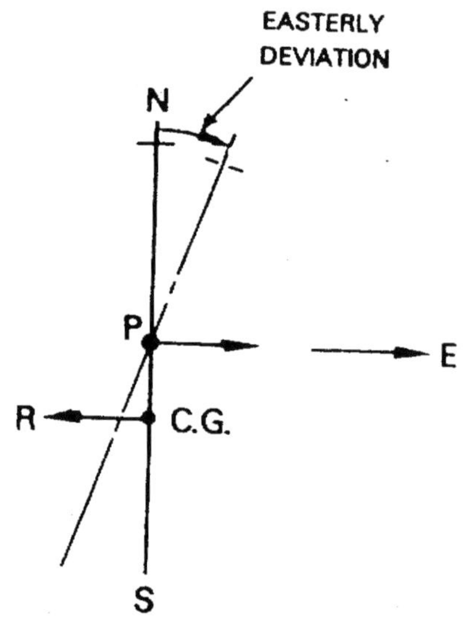

Acceleration on easterly heading

Action of R also causes the magnet system to tilt in the direction of acceleration, and thus the pivot and C of G are no longer in line with the magnet meridian. The magnets come under the influence of Z, as shown below, providing a further turning moment in the same direction as the force P/R couple.

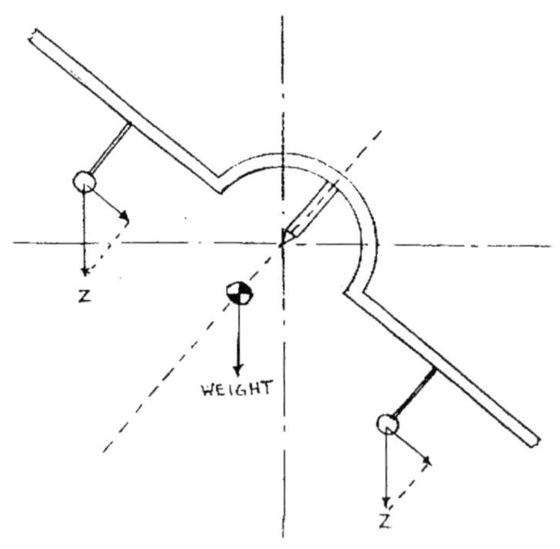

View through assembly looking North

Acceleration on East Clockwise Turning Moment due to "Z"

When the aircraft decelerates on east, the action and reaction of P and R respectively have the opposite effect, as shown below, causing the assembly to turn anti-clockwise with all forces again turning in the same direction.

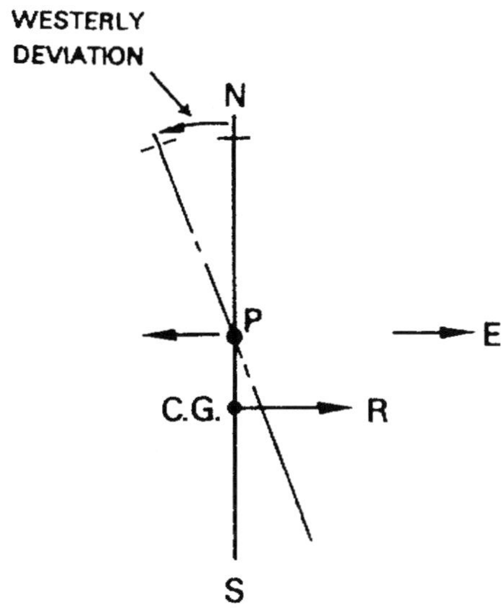

Deceleration on easterly heading

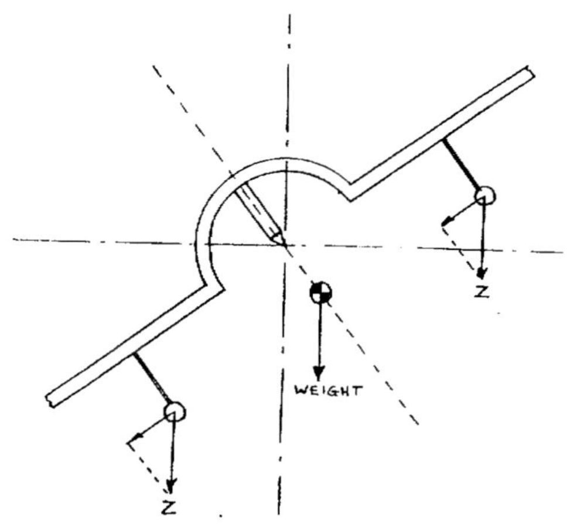

View through assembly looking North

Deceleration on East Anti-clockwise
Turning Moment due to "Z"

Here is a summary of errors due to acceleration and deceleration:

Heading	Speed	Needle Turns	Visual Effect
East	Increase	Clockwise	Apparent turn to the North
West	Increase	Anti-Clockwise	Apparent turn to the North
East	Decrease	Anti-Clockwise	Apparent turn to the South
West	Decrease	Clockwise	Apparent turn to the South

Note:

1. In the Southern Hemisphere, errors are in the opposite sense.
2. No error on north or south, as reaction force acts along the needle.
3. Similar errors can occur in turbulent flight conditions.
4. No errors on magnetic equator, as value of Z is zero and hence pivot and C of G are co-incident.

TURNING ERRORS

When an aircraft executes a turn, the compass pivot is carried with it along the curved path of the turn, but the centre of gravity is offset from the pivot to counter the effect of Z and is subject to the force of centrifugal acceleration acting outward from the centre of the turn. Further, in a correctly banked turn the magnet system tends to maintain a position parallel to the athwartship (wingtip to wing tip) plane of the aircraft and is now tilted in relation to the Earth's magnetic field. As before, the pivot and C of G is no longer in the plane of the local magnetic meridian and the needle is subject to a component of Z, as shown below, causing the system, when in the Northern Hemisphere, to rotate in the same direction as the turn and further increase the turning error.

The extent and direction of turning error is dependent upon the aircraft heading, the angle of bank (degree of tilt of the magnet system), and the local value of Z (dip). However, turning errors are maximum on north/south and are of significance within 35° of these headings.

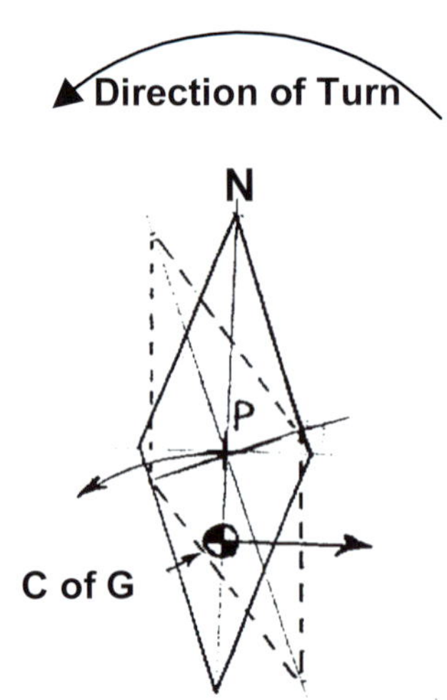

The preceding diagram shows the needle of a compass in an aircraft flying on a northerly heading in the Northern Hemisphere. The north-seeking end of the compass needle is coincident with the lubber line. The aircraft now turns west. As soon as the turn is commenced, centrifugal acceleration acts on the system C of G, causing it to rotate in the same direction as the turn and, since the magnet system is now tilted, the Earth's vertical component Z exerts a pull on the northern end, causing further rotation of the system.

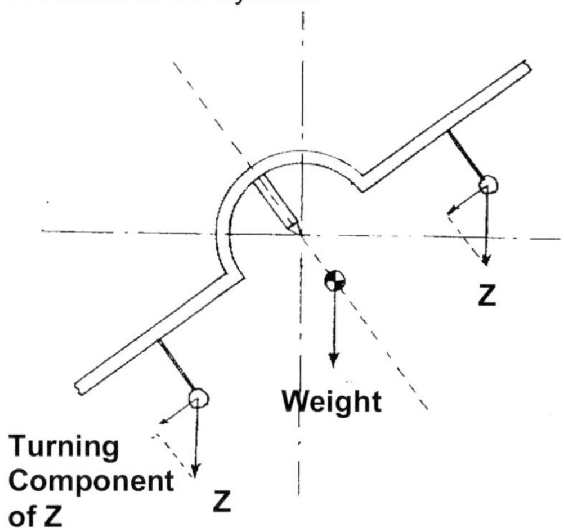

The same effect occurs if the heading change is from north to east in the Northern Hemisphere.

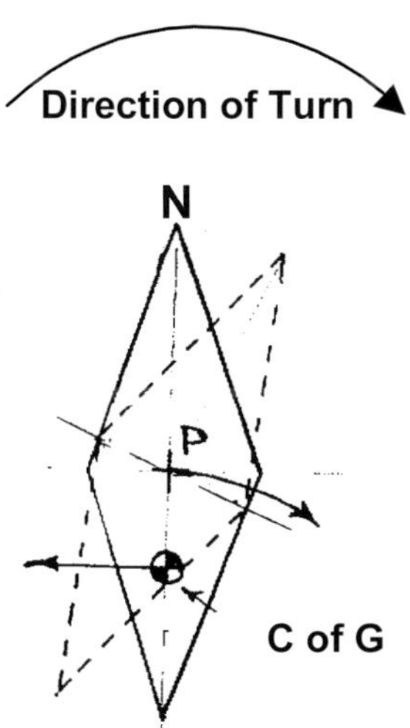

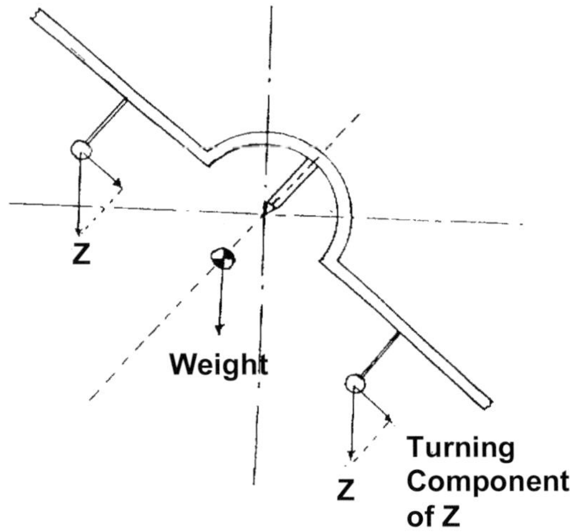

As mentioned earlier, the speed of system rotation is a function of the aircraft's bank angle and rate of turn, and, depending on those factors, three possible indications may be registered by the compass:

- A turn in the correct sense, but smaller than that carried out when the magnet system turns at a slower rate than the aircraft
- No turn when the magnet system turns at the same rate as the aircraft
- A turn in the opposite sense when the magnet system turns at a faster rate than the aircraft

When turning from a southerly heading in the Northern Hemisphere onto east or west, the rotation of the system and indications registered by the compass are the same as when turning from north, except that the compass over-indicates the turn.

In the Southern Hemisphere, the south magnetic pole is dominant and, in counter-acting its downward pull on the compass magnet system, the C of G moves to the northern side of the pivot. If an aircraft turns from a northerly heading eastward, the centrifugal acceleration acting on the C of G causes the needle to rotate more rapidly in the opposite direction to the turn, thus indicating a turn in the correct sense, but of greater magnitude than that which is carried out. The turn will be over-indicated. Turning from a southerly heading onto east or west in the Southern Hemisphere results in the same effect as turning through north in the Northern Hemisphere, because the C of G is still north of the compass pivot.

No mention has been made regarding motion of the liquid in the compass bowl. Ideally, it should remain motionless to act as a damping medium, preventing compass oscillation (aperiodicity). Regrettably, this is not so, and as the liquid turns with and in the same direction as the turn; its motion adds to or subtracts from needle error, depending on relative movement.

To summarise:

Turn Direction	Needle Movement	Visual Effect	Liquid Swirl	Corrective Action
Through North	Same as aircraft	Under-indication	Adds to error	Turn less than needle shows
Through South	Opposite to aircraft	Over-indication	Reduces error	Turn more than needle shows

Notes:

1. In the Southern Hemisphere, errors are of opposite value
2. In turns about east and west, no significant errors, since forces act along the needle
3. Northerly turning error is greater than southerly, as liquid swirl is additive to needle movement

GYRO-MAGNETIC COMPASSES

In their basic form, gyro-magnetic compasses were systems in which a magnetic-detecting element monitored a gyroscope-indicating element to provide a remotely displayed indication of heading. This combination of the better properties of a magnetic compass (determination of direction relative to a geographical location) and the gyroscope (rigidity) was a logical step in the development of heading display systems for use in aircraft.

Although the advent of the Remote Indicating Gyro-Magnetic Compass in the 1940 to 1950 period represented a major stride forward in instrumentation. The systems used in that era were not without errors and problems with the method of transmission from master units to remote heading indicators at crew stations. To reduce errors and to provide the modern compass with self-synchronous properties, new techniques were developed. The most notable of the improvements was the change from the traditional meridian-seeking permanent magnet to a meridian-sensing detector element, employing electro-magnetic induction to determine the direction of the Earth's magnetic field, the use of a modern synchronous transmission system, application of modern electronic techniques, and improved gyroscopes.

BASIC PRINCIPLE OF OPERATION

The manner in which the modern techniques are applied to gyro compass systems depends on the particular manufacturer. For the same reason, the number of components comprising an individual system may vary. However, the fundamental operating principles of the main components, as seen below, are the same and are dealt with in this chapter in general terms, rather than the specifics of a particular manufacturer's instrument.

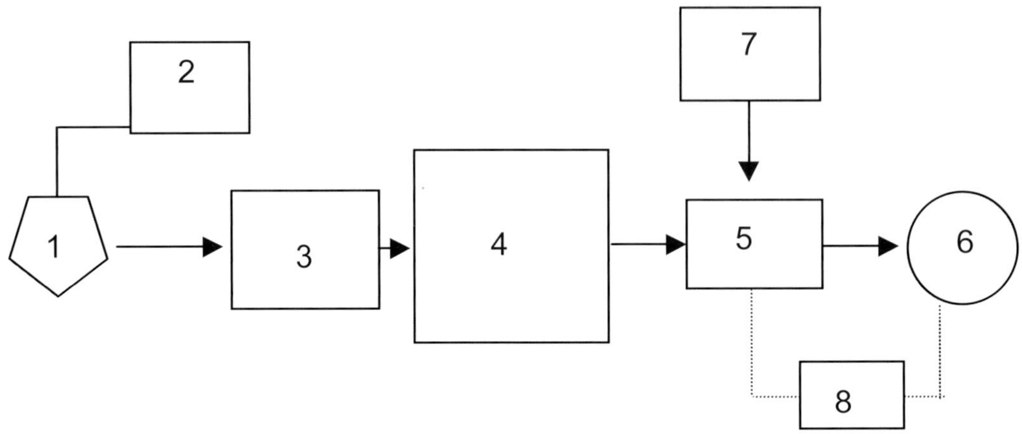

COMPONENTS

1. Flux detector element
2. Deviation compensator
3. Slaving system
4. Amplifier
5. Precession device and Gyroscope
6. Indicating element
7. Levelling system
8. Servo system

FLUX DETECTOR ELEMENT

Unlike the detector element of the simple magnetic compass, the element used in all remote-indicating compasses is of the fixed-in-azimuth type which senses the effect of the Earth's magnetic field as an electromagnetically-induced voltage.

Coil in Magnetic Field

(a) Components of "H"

(b) Total Flux

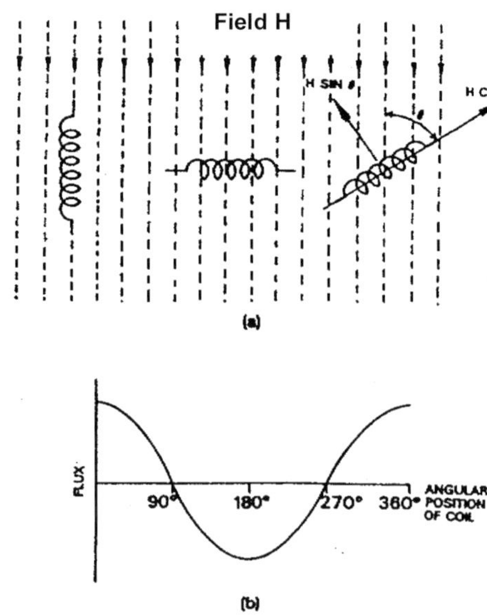

If a highly permeable magnetic bar is exposed to the Earth's magnetic field, the bar acquires magnetic flux. The amount of flux so produced depends on the magnetic latitude, which governs the strength of the Earth's horizontal component H and the direction of the bar relative to the direction of component H. In the diagram above, the bar is replaced with a single-turn coil, which is placed in the Earth's field with its longitudinal axis parallel to the magnetic meridian. In this case, the magnetic flux passing through the coil is maximum. Rotating the coil through 90°, so that it is at right angles to the field, produces zero magnetic flux, while rotating through a further 90°, to re-align the coil with field H, but this time in the reverse direction again produces maximum flux, but in the opposite algebraic sense.

The diagram above summarises this and shows a cosine relationship (zero flux at 90° and maximum flux at 0°) between field direction and coil alignment. If the aircraft was on a heading of 030°(M), the flux intensity would be H Cos 30°. Similarly, the flux intensity due to the Earth's magnetic field on a heading of 150°(M) is again H Cos 30°, but the direction of flow has reversed (Cos 150° is negative). However, on a heading of 330°(M), the induced flux would be of the same sign and value as for a heading of 030°(M).

It can be seen, therefore, that such a simple system is impracticable. First, in order to determine the magnetic heading, it is necessary to measure the magnetic flux in the coil. There is no simple way of doing this. Second, the ambiguity in heading must be solved. However, there is a basic principle which may be adapted to give direction measurement.

The problem of converting flux into a measurable electrical current is simple if the flux produced was a changing flux, for, according to Faraday:

"Whenever there is a change of flux linked with a circuit, an EMF is induced in the circuit".

For an aircraft at any given position and direction, the flux produced is constant in value. If this steady flux could be converted to a changing one, a current representing heading would flow. This is achieved in the gyro-magnetic compass through a device called a Flux Valve.

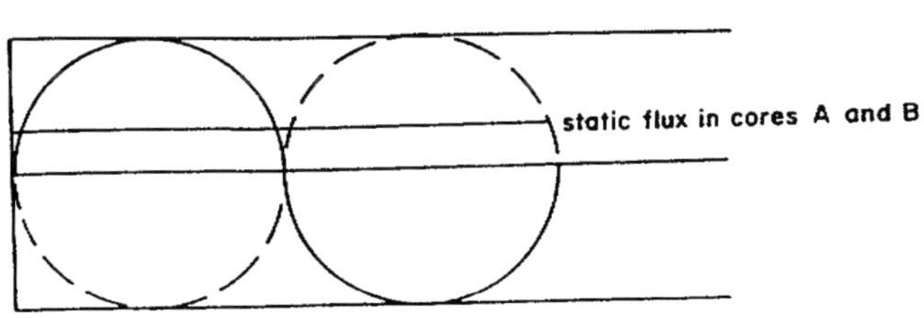

Schematic View of Flux Value

The diagram above shows a flux valve in diagrammatic form. The flux valve consists of two bars of highly permeable (easily magnetised and de-magnetised) material, bars A and B.

Both bars are wound with a coil, known as the Primary Coil, which is connected in series to an AC power source at 400 Hz. A pick-up coil, called the secondary coil, is wound around the primary coil and both bars. The effect of passing an AC current through the primary coil is shown below.

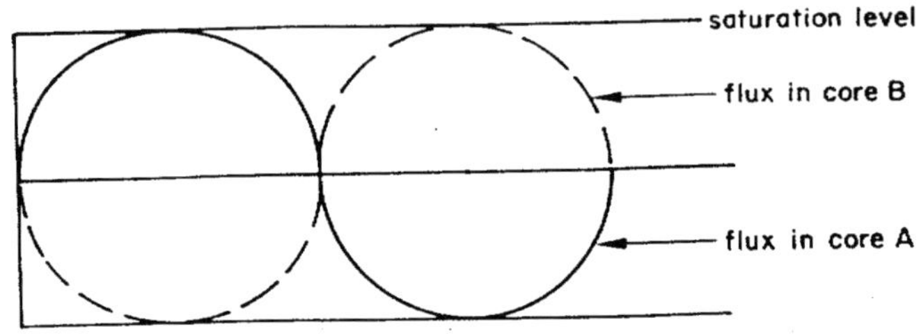

Total Saturation of Primary Coil

The current used is of such strength that at the peak it saturates both the primary and secondary coils. However, the flux produced will have no effect on the secondary coil, since at an instant of time the two bars produce flux of equal and opposite (sign) intensity, such that the total flux is zero. In practice, this situation does not occur since a bar placed horizontally in the Earth's magnetic field always has the field component H present (unless the aircraft is near the north or south magnetic pole). The component of H produces a static flux in both bars of the flux valve, as seen below.

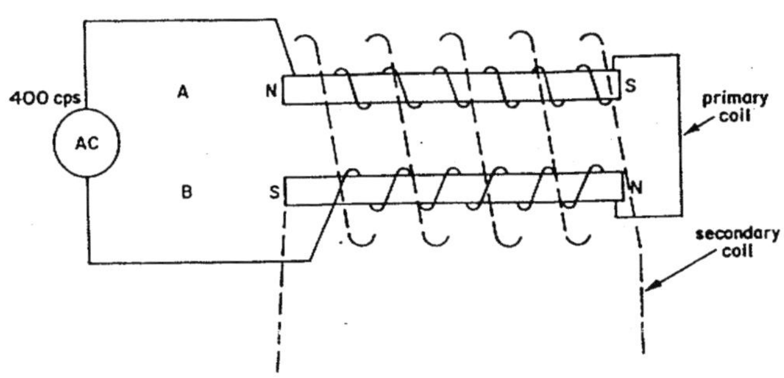

Introduction of Static Flux due to Earth's Magnetic Field

The effect of the static flux, when added to the variable flux produced by the AC current, is to saturate the bars (cores) of the flux valve before the AC current reaches its peak, as shown in the diagram below.

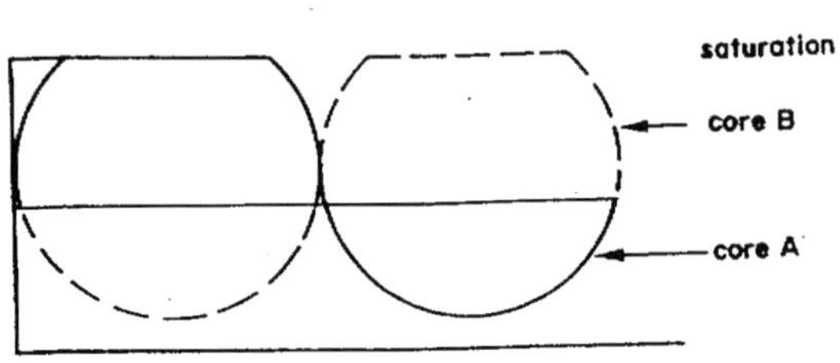

Pictorial Summation of Total Flux

Thus, the coils become saturated before the AC current has peaked. Because of this, the moment total saturation is reached, the flux resulting from intake of Earth magnetism starts to fall. On a graph of total flux in cores A and B, this shows as a curved variation to the straight line, or more simply, as a change in flux, as shown below.

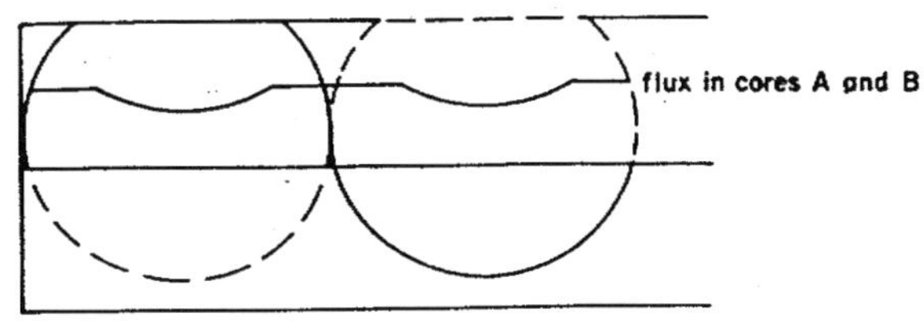

Change of Flux producing EMF in Secondary Coil

This changing flux (Faraday's Law) results in an EMF or voltage produced in the secondary coil and a measurable current flows.

After solving the problem of flux detection, solving for resolution of direction is relatively simple.

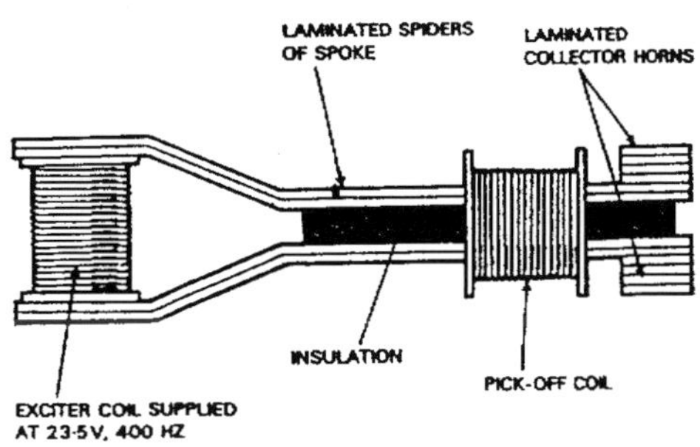

Single Flux Valve

The diagram above shows a single flux valve in practical form, which has ambiguity over four headings, although two of these have different algebraic signs than the remaining two.

The solution used in the gyro-magnetic compass is to employ three separate flux valves spaced 120° apart, as shown below, thereby removing ambiguity between headings.

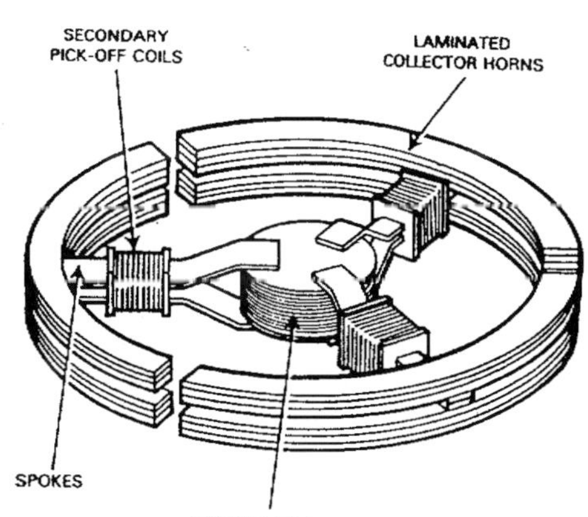

Multi-spoke Detector Head

It is still possible, however, to align the compass 180° in error, but the instrument itself detects this and immediately starts to precess to the correct heading.

DETECTOR UNIT

Construction of the flux detector element is shown in the diagram below.

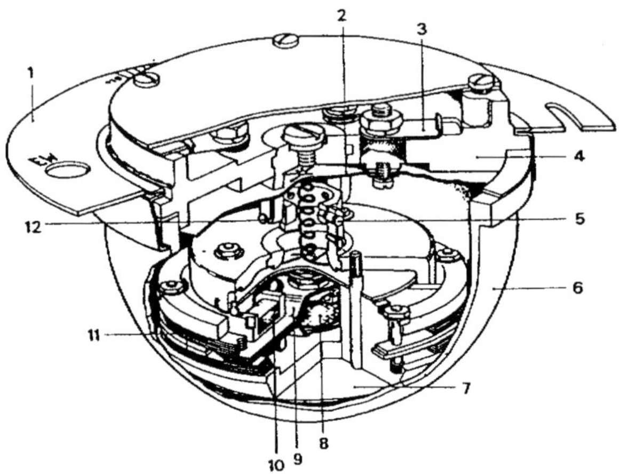

Sectional View of Detector

Head

A centrally-located exciter coil serving all three spokes replaces the primary windings of the single-spoke flux valve. A laminated collector horn is located at the outer end of each flux valve to concentrate the lines of Earth's magnetic force along the parent spoke, thereby increasing sensitivity.

COMPONENTS OF THE FLUX-DETECTOR ELEMENT

1. Mounting flange
2. Contact assembly
3. Terminal
4. Cover
5. Pivot
6. Bowl
7. Pendulous weight
8. Primary coil
9. Spider leg
10. Secondary coil
11. Collector horns
12. Pivot

The diagram is a sectional view of a typical practical detector unit. The spokes and coil assemblies are pendulously suspended from a universal joint, which permits limited freedom in pitch and roll to enable the element to sense the maximum value of H. There is no freedom in azimuth. The unit is hermetically sealed and partially filled with fluid to damp out oscillation of the element. The complete unit is secured in the aircraft structure, in a wing or fin tip, well away from the deviating influence of electronic circuits and the main body of the airframe. It is held in place with a flange containing three slots for screws. One slot has calibration marks to permit correction for A error. The top of the instrument case is equipped for installation of a deviation compensating device.

TRANSMISSION SYSTEM

Use of a remotely-located detector unit requires that the directional reference established by the unit is electronically transmitted to another location in the aircraft, where it is used to monitor the action of a gyro or displayed on an indicator as a value of aircraft heading. The principle of monitoring through transmission systems is essentially the same for all types of gyro-magnetic compass and may be understood by reference to the diagram below.

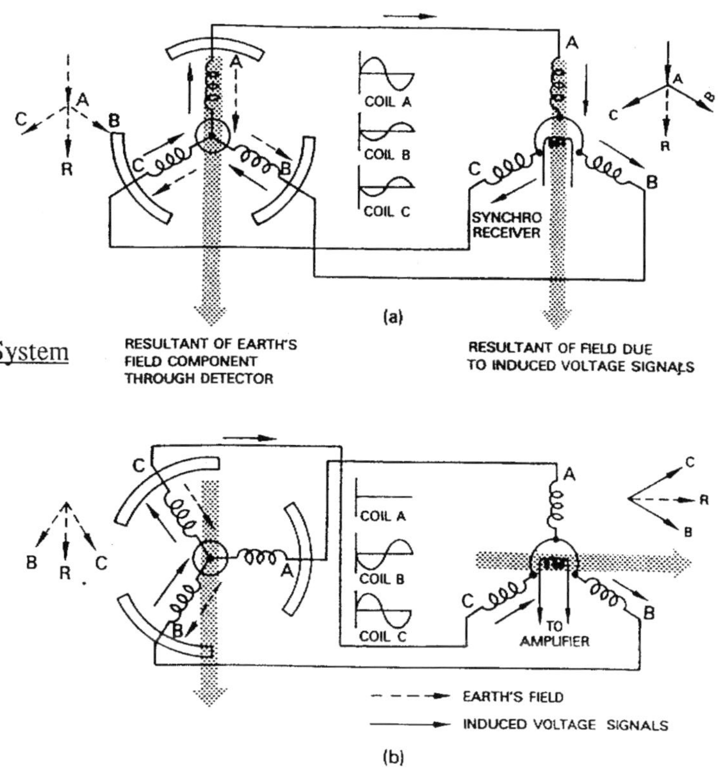

Synchro Transmission/Receiver System

When the flux detector is positioned steady on one heading, say 000°, figure (a), a maximum voltage signal is induced in the pick-off coil (secondary winding) A, while coils B and C have voltages of half strength and opposing phases induced in them. These signals are fed to the corresponding legs of the stator of a synchro receiver, where reproduced voltages combine to establish a resultant field across the centre of the stator. The resultant is in exact alignment with the Earth's field passing through the detector unit. If the rotor of the synchro receiver is at right angles to the resultant, no voltage is induced in the windings. In this position, the synchro is in a null position, and the directional gyro being monitored is also aligned with the Earth's field resultant vector; thus, the heading indicator shows 000°.

In figure (b), the aircraft, and the flux detector unit, have turned through 90°; the disposition of the pick-off coils are therefore as shown. No signal voltage will be induced in coil A, but that in coils B and C have increased voltages, with that in C being opposite in phase to B. The resultant voltage across the receiver synchro stator has rotated through 90°, and assuming that the synchro and gyro were still in their original positions, the resultant is now in line with the synchro rotor and therefore, induces a maximum voltage in the rotor. This error voltage signal is fed to a slaving amplifier, in which it is phase-detected and amplified before being passed to a slaving torque motor, the action of which precesses the gyro and synchro rotor until the synchro rotor reaches a null position at right angles to the resultant of the field induced in the synchro receiver. The system is now again in a position of stability, as in figure (a), the aircraft having turned through 90°.

In practice, of course, the rotation of the field in the receiver synchro and slaving of the gyro occur simultaneously with yawing of the aircraft and detector head, so that synchronisation between detector head (direction of Earth's magnetic field) and gyroscope is continuously maintained.

GYROSCOPE AND INDICATOR MONITORING

The synchronous transmission link between the three principle components of a modern gyro magnetic compass system is shown below.

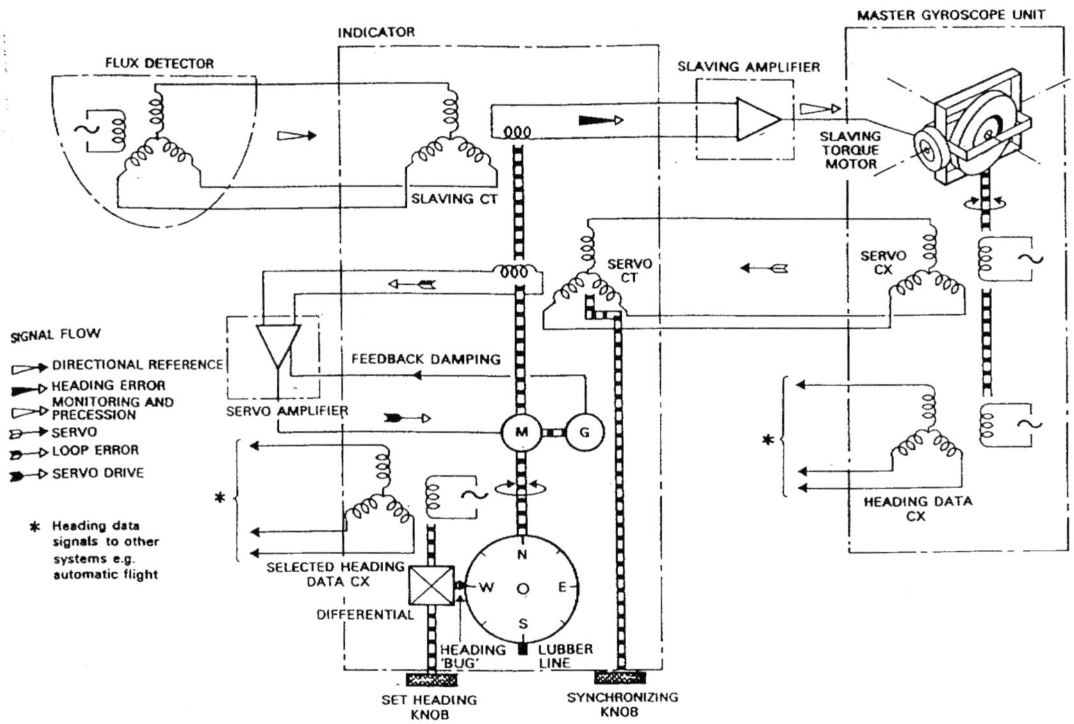

The basic principles of monitoring already described apply to this system, but because the indicator is a separate unit, additional synchros are incorporated into the system, to form what is called a servo-loop. The rotor of the loop transmitter synchro (CX), mounted in the master gyro unit, is rotated whenever the gyro is precessed, or slaved, to the directional reference (detector head). The rotor of the transmitter synchro in the gyro unit is fed with AC current, and thus a voltage is induced in each of the legs of the stator, which is reproduced in the legs of the receiver synchro (CT), located in the indicator unit. If the rotor of the CT synchro does not lie in the null of the induced field, a voltage is created in the rotor, which is fed to the servo-amplifier and, following amplification, to a motor which is mechanically coupled to the CT servo-rotor and the rotor of the slaving synchro (CT). Thus, both rotors and the dial of the heading indicator are rotated, the latter to indicate the correct heading. The rotor of the receiver synchro and that of the slaving synchro are so coupled that when rotation is complete, both rotors lie in the null position of the fields produced in their stators, and hence, no current flows. The servomotor also drives a tacho-generator which supplies feedback signals to the servo-amplifier, to damp out any oscillations in the system. Provision is made to transmit heading information to other locations in the aircraft through the installation of additional servo-transmitters in the master gyro unit and the heading indicator.

GYROSCOPE ELEMENT

In addition to the use of efficient synchro transmitter/receiver systems, it is also essential to employ a gyroscope which maintains its spin axis in a horizontal position at all times. A gyro erection mechanism is essential. This consists of a torque motor mounted horizontally on top of the outer gimbal with its stators fixed to the gimbal and its rotor attached to the gyro casing. The torque motor switch is generally of the liquid level type, as below, and is mounted on the gyro rotor housing, or inner gimbal, so as to move with it.

Gyro Levelling System

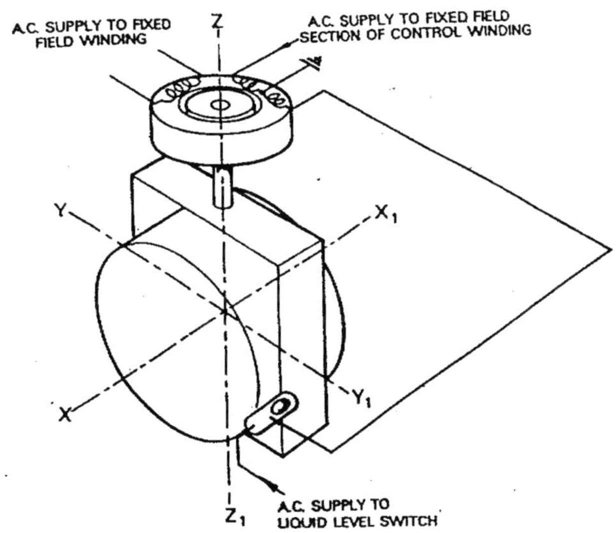

When the gyro axis is horizontal, the liquid switch is open and no current flows to the levelling torque motor. When the axis is tilted, however, the liquid completes the contact between the switch centre electrode and an outer electrode, providing power in one direction or another to the torque motor. The direction of current decides the direction of torque. The torque applied precesses the gyro axis back into the horizontal, at which time the liquid switch is broken.

Depending on the type of compass system, the directional gyroscope element may be contained in a panel-mounted indicator, or it may be an independent master gyro located at a remote part of the aircraft. Systems adopting the master gyro are now the most commonly used, because in serving as a centralised heading source, they provide for more efficient transmission of the data to flight director systems and automatic flight control systems with which they are now closely linked.

HEADING INDICATOR

In addition to displaying magnetic heading, the heading indictor is also capable of showing the magnetic bearing to the aircraft, with respect to ground stations of the radio navigation system - ADF (Automatic Direction Finding) and VOR (very high frequency omnidirectional range). For this reason the indicator is generally referred to as a Radio Magnetic Indicator (RMI).

In order that the pilot may set a desired heading, a set heading knob is provided. It is mechanically coupled to a heading bug, so that rotation of the knob causes the bug to move with respect to the compass card. For turning under automatically controlled flight, rotation of the set heading knob also positions the rotor of a CX synchro, which then supplies twin commands to the auto-pilot system.

MODES OF OPERATION

All gyro compass systems provide for the selection of two modes of operation:

> **Slaved**, in which the gyro is monitored by the detector element
>
> **DG (Free Gyro),** in which the gyro is isolated from the detector unit and functions as a straightforward directional gyroscope

The latter operating mode is selected when a malfunction in the monitoring mode occurs or the aircraft is flying in latitudes where the value of H is too small to be used as a reliable reference.

SYNCHRONISING INDICATORS

The function of the synchronising indicator, or annunciator as it is more usually known, is to indicate to the user that the gyro is synchronised with the directional reference sensed by the detector unit. The synchronisation indicator may be part of the heading indicator, or it may be a separate unit mounted on the aircraft instrument panel. Monitoring signals from the detector head to the gyro slaving torque motor activates the annunciator; hence, the annunciator is connected into the gyro slaving circuit.

The annunciator consists of a small flag marked with a dot and a cross which is visible through a window in one corner of the heading indicator (if so mounted). A small magnet is located at the other end of the shaft, positioned adjacent to two soft iron cored coils, and connected in series with the precession circuit. When the gyro is out of synchronisation with the detector head, a current flows through the coils, attracting the magnet in one direction or the other, such that either a dot or a cross show in the annunciator window. With a synchronised system, the annunciator window should be clear of an image; however, in practice, the flag moves slowly from dot to cross and back again, serving as a most useful indication that the system is working correctly.

MANUAL SYNCHRONISATION

When electrical power is initially applied to a compass system operating in the slaved mode, the gyroscope may be out of alignment from the detector head by a large amount. The system starts to synchronise, but as the rate of precession is normally low (1° to 2° per minute), some time may elapse before synchronisation is achieved. To speed up the process, there is always a manual synchronisation system.

The heading indicator has a manual synchronisation knob, the face of which is marked with a dot and a cross. It is coupled mechanically to the stator of the servo (CT) synchro. When the knob is pushed in and rotated in the direction indicated by the annunciator, the synchro stator is turned, inducing an error voltage into its rotor. This is fed to the servo-amplifier and motor, which drives the slave heading synchro rotor and gyro via the slaving amplifier and precession torque motor, into synchronisation with the detector head. At the same time, the synchro (CT) rotor is driven to the null position and all error signals are removed; the system is synchronised.

OPERATION IN A TURN

To better understand the operation of the gyro-magnetic compass, study its performance in a turn.

As the aircraft enters a turn, the gyroscope maintains its direction with reference to a fixed point (rigidity) and the aircraft turns around the gyro. The rotor of the servo synchro CX is rotated, and error signals are generated in the stator which are passed to and reflected in the stator of the servo synchro CT located in the heading indicator. The rotor of the servo synchro CT is now no longer in the null of the induced field and a voltage is generated, which is passed via the servo amplifier to the servo-motor M. The servo-motor drives the face of the indicator round, so that the compass card keeps pace with the turn and, at the same time, drives the rotor of the servo-synchro CT and the slaving synchro round again, keeping pace with the turn. During all this time, the detector unit, which is fixed in azimuth, is being turned in the Earth's magnetic field; therefore, the flux induced in each spoke of the detector unit is continuously changing. This results in a rotating field being produced in the stator of the slaving synchro CT, which would normally result in a change in flux being detected by the rotor of the slaving synchro and passed as an error signal to the precession circuit. However, the rotor of the slaving synchro is already rotating under the influence of the synchro motor, and the speed and direction of rotation of the rotor matches that of the stator field, hence no error signal is present for transmission to the precession circuit and no gyro precession occurs.

When the aircraft resumes straight and level light, rotation of the servo-synchro CX rotor ceases. There is no further field change between stators and no current flow in the servo-loop. Rotation of the heading indicator display ceases, and the system is now electrically at rest, but still in a fully synchronised condition.

In a steep and prolonged turn, a slight de-synchronisation may occur due to the introduction of a small component of Z, while the detector head is out of the horizontal for a protracted period of time. However, on coming out of the turn, the compass card will rapidly resume the correct heading through the normal precession process. Apart from this small error, the system is virtually clear of turning and acceleration errors.

ADVANTAGES OF THE REMOTE INDICATING GYRO MAGNETIC COMPASS

The advantages of the gyro magnetic compass over a DI or direct reading instrument are:

- The DI suffers from slow drift and has to be reset in flight. Also, when resetting to the magnetic compass, the aircraft must be flown straight and level, whereas a detector unit constantly monitors the gyro-magnetic compass.
- The detector unit can be installed in a remote part of the aircraft, well away from electrical circuits and other influences due to airframe magnetism.
- The flux valve technique used in the detector unit senses the Earth's meridian rather than seeking, which makes the system more sensitive to small components of H. It also minimises the effect of turning and acceleration errors.
- The compass may be detached from the detector unit by a simple switch selection to work as a DI. Therefore a normal DI is not required.
- The system can readily be used to monitor other equipment: autopilot, Doppler, RMI, etc.
- Repeaters can be made available to as many crew stations or equipment as is desired.

DISADVANTAGES OF THE REMOTE INDICATING GYRO MAGNETIC COMPASS

- It is much heavier than a direct-reading compass.
- It is much more expensive.
- It is electrical in operation, and therefore, susceptible to electrical failure.
- It is much more complicated than a DI or a direct-reading compass.

Chapter 22
Inertial Navigation

ACCELEROMETERS

The basis of an Inertial Navigation System (INS) is the measurement of acceleration in known directions. Accelerometers detect and measure acceleration along their sensitive (input) axes; the output is integrated, first to provide velocity along the sensitive axis, and a second time to obtain the distance along the same axis. The process of integration is used because acceleration is rarely a constant value.

For navigation in a horizontal plane, two accelerometers are necessary and are placed with their sensitive axes at 90° to each other. It is customary to align these accelerometers with True North and True East and this alignment has to be maintained throughout flight if the correct accelerations are to be measured. To avoid contamination by gravity, the accelerometers must be maintained in the local horizontal, with no influence from gravity along the sensitive axes. To keep this reference valid, the accelerometers are mounted on a gyro stabilised platform capable of maintaining the correct orientation as the aircraft manoeuvres.

PRINCIPLES AND CONSTRUCTION

The principle of an accelerometer is the measurement of the inertial force, which displaces a mass when acted on by an external force (acceleration). The simplest form is shown in the diagram below; the mass is suspended on a cylindrical casing in such a way that it can move relative to the case when the case (aircraft) is accelerated.

The retaining springs dictate the position of the mass. At rest it is centrally placed and the mass will appear to remain stationary when a horizontal force is applied. The final position of the mass is controlled by the pull of the springs, and the displacement of the mass is proportional to acceleration.

Another form of accelerometer is based on the angular displacement of a pendulum under acceleration at the pivot point. The diagram below shows such a Force Rebalance Accelerometer.

With the outer case at rest (and horizontal) or when moving at a constant velocity, the pendulum is central and no pick-off current flows. When accelerated left or right, the pendulum deflects, and this is detected by the pick-off coils. By feeding the current to the restorer coils, the pendulum is drawn back to the central position, and the magnitude of the current to hold the pendulum central is now proportional to acceleration. In practice, the movement of the pendulum is very small indeed — the reason for this is to prevent cross-coupling, which occurs when the pendulum departs from the vertical and is subject to gravity.

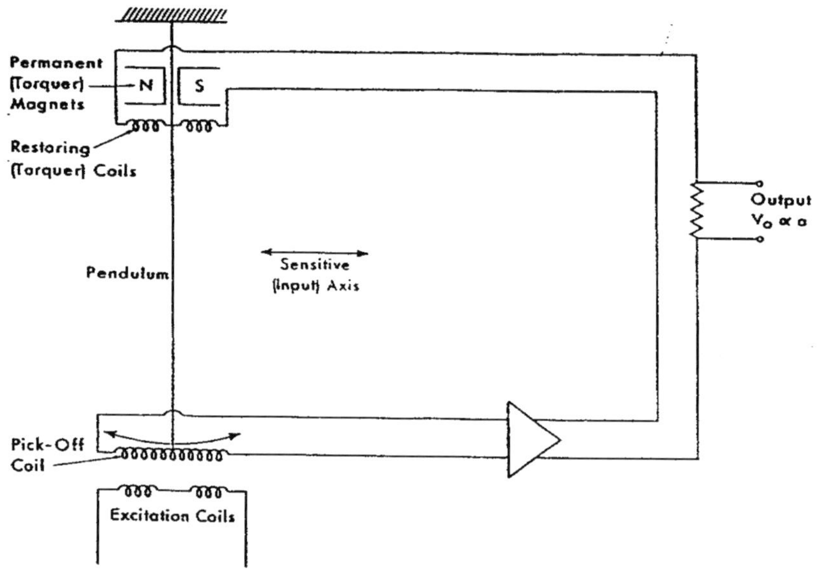

The inner tube is the pendulum arm, and the restorer coil and the pick-off coil form the bob. In all the types described, the current in the restorer circuit is proportional to the acceleration along the sensitive axis. This is known as the output.

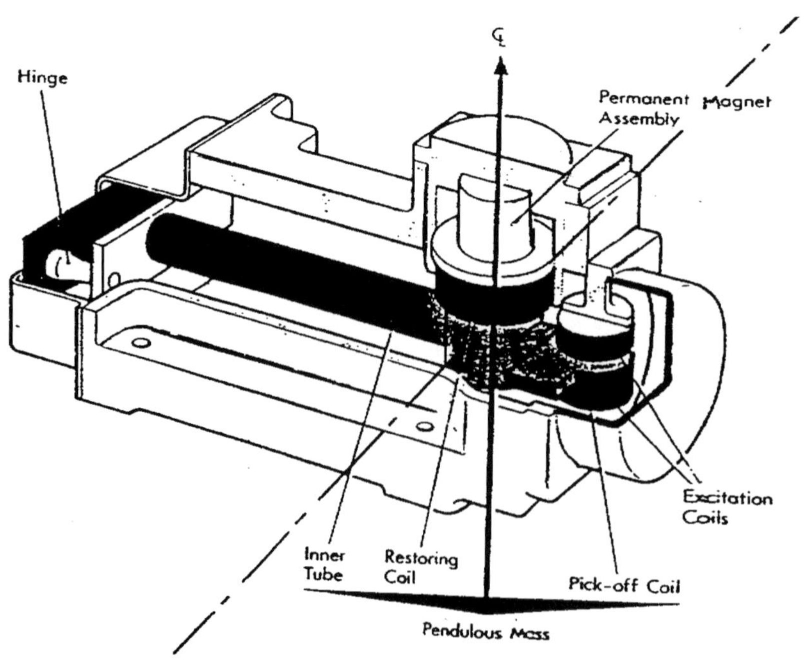

PERFORMANCE

Accelerometers used in INS applications should meet the following requirements:

Sensitivity Range	Be accurate over the range -10g to + 10g
Input/Output	Tolerance of 0.00001%
Scaling Factor	Amplification of restorer current of about 5 ma/g
Zero Stability	(Null uncertainty) The perfect accelerometer has zero output where input is also zero. However, instrument error may result in an output when input is zero. The null position should be defined within ±0.00002g
Small and Light	
Shock Loading	Withstand 60g shock loading and have a low response to vibration

GYRO STABILISED PLATFORM

For navigation in a horizontal plane, the sensing accelerometers must be aligned North and East and must also be mounted on a platform which is independent of aircraft manoeuvre and which is maintained in the local horizontal. Rate gyros are used as sensors to detect any departure of the platform from the level and from the desired alignment. Three single degree-of-freedom gyros are normally used; one detects rotation about the North datum, another about East, and the third about the vertical. Any platform rotation detected by these gyros is made to generate a correction signal which powers the relevant torque motor turning the platform back to its correct orientation.

RATE GYROS/PLATFORM STABILISATION

The accelerometers in an INS are mounted on a platform that is kept level and aligned (normally) with true North. To maintain this stabilisation, rate gyros are mounted on the platform and are oriented so that they sense manoeuvres of the aircraft in pitch, roll, and change in heading. Rate gyros are used in INS. They achieve high accuracy by reducing gimbal friction. The gimbal and rotor assemblies are floated in fluid. An example is shown below.

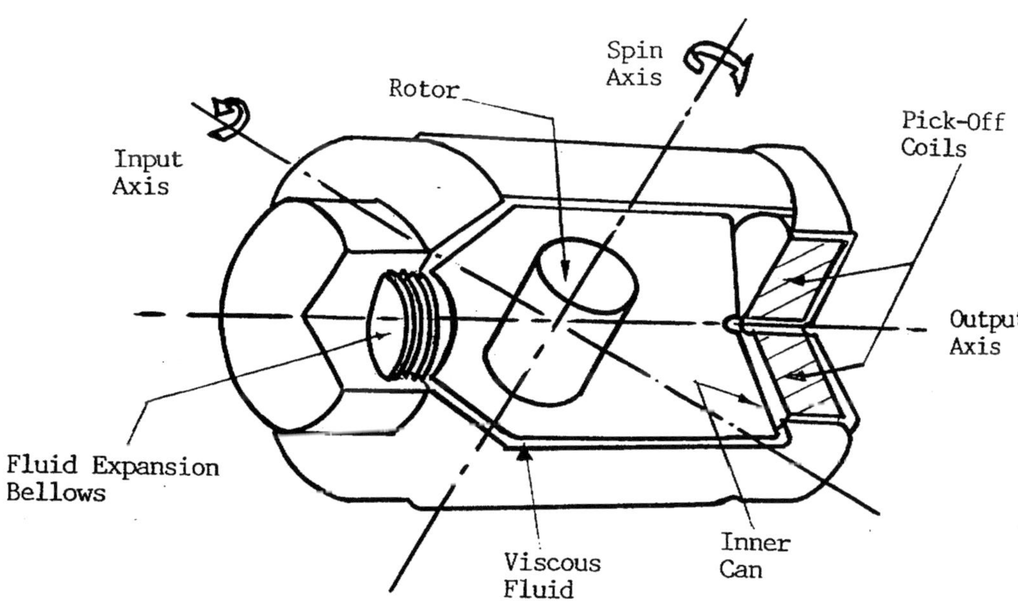

Any torque (rotation) about the input (sensitive) axis causes the inner can to precess about the output axis (i.e. there is relative motion between the inner and outer cans). The pick-off coils sense this, and the output is proportional to the input turning rate. To avoid any temperature errors, the whole unit is closely temperature controlled.

The operation of INS depends on the N/S and E/W accelerometers being held horizontal and correctly aligned. To achieve this, the accelerometers are placed on a platform which is mounted within a gimbal system. The diagrams below show a stable platform for one aircraft heading North and one heading East.

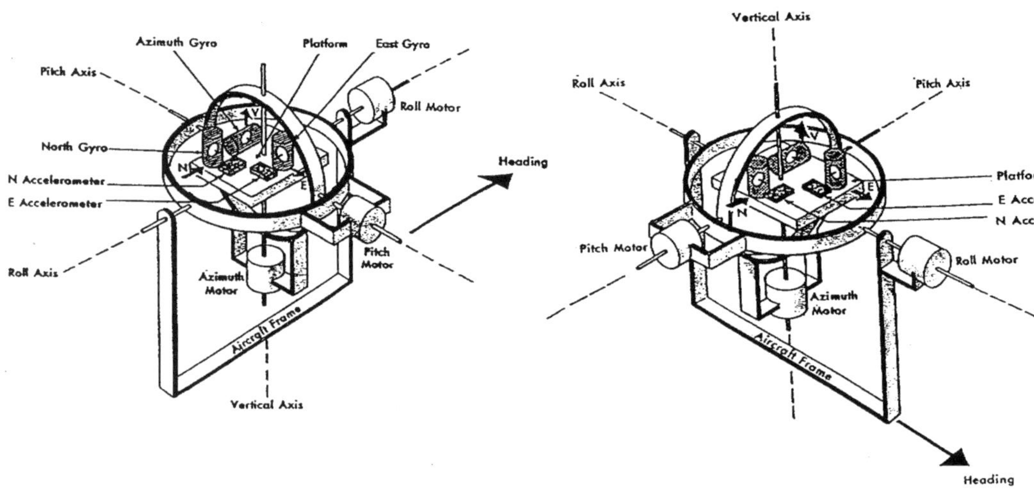

The platform is isolated from aircraft manoeuvres of roll and pitch by the gimbals. Thus, by the sensing gyros and follow-up torque systems, the platform is maintained Earth-horizontal and directionally aligned.

In the left diagram, the North gyro is sensitive to roll and the East gyro to movements in the pitch axis. Any yaw is detected by the azimuth gyro and all 3 rate gyros turn the respective motors to maintain alignment. In the right-hand diagram, the East gyro senses roll and the North senses pitch; for all intermediate headings, the simultaneous action of the rate gyros/torque motors is computed and the appropriate corrections applied. In summary, the platform isolates the accelerometers from angular rotations of the aircraft and maintains the platform in a fixed orientation relative to the Earth. This assembly, including accelerometers, rate gyros, torque motors, platform, and gimbal system, is known as the stable element.

SETTING-UP PROCEDURES

The accuracy of an INS depends on the alignment in azimuth and attitude of the stable element (i.e. it must be horizontal and aligned to the selected heading datum, normally True North). The levelling and alignment processes must be conducted on the ground when the aircraft is stationary.

As already indicated, gyros and accelerometers used in INS are normally fluid filled, and it is necessary to bring the containing fluid to its correct operating temperature before the platform is aligned. Thus, the first stage in the sequence is a warm-up period where the gyros are run up to their operating speeds, and the fluid is temperature controlled. When these have been achieved, the alignment sequence begins.

LEVELLING

Coarse levelling is achieved by driving the pitch and roll gimbals until they are at 90° to each other; the platform is then erect to the aircraft frame.

The aircraft may be tilted at a slight angle and fine levelling is then carried out. This process takes place if there is a gravity component sensed by the accelerometers. The output(s) are used to drive the appropriate torque motors until there is zero acceleration sensed.

ALIGNMENT

Gyro compassing, or fine alignment, is automatically initiated once the platform has been levelled. Where the platform is not accurately aligned with True North, the E/W gyroscope senses the rotation of the Earth; if it is lying with the sensitive axis exactly E/W, the Earth's rotation has no effect. But, and this is normally the case when the INS is switched on, if the alignment is not accurate, there is an E/W output and this is used to torque the platform until the E/W output is reduced to nil.

Note: Within the value of Earth rate affecting the E/W gyroscope is a component dependent on the cos.lat. Therefore, for an aircraft at very high latitudes, this component gets very close to zero and makes alignment to True North virtually impossible. Be warned that the effect of latitude on the fine alignment process limits the initial alignment to mid-latitudes and equatorial regions.

The inter-relationship between levelling and alignment is complex. Any slight discrepancy in the one affects the other. Therefore, it is important from the moment fine levelling is completed that the necessary corrections be applied to keep the platform horizontal with respect to the Earth. Remember that this is a gyro stabilised device and the gyros want to maintain spatial rather than terrestrial rigidity. The Earth rotates continuously, so the platform has to be tilted as the Earth moves round to maintain terrestrial horizontality.

INERTIAL NAVIGATION SYSTEM (CONVENTIONAL GYRO)

Inertial Navigation Systems (INS) provide aircraft velocity and position by continuously measuring and integrating aircraft acceleration. INS use no external references, are unaffected by weather, operate day and night, and all corrections for Earth movement and for transporting over the Earth's surface are applied automatically. The products of an INS are:

- Position (lat/long)
- Speed (knots)
- Distance (nautical miles)
- Other navigational information

The quality of information is dependent on the accuracy of initial (input) data and the precision with which the platform is aligned (to True North).

The final step toward an integrated INS is to provide the necessary corrections to keep the stable element in the local horizontal and to process the output of the accelerometers.

A simple INS is shown in schematic form below. The N/S distance is added to initial latitude to give present latitude, while the departure E/W has to be multiplied by the secant of the latitude to obtain change in longitude. The accelerometer outputs are integrated with respect to time to obtain velocity, and then a second time to obtain distance. The accelerometer output may be either in voltage (or analogue) form, or in pulse form, for analogue and digital systems, respectively. Remember, the output of first stage integration is the value velocity and of the second is distance along the sensitive axis of the accelerometer. The translation of detection by the accelerometers at 90° to each other into present position expressed in lat/long is also shown.

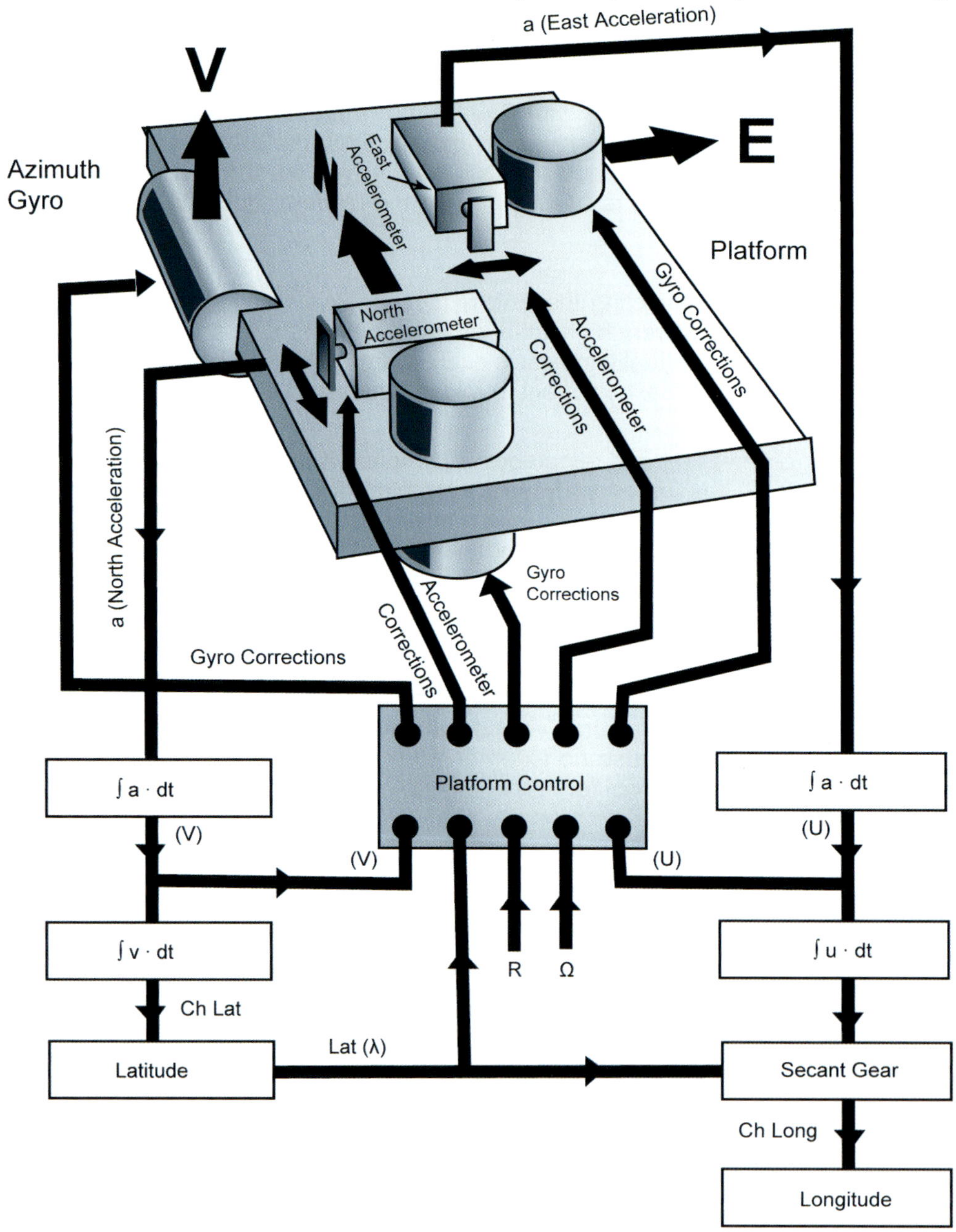

V	Velocity North
U	Velocity East
λ	Latitude
R	Radius of Earth
⦸	Rotation of Earth (15.04°/hr)

CORRECTIONS

Accelerometers and gyros have sensitive axes which extend infinitely in straight lines, i.e. they operate with respect to inertial space. But the Earth is not like that — local vertical axes are not constant because the Earth is a curved surface which also rotates. Corrections for Earth rate and transport wander have to be made, as do those for accelerations caused by the Earth's rotation. Any control gyro is rigid in space and, in order to maintain an Earth reference, it must be corrected for both Earth rate and transport wander. Further correction must be applied for coriolis (sideways movement caused by Earth rotation, except at the equator), and the central acceleration. The latter is caused by rotating the platform to maintain alignment with the local vertical reference frame.

GYRO CORRECTIONS:

Due to Apparent Wander

Earth Rate Drift

The azimuth gyro must be torqued by a compensating force to keep the spin axis aligned with True North. The value is the familiar 15 sin lat°/hr.

Earth Rate Topple

The North gyro must be torqued by a compensating force of 15 cos lat°/hr.

Note: For a correctly aligned platform, the East gyro requires no correction for Earth rate.

Due to Transport Wander

Transport Wander Drift

Transport wander causes misalignment of the gyro spin axis at a rate varying directly with speed (along the sensitive axis) and latitude. For a correctly aligned platform, the speed in an E/W direction is the first integral of easterly acceleration (i.e. the output of the East accelerometer). Latitude is also calculated by the platform and, given these two values, the INS computer can calculate and apply the correction for transport wander drift.

Transport Wander Topple

A stabilised platform which is transported across the surface of the Earth appears to topple in both the E/W and N/S planes. To keep the platform locally horizontal, transport wander corrections are applied to the pitch/roll torque motors by the appropriate amounts.

Acceleration Corrections

Applying the apparent wander corrections implies turning the platform, even though it is only by small amounts, about its axes. Moving the spatial reference to make the platform keep up with the changing Earth reference causes acceleration errors. To remove these, acceleration error corrections are applied.

Coriolis

This sideways force affects the output of both N/S and E/W accelerometers; it is caused by the rotation of the Earth about its axis. An aircraft following an Earth-referenced track follows a curved path in space. The very small error is computed, and the necessary corrections applied to the outputs of the accelerometers.

Centripetal Acceleration

A body moving at a constant speed in a circle (such as an aircraft flying over the surface of the Earth, where the centre of the Earth is the centre of the circle) has a constant acceleration toward the centre of the Earth. This acceleration affects the accelerometers on an inertial platform and corrections to compensate for this movement are made and applied to the outputs of the accelerometers.

The corrections to the gyros and the accelerometers in an INS are below. It is unlikely that you would be required to calculate the corrections, but you are expected to be aware that they exist.

Axis	Gyros		Accelerometers	
	Earth Rate	Transport Wander	Central	Coriolis
North	$\Omega \cos \lambda$	$^{U}/_{R}$	$\frac{-U^2 \tan \lambda}{R}$	$-2 \Omega U \sin \lambda$
East	NIL	$^{-V}/_{R}$	$\frac{UV \tan \lambda}{R}$	$2 \Omega V \sin \lambda$
Azimuth/Vertical	$\Omega \sin \lambda$	$\frac{U \tan \lambda}{R}$	$\frac{U^2 + V^2}{R}$	$-2 \Omega U \sin \lambda$

V Velocity North
U Velocity East
λ Latitude
R Radius of Earth
Ω Rotation of Earth (15.04°/hr)

ERRORS

The errors of INS fall into three categories:

- Bounded Errors
- Unbounded Errors
- Inherent Errors

THE SCHULER PERIOD

Schuler postulated an Earth pendulum with length equal to the radius of the Earth, its bob at the Earth's centre and point of suspension at the Earth's surface. If the suspension point of such a pendulum were to be accelerated over the Earth's surface, inertia and gravity would combine to hold the bob stationary at the Earth's centre, and the shaft of the pendulum would remain vertical throughout. If the bob of an Earth pendulum were disturbed, as it is when the aircraft is the suspension point, it would oscillate with a period of 84.4 minutes.

It can be shown that an INS platform which is tied to the Earth's vertical possesses the characteristics of an Earth pendulum; once disturbed, it oscillates with a Schuler Period of 84.4 minutes.

Bounded Errors

Errors which build up to a maximum and return to zero within each 84.4 minutes Schuler Cycle are termed bounded errors. The main causes of these errors are:

- Platform tilt, due to initial misalignment
- Inaccurate measurement of acceleration by accelerometers
- Integrator errors in the first integration stage

In practical terms, to the aviator this means that the output of the INS is correct three times every Schuler Period; once when the period starts and then again at the end. In the middle, at 42.2 minutes, it is again correct. At 21.1 minutes the error will be a maximum high (say) and at 63.3, a maximum low. So, for an INS, where the platform has been slightly disturbed, the real groundspeed is 500 kt and the bounded error is carrying maximum variation of 7 kt in groundspeed, then:

Period (min)	0	21.1	42.2	63.3	84.4
INS G/S (kt)	500	507	500	493	500

The error averages out over time.

Unbounded Errors

Cumulative Track Errors

These errors arise from misalignment of the accelerometers in the horizontal plane resulting in track errors. The main causes of these errors are:

- Initial azimuth misalignment of the platform
- Wander of the azimuth gyro

Cumulative Distance Errors

These errors give rise to cumulative errors in the recording of distance run. The main causes are:

- Wander in the levelling gyros

  Note: Wander causes a Schuler oscillation of the platform, but the mean recorded value of distance run is increasingly divergent from the true distance nm.

- Integrator errors in the second stage of integration

In both cases above, position error is the most obvious result. The largest single contribution is real wander of the gyros. The sensitivities of an INS system expose any inaccuracies in the manufacture of rate integrating gyros and despite tight tolerances, less than 0.01°/hr is normal, real wander is the culprit in unbounded error.

Inherent Errors

The irregular shape and composition of the Earth, the movement of the Earth through space, and other factors provide further possible sources of error. Such errors vary from system to system, depending upon the balance achieved between accuracy and simplicity of design, reliability, ease of construction and cost of production.

Radial Error

The radial error of an INS is a common question in licensing examinations. It is:

$$\frac{\text{Distance of ramp position from INS position}}{\text{Elapsed time in hours}}$$

Watch out when calculating the distance between two positions; latitude must be considered.

ADVANTAGES OF THE INERTIAL SYSTEM

- Indications of position and velocity are instantaneous and continuous
- Self-contained; independent of ground stations
- Navigation information is obtainable at all latitudes and in all weathers
- Operation is independent of aircraft manoeuvres
- Given TAS, the W/V can be calculated and displayed on a continuous basis
- If correctly levelled and aligned, any inaccuracies may be considered minor, as far as civil air transport is concerned
- Apart from the over-riding necessity for accuracy in pre-flight requirements, there is no possibility of human error

DISADVANTAGES OF THE INERTIAL SYSTEM

- Position and velocity information does degrade with time
- Expensive and difficult to maintain and service
- Initial alignment is simple enough in moderate latitudes when stationary, but difficult above 75° latitude and in flight

OPERATION OF INS

The following pages describe the control, operation, and displays of a current conventional INS.

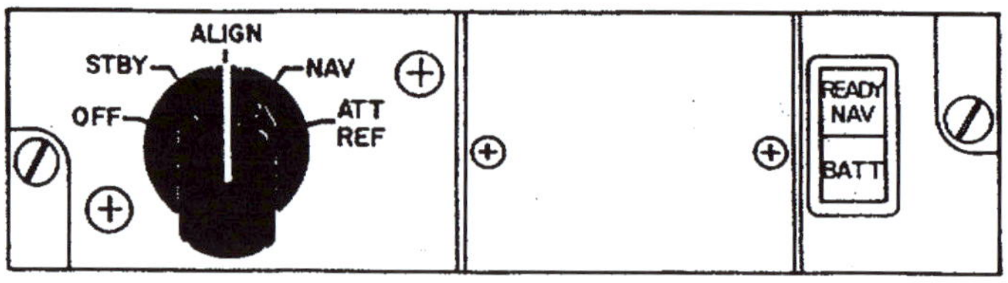

Selection	Meaning
OFF	Power OFF
STBY	Power ON; TEST or INSERT (data) may be carried out Platform erect to aircraft axes System not affected by aircraft movement
ALIGN	Automatic alignment commences Aircraft must not be moved when ALIGN mode is selected System can withstand loading/gust movement READY NAV light (green) illuminates at end of alignment sequence
NAV	READY NAV extinguished Platform in operational mode, all gyro and accelerometer corrections applied Selector switch heavily indented in NAV position to prevent accidental movement of switch to any other position
ATT REF	Selected if NAV mode fails Continues to provide pitch, roll, heading CDU L/R displays go blank Extinguishes red WRN lamp on CDU
BATT	Red battery warning lamp informs that back-up power is in action

CDU

The diagram below shows the principal controls and displays on the CDU.

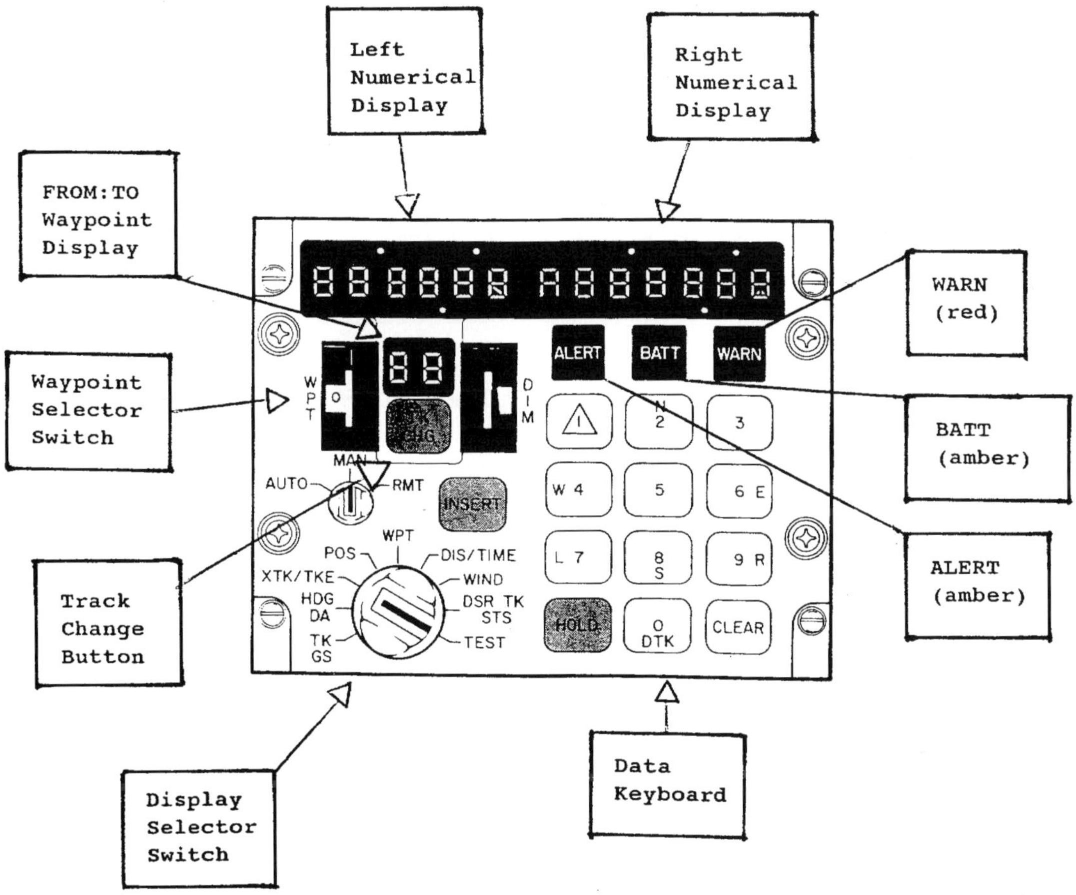

The following diagrams refer to character numbers in the left and right displays. The characters are numbered as follows:

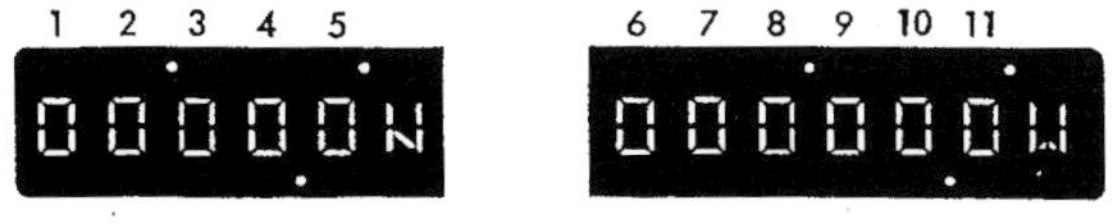

DISPLAY SELECTION – TK/GS

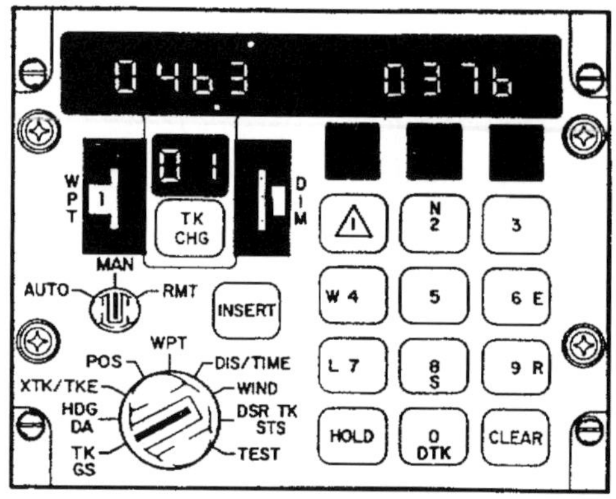

Function		Computes and displays track and aircraft groundspeed
Display	**LH**	Track (°T) Character 1 blank Characters 2 to 5 read track in 0.1° increments Decimal point shown
	RH	Aircraft groundspeed in knots Characters 6 and 7 blank Characters 8 to 11 read 0–3999 knots in one knot increments
Other		If TK/GS selected, the INS continues to make AUTO track leg switching if AUTO selected on AUTO/MAN/RMT selector Operates only in the NAV mode

DISPLAY SELECTION – HDG/GA

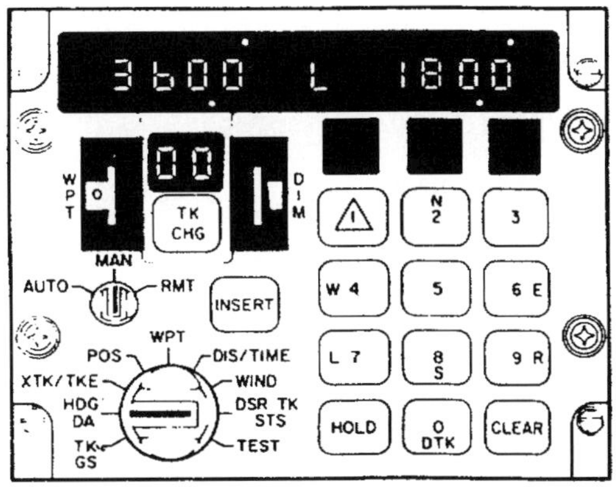

Function		Computes heading and calculates drift angle
Display	**LH**	True heading Character 1 blank Characters 2 to 5 read heading in 0.1° increments Decimal point shown
	RH	Difference in aircraft heading and track Characters 6 is L or R Character 7 is blank Characters 8 to 11 read 0 – 180° in 0.1° increments
Other		Operates only in the NAV mode

DISPLAY SELECTOR – XTK/TKE

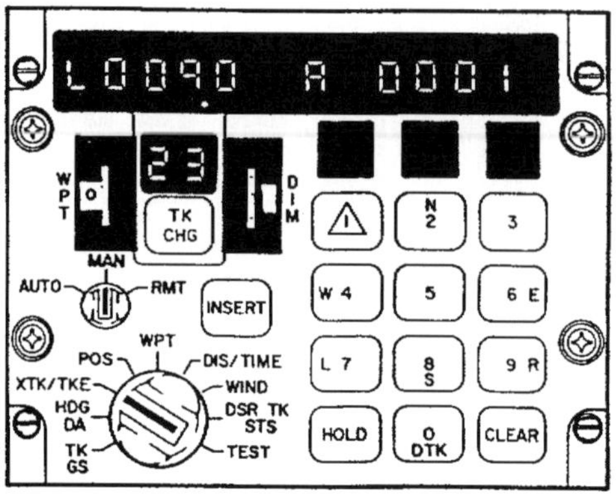

Function		Calculates both cross track distance from great circle track between selected waypoint and the angular difference between track and desired course between selected waypoints
Display	**LH**	Cross track distance (nm) Character 1 reads L or R Characters 2 to 5 read track in 0 to 399.9 nm in 0.1° increments Decimal point shown
	RH	Track error angle Characters 6 reads L or R Character 7 is blank Characters 8 to 11 read 0 – 180° in 0.1° increments
Other		The RMT selection on the AUTO/MAN/RMT switch permits insertion of a desired cross track distance for example parallel tracking Operates only in the NAV mode

DISPLAY SELECTION – POS

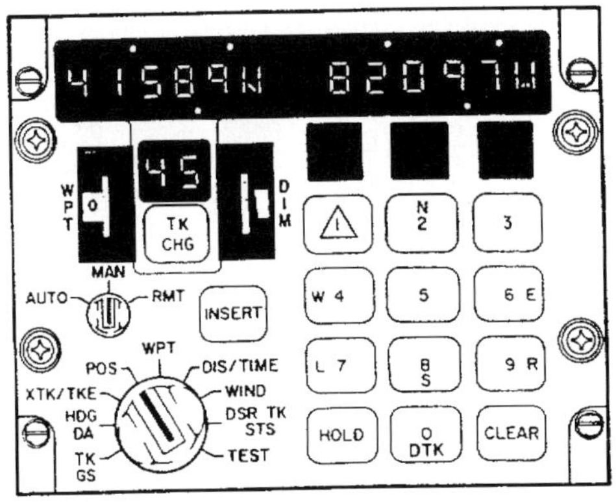

Function		Permits insertion of lat/long for aircraft position and updates to aircraft position
Display	**LH**	Characters 1 to 5 reads latitude 0 to 90° in 0.1° increments N or S shown between character 5 and 6
	RH	Characters 6 to 11 reads longitude 0 to 180° in 0.1° increments E or W shown following 11
Other		The values of latitude and longitude can be altered in the STBY, ALIGN and NAV modes of operation

DISPLAY SELECTION – WPT

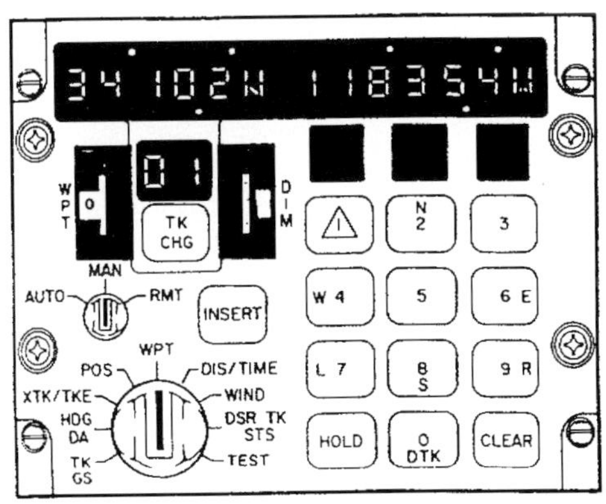

Function		Displays the latitude and longitude of stored waypoints
Display	**LH** **RH**	Both LH and RH displays are the same as the above
Other		The values of latitude and longitude can be altered in the STBY, ALIGN and NAV modes of operation

DISPLAY SELECTION – DIS/TIME

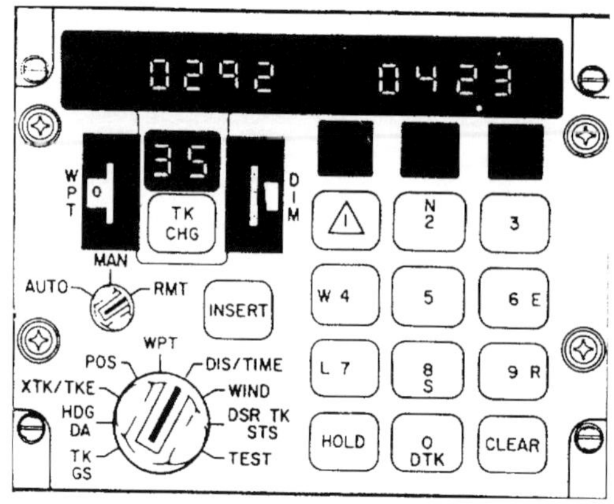

Function		Computes and displays great circle distance and time to a selected waypoint. Present groundspeed is assumed
Display	**LH**	Character 1 blank Characters 2 to 5 read 0 to 9999 nm in 1 nm increments
	RH	Characters 6 and 7 blank Characters 8 to 11 read 0 to 799.9 minutes in 0.1 minute increments
Other		Operates only in NAV mode When RMT is selected, displays data for any leg between any waypoints as above The 35 refers to FROM waypoint 3 to waypoint 5 If 0 is selected, the computation is for aircraft present position to the waypoint selected

DISPLAY SELECTION – WIND

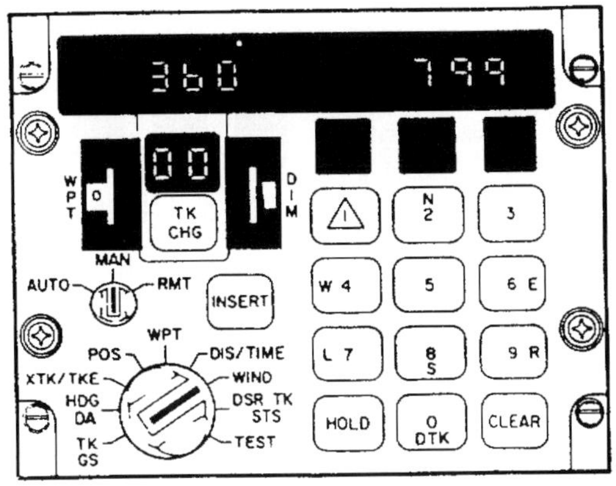

Function		Given a TAS input, the INS computes wind velocity
Display	**LH**	Character 1 and 2 blank Characters 3 to 5 read 0 to 360° nm in 0.1° increments
	RH	Characters 6 to 8 blank Characters 9 to 11 read 0 to 799 knots in 1 knot increments
Other		Operates only in NAV mode

DISPLAY SELECTION - DSR TK/STS

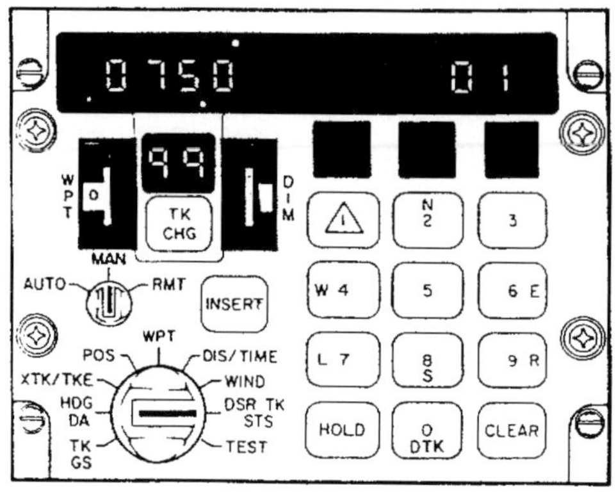

Function		Computes and displays great circle track between two waypoints Advises the status of operation of the system
Display	**LH**	Character 1 blank Characters 2 to 5 read 0 to 360° in 0.1° increments
	RH	A series of codes are displayed: Alignment status, or Action required Malfunction
Other		Status counts down from 90 to 10 in increments of 10 as alignment proceeds. Reads 02 at READY NAV Reads 01 in NAV mode

DISPLAY FUNCTION – TEST

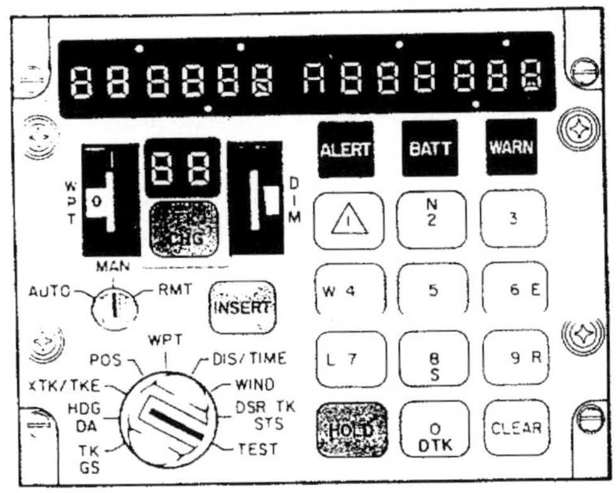

Function All segments of numerical and FROM/TO displays illuminate

DISPLAY FORMAT

Most INS are capable of interfacing with other instrumentation such as:

- FDI
- HSI
- Area Navigation Systems
- EFIS

SOLID STATE GYROS

Up to now, studies of gyros have been confined to air or electrically driven spinning wheel gyros contained within a basic gimbal configuration, the purpose of which is to isolate the gyro from aircraft manoeuvres. Comparison between the relative positions of the gyro axes and the relevant gimbal gives the degree of pitch, roll or yaw being generated by the aircraft manoeuvre. The conventional gyro has several physical constraints: it requires space, freedom, and an axis for the spin axis. This means that manoeuvres in all three axes cannot be detected by a single gyro instrument. Thus, basic flight instrumentation requires both an artificial horizon and a DGI to cover all manoeuvres, even though the outputs of these instruments can be shown on a single display.

TYPES OF SOLID STATE GYROS

There are currently three types of solid state gyro suitable for aviation applications. Of these, only one is not yet available for commercial aviation, namely the Nuclear Magnetic Resonance Gyro (NMRG). The Ring Laser Gyro (RLG) and the Fibre Optic Gyro (FOG) are both available and operate on similar principles. Accordingly, the RLG is explained in some detail and a brief mention is made of the FOG toward the end of this chapter.

RING LASER GYRO

Unlike conventional, or spinning wheel, gyros which are maintained in a level attitude by a series of gimbals, the RLG is fixed in orientation to the aircraft axes. Changes in orientation caused by aircraft manoeuvre are sensed by measuring the frequencies of two contra-rotating beams of light within the gyro.

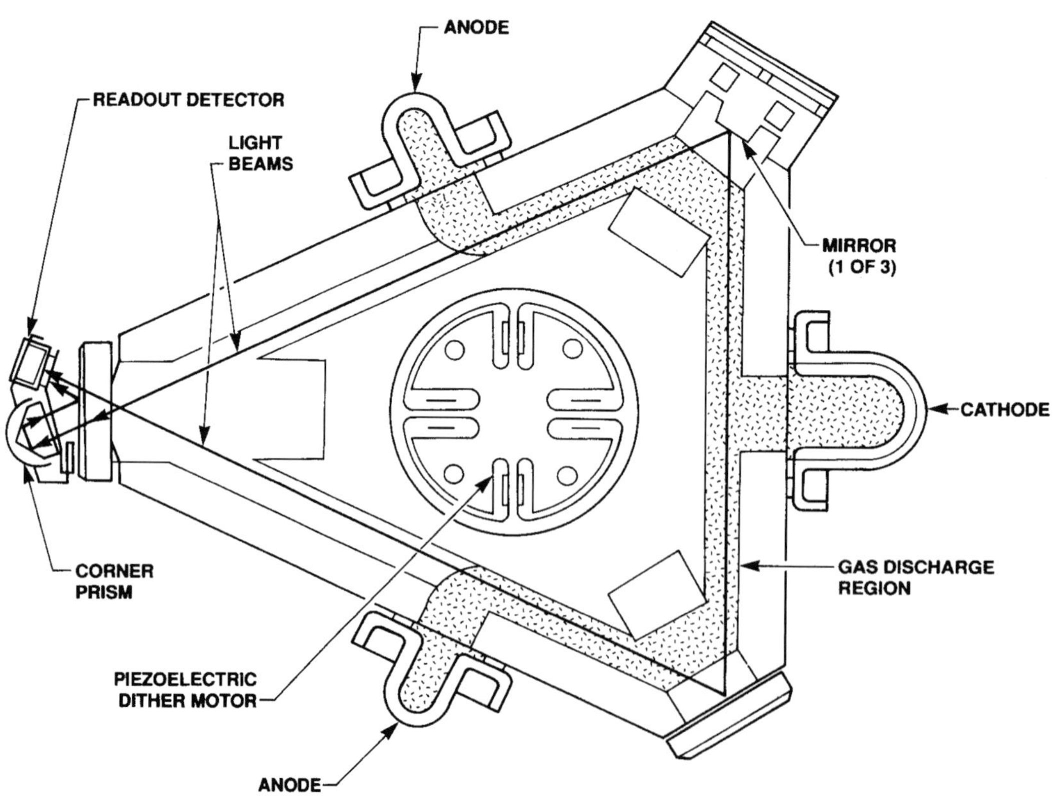

The example shown has a triangular path of laser light. The path length is normally 24, 32, or 45 cm. Other models have a square path (i.e. one more mirror). The RLG is produced from a block of a very stable glass ceramic compound with an extremely low co-efficient of expansion. The triangular cavity contains a mixture of helium and neon gases at low pressure, through which a current is passed. The gas (or plasma) is ionised by the voltage causing helium atoms to collide with, and transfer energy to, the neon atoms. This raises the neon to an inversion state, and the spontaneous return of neon to a lower energy level produces photons, which then react with other excited neon atoms. This action repeated at speed creates a cascade of photons throughout the cavity (i.e. a sustained oscillation), and the laser beam is pulsed around the cavity by the mirrors at each corner.

The laser beam is made to travel in both directions around the cavity. Thus, for a stationary block, the travelled paths are identical, and the frequencies of the two beams are the same at any sampling point. But, if the block is rotated, the effective path lengths differ — one increases and the other decreases. Now sampling at any point gives different frequencies, and the frequency change can be processed to give an angular change AND a rate of angular change.

By processing the frequency difference between the two pulsed light paths, the RLG can be used as both a displacement and a rate gyro. There is a limit of rotation rate below which the RLG does not function: because of minute imperfections (instrument error) in the mirrors, one laser beam can lock-in to the other, and therefore, no frequency change is detected — the RLG has ceased to be a gyro. The situation is the RLG equivalent of gimbal-lock in a conventional gyro. One solution is to gently vibrate the RLG. The complete block is vibrated, or dithered, by a piezo-electric motor at about 350 Hz. The dither mechanism, literally the only moving part of the PLO, prevents “lock-in” of the two laser beams. The outputs of the RLG are digital, not mechanical, and the reliability and accuracy should exceed those of a conventional gyro by a factor of several times.

FIBRE OPTIC GYROS

Like the RLG, the FOG comprises a triad of gyros mutually perpendicular to each other and similarly three accelerometers. The FOG senses the phase shift proportional to angular rate in counter-directional light beams travelling through an optical fibre. Although dimensionally similar, the FOG benefits from less weight and is cheaper, but the fibre optic is not quite as rugged or efficient (more instrument error) as the RLG.

ADVANTAGES OF RLG’S:

- High reliability
- Very low g sensitivity
- No run-up (warm-up) time
- Digital output
- High accuracy
- Low power requirement
- Low life-cycle cost

DISADVANTAGE OF RLG’S

- High capital cost

STRAP-DOWN INS

SYSTEM DESCRIPTION

Strap-down systems dispense with the gimbal mounted stable element. The sensitive axes of both the accelerometers and the RLGs are in line with the vehicle body axes. There is no isolation from vehicle movement, and so the outputs represent linear accelerations (accelerometers) and angular rates (RLGs) with respect to the three axes of the aircraft.

The RLGs are not required to stabilise the accelerometers but provide vehicle orientation — the already familiar horizontal and True North alignment are the reference axes. The orientation data is used to process (modify) the accelerometer outputs to represent those, which under the same conditions, would be output by accelerometers actually in the N, E, and vertical planes. The transform matrix (a quaternion) can only be generated by digital computation (i.e. the quaternion is the analytical equivalent of a gimballed system).

ALIGNMENT

Although the assembly is bolted to the aircraft frame, an RLG INS still needs to be aligned to an Earth reference. Instead of levelling and aligning a stable platform, the speed and flexibility of a digital computer allows a transform to be calculated and compiled. The transform is a mathematical solution as to where the horizontal and True North lie with respect to the triad of RLGs and accelerometers. Full alignment takes about 10 minutes at most, at the end of which an offset to each output of the RLGs and accelerometers is established which determine local horizontal and True North references. These initial calculated values are applicable at that place on that heading at that time. The Earth certainly moves on, and if the aircraft moves as well, the vital references must be safeguarded. The complexities of 3-D motion (i.e. the interactions of pitch, roll, and yaw), require a fairly extensive mathematical/trigonometrical juggle to be conducted at speed. The answer lies in a series of functions which make up a mathematical matrix — these are big words for lots of factors being calculated and their inter-relating effects being taken care of.

It's all a bit difficult to imagine, but try to think of it as the reverse of the techniques in a conventional INS. Instead of creating a reference from a gimballed system, a reference is created from data taken from a completely different set of values. If the aircraft heading has not been altered since the RLG INS was last used, then a rapid alignment, taking 10-15 seconds is possible. If the aircraft is also fitted with Global Positioning Systems (satellite positional systems), it is possible to re-align an RLG INS in flight, a significant advantage over conventional systems.

PERFORMANCE

The performance of RLG INS is generally slightly better than that of a conventional INS, the principal advantage being reliability:

Position accuracy	2 nm/hr *
Pitch/roll	0.05°
Heading (T)	0.40°
Groundspeed	± 8 kt
Vertical velocity	30'/second
Angular rates	0.1°/second
Acceleration	0.01g

* 95% probability assuming no update to other navigation source